Recent Advances in Machine learning and Deep Learning Theories: Towards Intelligent Fault Diagnosis

Recent Advances in Machine learning and Deep Learning Theories: Towards Intelligent Fault Diagnosis

Guest Editors

Heung Soo Kim
Salman Khalid
Ananda Shankar
Prashant Kumar

MDPI

Basel • Beijing • Wuhan • Barcelona • Belgrade • Novi Sad • Cluj • Manchester

Guest Editors
Heung Soo Kim
Department of Mechanical, Robotics and Energy Engineering
Dongguk University
Seoul
Republic of Korea

Salman Khalid
Department of Mechanical, Robotics and Energy Engineering
Dongguk University
Seoul
Republic of Korea

Ananda Shankar
Indian School of Mines
Indian Institute of Technology Dhanbad
India

Prashant Kumar
Department of Mechanical, Robotics and Energy Engineering
Dongguk University
Seoul
Republic of Korea

Editorial Office
MDPI AG
Grosspeteranlage 5
4052 Basel, Switzerland

This is a reprint of the Special Issue, published open access by the journal *Mathematics* (ISSN 2227-7390), freely accessible at: https://www.mdpi.com/si/mathematics/F7X1E5JT8L.

For citation purposes, cite each article independently as indicated on the article page online and as indicated below:

Lastname, A.A.; Lastname, B.B. Article Title. *Journal Name* **Year**, *Volume Number*, Page Range.

ISBN 978-3-7258-5951-1 (Hbk)
ISBN 978-3-7258-5952-8 (PDF)
https://doi.org/10.3390/books978-3-7258-5952-8

Contents

About the Editors

Heung Soo Kim

Heung Soo Kim received his B.S. and M.S. degrees from the Department of Aerospace Engineering at Inha University, Korea, in 1997 and 1999, respectively. He earned his Ph.D. from Arizona State University in 2003, conducting research supported by NASA Langley Research Center and the US Air Force Research Laboratory on smart composite modeling and computational structural analysis. He is currently a Professor in the Department of Mechanical, Robotics, and Energy Engineering at Dongguk University, Seoul, Republic of Korea. Prof. Kim's research interests include Prognostics and Health Management (PHM) of composite structures, power plants, industrial robots, and mobility batteries. He is also interested in biomimetic actuators, adaptive structures, and structural analysis. He serves as director of the BK21 AIMS Center and the DGU Global Intelligent Robot Center, leading significant research initiatives. He has published 245 SCIE journal papers, achieving an H-index of 46 with over 9,000 citations. His outstanding research contributions have been recognized through numerous Academic Achievement Awards from various academic societies in the PHM field.

Salman Khalid

Salman Khalid is a Research Fellow in the Department of Civil and Environmental Engineering at the University of Michigan, Ann Arbor, USA. He previously served as an Assistant Professor in the Department of Mechanical, Robotics, and Energy Engineering at Dongguk University, Seoul, Republic of Korea. His research spans the fields of prognostics and health management (PHM), machine learning, and smart infrastructure systems, with particular emphasis on fault detection, predictive maintenance, and intelligent monitoring of industrial and structural assets. He has authored and co-authored numerous journal articles and book chapters on intelligent diagnostic frameworks, data-driven modeling, and the integration of AI techniques into complex engineering systems. His ongoing research at the University of Michigan focuses on developing computational intelligence methods for reliability assessment and risk-informed decision making in large-scale civil infrastructure.

Ananda Shankar

Ananda Shankar Hati earned his Ph.D. degree in electrical engineering from the Indian Institute of Technology (IIT) [Indian School of Mines (ISM)], Dhanbad, India in 2016. He is an assistant professor at IIT (ISM), Dhanbad 826004, India. His research interests include prognostic health management of electrical machines, drive systems, and energy efficiency in motors. He is a Fellow of the Royal Society of Arts (U.K.) and the Institute of Electronics and Telecommunication (India), and a Senior Member of IEEE.

Prashant Kumar

Prashant Kumar is an Assistant Professor in the Department of AI and Big Data at Woosong University, Daejeon, South Korea. He earned his B.Tech in Electrical Engineering (2014), M.Tech in Electrical Engineering (2017) from Indian Institute of Technology (Indian School of Mines) Dhanbad, India, and completed his Ph.D. in February 2022 from Indian Institute of Technology (Indian School of Mines) Dhanbad, India. His research interests include prognostics and health management (PHM), smart manufacturing, application of artificial intelligence to fault diagnosis of rotating machinery and e-mobility systems, mine winder drives, and mine electrical safety. He serves as reviewer for high-impact journals including *IEEE Transactions on Industrial Electronics, IEEE Transactions on Industry Applications, IEEE Transactions on Power Electronics, IEEE Transactions on Instrumentation and Measurement, IEEE Systems Journal, ISA Transactions, and Neural Networks.*

Preface

The rapid evolution of artificial intelligence has transformed the landscape of fault diagnosis and condition monitoring across industrial systems. Machine learning and deep learning algorithms have enabled engineers and researchers to move beyond traditional rule-based diagnostics toward autonomous, data-driven decision-making frameworks. This transformation has been particularly significant in safety-critical domains such as robotics, manufacturing, energy systems, and rotating machinery, where early fault detection is essential for ensuring reliability and minimizing operational downtime.

This Reprint compiles a selection of peer-reviewed studies that demonstrate the growing influence of machine learning and deep learning theories in the development of intelligent fault diagnosis systems. The collected works span fundamental theoretical advancements, novel algorithmic approaches, and practical implementations that bridge the gap between computational intelligence and engineering reliability. Together, they illustrate how data-centric paradigms are reshaping prognostics and health management (PHM) in the context of Industry 4.0.

The motivation behind this Reprint is to provide a unified platform for disseminating multidisciplinary research efforts that advance fault diagnosis methodologies. By bringing together contributions from leading experts, this collection aims to inspire continued innovation in intelligent fault diagnosis and promote collaboration among researchers in artificial intelligence, mechanical and electrical engineering, and industrial automation. It is intended for academics, practitioners, and students who seek to understand both the theoretical underpinnings and real-world implications of AI-driven diagnostic technologies.

We sincerely thank all authors, reviewers, and the editorial staff for their invaluable contributions to the success of this Reprint.

Heung Soo Kim, Salman Khalid, Ananda Shankar, and Prashant Kumar
Guest Editors

mathematics

MDPI

Article

An Interpretable Time Series Forecasting Model for Predicting NOx Emission Concentration in Ferroalloy Electric Arc Furnace Plants

Youngjin Seol [1], Seunghyun Lee [1], Jiho Lee [1], Chang-Wan Kim [2], Hyun Su Bak [3], Youngchul Byun [3] and Janghyeok Yoon [1,*]

1 Department of Industrial Engineering, Konkuk University, 120 Neungdong-ro, Gwangjin-gu, Seoul 05029, Republic of Korea; syj6151@konkuk.ac.kr (Y.S.); ant6836@konkuk.ac.kr (S.L.); oscar@neopons.com (J.L.)
2 School of Mechanical Engineering, Konkuk University, 120 Neungdong-ro, Gwangjin-gu, Seoul 05029, Republic of Korea; goodant@konkuk.ac.kr
3 Particulate Matter Research Center, Research Institute of Industrial Science and Technology (RIST), Gwangyang 57801, Republic of Korea; hsbak@rist.re.kr (H.S.B.); ycbyun@rist.re.kr (Y.B.)
* Correspondence: janghyoon@konkuk.ac.kr

Abstract: Considering the pivotal role of ferroalloys in the steel industry and the escalating global emphasis on sustainability (e.g., zero emissions and carbon neutrality), the demand for ferroalloys is anticipated to increase. However, the electric arc furnace (EAF) of ferroalloy plants generates substantial amounts of nitrogen oxides (NOx) because of the high-temperature combustion processes. Despite the substantial contributions of many studies on NOx prediction from various industrial facilities, there is a lack of studies considering the environmental condition of the EAF in ferroalloy plants. Therefore, this study presents a deep learning model for predicting NOx emissions from ferroalloy plants and further can provide guidelines for predicting NOx in industrial sites equipped with electric furnaces. In this study, we collected various historical data from the manufacturing execution system of electric furnaces and exhaust gas systems to develop a prediction model. Additionally, an interpretable artificial intelligence method was employed to track the effects of each variable on the NOx emissions. The proposed prediction model can provide decision support to reduce NOx emissions. Furthermore, the interpretation of the model contributes to a better understanding of the factors influencing NOx emissions and the development of effective strategies for emission reduction in ferroalloys EAF plants.

Keywords: NOx emission; electric arc furnace; deep learning; explainable artificial intelligence

MSC: 68T05; 68T07; 68T37

1. Introduction

The escalating global emphasis on sustainability, such as zero emissions, has led to changes in various industries, including the steel industry [1]. A wide range of policies, strategies, protocols, and interventions related to emission reductions for specific air pollutants have been implemented globally [2]. Particularly, in the Republic of Korea, owing to increasingly stringent environmental regulations, government agencies have installed sensors in stacks for telemonitoring and regulating factories that emit environmental pollutants [3]. Additionally, the demand for ferroalloy, which is an essential raw material for the steel industry, is anticipated to increase not only because of its importance in manufacturing steel but also because of evolving production technologies aimed at reducing emissions [1]. Ferroalloys are iron alloys with a high proportion of one or more elements, such as manganese (Mn), aluminum (Al), and silicon (Si), which enhance the characteristics of steel and cast iron or serve essential functions in the manufacturing process [4]. Although ferroalloy production using electric arc furnaces (EAFs) results in lower emissions than steel production using blast furnaces, the ferroalloy production process still generates a considerable amount of NOx emissions, a substantial portion of which originates from EAFs themselves [5]. As NOx is a major contributor to air pollution and a factor that affects human health [6], there has been an increasing focus on research to predict and reduce NOx emissions from various facilities [7–9]. However, despite the high demand for ferroalloys and the significant NOx emissions associated with their production, there is a lack of research on predicting NOx emissions from EAFs, which are the primary sources of NOx at production sites. In this study, we developed a deep learning-based time series prediction model to predict NOx emissions from electric furnaces. For this purpose, data were collected from electric furnace and exhaust gas equipment at a ferroalloy production site. Furthermore, to interpret the deep learning-based prediction model, we used interpretable artificial intelligence techniques to identify the variables that have a significant impact on NOx prediction in the electric furnace environment.

Predicting NOx emissions in EAFs can facilitate the reduction in emissions through both pre-management, by adjusting key operating variables in production facilities, and post-management, by enhancing denitrification facilities for efficient NOx removal from exhaust gases. However, predicting NOx emissions in EAFs is challenging, owing to the severe internal environment and complex combustion reactions [10,11]. EAFs produce various exhaust gases and particulate matter during high-temperature combustion. Additionally, the inside of the furnace chimney is exposed to a hot, humid environment containing a mixture of various gases. Owing to these conditions, it is difficult to accurately predict the NOx concentration within EAFs. There are two main approaches to predicting NOx emissions [9,12]. The first one is the mechanism-based calculation approach, which involves various parameters and empirical formulas for heat transfer, combustion, and turbulence [12–15]. However, this approach to NOx prediction requires various assumptions and time to simulate the combustion process and predict NOx emissions, making it challenging to model a combination of various factors inside EAFs [9,12,16].

The second approach is a data-driven method that establishes the relationships between NOx emissions and output variables based on data [9,10]. Compared with the first approach, this data-driven approach does not need to solve complex equations [12]. In this regard, many studies have employed data-driven methods to predict NOx emissions by applying a deep belief network (DBN) [9], artificial neural network (ANN) [17], extreme learning machine (ELM) [8], and long short-term memory (LSTM) [7] to various facilities such as coal-fired boilers, cement precalcining kilns, and industrial waste incinerators [7,17,18]. Although these data-based approaches have proven to be effective in predicting NOx emissions in diverse applications, applying data-based approaches to the EAFs of ferroalloy production facilities has certain limitations. First, these approaches were designed without considering the specific environment of the EAFs in ferroalloy production facilities. EAFs have unique environmental conditions compared to other high-temperature industrial settings, including higher temperatures from electric arcs (commonly reach 2000 °C) and reliance on electrical energy instead of fossil fuels [19,20]. Unlike the constant conditions found in other combustion processes, EAFs involve a dynamic process for producing products. This includes adding raw materials, removing slag, and adjusting alloy compositions even during operation. In addition, the absence of a data collection system to gather the necessary information from ferroalloy production systems presents another challenge. Identifying the data that are essential for the accurate prediction of NOx emissions from EAFs remains unclear. Therefore, further research is required to develop NOx emission prediction models that account for the unique conditions within EAFs. Second, many previous studies have employed machine learning-based models for NOx prediction, focusing only on predictive performance analysis. For the successful collaboration between experts and machine learning technology, the key factor is interpretability [21]. This ensures that behaviors of the model and predictions are understandable to humans, facilitating further application for EAFs. Accordingly, for NOx prediction and reduction, it is necessary to analyze the critical factors for NOx prediction and to understand the behaviors of the predictive models.

This study conducts a data-driven NOx emission prediction that is suitable for the exhaust gas generation mechanism in the EAFs of ferroalloy production facilities. Additionally, the study employs interpretable artificial intelligence (AI) algorithms to identify variables that contribute significantly to NOx emissions, thereby proposing an interpretable model that considers the characteristics of EAFs to predict NOX emissions. Therefore, this study provides guidance for constructing NOx prediction systems and data collection systems for EAFs and can also be utilized to support the installation and operation of denitrification equipment for NOx reduction by providing NOx emissions from EAFs and furnishing data on NOx emissions from EAFs. It also offers insights into the factors influencing these emissions, facilitating the environmental management and efficient control of NOx emissions during ferroalloy production.

2. Background

2.1. Operation and Gas Exhaustion Process of the Electric Arc Furnace

EAFs are primarily used to produce ferroalloys. The ferroalloy production process consists of raw material transportation, raw material pretreatment, electric furnace melting, refining, and casting. In EAFs, raw materials such as iron scrap are melted and refined; subsequently, oxidizing slag is produced to remove impurities from the molten pool [20]. An EAF is a sealed structure in which raw materials are charged and electrodes are inserted after sealing with a cover. As illustrated in Figure 1, the melting of the raw materials begins with an arc discharge. Electrical energy is supplied through the graphite electrodes, creating a powerful electric arc between the electrodes and raw materials. This intense electric arc, with its strong voltage, serves as the primary heat source for melting the material. The internal temperature of the furnace is controlled by adjusting the position of the electrodes. During the melting process, EAFs emit thermal NOx and other gases because of the high temperatures generated, and NOx emission is predominantly concentrated in this melting process.

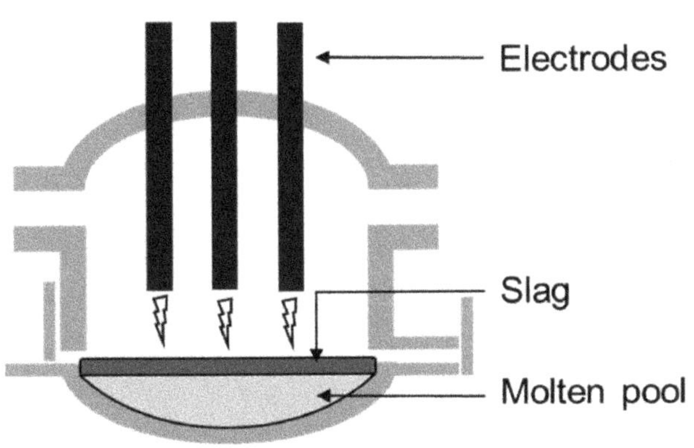

Figure 1. Schematic of an electric arc furnace.

In this study, we collected data from EAFs and exhaust gas emission facilities at a ferroalloy production site in South Korea. Figure 2 illustrates the exhaust gas emissions generated in the EAFs considered in this study. By melting the raw materials, EAFs generate a significant amount of thermal NOx. Subsequently, the dust duct captures and collects the exhaust gases and fine particulates generated in the preceding processes. The exhaust gases are then directed to a semi-dry reactor (SDR), where water is injected to control the temperature of the exhaust gas. In the SDR, further treatment, such as desulfurization, occurs to remove additional pollutants from the exhaust before release.

The role of SDRs extends beyond temperature control to actively reduce the concentrations of various harmful substances in exhaust gas. Bag filters remove particulate pollutants (e.g., dust) but not gaseous pollutants (e.g., NOx and SOx). This phase primarily focuses on eliminating fine particulates from the gas stream. An induced draft fan (IDF) is operated to expel gases from outside the stack using pressure. The IDF creates a suction effect that ensures the efficient and effective discharge of gases, thereby minimizing the emission of untreated or partially treated exhaust gases into the environment.

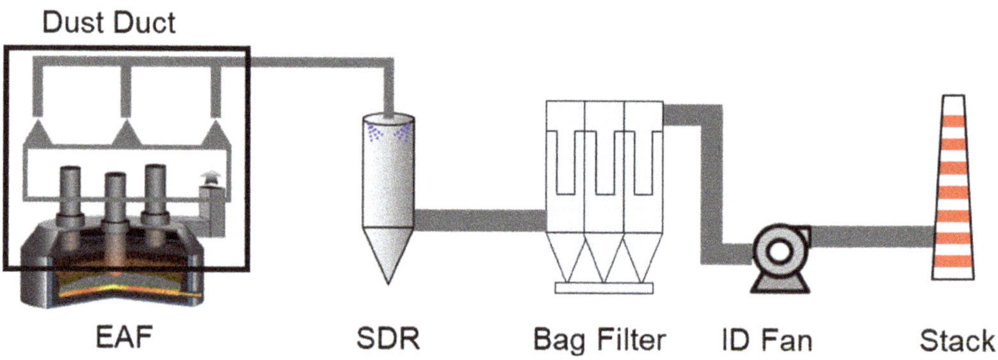

Figure 2. Schematic of the NOx emission process from the electric arc furnace to the chimney.

2.2. Data-Driven NOx Emissions Prediction Research

Owing to the complex mechanism of NOx emissions from facilities involving high-temperature processes, such as coal-fired power plants, research has been conducted on predicting NOx emissions from exhaust gases (Table 1). Research has been conducted to predict NOx emissions by utilizing computational fluid dynamics (CFD) simulations to generate data on flow, temperature, and chemical reactions within the furnace. Faravelli et al. [22] proposed a method for predicting NOx emissions from gas/oil boilers by utilizing CFD to obtain data on flow, temperature, and stoichiometry within the furnace. They simplified the conditions with an ideal reactor network which is interconnected and perfectly stirred or plug flow reactors to predict NOx emissions using a detailed kinetic scheme. Likewise, Lv et al. [23] utilized CFD simulations to generate 3D NOx spatial distribution data and applied extreme learning machine modeling for accurate predictions of NOx distribution in the furnace. This study partitioned data based on NOx generation mechanisms for enhancing model accuracy and provided a detailed approach for NOx prediction in furnace environments. However, a potential limitation of these studies is the requirement for fluid dynamics experts to effectively use CFD, requiring expertise in handling diverse parameters and empirical formulas for heat transfer, combustion, and turbulence specific to each facility's environmental conditions. This complexity can pose challenges for implementation in areas with limited research, such as EAFs, due to the variability in environmental conditions across different facilities.

Compared to the challenges associated with CFD studies, research utilizing data-driven methods has been conducted to establish the relationship between operational variables and NOx generation, thereby enabling the prediction of NOx emissions from various facilities with less difficulty. Wang, Ma, Wang, Li, and Zhang [9] proposed a method for data acquisition and NOx emission prediction in coal-fired power plants using DBN-based models utilizing historical operating data. Tang, Wang, Chai, Cao, Ouyang, and Li [8] proposed an autoencoder ELM model to predict NOx emission concentrations from a coal-fired boiler. In their study, an autoencoder was utilized to extract hidden features from the variables of operational data, and an ELM model was then applied to predict NOx emissions from the hidden features. Zhang, Wang, Shao, Duan, and Hou [17] utilized an ANN to predict NOx in cement precalcining kilns and a genetic algorithm to search for optimal operation parameters to achieve the lowest concentration of nitrogen oxide emissions.

Table 1. Prior NOx prediction studies in facilities with combustion process.

Facility	Data	Prediction Method	Reference
Gas/oil-fired boiler	Fluent-based simulation data	Computer fluid dynamics, ideal reactor network	Faravelli, Bua, Frassoldati, Antifora, Tognotti, and Ranzi [22]
Coal-fired boiler	Fluent-based simulation data	Computer fluid dynamics, extreme learning machine	Lv, Zhao, Cao, and Shen [23]
Coal-fired boiler	Historical operation data, fluent-based simulation data, and experimental data	Deep belief network	Wang, Ma, Wang, Li, and Zhang [9]
Coal-fired boiler	Historical operation data	Auto-encoder, extreme learning machine	Tang, Wang, Chai, Cao, Ouyang, and Li [8]
Cement precalcining kiln	Historical operation data	Artificial neural network	Zhang, Wang, Shao, Duan, and Hou [17]
Coal-fired boiler	Historical operation data	Recurrent neural network	Safdarnejad, Tuttle, and Powell [24]
Coal-fired boiler	Historical operation data	Long short-term memory network	Yang, Wang, and Li [7]
Diesel engine	World harmonized transient cycle (WHTC) emission test data	Convolutional neural network, long short-term memory network	Shen, Wang, Wang, Zeng, Yu, and He [25]
Coal-fired boiler	Historical operation data	Random forest algorithm, lightweight convolutional neural network	Wang, Peng, Cao, Zhou, Fan, Li, and Huang [12]
Coal-fired boiler	Historical operation data	Convolutional neural networks, channel Attention mechanism	Li et al. [26]

However, previous studies utilizing ANN-based models have certain limitations. This is because they do not utilize the temporal dynamics of the operating variables in facilities, which can contribute to NOx emissions. As the combustion of an EAF is a dynamic process, EAFs' working conditions are correlated with historical NOx emissions. Given that manufacturing execution systems (MESs) and telemonitoring systems (TMSs) store dynamic time series data, previous time series data can be leveraged to develop prediction models. Safdarnejad et al. [24] developed a dynamic data-driven model for a coal-fired utility boiler to estimate NOx and CO emissions simultaneously, utilizing recurrent neural networks to capture time series characteristics of the data. Yang, Wang, and Li [7] focused on using LSTM networks to model the relationship between the operational parameters and NOx emissions in a 660 MW boiler. To enhance NOx emissions prediction in diesel engine transient environments, Shen et al. [25] proposed a prediction model based on a hybrid neural network architecture that combines the feature extraction capabilities of a convolutional neural network (CNN) with the time series prediction proficiency of LSTM networks. In addition to models considering the temporal dynamics of the operating variables in facilities, research has been conducted to modify the characteristics and purposes of prediction in facilities or enhance the performance of existing models. To improve the efficiency of the denitrification process in power plants, Wang, Peng, Cao, Zhou, Fan, Li, and Huang [12] proposed a modeling method using a random forest algorithm for the dimensionality reduction in input data and a lightweight CNN. In their study, satisfactory NOx predictive performance was obtained. A lightweight CNN is preferred over a high-performance CNN, which requires numerous parameters and floating-point operations. Lightweight CNN could offer the advantage of efficient computation and reduced complexity, making them more suitable for real-time NOx emission prediction tasks in coal-fired boilers. Li et al.'s [25] study presents a CNN-based model for the accurate prediction of NOx emissions from a coal-fired power plant boiler. An attention mechanism was integrated into the CNN-based model, with the attention module focusing on the interdependencies between channels in the input feature maps to capture important information in latent space.

Though previous studies have proposed data-driven NOx prediction methods for facilities with combustion systems, research on predicting NOx emissions from EAFs is still lacking. Consequently, data-acquisition systems tailored for NOx prediction in EAF environments are lacking. An EAF generates extremely high temperatures to melt raw materials, and owing to the characteristics of the molten pool during ferroalloy production, noise is generated when measuring the exhaust gases emitted during ferroalloy production. As the gas trapped beneath the slag layer in the molten pool and the collapse of charged raw materials can lead to sudden explosions and a rapid increase in NOx emissions, it is necessary to smooth the NOx emission values before utilizing them as training data for the prediction model. In addition, exhaust gases in ferroalloy production facilities motion at high speeds in hot and humid environments. In such an environment, data collected by IoT sensors in a pipe may contain noise, owing to various factors. Thus, data preprocessing techniques are required to construct training data for the prediction mode by smoothing the noise. To smooth out noise or outliers, a Kalman filter is used to estimate the current state from past measurements and correct outlier data based on the distribution of the given data.

2.3. Interpretable Prediction Models

Despite the contributions of previous studies to the prediction of NOx emissions in various combustion processes, an interesting yet unexplored angle still exists. In the case of deep-learning-based prediction models, numerous studies have focused on performance analysis, making it difficult to track the impact of input variables on NOx emissions. As deep learning-based predictions rely solely on black-box models with undisclosed internal mechanisms, experts in decision making have experienced challenges in utilizing these predictive models [27].

Interpretable artificial intelligence methods are processes that provide interpretability in a form understandable by humans, based on the explainability of how a model works [28]. They can be classified based on the complexity of the model into post hoc and intrinsic approaches [29]. The intrinsic approach involves models that are naturally interpretable due to their simple structure (e.g., decision trees, linear SVMs). On the other hand, the post hoc approach is applied after the model has been trained, focusing on the analysis and interpretation of the model's behavior. LIME (local interpretable model-agnostic explanations) and SHAP (SHapley Additive exPlanations) are well-known methods, offering insights into how the model makes its predictions. Both approaches are model-agnostic and can be utilized across various models. LIME focuses on local explanations, offering insights into the interpretation process for specific data points, but it has limitations in providing global interpretations and consistency in the contribution of input variables [30]. SHAP similarly allows for an understanding of individual contributions to predictions across the entire dataset, but this approach can offer a broader analysis of model predictions, such as feature importance [31]. Consequently, it has been utilized across various domains for its comprehensive insights into model behavior [32,33].

Considering the ability to provide model-agnostic interpretations and both global and local explanations [21,31], therefore, this study utilizes SHapley Additive exPlanations (SHAP) to uncover the inner workings of a machine learning model for time series data to predict NOx emissions from EAFs. This study constructs a model that reflects the relationships between input variables over time and employs preprocessing techniques specific to the features of EAFs to build the training dataset. Additionally, interpretable AI is utilized to analyze the impact of the input variables on NOx emission predictions.

3. Methodology

3.1. Kalman Filter-Based Smoothing Algorithm

Owing to the extreme environment in the chimney, the NOx data collected by the sensors often contain noise. To address this issue, a Kalman-filter-based smoothing algorithm is introduced to mitigate sensor noise, remove outliers, and enhance the quality of the collected data to train the prediction model [34]. Kalman filtering is a method for estimating the state of a dynamic system [35,36]. It predicts the next state based on the current state and subsequently updates the predicted state using new measurements. The mathematical model can be expressed as follows:

X_k is the state vector representing the system's state at time k.

Y_k is the measurement at time k.

Q is the process noise variance.

R is the measurement variance.

P_k is the error covariance matrix at time k.

K_k is the Kalman gain at time k.

The Kalman gain adjusts the confidence between the current prediction and observed data, thereby determining the optimal state correction. Therefore, a higher Kalman gain value places more trust in the observed data and less emphasis on prediction, allowing the Kalman filter to estimate and predict the system state more accurately. The state variables of the system are estimated using measured data. The measurement data sequence is used as the input to estimate the state of the system, and the Kalman filter-based smoothing algorithm is performed as follows (Algorithm 1):

$$\hat{X}_{k+1|k} = X_k \tag{1}$$

$$P_{k+1|k} = P_k + Q \tag{2}$$

$$e_k = Y_{k+1} - \hat{X}_{k+1|k} \tag{3}$$

$$K_k = \frac{P_{k+1|k}}{P_{k+1|k} + R} \tag{4}$$

$$X_{k+1} = \hat{X}_{k+1|k} + K_k \cdot e_k \tag{5}$$

$$P_{k+1|k} = (I - K_k) \cdot P_{k+1|k} \tag{6}$$

Algorithm 1. Kalman filter-based smoothing algorithm

Input: X_k, Y_{k+1}, P_k
Output: X_{k+1}, P_{k+1}
Prediction:
(a) State prediction (Equation (1)).
(b) Error covariance prediction (Equation (2)).
Update:
(c) Innovation (Equation (3))
(d) Kalman gain (Equation (4))
(e) State update (Equation (5))
(f) Error covariance update (Equation (6))

3.2. NOx Emission Prediction

3.2.1. Long Short-Term Memory Network

NOx emissions in EAFs represent a time series issue because of the relationship between the past operating conditions and the current state. Since NOx emissions during combustion in an EAF is a non-linear and complex process [15], variables and temporal factors should be considered. Given the time series nature of NOx emissions in EAFs, an LSTM neural network-based model is adopted (Figure 3). Owing to the ability of the LSTM network to remember long-term dependencies, it can capture patterns in emission data [7], and it has been increasingly utilized in various time series prediction domains [7,34,37]. LSTM networks employ an unique architecture that uses structures known as gates to regulate a value called the cell state (C). The cell state acts as the memory for the network, which is crucial for retaining and carrying relevant information throughout the data sequence. The ability of LSTM networks to use gates to regulate cell states is crucial, and this mechanism allows the network to selectively retain or discard information, thereby enhancing its efficiency in analyzing time series data. The forget gate in LSTM networks uses a sigmoid function to assess previous outputs (h_{t-1}) and current inputs (i_t), determining which past information to retain or discard from the cell state. The input gate in the LSTM network updates cell state C_t. It employs a sigmoid function to identify which elements of the current input are significant and identifies a tangent hyperbolic function to generate a vector of new candidate values, $\widetilde{C}_t$. These elements are integrated to update C_t using essential new information. The output gate determines the final output h_t by filtering the cell state $\widetilde{C}_t$ through a tangent hyperbolic function and then multiplying it by the output of the sigmoid function. This selectively updates h_t with the relevant information from C_t. Each gate in the LSTM network operates according to the following formula:

$$\text{The forget gate}: \ f_t = \sigma\left(W_f \cdot [h_{t-1}, x_t] + b_f\right) \tag{7}$$

$$\text{The input gate}: \ i_t = \sigma(W_i \cdot [h_{t-1}, x_t] + b_i) \tag{8}$$

$$\text{Alongside } \widetilde{C}_t = tanh(W_C \cdot [h_{t-1}, x_t] + b_C) \tag{9}$$

$$C_t = f_t \otimes C_{t-1} + i_t \otimes \widetilde{C}_t \tag{10}$$

$$\text{The output gate}: \ O_t = \sigma(W_O \cdot [h_{t-1}, x_t] + b_o) \tag{11}$$

$$h_t = O_t \otimes tanh(C_t) \tag{12}$$

$$\sigma(x) = \frac{1}{1+e^{-x}} \tag{13}$$

$$tanh(x) = \frac{e^x - e^{-x}}{e^x + e^{-x}} \tag{14}$$

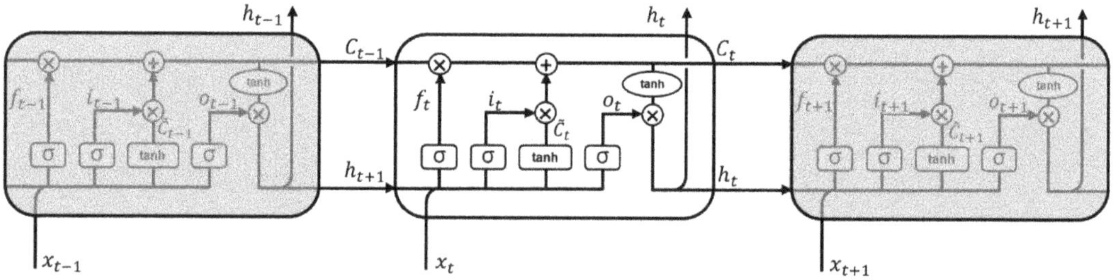

Figure 3. Structure of LSTM.

C_t denotes the state of the LSTM cells at time t, and h_t denotes the output of the unit at time t. W denotes the weight parameter metrics. f_t, i_t, and o_t denote the forget, input, and output gates and state vector at time t. ⊗ represents element-wise multiplication. When applied to EAFs, utilizing their strengths in learning the sequence of features [7,25,34,37], the LSTM network can offer advantages in improving the accuracy of predicting NOx emissions typically associated with the operations of these furnaces.

3.2.2. Delay Time Determination

At Korean ferroalloy production sites, TMSs are commonly used to measure the NOx concentrations in EAFs [3]. Throughout the processes of NOx generation, detection, and control, numerous parameters are monitored using the MES, as depicted in Figure 2. However, these parameters are not measured simultaneously by the sensors, which leads to inherent delays in data acquisition. In addition, the combustion processes in EAFs involve complex reactions that occur over time and can influence NOx emissions. Given that changes in the variables within the process do not immediately affect the NOx emissions, it is necessary to select an appropriate delay time between the variables. This helps determine the suitable length of the sequence to be input into the LSTM model, which is suitable for processing and predicting events with intervals and delays in a time series [38]. The delay time selection method based on mutual information (MI) focuses on identifying the most effective sequence length from the operation variables to predict NOx emissions. Tang, Wang, Chai, Cao, Ouyang, and Li [8] determined the delay time between each feature and NOx emission concentration using the MI method. This is achieved by maximizing the combined MI between the input features and target variable. MI is an information theory measure that quantifies the amount of information obtained from one random variable by observing another [39]. MI is frequently used to evaluate the dependence or correlation between variables, capturing insights that traditional regression analyses may not reveal. Here, MI serves as a metric for measuring the extent to which one variable informs another, thereby indicating their level of interdependence. $X = [x_1, x_2, \ldots, x_n]$, and n is the number of samples in dataset X. $H(X)$ represents the information entropy of random variable x. The probability distribution of x_i is $p(x_i)$. $H(X,Y)$ is the joint entropy of X and Y. The probability density functions of x and y are $p(x)$ and $p(y)$. The degree of correlation between the two random variables can be expressed by the MI as follows [40]:

$$H(X) = -\sum_{i=1}^{n} p(x_i)\log p(x_i) \tag{15}$$

$$I(X;Y) = H(X) + H(Y) - H(X,Y) \tag{16}$$

$$I(x;y) = \sum_{y} \sum_{x \epsilon X} p(x,y) log \frac{p(x,y)}{p(x)p(y)} \tag{17}$$

To determine the delay time, it is varied starting from one step, and the time step that yields the highest MI is selected. By analyzing the MI between the variables and the NOx emission concentration, it is possible to determine the maximum feasible delay time for all input variables.

3.2.3. NOx Emission Prediction Model Development

This study develops a model to predict future NOx emissions using a sequence of data comprising 19 variables, including NOx emissions. To capture the trend of previously emitted NOx levels, NOx emissions are utilized as predictive variables. The performance of the NOx prediction model is assessed using quantitative performance evaluation metrics. The mean absolute percentage error (MAPE) measures the average percentage error between predicted and actual values. The R-squared (R^2) score, or the coefficient of determination, indicates how well the predicted values fit the actual data, with a score of 1 representing a perfect fit. The mean squared error (MSE) quantifies the average of the squares of errors and measures the variance of the prediction errors. The mean absolute error (MAE) measures the average magnitude of errors between the predicted and actual values without considering direction.

$$MAPE = \frac{100}{n} \sum_{i=1}^{n} \frac{y_i - \hat{y}_i}{\hat{y}_i} \tag{18}$$

$$R^2 = \frac{\sum_{i=1}^{n} (\hat{y}_i - \overline{y_i})^2}{\sum_{i=1}^{n} (y_i - \overline{y_i})^2} \tag{19}$$

$$MSE = \frac{1}{n}\sum_{i=1}^{n}(\hat{y}_i - y_i)^2 \tag{20}$$

$$MAE = \frac{1}{n}\sum_{i=1}^{n}|\hat{y}_i - y_i| \tag{21}$$

3.3. Interpretation of the NOx Emissions Prediction

Although machine-learning-based models have been adopted in various domains, their black-box nature, which enables powerful predictions, presents a key impediment in that AI-based systems often lack interpretability and need interpretable machine learning [27]. To address the lack of interpretability of complex and nonlinear machine-learning-based models, the post hoc interpretation method employs a model-agnostic method to explain how certain features contribute to predictions and the model's behavior [21]. Among the various interpretation methods, SHAP is a widely used framework for interpreting the predictions of machine learning models based on the Shapley value of the conditional expectation of a model [41,42].

SHAP evaluates the feature importance using additive feature attribution methods, as illustrated in Equation (22).

$$g(z') = \phi_0 + \sum_{i=1}^{M}\phi_i z'_i \tag{22}$$

Let f be the original predictive model to be explained and g be the explanation model. Where $z' \in \{0,1\}^M$ is a coalition vector that indicates whether the ith feature is present (=1) or absent (=0), M is the number of features, $\phi_i \in \mathbb{R}$ is the importance value of the ith feature, and ϕ_0 is the baseline outcome without any feature. Specifically, SHAP identifies the importance of each feature as a change in the expected model prediction when conditioning on that feature and explains how to change from the base value $E[f(z)]$ to the current output $f(x)$. SHAP averages the ϕ_i values across all possible ordering. Hence, when defining $f_x(S) = E[f_x|x_s]$ for a subset of features (S), the SHAP value (ϕ_i) is expressed as in Equation (23).

$$\phi_i = \sum_{S\subseteq\{x_1,\ldots,x_m\backslash\{x_i\}}\frac{|S|!(M-|S|-1)!}{M!}\left(f_x\left(S\bigcup\{x_i\}\right) - f_x(S)\right) \tag{23}$$

where $f_x(S\bigcup\{x_i\})$ and $f_x(S)$ are the model prediction with and without the ith feature. SHAP is an additive feature attribution method when ϕ_0 equals $f_x(\phi)$, representing the baseline prediction with no features. The original model's prediction for each sample is equal to the sum of all the feature SHAP values. Thus, the SHAP values indicate the contribution of each feature to the predictions of the model.

Calculating the precise SHAP value poses a challenge due to the necessity of evaluating each potential feature subset, resulting in exponential computational complexity [21]. Therefore, we utilized deep SHAP, a method that aggregates SHAP values calculated for individual network components to derive SHAP values for the entire network [42,43]. Using deep SHAP, we obtained the SHAP values for each feature. The absolute SHAP value of the ith feature for the jth time-steps is expressed as in $|\phi_{i,j}|$, and the SHAP value of the ith feature ϕ_i is the average of $\phi_{i,j}$.

4. Analyses and Results

4.1. Data Preparation

Data were collected from the MES and TMS of EAFs, and 18,834 data points were collected from 1 May 2023 to 7 July 2023. Among them, 17,422 data points were used for training and 1412 for validation; 1412 data points were collected from 12 July to 17 July for the test dataset. Given that the model based on deep learning demands numerous variables and substantial data, long-term observation and data collection are essential. However, due to the nature of the data collected by sensors, there can be gaps, and there may be times when data are not collected due to operational schedules. Therefore, for research purposes, it is crucial to collect long-term data without gaps across many variables. To build the training dataset for model learning, the NOx emission measurement data were smoothed using a Kalman filter-based smoothing algorithm. Increasing the value of the measurement variance (R) gives more weight to noise in the observed data. In this case, the Kalman filter is less influenced by the predicted values, and the resulting graph is smoother, following the volatility of the observed data more closely. In this study, R was set as 10^2. Increasing the value of the process noise variance (Q) results in greater uncertainty in the system. In this case, the Kalman filter considered the predictions to be more uncertain. Consequently, the graph maintains higher volatility in the predictions. In this study, Q was set as 5^2. The initial error covariance matrix (P) affected the initial state prediction of the Kalman filter. Increasing the initial error covariance matrix (P) value increases the uncertainty of the initial prediction, resulting in a larger initial prediction error. In this study, hyperparameters R, P, and Q were selected as trials and errors. We set the sum of the R and Q so as not to exceed the actual variance of NOx, which is 17.75^2. To smooth the fluctuations in the graph, R was maintained larger than Q. P was set to 0.7, based on the initial measurements' difference, which was approximately 1.3. The smoothed NOx data are shown in Figure 4. We selectively illustrated key examples, as visualizing all data points would obscure this effect.

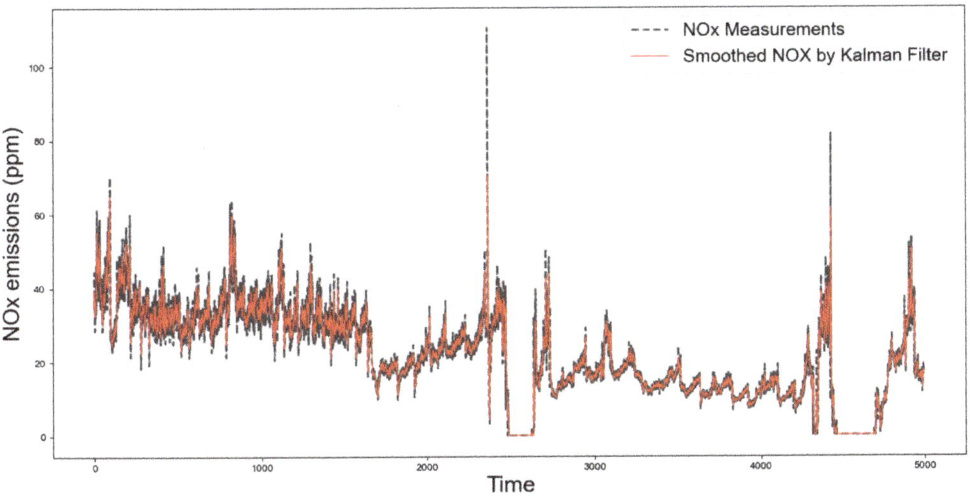

Figure 4. The denoised results of the NOx data using the Kalman filter-based smoothing algorithm.

4.2. NOx Emission Prediction

A comparison of the MI between NOx emissions and variables was conducted to determine the appropriate sequence length for the prediction model input. As shown in Table 2, each variable had a range of delay times from 1 to 6 steps, and each step was 5 min. This design, resulting in a maximum delay time of 30 min, was influenced by regulatory standards mandating emissions monitoring over 30 min intervals in Korea.

To capture the changes in each variable over time, we selected six steps as inputs for the prediction model. The number of units was chosen from the range [64, 128, 256, 512], and the numbers of LSTM and dense layers were varied to identify the optimal number of units that yielded the highest performance. The output of an LSTM layer is a high-dimensional feature vector that cannot be directly used to predict a single NOx emission value. Therefore, a dense layer was employed, wherein each input node was connected to every output node. This setup transformed the LSTM layer's output into a single, predictive NOx emission value. After analyzing the performance evaluation metrics in the pilot experiments, two LSTM layers and one dense layer were used (Figure 5), and the optimal units for each layer were determined as follows: LSTM1 (128), LSTM2 (64), and dense layer (64). As illustrated in Figure 6, the red line representing the predicted values from the model closely followed the dotted line representing the actual NOx emissions. The alignment of these two lines suggests that the model can effectively predict NOx emissions. Figure 7 shows a scatter plot of the prediction models from the test data, where each dot represents an individual prediction against the actual value. The linear fit line indicates the trajectory of the predicted value, and the perfect prediction line in dashed red represents the ideal points at which the predicted values would match the actual values. The 95% prediction band indicates the area in which 95% of the predicted values lie, thus demonstrating the consistency of the model. A narrow 95% prediction band signifies concentrated, accurate predictions within the confidence interval, reflecting a model's consistent output. Conversely, a wide band indicates greater uncertainty and dispersed predictions. The performance of the prediction model is shown in Table 3, and a comparison analysis was conducted to observe the effects of the presence of previous NOx emissions and temporal factors. This analysis revealed that incorporating the previous NOx emissions and temporal factors yielded better results, as reflected by the improved performance metrics. The 'Model without NOx' did not utilize the previous NOx emissions values, indicating that incorporating past NOx emissions data is indeed valuable. The 'Model with only NOx' showed satisfactory performance. It seems that including NOx as a feature is crucial. 'Linear Regression', 'Deep Neural Network (DNN)', 'Gradient Boosting Regression', and 'Random Forest Regression' employed the same variables as the proposed model. However, due to the nature of their models, they did not incorporate the temporal aspect. This table demonstrates the effectiveness of using a model capable of reflecting temporal elements and leveraging previous NOx emissions data.

Table 2. Highest MI according to the delay time of each feature.

Data Description	Mutual Information	Delay Time (5 min)	Data Description	Mutual Information	Delay Time (5 min)
Electrode Depth-A	0.2646	3	Dust Duct Temperature-A	0.8403	1
Electrode Depth-B	0.2283	1	Dust Duct Temperature-B	0.7489	1
Electrode Depth-C	0.2538	1	Dust Duct Temperature-C	0.7651	1
Electrode Supply Water Flow	0.1457	4	Semi Dry Reactor Inlet Temperature	0.7935	1
Press Down Elevation-A	0.2590	3	Semi Dry Reactor Outlet Temperature	0.5817	2
Press Down Elevation-B	0.2992	3	Bag Filter Inlet Pressure	0.2683	6
Press Down Elevation-C	0.3053	3	Bag Filter Differential Pressure	0.2290	6
Power Use	0.5097	3	Induced Draft Fan Inlet Pressure	0.5280	1
Shell Cooling Water Supply Flow	0.2129	2	Induced Draft Fan Power	0.5765	2

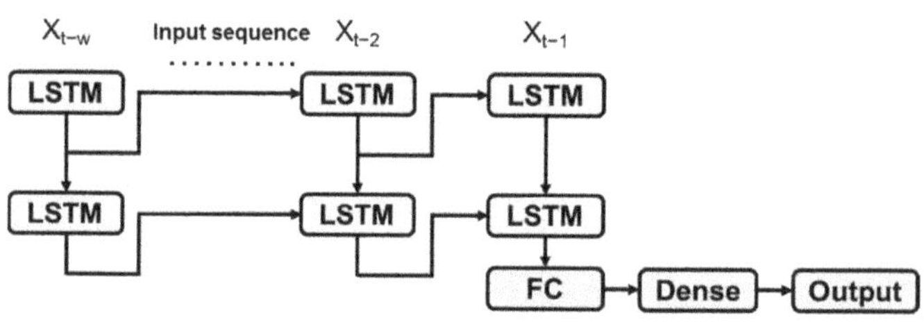

Figure 5. Schematic of the proposed NOx emissions prediction model.

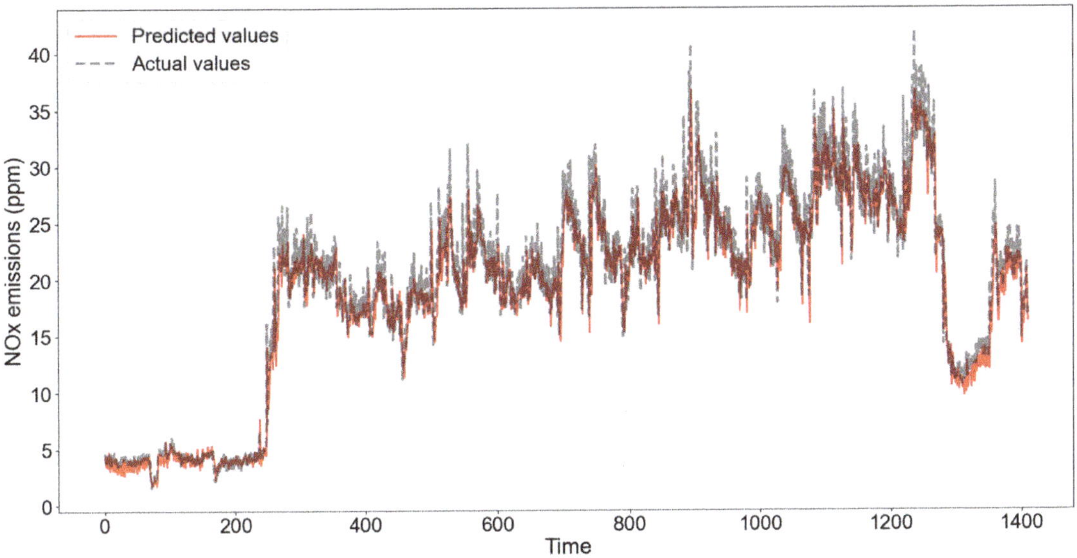

Figure 6. Comparison of predicted and actual NOx emission.

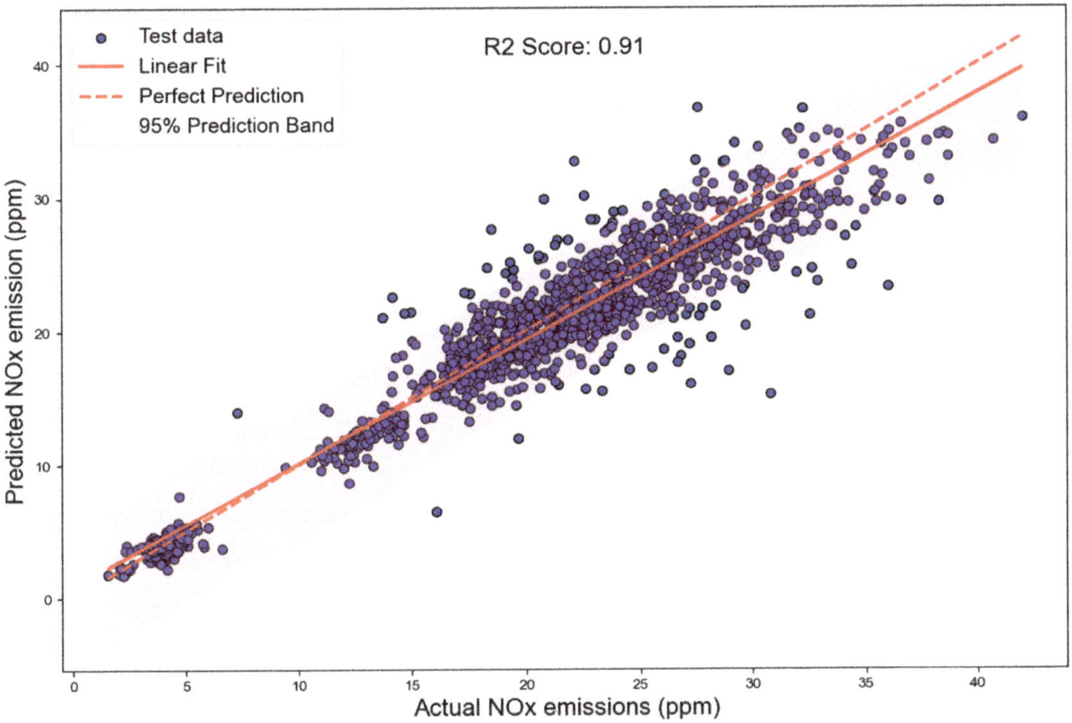

Figure 7. Scatter plots of the prediction model on the test set.

Table 3. Impacts of incorporating temporal factors or previous time-step NOx emissions on the performance (bold: indicates the best model).

Model	MAPE	R^2	MAE	MSE
Proposed Model (NOx)	**9.4506**	**0.9145**	**1.7823**	**6.4525**
Model without NOx	42.6532	0.5859	4.8642	31.2548
Model with only NOx	12.7176	0.5655	2.3918	10.1512
Linear Regression	14.5906	0.8841	2.2690	8.7988
Deep Neural Network (DNN)	14.1423	0.8751	2.3234	9.4811
Gradient Boosting Regression	19.4197	0.7903	3.1028	15.9172
Random Forest Regression	16.0896	0.8777	2.3040	9.2833

4.3. *Interpretation of the NOx Emission Prediction*

The SHAP algorithm was applied to the constructed model to calculate the importance of each variable over time. Specifically, SHAP assigns an importance value to each feature for each prediction, based on additive feature attribution methods that comply with a set of variables. In the test dataset, 1000 data points were randomly selected to derive SHAP values. The results of SHAP analysis provide information on how variables influence the model's predictions but do not directly indicate causality. Therefore, it is important to be aware of this limitation when interpreting the results obtained from SHAP analyses. The average absolute SHAP values for each variable were calculated and plotted to visually represent the impact of these variables on the NOx prediction at different time points (Figure 8). The purpose of the various colors is to distinguish between variables, and therefore, colors are unrelated to whether something is worse or better. Based on the SHAP analysis, the temperature measured in the dust duct and SDR before passing through the SDR device and the NOx emissions at the previous time-steps contributed to the predictions. In the semi-dry reactor (SDR), there is a process where liquid is sprayed into the exhaust gas to lower its temperature. Indeed, a noticeable difference in the area between the SDR inlet temperature and the SDR outlet temperature can be observed. This suggests that the contributions of the semi-dry reactor inlet temperature and the dust duct temperature, which are related to the temperature of the exhaust gas before passing through the semi-dry reactor, may be linked to the actual NOx emissions.

Summary and bar plots were employed to illustrate how the input features contributed to the predicted output values (Figures 9 and 10). Summary plots allow us to understand the global trend of the SHAP values of a feature. Specifically, the summary plots show the distribution of SHAP values for each feature. Each point represents the SHAP value of the feature for an individual prediction. Points moving to the right indicate a positive impact on the model output, whereas points to the left indicate a negative impact. Red points represent "high" NOx emissions, whereas blue points represent "low" NOx emissions. The bar plots represent the importance of the features; their importance decreases from top to bottom. Figure 8 depicts how different variables affect NOx predictions across time. Figure 9 examines the variables' impact on lower NOx emission data points, whereas Figure 10 focuses on higher emission points. Thus, while Figure 8 offers a global view of variable impacts over time, Figures 9 and 10 provide more local insights into their effects at particular emission levels. Figures 9 and 10 show the average SHAP values for each feature in the bar graph. The bar lengths indicate the importance of the features, with longer bars indicating more important features. To derive the SHAP values for both low and high NOx emission levels, we selected 200 data points for each category from the test dataset. The first 200 data points were designated to represent the low NOx emission level, while data points from the 1000th to the 1200th position were chosen to represent the high NOx emission level. Figure 9a shows the summary plots, and Figure 9b shows the bar plots when the NOx emissions are low. Features such as the induced draft fan power, induced draft fan inlet pressure, and bag filter differential pressure were identified as important features when NOx emissions were low. Figure 9b illustrates the variables with high contributions at points of low NOx emissions. The exhaust gas facilities maintain pressure to discharge exhaust gas outside the chimney. Observing that variables such as induced draft fan power, induced draft fan inlet pressure, and bag filter differential pressure have high contributions, it is apparent that at points of low NOx emissions, the internal pressure of the exhaust gas facilities has a greater influence than temperature or operational variables. Figure 10a shows the summary plots, and Figure 10b shows the bar plots when the NOx emissions are high. Features such as exhaust NOx, bag filter differential pressure, and bag filter inlet pressure were identified as important when the NOx emissions were high. As can be seen in Figure 10b, the NOx emissions from previous points have a very high impact. Therefore, it can be inferred that there is some inertia effect with the emissions at a particular level. Figure 11 represents the actual temperature of the dust duct at data points where NOx levels are low and high. In Figure 11, when comparing the temperature in the dust duct, which collects gases emitted from the electric arc furnace (EAF), across two segments, it is observed that there is about a twofold difference. Considering both Figures 8 and 11, they suggest a possible correlation between NOx emissions and the temperature in the exhaust gas system. However, the direct comparison of the SHAP value between low and high emission levels may not entirely reflect an equal analysis due to the dataset containing a higher number of samples at high NOx emission levels. Despite the dataset's imbalance, the figures reveal the relationships between features and the target, offering insights into the variables' impacts on low or high NOx emissions.

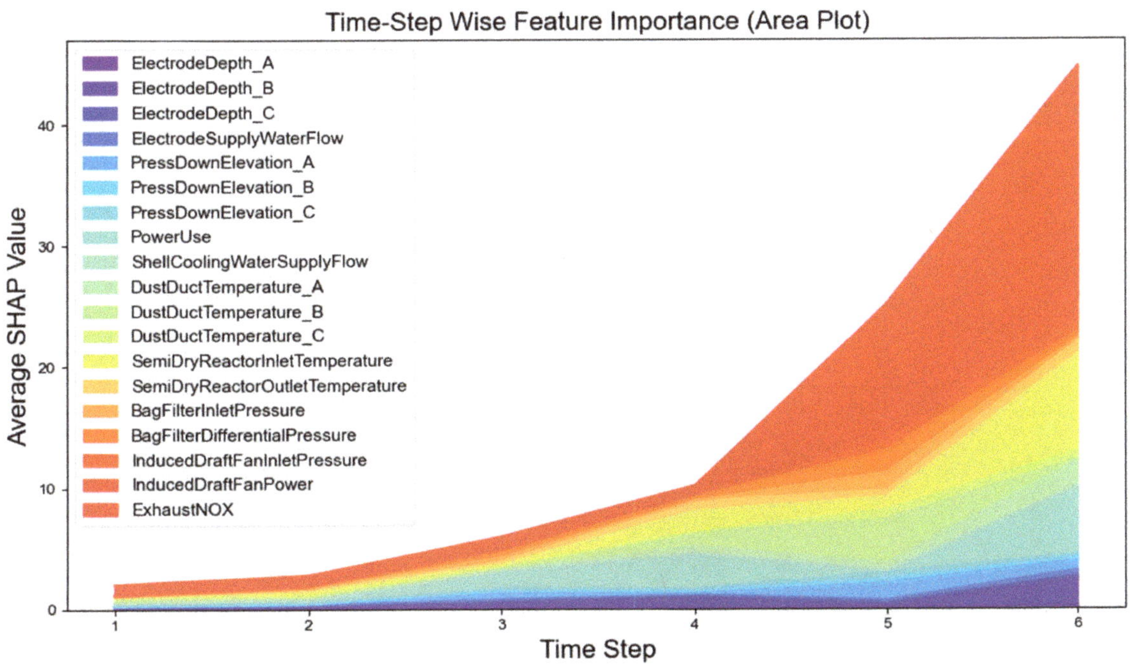

Figure 8. The absolute SHAP value of each variable for time-wise steps.

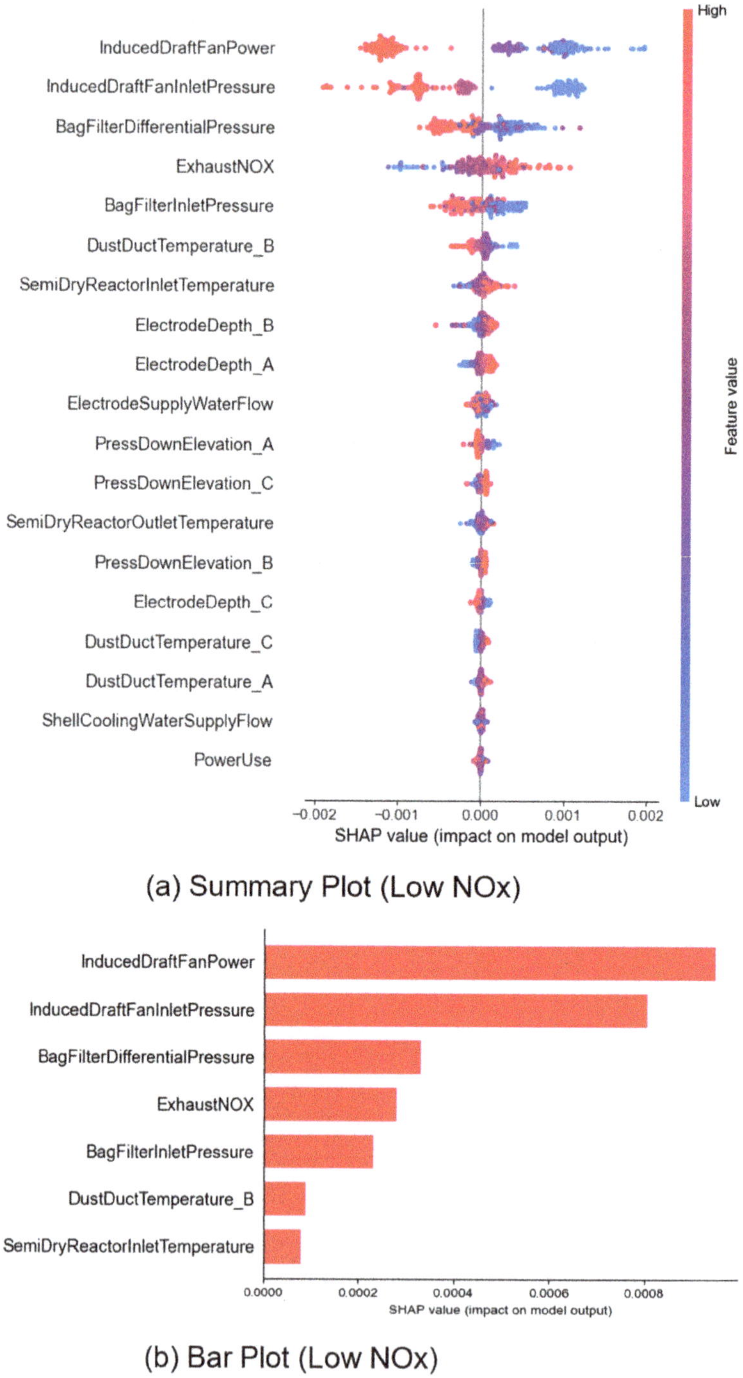

Figure 9. Summary and bar plots with low NOx emissions.

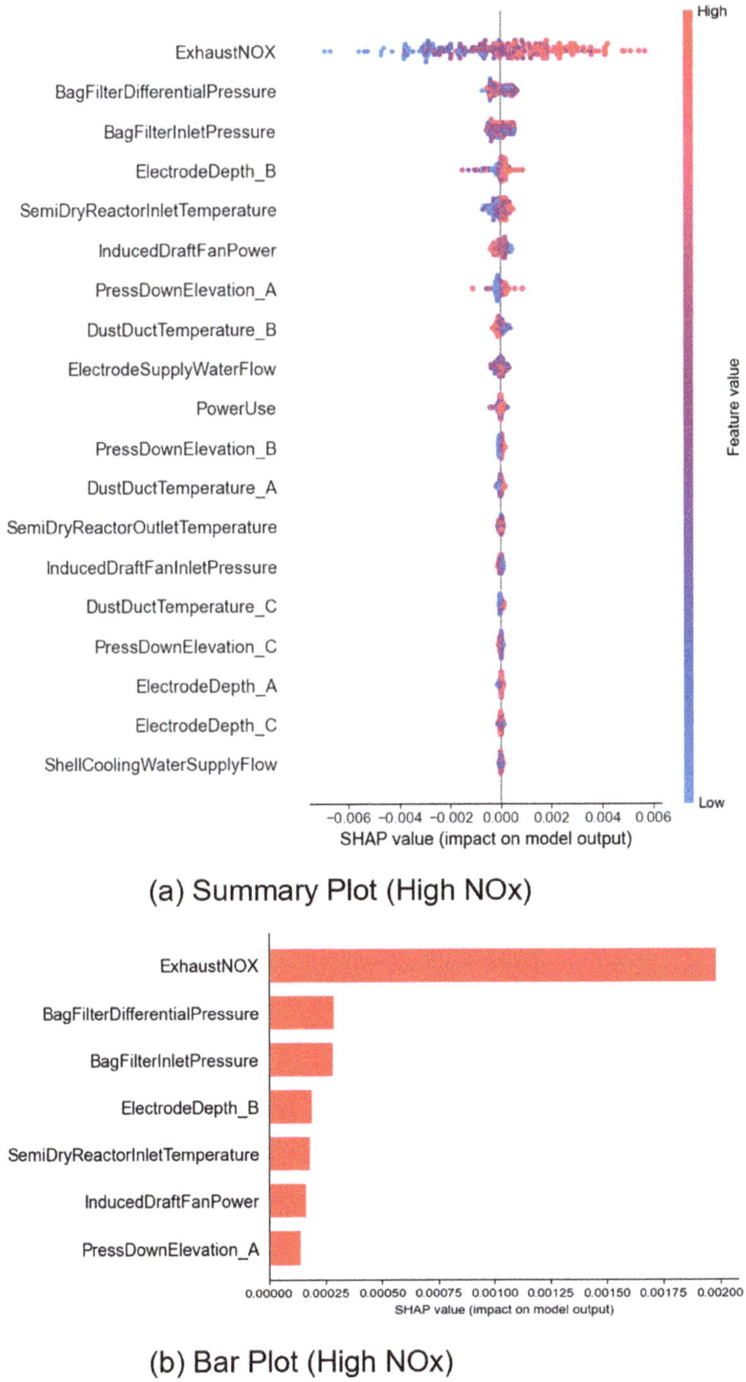

Figure 10. Summary and bar plots with high NOx emissions.

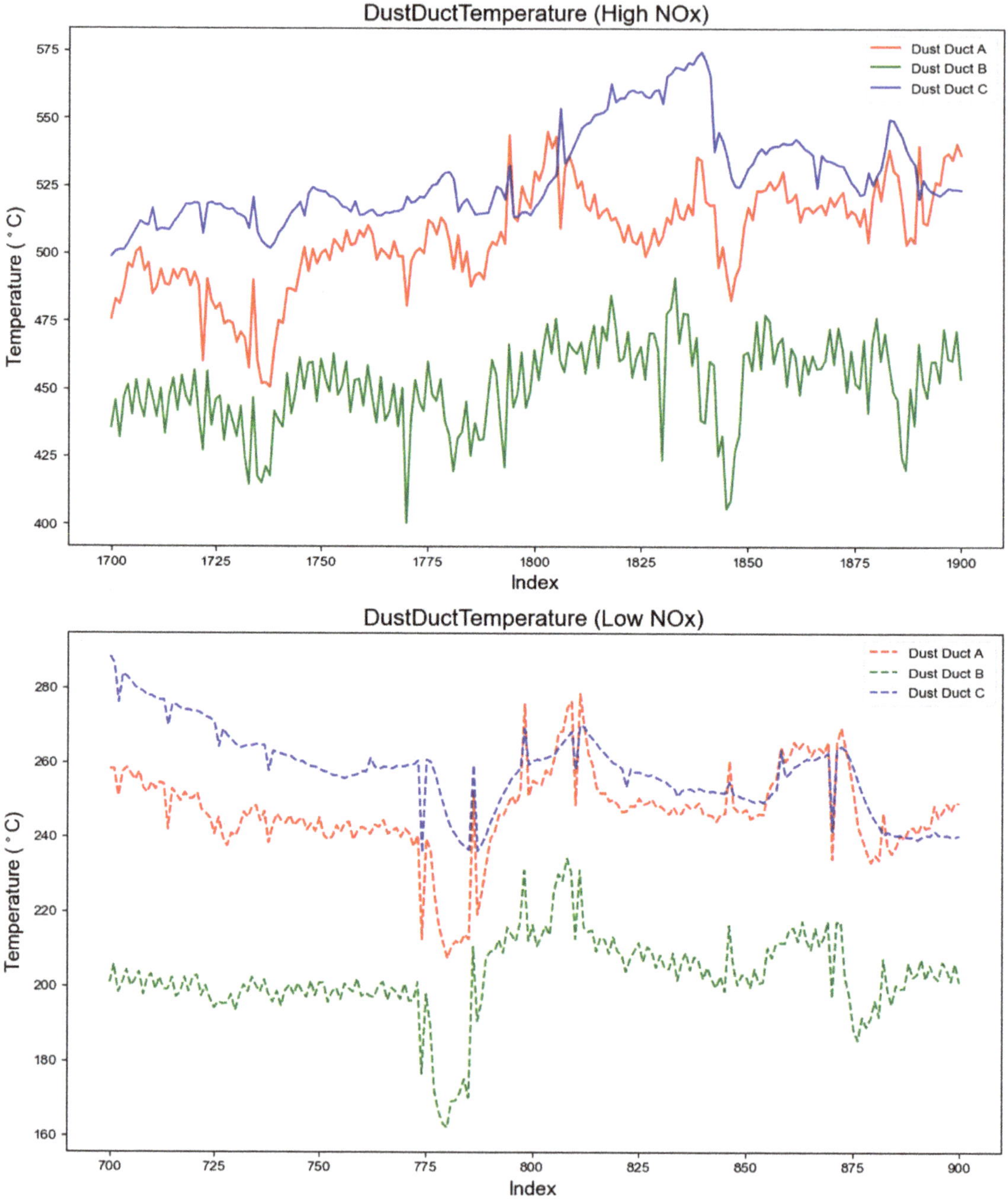

Figure 11. Comparison of dust duct temperature at different NOx emission levels.

5. Discussion and Conclusions

This study proposes a model for predicting NOx emissions suitable for the EAFs of ferroalloy production sites. A Kalman-filter-based smoothing algorithm was used to denoise the NOx emission data from the EAFs and construct the training data. The study presented an interpretable model using variables collectable from EAFs at ferroalloy production sites and was able to identify key influencing variables in prediction through the utilization of explainable AI. The NOx emission prediction model employs real-time data collected from the EAFs of the ferroalloy production workplace, thereby offering insights for practitioners aiming to establish a real-time prediction system with data collection and NOx prediction capability. With increasing environmental regulations, practitioners involved in related industries need to prepare for these changes, which can serve as a basis for proactive adaptation in ferroalloy production.

This study developed an interpretable model for predicting NOx emissions in EAFs by adopting LSTM and identified the variables with a significant impact on NOx emission predictions from the collected data through explainable AI methods. Owing to this research, it is possible to provide guidance for building a NOx prediction system in EAFs, and it hints at ways to reduce NOx emissions at ferroalloy production sites through NOx prediction. For practical applications, NOx prediction can be implemented in real-world settings, with potential expansion to both chimney and internal exhaust gas emissions. However, the key to effective NOx emission prediction lies in the ability to collect data. Real-time data transmission from manufacturing and exhaust gas facilities to systems capable of immediate data management and collection is essential. From the perspective of building an NOx emission prediction system, this study can be helpful in establishing a system for the prediction of EAFs at ferroalloy production sites, where a data collection system has not yet been implemented. This study outlines the collected data, key variables, and data collection locations, offering guidance for workplaces looking to initiate data collection and management for NOx prediction. Many EAFs in ferroalloy production face challenges in establishing a data collection system for real-time historical processes and observational data from chimneys. Moreover, identifying the specific data required for accurate real-time NOx emissions prediction from the collectable data is necessary to these facilities. Owing to the limited prior research on predicting NOx emissions from EAFs, it is necessary to identify data that can be collected and that are essential for the prediction of EAFs at ferroalloy production.

Regarding potential impacts, this research can assist ferroalloy plant operators planning to reduce NOx emissions. NOx prediction can significantly contribute to NOx reduction efforts, both pre- and post-management. For pre-management, by identifying key operating variables during the NOx prediction process, it is possible to apply them to the operating systems of production facilities, attempting to adjust variables for the reduction in NOx emissions. In this study, through SHAP analysis, the operational variables were determined when the NOx emission levels were high and low. However, the variables with high importance values were measurements, whereas the actual operational variables, such as the depth of the electrode bars and power usage, showed low importance. If future research develops a high-performance predictive model based on operational variables, it will be possible to identify combinations of operational variables to reduce NOx emissions using an interpretable method. In post-management techniques, NOx prediction can contribute to exhaust systems using selective catalytic reduction (SCR) facilities. Denitrification facilities (e.g., SCR) remove NOx emissions from exhaust gases through chemical reactions, and the rate of NOx removal varies depending on the amount of ammonia used as a reducing agent. The excessive injection of ammonia can cause ammonia slip, leading to potential equipment failure and reduced dust collection efficiency, whereas too little ammonia reduces the NOx reduction. Therefore, a system that can adjust the amount of ammonia injection by predicting NOx emissions in real time is required.

Despite these contributions, further studies are required. First, the study could be applied to various EAF environments as the types, variables, and specifications of EAFs can vary, and broader application in diverse settings could enhance the generalizability of this research. By expanding our collection of operational variables and enhancing the depth of interpretable AI analysis in future research, NOx prediction can transform into a proactive management tool. This progress is expected to facilitate the implementation of operational strategies specifically targeted at reducing NOx emissions, thereby advancing toward active environmental management. Second, as this study was conducted between May and July, there is a need to use data over a more extended period. With significant seasonal temperature variations in Korea, collecting more data to consider seasonality could improve the applicability of this study. Continued research in this area could lead to broader and more universal applications of this study for various EAFs at ferroalloy production sites. Third, a systematic approach to assign hyperparameters of the Kalman Filter smoothing algorithm is required. In this study, they are designed based on trial-and-error methods. An enhanced and systematic approach can improve this study. Finally, the intrinsic limitation of SHAP should be acknowledged. Because SHAP is a model-agnostic method utilizing the average value of the local one, the derived values are inherently influenced by the specific samples used. This challenge is not exclusive to this particular issue but is relevant to the interpretation of deep learning models at large. Further research into the interpretation of NOx prediction is necessary to deepen our understanding of NOx generation from EAFs.

This study was implemented using the Python 3.8.18 programming language, alongside TensorFlow 2.10.0 for deep learning model development and SHAP 0.42.1 for interpretability analysis.

Author Contributions: Conceptualization, Y.S., S.L., J.L., C.-W.K., H.S.B., Y.B., and J.Y.; methodology, Y.S., S.L., J.L., and J.Y.; software, Y.S., S.L., C.-W.K., and J.Y.; validation, J.L., C.-W.K., and J.Y.; formal analysis, S.L.; investigation, Y.S., S.L., J.L., C.-W.K., J.Y., H.S.B., Y.B., and J.Y.; resources, C.-W.K. and J.Y.; data curation, Y.S., H.S.B., and Y.B.; writing—original draft preparation, Y.S., S.L., J.L., and J.Y; writing—review and editing, C.-W.K., H.S.B., Y.B., and J.Y.; visualization, Y.S., S.L., and H.S.B.; supervision, J.Y.; project administration, C.-W.K., J.Y., H.S.B., Y.B., and J.Y.; funding acquisition, Y.B. and J.Y. All authors have read and agreed to the published version of the manuscript.

Funding: This work was supported by the Korea Environment Industry & Technology Institute (KEITI) through the R&D Project for Intelligent Optimum Reduction and Management of Industrial Fine Dust funded by the Korea Ministry of Environment (MOE) (2022003580004), the Human Resources Program in Energy Technology of the Korea Institute of Energy Technology Evaluation and Planning (KETEP), and the Ministry of Trade, Industry & Energy (MOTIE) of the Republic of Korea (No. 20204010600220).

Data Availability Statement: The datasets presented in this article are not readily available because the data were provided by the ferroalloy plants in Gwangyang. Requests to access the datasets should be directed to RIST.

Conflicts of Interest: The authors declare no conflicts of interest.

References

1. Agency, I.E. *Iron and Steel Technology Roadmap: Towards More Sustainable Steelmaking*; OECD Publishing: Berlin, Germany, 2020.
2. Jonidi Jafari, A.; Charkhloo, E.; Pasalari, H. Urban air pollution control policies and strategies: A systematic review. *J. Environ. Health Sci. Eng.* **2021**, *19*, 1911–1940. [CrossRef]
3. Trnka, D. *Policies, Regulatory Framework and Enforcement for Air Quality Management: The Case of Korea*; OECD Publishing: Berlin, Germany, 2020.
4. Fichte, R. *Ferroalloys. Ullmann's Encyclopedia of Industrial Chemistry*; John Wiley & Sons, Inc.: Hoboken, NJ, USA, 2000.
5. Kirschen, M.; Voj, L.; Pfeifer, H. NO x emission from electric arc furnace in steel industry: Contribution from electric arc and co-combustion reactions. *Clean Technol. Environ. Policy* **2005**, *7*, 236–244. [CrossRef]
6. Weschler, C.J. Ozone's impact on public health: Contributions from indoor exposures to ozone and products of ozone-initiated chemistry. *Environ. Health Perspect.* **2006**, *114*, 1489–1496. [CrossRef]
7. Yang, G.T.; Wang, Y.N.; Li, X.L. Prediction of the NO emissions from thermal power plant using long-short term memory neural network. *Energy* **2020**, *192*, 116597. [CrossRef]

8. Tang, Z.H.; Wang, S.K.; Chai, X.Y.; Cao, S.X.; Ouyang, T.H.; Li, Y. Auto-encoder-extreme learning machine model for boiler NO emission concentration prediction. *Energy* **2022**, *256*, 124552. [CrossRef]
9. Wang, F.; Ma, S.; Wang, H.; Li, Y.; Zhang, J. Prediction of NOx emission for coal-fired boilers based on deep belief network. *Control Eng. Pract.* **2018**, *80*, 26–35. [CrossRef]
10. Yuan, Z.; Meng, L.; Gu, X.; Bai, Y.; Cui, H.; Jiang, C. Prediction of NOx emissions for coal-fired power plants with stacked-generalization ensemble method. *Fuel* **2021**, *289*, 119748. [CrossRef]
11. Korpela, T.; Kumpulainen, P.; Majanne, Y.; Häyrinen, A.; Lautala, P. Indirect NOx emission monitoring in natural gas fired boilers. *Control Eng. Pract.* **2017**, *65*, 11–25. [CrossRef]
12. Wang, Z.; Peng, X.; Cao, S.; Zhou, H.; Fan, S.; Li, K.; Huang, W. NOx emission prediction using a lightweight convolutional neural network for cleaner production in a down-fired boiler. *J. Clean. Prod.* **2023**, *389*, 136060. [CrossRef]
13. Wang, H.; Zhang, C.; Liu, X. Heat transfer calculation methods in three-dimensional CFD model for pulverized coal-fired boilers. *Appl. Therm. Eng.* **2020**, *166*, 114633. [CrossRef]
14. Belošević, S.; Tomanović, I.; Beljanski, V.; Tucaković, D.; Živanović, T. Numerical prediction of processes for clean and efficient combustion of pulverized coal in power plants. *Appl. Therm. Eng.* **2015**, *74*, 102–110. [CrossRef]
15. Chan, E.; Riley, M.; MJ, T.; EJ, E. Nitrogen oxides (NOx) formation and control in an electric arc furnace (EAF): Analysis with measurements and computational fluid dynamics (CFD) modeling. *ISIJ Int.* **2004**, *44*, 429–438. [CrossRef]
16. Zhou, H.-C.; Lou, C.; Cheng, Q.; Jiang, Z.; He, J.; Huang, B.; Pei, Z.; Lu, C. Experimental investigations on visualization of three-dimensional temperature distributions in a large-scale pulverized-coal-fired boiler furnace. *Proc. Combust. Inst.* **2005**, *30*, 1699–1706. [CrossRef]
17. Zhang, Y.; Wang, W.; Shao, S.; Duan, S.; Hou, H. ANN-GA approach for predictive modelling and optimization of NOx emissions in a cement precalcining kiln. *Int. J. Environ. Stud.* **2017**, *74*, 253–261. [CrossRef]
18. Ding, X.; Feng, C.; Yu, P.; Li, K.; Chen, X. Gradient boosting decision tree in the prediction of NOx emission of waste incineration. *Energy* **2023**, *264*, 126174. [CrossRef]
19. Fleuriault, C.; Grogan, J.; White, J. Electric arc smelting. *JOM* **2019**, *71*, 321–322. [CrossRef]
20. Singh, R. *Applied Welding Engineering: Processes, Codes, and Standards*; Butterworth-Heinemann: Oxford, UK, 2020.
21. Kim, J.; Lee, G.; Lee, S.; Lee, C. Towards expert–machine collaborations for technology valuation: An interpretable machine learning approach. *Technol. Forecast. Soc. Chang.* **2022**, *183*, 121940. [CrossRef]
22. Faravelli, T.; Bua, L.; Frassoldati, A.; Antifora, A.; Tognotti, L.; Ranzi, E. A new procedure for predicting NOx emissions from furnaces. In *Computer Aided Chemical Engineering*; Elsevier: Amsterdam, The Netherlands, 2000; Volume 8, pp. 859–864.
23. Lv, M.; Zhao, J.; Cao, S.; Shen, T. Prediction of the 3D Distribution of NOx in a Furnace via CFD Data Based on ELM. *Front. Energy Res.* **2022**, *10*, 848209. [CrossRef]
24. Safdarnejad, S.M.; Tuttle, J.F.; Powell, K.M. Dynamic modeling and optimization of a coal-fired utility boiler to forecast and minimize NOx and CO emissions simultaneously. *Comput. Chem. Eng.* **2019**, *124*, 62–79. [CrossRef]
25. Shen, Q.; Wang, G.; Wang, Y.; Zeng, B.; Yu, X.; He, S. Prediction Model for Transient NOx Emission of Diesel Engine Based on CNN-LSTM Network. *Energies* **2023**, *16*, 5347. [CrossRef]
26. Li, N.; Lv, Y.; Hu, Y. Prediction of NOx Emissions from a Coal-Fired Boiler Based on Convolutional Neural Networks with a Channel Attention Mechanism. *Energies* **2022**, *16*, 76. [CrossRef]
27. Adadi, A.; Berrada, M. Peeking inside the black-box: A survey on explainable artificial intelligence (XAI). *IEEE Access* **2018**, *6*, 52138–52160. [CrossRef]
28. Doshi-Velez, F.; Kim, B. Towards a rigorous science of interpretable machine learning. *arXiv* **2017**, arXiv:1702.08608.
29. Molnar, C. *Interpretable Machine Learning*; Lulu.Com: Raleigh, NC, USA, 2020.
30. Das, A.; Rad, P. Opportunities and challenges in explainable artificial intelligence (xai): A survey. *arXiv* **2020**, arXiv:2006.11371.
31. Lundberg, S.M.; Erion, G.; Chen, H.; DeGrave, A.; Prutkin, J.M.; Nair, B.; Katz, R.; Himmelfarb, J.; Bansal, N.; Lee, S.-I. From local explanations to global understanding with explainable AI for trees. *Nat. Mach. Intell.* **2020**, *2*, 56–67. [CrossRef] [PubMed]
32. Jiang, P.; Liu, Z.; Abedin, M.Z.; Wang, J.; Yang, W.; Dong, Q. Profit-driven weighted classifier with interpretable ability for customer churn prediction. *Omega* **2024**, *125*, 103034. [CrossRef]
33. Liu, Z.; Jiang, P.; Wang, J.; Du, Z.; Niu, X.; Zhang, L. Hospitality order cancellation prediction from a profit-driven perspective. *Int. J. Contemp. Hosp. Manag.* **2023**, *35*, 2084–2112. [CrossRef]
34. Rabby, M.F.; Tu, Y.; Hossen, M.I.; Lee, I.; Maida, A.S.; Hei, X. Stacked LSTM based deep recurrent neural network with kalman smoothing for blood glucose prediction. *BMC Med. Inform. Decis. Mak.* **2021**, *21*, 101. [CrossRef]
35. Xue, G.; Qi, C.; Li, H.; Kong, X.; Song, J. Heating load prediction based on attention long short term memory: A case study of Xingtai. *Energy* **2020**, *203*, 117846. [CrossRef]
36. Staal, O.M.; Sælid, S.; Fougner, A.; Stavdahl, Ø. Kalman smoothing for objective and automatic preprocessing of glucose data. *IEEE J. Biomed. Health Inform.* **2018**, *23*, 218–226. [CrossRef]
37. Song, M.; Xue, J.; Gao, S.; Cheng, G.; Chen, J.; Lu, H.; Dong, Z. Prediction of NOx concentration at SCR inlet based on BMIFS-LSTM. *Atmosphere* **2022**, *13*, 686. [CrossRef]
38. Wen, X.; Li, K.; Wang, J. NOx emission predicting for coal-fired boilers based on ensemble learning methods and optimized base learners. *Energy* **2023**, *264*, 126171. [CrossRef]

39. Bostani, H.; Sheikhan, M. Hybrid of binary gravitational search algorithm and mutual information for feature selection in intrusion detection systems. *Soft Comput.* **2017**, *21*, 2307–2324. [CrossRef]
40. Kraskov, A.; Stögbauer, H.; Grassberger, P. Estimating mutual information. *Phys. Rev. E* **2004**, *69*, 066138. [CrossRef] [PubMed]
41. Shapley, L.S. *Additive and Non-Additive Set Functions*; Princeton University: Princeton, NJ, USA, 1953.
42. Lundberg, S.M.; Lee, S.-I. A unified approach to interpreting model predictions. *Adv. Neural Inf. Process. Syst.* **2017**, *30*, 4765–4774.
43. Chen, H.; Lundberg, S.; Lee, S.-I. Explaining models by propagating Shapley values of local components. In *Explainable AI in Healthcare and Medicine: Building a Culture of Transparency and Accountability*; Springer: Cham, Switzerland, 2021; pp. 261–270.

mathematics

MDPI

Article

Defect Detection Model Using CNN and Image Augmentation for Seat Foaming Process

Nak-Hun Choi [1], Jung Woo Sohn [2] and Jong-Seok Oh [1,3,*]

[1] Department of Future Convergence Engineering, Kongju National University, Cheonan 31080, Chungnam, Republic of Korea; nnk_0950@naver.com
[2] Department of Mechanical Design Engineering, Kumoh National Institute of Technology, Gumi 39177, Gyeongbuk, Republic of Korea; jwsohn@kumoh.ac.kr
[3] Department of Future Automotive Engineering, Kongju National University, Cheonan 31080, Chungnam, Republic of Korea
* Correspondence: jongseok@kongju.ac.kr

Abstract: In the manufacturing industry, which is facing the 4th Industrial Revolution, various process data are being collected from various sensors, and efforts are being made to construct more efficient processes using these data. Many studies have demonstrated high accuracy in predicting defect rates through image data collected during the process using two-dimensional (2D) convolutional neural network (CNN) algorithms, which are effective in image analysis. However, in an environment where numerous process data are recorded as numerical values, the application of 2D CNN algorithms is limited. Thus, to perform defect prediction through the application of a 2D CNN algorithm in a process wherein image data cannot be collected, this study attempted to develop a defect prediction technique that can visualize the data collected in numerical form. The polyurethane foam manufacturing process was selected as a case study to verify the proposed method, which confirmed that the defect rate could be predicted with an average accuracy of 97.32%. Consequently, highly accurate defect rate prediction and verification of the basis of judgment can be facilitated in environments wherein image data cannot be collected, rendering the proposed technique applicable to processes other than those in this case study.

Keywords: defect detection; defect prediction; manufacturing process; seat foaming process; deep learning; convolutional neural network; image augmentation; artificial neural network

MSC: 37M20

1. Introduction

Recently, the "4th Industrial Revolution" has emerged as a major keyword for economic growth and has had a great effect in various fields, including manufacturing. In particular, the concept of Industry 4.0, which enables factories to become independent and self-adaptive depending on input from data that are gathered, is known in manufacturing as smart manufacturing. Smart factories are production systems wherein factory devices and parts are connected and interact with each other by combining existing production manufacturing technologies with technologies such as the Internet of things, big data, and cloud computing. A key feature of smart manufacturing is to assess and extract relevant information from collected data using deep learning [1–3].

Because deep learning can analyze raw data and automatically identify feature representations of data across several levels of abstraction, it has attracted interest as a tool in smart manufacturing. The application of deep learning is not limited to process fault monitoring [4–6] or state estimation [7,8]; several studies have explored its potential for various other manufacturing applications [9,10]. In deep learning, artificial neural networks (ANNs) and convolutional neural networks (CNNs) are widely acknowledged as the leading technologies for pattern recognition from tabular and image data, respectively.

Each layer of an ANN is made up of a collection of several perceptrons or neurons. Because an ANN only processes inputs in a forward manner, it is often referred to as a feedforward neural network. It can easily be used to process image, textual, and tabular data. Such neural networks are among the simplest variants. They pass information in one direction through various input nodes until sending it to an output node. The network may or may not have hidden node layers, rendering their functions more interpretable. Several studies have shown that ANNs can implicitly detect complex nonlinear relationships between dependent and independent variables. However, proper feature selection is crucial when applying an ANN. The features input into the model must be well designed according to the problem at hand. A CNN comprises convolution, pooling, and fully connected layers. A CNN is best used when millions of features need to be retrieved, since the convolutional layer generates feature maps that capture an area of an image that is then divided into rectangles and transmitted for nonlinear processing. The CNN automatically aggregates these characteristics rather than measuring each one separately. The fully connected layers use the extracted features to identify the input picture after the pooling layer reduces the number of the collected features [11,12]. CNNs based on auto-feature extraction have been used in various systems for fault detection, material degradation, and other applications. Glaeser et al. developed a fault-detection algorithm for industrial cold forging. Based on a CNN, the algorithm can detect faults with 99.02% accuracy, and classify each fault with 92.66% accuracy [13]. Nakazawa and Kulkarni proposed a CNN with a SoftMax activation function to classify 22 WM defect patterns [14]. Saqlain et al. proposed a deep learning-based CNN for automatic wafer defect identification (CNN-WDI) in semiconductor manufacturing processes [15]. However, CNNs are better suited for processing image data rather than tabular data. Accordingly, several studies have utilized the conversion of tabular data into image data to leverage the advantages of CNNs, such as automatic feature extraction. Numerous time–frequency analysis techniques, including short-time Fourier transform (STFT), continuous wavelet transform (CWT), and wavelet packet transform (WPT), were combined with CNNs to convert tabular time-series data [16]. These techniques use deep learning techniques to extract discriminative features from time–frequency representations rather than the time domain and convert continuous time-series data to two-dimensional (2D) representations using time–frequency analysis [17–21]. The second method involves the conversion of numbers into images for noncontinuous time-series data. Sezer et al. [22] generated 15×15 pixel images using 15 technical indicators related to stock prices. A CNN was adopted as the classification and prediction model to classify financial data as images and predict buy, sell, or hold signals for stocks. They evaluated the performance of their proposed model on Dow 30 stocks. In addition, Lee et al. [23] converted tabular data, such as vehicle spare parts, into 3D voxel images and applied them to a 3D CNN to perform demand forecasting for spare parts. By comparing them with other methods, they concluded that the proposed method exhibited good prediction performance. However, there has been no research related to the application of CNNs using the dataset conversion of numbers into images for manufacturing processes. In addition, many manufacturing process data are recorded as noncontinuous time-series and tabular data types.

Consequently, the main contribution of this study is to detect defects in manufactured products by applying data obtained from the seat foam manufacturing process to the CNN algorithm. Since the data obtained from the manufacturing process are numerical data in tabular form, they were normalized, converted to gray images, and applied to the CNN algorithm. To solve the imbalanced data problem, data augmentation and hyperparameter optimization were also performed. In order to confirm the excellence of the proposed method, defect detection was performed by applying the features extracted from tabular numerical data to the ANN algorithm and then comparing the results with the results of the proposed method. Consequently, it was possible to develop a defect detection model with an accuracy of 98.33%, and the results confirmed the effectiveness of the proposed technique.

2. Data Collection and ANN

2.1. Data Collection and Processing Method

The validity of this study was verified using a polyurethane foaming process for automobile seats. The manufacturing equipment used for the foaming process is shown in Figure 1. The study was conducted using data recorded during the actual foaming process.

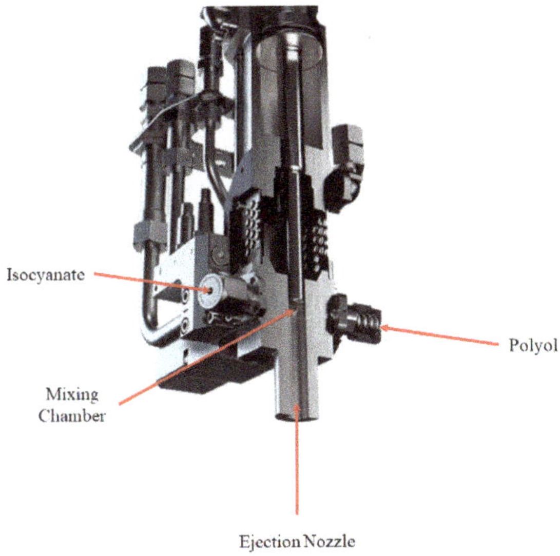

Figure 1. Configuration of foaming machine.

The foaming process involves the production of polyurethane foam constituting automobile seat cushion foam or automobile interior parts by mixing and foaming polyol and isocyanate. This process was performed within 1.11 s, and the mixing and foaming processes occurred when each raw material was foamed rather than generating and foaming a mixed solution. Therefore, information regarding the mixed raw materials is unknown. Thus, the process data for each raw material were collected by attaching flow, pressure, and temperature sensors to the part closest to the mixing head [24].

To measure the flow, pressure, and temperature of isocyanate and polyol, Kracht VC1 F4 PS, Keller PA-21Y, and PT 100 Ω type were used. In this study, the average value of the data measured for 1.11 s, which is the one-time foaming time, was calculated and used. The collected data were divided into two types: normal and defective. The classification was based on ±3% of the mass reference value, which was the same as the quality requirement of the finished-vehicle company. In the case of the mass of the produced polyurethane foam being higher than the reference value, the density of the tissue inside the cushion was high, resulting in poor ride comfort. However, if the mass of the produced polyurethane foam was lower than the reference value, the density of the tissue inside the cushion decreased, and the passenger's body was not well supported.

The mass of the final polyurethane foam product is related to the flow rate, temperature, and pressure. However, because each factor exhibits a nonlinear relationship with the others, this study considered these three factors; the labels are listed in Table 1. As various process data were collected, the dimensions of each factor differed. Furthermore, the algorithm being developed was not process-specific but general-purpose. To offset the characteristics of each factor, a normalization process was performed using the equation below, such that the maximum and minimum values of each factor were the same.

$$M = \frac{C - (C_{min} - W_n \times D)}{\{(C_{max} + W_n \times D) - (C_{min} - W_n \times D)\}} \quad (1)$$

where M is a normalized value, C is the data to be normalized, C_{max} and C_{min} are the maximum and minimum values of each factor, respectively, and D is the difference between C_{max} and C_{min}. This equation allows a value between 0 and 1 to be derived based on the maximum and minimum values for each factor. Here, normalization may be performed in a narrower range than 0–1 by adjusting the W_n factor. Based on previous research that has reported the possibility of deriving results with higher prediction performance and reliability by avoiding the normalization range of 0–1, this study employed a W_n value of 0.125 to limit the normalization range to a range from 0.1 to 0.9 [25]. The lower row in Table 1 shows the results of the normalization in Equation (1).

Table 1. Collected foaming process data.

	Isocyanate			Polyol			Label
	Flow	**Pressure**	**Temperature**	**Flow**	**Pressure**	**Temperature**	
Original Dataset	42.6	92.2	24.4	133.3	109.1	26.4	Fine
	42.1	93.4	24.4	133.3	109.7	26.3	Fine
	41.7	105	24.4	134.4	109.6	26.3	Fine
	42.1	100.9	24.8	135.4	109.6	26.3	Fine
	42.1	94.9	24.3	133.3	108.7	26.4	Defect
	41.2	90.7	24.	133.3	107.5	26.9	Defect
	41.2	109.5	24.9	133.3	108.6	26.5	Defect
	41.7	90	24.7	134.4	109.4	26.3	Defect
Normalized Dataset	0.616667	0.537258	0.493846	0.741975	0.338596	0.841935	Fine
	0.602778	0.55413	0.493846	0.741975	0.366667	0.835484	Fine
	0.591667	0.717223	0.493846	0.796296	0.361988	0.835484	Fine
	0.602778	0.659578	0.543077	0.845679	0.361988	0.835484	Fine
	0.602778	057522	0.481538	0.741975	0.319883	0.841935	Defect
	0.577778	0.516169	0.506154	0.796296	0.319883	0.848387	Defect
	0.577778	0.780492	0.555385	0.741975	0.315205	0.848387	Defect
	0.591667	0.506327	0.530769	0.796296	0.35632	0.835484	Defect

An overview of the data processing and defect detection methods is shown in Figure 2. The numbers of fine and defective data are 8474 and 187, respectively. Some labeled data are listed in Table 1. Tabular data were converted into image data. The tabular and image datasets were augmented using the synthetic minority oversampling technique (SMOTE) and cutout. Following preprocessing and augmentation, the tabular and image datasets were passed through an ANN and CNN for defect detection.

2.2. ANN

When addressing data imbalance problems using seat foam manufacturing process data, a challenge often arises in the case of an abundance of normal data, but a scarcity of defective data. This imbalance can result in biased and inaccurate machine learning models, particularly for minority labels. To address this issue, typically, oversampling techniques are employed, particularly to augment existing defective data. There are various methods for oversampling based on the nature of the data to be augmented. In this study, SMOTE was applied to augment the numerical data in the tabular datasets, and a cutout was utilized to augment the image data.

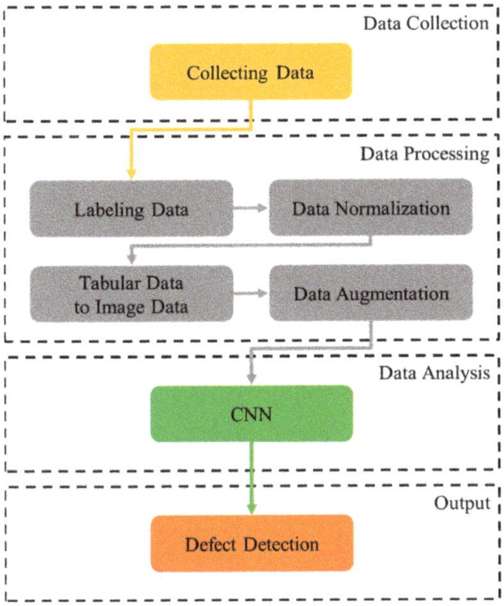

Figure 2. A flowchart representing the proposed defect detection method.

The synthetic minority oversampling SMOTE is used to address the issue of class imbalance in machine learning. Class imbalance occurs when certain classes in the dataset have significantly fewer instances than others, causing the model to be biased towards the majority class. SMOTE helps to mitigate this problem.

First, SMOTE begins by selecting data points from a minority class. Subsequently, it identifies the k-nearest neighbors for each selected data point and generates new data points by interpolating the selected data point and its neighbors. A random number between 0 and 1, denoted as λ, is chosen. The new data points are calculated as follows:

$$\text{Synthetic Data} = X + \lambda\,(X_{nn} - X) \tag{2}$$

Finally, the newly generated data points are added to the existing dataset. In this study, the values of k are chosen as 65, 98, and 130.

An ANN is a computational model inspired by biological neural networks in the human brain. ANNs typically comprise three main types of layers: input, hidden, and output. The input layer receives the initial data or features fed into the neural network. The number of neurons in the input layer corresponds to the number of input features. The neurons in the hidden layers perform computations on the input data. The network learns and extracts features from the input data in these hidden layers. Consequently, the output layer produces the final predictions or outputs of the neural network.

The ANN architecture in Figure 3 is simulated via Matlab 2022b on Windows 10. The model parameters for each layer and activation functions are listed in Table 2. In this process, the batch normalization layer and ReLU activation function were applied after the previous fully connected layer. This process was repeated three times to analyze the numerical data. Subsequently, to prevent overfitting, the model was passed through a dropout layer, and the results of the fully connected layer were output to the classification layer using the SoftMax activation function.

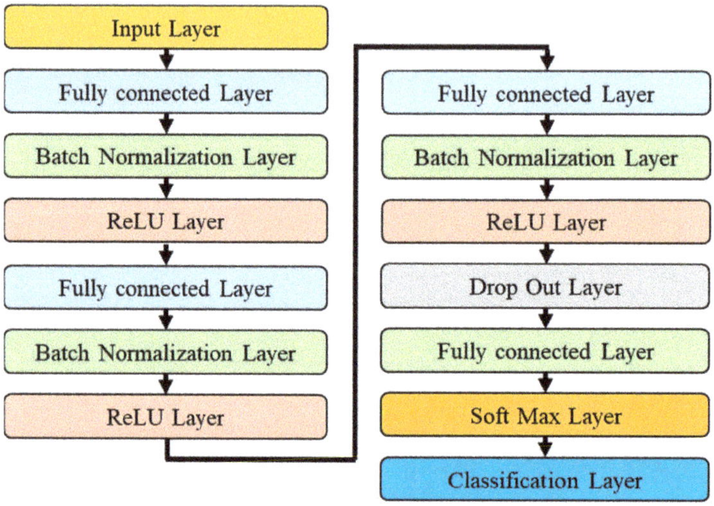

Figure 3. ANN model.

Table 2. ANN model parameters.

Layer	Feature Map	Learnables	Activation
Input Layer	6	-	
Fully Connected Layer	100	Weight 100×6, Bias 100×1	
Batch Normalization Layer	100	Offset 100×1, Scale 100×1	ReLU
Fully Connected Layer	50	Weight 50×100, Bias 50×1	
Batch Normalization Layer	50	Offset 50×1, Scale 50×1	ReLU
Fully Connected Layer	10	Weight 10×50, Bias 10×1	
Batch Normalization Layer	10	Offset 10×1, Scale 10×1	ReLU
Dropout Layer	10	-	
Fully Connected Layer	2	Weight 2×10, Bias 2×1	
Classification Layer	2	-	SoftMax

3. Proposed CNN Architecture

3.1. Data Creation and Augmentation for CNN

The process of changing the data from a normalized table to images was applied to a 2D CNN. In the image-creation phase, a 2×3 image was generated using six factors. Each image was labeled as fine or defective. Because alternative ordering results occur in diverse image forms, the order of the elements is crucial. To produce a coherent and significant visual depiction, we grouped the factors and exhibited factors collectively or in close proximity. Sample 2×3 images produced during image production are shown in Figure 4. The process of converting the data into an image was performed such that the normalized value could be composed of a grayscale value between 0 and 1. To specify a value for grayscale, the following was used: 0 means black, 1 means white. The determined gray color was then displayed in the generated image.

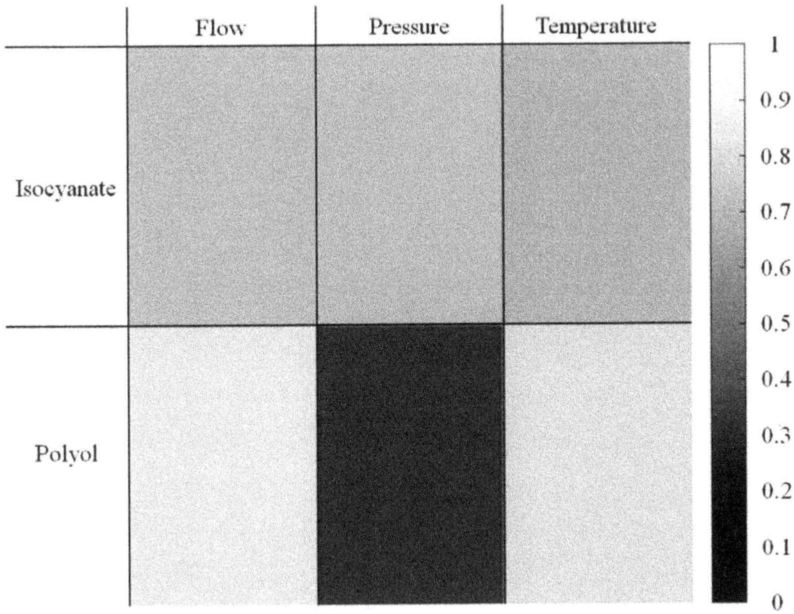

Figure 4. Image data creation from tabular data.

While collecting actual process data, there may be an imbalance in the number of normal and defective data points or a lack of collected data. Moreover, when learning is performed using such a dataset, an overfitting problem can occur with a high validation accuracy but low test accuracy. The simplest method to address this challenge involves increasing the amount of data artificially before proceeding with learning. This method is referred to as "data augmentation", and there exist methods to change the basic characteristics of an image, such as cropping a portion of the image, rotating the image, flipping the image symmetrically in the horizontal or vertical direction, and injecting noise in the image. Various studies have focused on methods for changing the geometrical features of an image, such as mix-up, which mixes two images into one, and random erase, which masks a part of the existing image with a random grayscale image [26]. The data augmentation method used in this study was eliminated, and the existing image was masked by a randomly sized white rectangle within the range of a minimum of 1×1 to a maximum of 112×112. When masked at the maximum size, 1/4 of the total image was covered. Furthermore, the masked position was randomly designated to prevent the problem of concentrated masking at a specific position [27].

In contrast to other methods, the image augmentation method using a white rectangular cutout is suitable for this study, where the classification results may vary depending on the grayscale values for each location in the image. Moreover, there is no change in or movement of normalized values for each location because the scale of an image does not change or the image is not augmented, such as in symmetric movement and rotation.

The augmentation results were used to generate the image shown in Figure 5. The figure (a) presents the result of augmenting the fine data, and (b) presents the result of augmenting the defect data. To solve the data shortage problem, the original image dataset is increased by factors of 2, 5, and 10.

(**a**) (**b**)

Figure 5. Augmented image data: (**a**) augmented fine data; (**b**) augmented defect data.

3.2. Two-Dimensional CNN Model

Through this process, sensor data from industrial sites, where image data could not be collected, were visualized and applied to the 2D CNN algorithm. The 2D CNN algorithm is a deep neural network algorithm conceived based on the working principle of the optic nerve in animals and is designed with a structure suitable for image data processing. A 2D CNN extracts the features of the data by reducing the size of the overall image and increasing the image dimensions as the image is input to the feature extraction layer and then passes through the sequentially constructed convolution and pooling layers. The extracted features are finally entered into the fully connected layer, and a final judgment is made. The algorithm used was based on CNN-WDI, which is a 2D CNN model proposed by Saqlain et al., and the number of nodes in the fully connected layer was changed to make it suitable for this study [15]. The structure of the 2D CNN model in Figure 6 is simulated through Matlab on Windows 10. The parameters such as the output size and activation function of each layer are listed in Table 3.

3.3. Optimization of Hyperparameters

CNNs contain several hyperparameters that must be carefully tuned to achieve an optimal performance in various tasks. Certain key hyperparameters in CNNs include the minibatch size, max epoch, learning rate, and dropout. The minibatch size is the number of data samples used in one training iteration. This balances efficiency and accuracy, thereby affecting the convergence speed. The max epoch signifies the maximum number of training cycles through the dataset, which is crucial for model learning to avoid underfitting or overfitting. The learning rate dictates the step size for updating the neural network weights during training. This influences the convergence and model accuracy, which require careful tuning. Dropout is a regularization method that prevents overfitting. It randomly drops neurons, thereby enhancing model generalization. The dropout rate controls the fraction of dropped neurons, which is crucial for robustness.

The selection of hyperparameter values significantly affects the performance of machine learning models. In this study, the grid search method, which is a systematic approach for determining the best combination of hyperparameters by evaluating all possible combinations within a specified range for each hyperparameter, was used. The ranges of the hyperparameters are listed in Table 4. Subsequently, a grid containing all possible combinations of the specified hyperparameters was generated. For each combination in the grid, the model was trained on the training data, and its performance was evaluated using cross-validation techniques (such as k-fold cross-validation). This provided an unbiased estimate of model performance for each set of hyperparameters. Thus, the combination of hyperparameters resulted in the best performance based on the loss function. This combination represents the optimal set of hyperparameters for the proposed model. Once the optimal hyperparameters were determined, the final model was trained using these values for the entire training dataset. The range of hyperparameters was determined through experiments and theories and by randomly substituting values within the range [28]. To reduce the computational time required for iterative operations during this process, the size of the images was reduced to 25 × 25 × 3. Table 5 provides the optimized values of the hyperparameters used in the optimization method. After the hyperparameters were determined, the model was trained with image data of the original size (224 × 224 × 3). The training time for the CNN model was approximately 4 h.

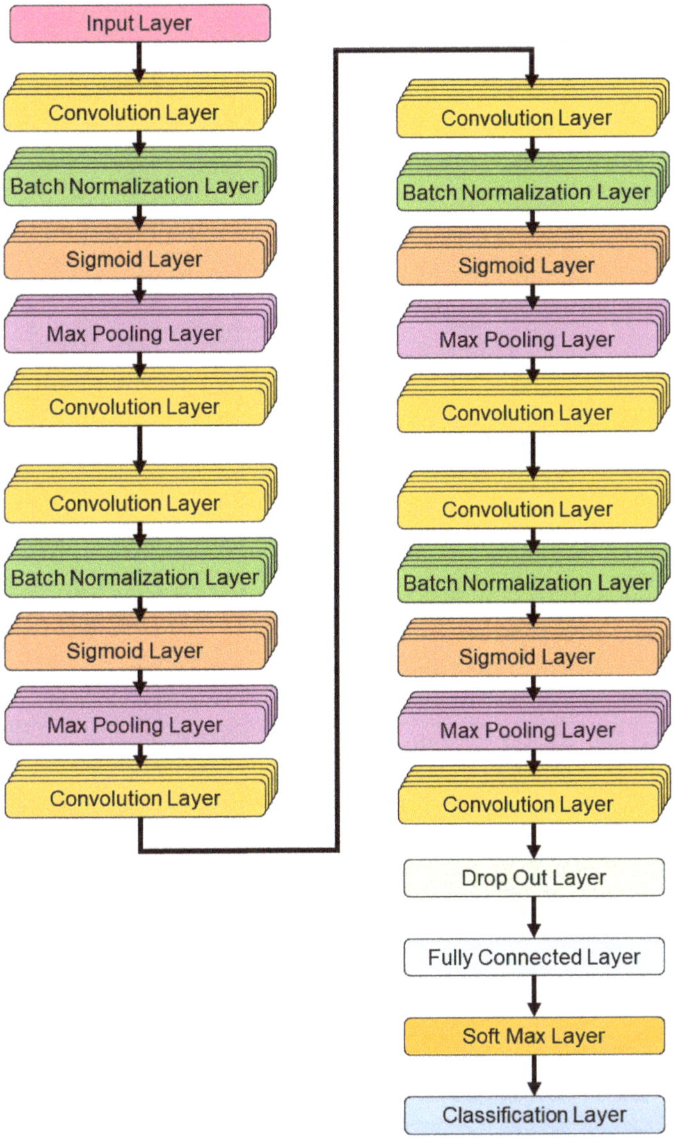

Figure 6. CNN-WDI model.

Table 3. CNN model parameters.

Layer	Activation	Learnables	Activation
Image Input Layer	224 × 224 × 3	-	
Convolution Layer	224 × 224 × 16	Weight 3 × 3 × 3 × 16, Bias 1 × 1 × 16	
Batch Normalization Layer	224 × 224 × 16	Offset 1 × 1 × 16, Scale 1 × 1 × 16	Sigmoid
Max Pooling Layer	112 × 112 × 16	-	
Convolution Layer	112 × 112 × 16	Weight 3 × 3 × 16 × 16, Bias 1 × 1 × 16	
Convolution Layer	112 × 112 × 32	Weight 3 × 3 × 16 × 32, Bias 1 × 1 × 32	
Batch Normalization Layer	112 × 112 × 32	Offset 1 × 1 × 32, Scale 1 × 1 × 32	Sigmoid
Max Pooling Layer	56 × 56 × 32	-	
Convolution Layer	56 × 56 × 32	Weight 3 × 3 × 32 × 32, Bias 1 × 1 × 32	
Convolution Layer	56 × 56 × 64	Weight 3 × 3 × 32 × 64, Bias 1 × 1 × 64	
Batch Normalization Layer	56 × 56 × 64	Offset 1 × 1 × 64, Scale 1 × 1 × 64	Sigmoid
Max Pooling Layer	28 × 28 × 64	-	
Convolution Layer	28 × 28 × 64	Weight 3 × 3 × 64 × 64, Bias 1 × 1 × 64	
Convolution Layer	28 × 28 × 128	Weight 3 × 3 × 64 × 128, Bias 1 × 1 × 128	
Batch Normalization Layer	28 × 28 × 128	Offset 1 × 1 × 128, Scale 1 × 1 × 128	Sigmoid
Max Pooling Layer	14 × 14 × 128	-	
Convolution Layer	14 × 14 × 128	Weight 3 × 3 × 128 × 128, Bias 1 × 1 × 128	
Dropout	14 × 14 × 128	-	
Fully Connected Layer	1 × 1 × 2	-	
Classification Layer	1 × 1 × 2	-	SoftMax

Table 4. Range of grid search and step.

Hyperparameter	Range	Step
Initial Learning Rate	0.001~0.01	0.05
Max Epoch	10~50	10
Minibatch Size	10~300	50
Dropout Rate	0~0.3	0.1

Table 5. Optimized values of the hyperparameters.

Algorithm	Dataset	Optimization Hyperparameter			
		Minibatch	Max Epoch	Dropout	Learning Rate
ANN	k-65 SMOTE	100	50	0	0.005
	k-98 SMOTE	300	50	0	0.001
	k-130 SMOTE	150	50	0	0.005
CNN	2× Augmentation	100	50	0.2	0.001
	5× Augmentation	150	30	0.1	0.001
	10× Augmentation	100	20	0.3	0.001

4. Results and Discussion

To derive the test results of the learned model, a confusion matrix was configured, where Tp, Fp, Fn, and Tn represent the numbers of data points classified as true positive, false positive, false negative, and true negative, respectively.

It was evaluated using various performance measures, such as accuracy, precision, recall, and *F*1 score [29]. The *Accuracy* of a classifier defines the frequency with which it accurately predicts over the entire dataset, and is defined as follows:

$$Accuracy = \frac{Tp + Tn}{Tp + Tn + Fp + Fn} \tag{3}$$

Precision and *Recall* indicate that both performance measures are inversely proportional to each other, and each has various classification-measuring qualities.

$$Precision = \frac{Tp}{Tp + Fp} \tag{4}$$

$$Recall = \frac{Tp}{Tp + Fn} \tag{5}$$

The *F*1 score calculates the harmonic mean of precision and recall and is defined as follows: The *F*1 score is an interpretation of actual and predicted probabilities. If these probabilities are close to each other, then the *F*1 score exhibits a higher result, and vice versa.

$$F1\ score = \frac{2 \times Precision \times Recall}{Precision + Recall} \tag{6}$$

To evaluate the execution time of defect detection, we used the GPU Nvidia GeForce RTX 3070 and CPU Intel i9 10,900, resulting in an execution time of 0.089 s. The performance evaluation metrics are listed in Table 6. Applying the oversampled data to the ANN, the dataset with the k value set to 130 exhibited the highest accuracy of 84.82% and a fallout value of 0.2857. In the CNN utilizing cutout, the image data were augmented tenfold, resulting in an accuracy of 97.32% and a fallout value of 0.0357. Consequently, a performance comparison between an ANN applied to tabular data and a CNN utilizing tabular data converted into image data revealed the superior predictive accuracy and fallout values of the CNN.

Table 6. Performance evaluation index by dataset.

Algorithm	Dataset	Performance Index				
		Accuracy	Precision	Recall	F1 Score	Fallout
ANN	k-65 SMOTE	0.8304	0.7606	0.9643	0.8540	0.3036
	k-98 SMOTE	0.8393	0.7639	0.9821	0.8594	0.3036
	k-130 SMOTE	0.8482	0.7746	0.9821	0.8661	0.2857
CNN	2× Augmentation	0.9554	0.9474	0.9643	0.9558	0.0526
	5× Augmentation	0.9643	0.943	0.9643	0.9643	0.0357
	10× Augmentation	0.9732	0.9649	0.9821	0.9735	0.0357

This confirmed that the tabular data applied to the ANN were effectively transformed into grayscale images. Moreover, the spatial context information of these image files formed an efficient array for extracting the features of the seat-forming process. Employing convolution layers for feature extraction and max pooling layers for downsampling the image allowed the spatial hierarchical structure of the image data to be learned well. Consequently, the preservation of specific parts of the image and assistance in feature extraction were evident. The CNN model used in this study repeated the structure of the convolution layer–batch normalization–sigmoid–max pooling–convolution layer four times. In addition, previous studies have reported that accuracy escalates with each repetition, indicating effective feature extraction [30].

5. Conclusions

This study discussed the effectiveness of using deep learning, specifically 2D CNN algorithms, to predict defects in manufacturing processes with nonlinear characteristics. The focus was on predicting defects in seat foaming manufacturing using both ANNs and CNNs. To address data imbalances, oversampling techniques were employed, including SMOTE for the ANN and cutout augmentation for the CNN. The CNN outperformed the ANN in terms of prediction accuracy, particularly with the 10-fold augmented dataset using cutout, achieving 97.32% accuracy and a fallout value of 0.0357. Moreover, the importance of preprocessing techniques such as grayscale conversion for image data was emphasized and it was concluded that a CNN, with its ability to extract spatial features and repeated convolution layers, was more effective than an ANN in predicting defects using transformed image data in manufacturing processes.

Regarding the reliability of prediction or process analysis, it is effective to predict defects in processes with nonlinear characteristics using deep learning. In particular, utilizing a 2D CNN algorithm with excellent classification performance is effective, and data in image form are necessary to apply the 2D CNN algorithm. However, extracting distinct features, particularly when mixing raw materials, is challenging, and the process of injecting them into a mold is limited by the collection and analysis of image data. This process requires the conversion of numerical data into images. In this study, the concept of each factor's range or unit was eliminated through the normalization of the numerical data, thereby facilitating classification based on its location within the entire range. It is believed that these normalization results can be converted into grayscale values to allow a model to learn a range of converted grayscale values instead of specific numbers, thereby enhancing the classification performance. As a part of future work, we aim to explore and implement various methods to reduce the training time of the 2D CNN model. This will include investigating the impact of optimizing the size of the image dataset, among other potential strategies.

Author Contributions: J.-S.O. takes the primary responsibility for this research as the principal investigator and drafted the manuscript. N.-H.C. contributed to the analysis, algorithm, and writing of the manuscript. J.W.S. contributed to the investigation and writing—review and editing. All authors have read and agreed to the published version of the manuscript.

Funding: This results was partially supported by the "Regional Innovation Strategy (RIS)" through the National Research Foundation of Korea (NRF) funded by the Ministry of Education (MOE) (2021RIS-004) and the Korea government (MSIT) (No. 2022R1F1A1074691).

Data Availability Statement: The data used to support the findings of this study are included within the article.

Conflicts of Interest: The authors declare no conflict of interest.

References

1. Soualhi, M.; Nguyen, K.T.P.; Medjaher, K. Pattern recognition method of fault diagnostics based on a new health indicator for smart manufacturing. *Mech. Syst. Signal Process.* **2020**, *142*, 106680. [CrossRef]
2. Booyse, W.; Wilke, D.N.; Heyns, S. Deep digital twins for detection, diagnostics and prognostics. *Mech. Syst. Signal Process.* **2020**, *140*, 106612. [CrossRef]
3. Jang, I.; Bae, G.; Kim, H. Metal forming defect detection method based on recurrence quantification analysis of time-series load signal measured by real-time monitoring system with bolt-type piezoelectric sensor. *Mech. Syst. Signal Process.* **2022**, *180*, 109457. [CrossRef]
4. Chen, Y.; Rao, M.; Feng, K.; Zuo, M.J. Physics-Informed LSTM Hyperparameters Selection for Gearbox Fault Detection. *Mech. Syst. Signal Process.* **2022**, *171*, 108907. [CrossRef]
5. Han, T.; Xie, W.; Pei, Z. Semi-Supervised Adversarial Discriminative Learning Approach for Intelligent Fault Diagnosis of Wind Turbine. *Inf. Sci.* **2023**, *648*, 119496. [CrossRef]
6. Chen, Y.; Rao, M.; Feng, K.; Niu, G. Modified Varying Index Coefficient Autoregression Model for Representation of the Nonstationary Vibration from a Planetary Gearbox. *IEEE Trans. Instrum. Meas.* **2023**, *72*, 1–12. [CrossRef]
7. Yao, J.; Han, T. Data-Driven Lithium-Ion Batteries Capacity Estimation Based on Deep Transfer Learning Using Partial Segment of Charging/Discharging Data. *Energy* **2023**, *271*, 127033. [CrossRef]

8. Im, S.J.; Oh, J.S.; Kim, G.-W. Simultaneous Estimation of Unknown Road Roughness Input and Tire Normal Forces Based on a Long Short-Term Memory Model. *IEEE Access* **2022**, *10*, 16655–16669. [CrossRef]
9. Chien, J.C.; Wu, M.T.; Lee, J.D. Inspection and classification of semiconductor wafer surface defects using CNN deep learning networks. *Appl. Sci.* **2020**, *10*, 5340. [CrossRef]
10. Sahu, C.K.; Young, C.; Rai, R. Artificial intelligence (AI) in augmented reality (AR)-assisted manufacturing applications: A review. *Int. J. Prod. Res.* **2021**, *59*, 4903–4959. [CrossRef]
11. Schmidhuber, J. Deep learning in neural networks: An overview. *Neural Netw.* **2015**, *61*, 85–117. [CrossRef] [PubMed]
12. Krizhevsky, A.; Sutskever, I.; Hinton, G.E. ImageNet classification with deep convolutional neural networks. *Commun. ACM* **2017**, *60*, 84–90. [CrossRef]
13. Glaeser, A.; Selvaraj, V.; Lee, S.; Hwang, Y.; Lee, K.; Lee, N.; Lee, S.; Min, S.; Min, S. Applications of deep learning for fault detection in industrial cold forging. *Int. J. Prod. Res.* **2021**, *59*, 4826–4835. [CrossRef]
14. Nakazawa, T.; Kulkarni, D.V. Wafer map defect pattern classification and image retrieval using convolutional neural network. *IEEE Trans. Semicond. Manuf.* **2018**, *31*, 309–314. [CrossRef]
15. Saqlain, M.; Abbas, Q.; Lee, J.Y. A deep convolutional neural network for wafer defect identification on an imbalanced dataset in semiconductor manufacturing processes. *IEEE Trans. Semicond. Manuf.* **2020**, *33*, 436–444. [CrossRef]
16. Liu, J.; Shao, Y. Overview of dynamic modelling and analysis of rolling element bearings with localized and distributed faults. *Nonlinear Dyn.* **2018**, *93*, 1765–1798. [CrossRef]
17. Wang, L.-H.; Zhao, X.-P.; Wu, J.-X.; Xie, Y.-Y.; Zhang, Y.-H. Motor fault diagnosis based on short-time Fourier transform and convolutional neural network. *Chin. J. Mech. Eng.* **2017**, *30*, 1357–1368. [CrossRef]
18. Chen, K.; Zhou, X.-C.; Fang, J.-Q.; Zheng, P.-F.; Wang, J. Fault feature extraction and diagnosis of gearbox based on EEMD and deep briefs network. *Int. J. Rotating Mach.* **2017**, *2017*, 9602650. [CrossRef]
19. Guo, S.; Yang, T.; Gao, W.; Zhang, C. A novel fault diagnosis method for rotating machinery based on a convolutional neural network. *Sensors* **2018**, *18*, 1429. [CrossRef]
20. Sun, W.F.; Yao, B.; Zeng, N.; Chen, B.; He, Y.; Cao, X.; He, W. An intelligent gear fault diagnosis methodology using a complex wavelet enhanced convolutional neural network. *Materials* **2017**, *10*, 790. [CrossRef]
21. Zhao, M.; Kang, M.; Tang, B.; Pecht, M. Deep residual networks with dynamically weighted wavelet coefficients for fault diagnosis of planetary gearboxes. *IEEE Trans. Ind. Electron.* **2018**, *65*, 4290–4300. [CrossRef]
22. Sezer, O.B.; Ozbayoglu, A.M. Algorithmic financial trading with deep convolutional neural networks: Time series to image conversion approach. *Appl. Soft Comput.* **2018**, *70*, 525–538. [CrossRef]
23. Lee, E.; Nam, M.; Lee, H. Tab2vox: CNN-based multivariate multilevel demand forecasting framework by tabular-to-voxel image conversion. *Sustainability* **2022**, *14*, 11745. [CrossRef]
24. Choi, N.K. Defect Prediction Model of Automobile Interior Parts in Manufacturing Process. Master Thesis, Kongju National University, Cheonan, Choongnam, Republic of Korea, 2023.
25. Adnan, R.; Ruslan, F.A.; Samad, A.M.; Zain, Z.M. New Artificial Neural Network and Extended Kalman Filter Hybrid Model of Flood Prediction System. In Proceedings of the 2013 IEEE 9th International Colloquium on Signal Processing and its Applications, Kuala Lumpur, Malaysia, 8–10 March 2013; pp. 252–257. [CrossRef]
26. Shorten, C.; Khoshgoftaar, T.M. A survey on image data augmentation for deep learning. *J. Big Data* **2019**, *6*, 1–48. [CrossRef]
27. DeVries, T.; Taylor, G.W. Improved Regularization of Convolutional Neural Networks with Cutout. *arXiv* **2017**, arXiv:1708.04552.
28. Restrepo Rodríguez, A.O.; Casas Mateus, D.E.; Gaona García, P.A.; Montenegro Marín, C.E.; González Crespo, R. Hyperparameter optimization for image recognition over an ar-sandbox based on convolutional neural networks applying a previous phase of segmentation by color–space. *Symmetry* **2018**, *10*, 743. [CrossRef]
29. Sokolova, M.; Japkowicz, N.; Szpakowicz, S. *Beyond Accuracy, F-Score and ROC: A Family of Discriminant Measures for Performance Evaluation*; Springer: Berlin/Heidelberg, Germany, 2006; pp. 1015–1021.
30. He, K.; Zhang, X.; Ren, S.; Sun, J. Deep residual learning for image recognition. In Proceedings of the IEEE Conference on Computer Vision and Pattern Recognition, Las Vegas, NV, USA, 27–30 June 2016; pp. 770–778.

mathematics

MDPI

Article

Accuracy Is Not Enough: Optimizing for a Fault Detection Delay

Matej Šprogar * and Domen Verber

Faculty of Electrical Engineering and Computer Science, University of Maribor, 2000 Maribor, Slovenia; domen.verber@um.si
* Correspondence: matej.sprogar@um.si

Abstract: This paper assesses the fault-detection capabilities of modern deep-learning models. It highlights that a naive deep-learning approach optimized for accuracy is unsuitable for learning fault-detection models from time-series data. Consequently, out-of-the-box deep-learning strategies may yield impressive accuracy results but are ill-equipped for real-world applications. The paper introduces a methodology for estimating fault-detection delays when no oracle information on fault occurrence time is available. Moreover, the paper presents a straightforward approach to implicitly achieve the objective of minimizing fault-detection delays. This approach involves using pseudo-multi-objective deep optimization with data windowing, which enables the utilization of standard deep-learning methods for fault detection and expanding their applicability. However, it does introduce an additional hyperparameter that needs careful tuning. The paper employs the Tennessee Eastman Process dataset as a case study to demonstrate its findings. The results effectively highlight the limitations of standard loss functions and emphasize the importance of incorporating fault-detection delays in evaluating and reporting performance. In our study, the pseudo-multi-objective optimization could reach a fault-detection accuracy of 95% in just a fifth of the time it takes the best naive approach to do so.

Keywords: artificial neural networks; deep learning; fault detection; accuracy; multi-objective optimization

MSC: 68T07

1. Introduction

Modern industrial systems are increasingly more complex and prone to failure, which can lead to significant dangers or high costs. Detecting faults is crucial in these systems [1], but it is challenging due to the vast amount and complex nature of data the systems handle and produce. Once a fault is detected, further analysis and decision-making processes are necessary to identify the specific fault type and prevent it from spreading.

In recent years, deep learning (machine learning using neural networks with many hidden layers) has showcased its remarkable ability to learn complex data representations, revolutionizing various learning tasks. Deep learning was also successfully applied to fault detection, which must handle a broad range of multivariate data [2,3]. Multivariate data are a sequence of chronologically recorded observations of interrelated and interacting multidimensional variables.

Although deep learning has shown success in fault detection, it is important to acknowledge that researchers using deep fault-detecting models sometimes overlook the crucial temporal aspect of fault detection. Specifically, they fail to leverage the existing temporal dependencies among variables using only a single data sample in one time step or, conversely, too much data in too many time steps [4]. Consequently, they fail to optimize for the time it takes to detect a fault. In many applications, the fault-detection delay—the time gap between the actual occurrence of a fault and its recognition by the fault-detecting component—can be quite dangerous and therefore this delay should be as small as possible [5].

If attainable, fault prediction is better than fault detection as it allows us to prevent potentially expensive faults from occurring. We can consider fault prediction as a negative fault-detection delay. However, if predictions are unattainable, a low fault-detection delay is just as important as high sensitivity and a low false alarm rate.

Quick detection of faults while minimizing false alarms is paramount in fault-tolerant systems. A functional fault-detection system raises alarms with acceptable delays. Our objective is to demonstrate the inadequacy of approaches that ignore fault-detection delays when evaluating fault-detection (and prediction) performance. We experimented on a large and renowned synthetic dataset [6] and tried to identify the main factor influencing the accuracy and delay of the fault-detection process.

The main contributions of this paper are as follows:

(1) Emphasizing the significance of fault-detection delays when considering deep-learning fault-detection models. By disregarding the temporal aspect of the solution, standard loss functions produce solutions with little practical value.
(2) Introducing a methodology for estimating deep fault delays. In cases where the timestamps of faults are unknown, it is only possible to estimate the fault-detection delay to a certain extent.
(3) Proposing a pseudo-multi-objective approach to fault detection with any deep-learning model, although we have only validated it with Long Short-Term Memory on a single dataset. Deep models should only have access to short training sequences, or they will not learn short-term relations needed for short fault-detection delays.
(4) Providing a clear integration of machine learning concepts with fault detection. Bridging these two domains facilitates better knowledge exchange and helps prevent experimental errors.

This paper delves into the temporal aspect of deep fault detection. Additionally, we examined the influence of data windowing on fault-detection accuracy and delay. Section 2 introduces the concept of a monitoring component and provides an overview of artificial neural networks. Section 3 introduces a uniform notation for describing the context and data windows in sequential data and estimating fault-detection delays for any model. Section 4 presents a pseudo-multi-objective optimization approach that surpasses certain naive approaches observed in the literature. Finally, Section 5 illustrates the application of the proposed concepts using the widely used Tennessee Eastman Process (TEP) dataset [7].

2. Background

Fault handling commonly includes fault detection, fault identification, and fault diagnosis [8]. In general, fault detection evaluates the system's operational status to determine its normal functionality; fault identification determines the specific type of fault that has occurred; and fault diagnosis identifies the root cause of the fault and traces its potential propagation path. Sometimes it is possible to identify a fault during the fault-detection step. Regardless of the chosen approach, it is crucial to incorporate a component that monitors the entire system.

2.1. The Monitoring Component

To effectively address the system's complexity and safety concerns, we must design, evaluate, and implement the safety-related aspects independently and in parallel with the functional components. It is also essential to acknowledge the susceptibility to faults of the control process itself. An independent monitoring component (MC) is a general approach to overseeing the control function and assisting in fault handling.

The component actively monitors the inputs of the main system (a), the control system's response ($b = F(a)$), and, if available, the internal state variables (c) of the control system (refer to Figure 1). It is important to note that while the MC possesses the same information as the control function F, it does not perform the controlling task. The primary role of the component is to confirm the validity of its inputs $X = (a, b, c)$. Consequently, the MC reports the operational diagnosis $d = f(X)$ to a higher fault management layer with the necessary expertise to handle a fault. Although a binary diagnosis indicates the presence or absence of a fault, a more intricate output may even identify a specific fault.

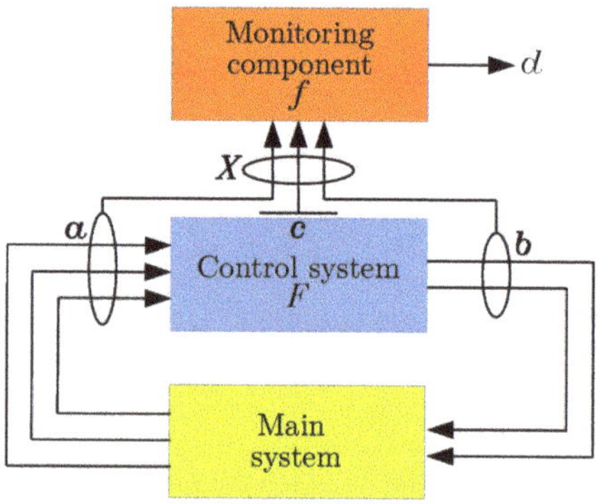

Figure 1. Data flows and the positioning of the monitoring component above the control system.

To ensure minimal interference with the control environment, the monitoring component should strive to employ physically separate and dedicated hardware exclusively for its operation. Furthermore, the monitoring component needs to operate at a speed that matches or surpasses the monitored system.

The most challenging aspect is developing a reliable decision model within the MC. This decision model is responsible for recognizing the system's state as either normal or abnormal. Deep learning with artificial neural networks has enabled many effective solutions that address this decision-making challenge [8,9].

2.2. *Artificial Neural Networks*

Modern machine learning encompasses a broad spectrum of approaches, among which artificial neural networks have emerged as a successful and widely adopted method. Artificial Neural Networks (ANNs) are computational models inspired by the complex network of biological neurons in animal and human brains. These networks are comprised of interconnected nodes with weighted connections that transmit signals (represented as real numbers) from one node to another. ANNs are highly suitable for addressing diverse problem domains. A general and detailed description of artificial neural networks is available in [10].

Although ANNs are fast to execute and can learn to compute nonlinear and complex functions, it is important to acknowledge the potential pitfalls associated with their use. Ref. [11] These pitfalls include:

- Data: ANNs rely on sufficient high-quality data that accurately represent the problem. Data availability and quality can be a challenge, particularly because obtaining large, labeled datasets may be impractical or costly [4].
- Learning: The success of the learning phase in ANNs is not guaranteed and can be influenced by factors such as the chosen network type and topology. Selecting the appropriate architecture and configuring the network hyperparameters can significantly impact its learning capabilities and overall performance [12].
- Verification and Overfitting: Validating the solutions produced by ANNs can be challenging. Due to the complexity of their internal workings, it can be difficult to understand how and why an ANN arrived at a specific output. Additionally, ANNs are susceptible to overfitting, resulting in reduced generalization of unseen data [11].

Addressing these issues requires careful consideration during the design and implementation of ANNs. Strategies such as data preprocessing, regularization techniques, cross-validation, and model evaluation can help mitigate these challenges and improve the reliability and generalizability of ANNs in real-world applications.

There are two general ANN architecture types, each with distinct advantages and disadvantages. The first type is feed-forward networks, which propagate signals directly from the input to the output layer. Due to their inherent simplicity, these networks can only extract cross-dimensional correlations from large, external sequence-encompassing contexts using more complex internal mechanisms, such as convolution [13] or attention [14]. It is worth noting that feed-forward designs require substantial amounts of data and significant offline learning efforts, but they are cost-effective to use afterward.

Recurrent neural networks (RNN) can naturally capture autocorrelations by utilizing recurrent connections that loop the propagated signals. As a result, RNNs are well-suited for handling sequential data, as they can effectively leverage an internal context that they build autonomously from the supplied inputs. Chung et al. [15] observed that many effective recurrent neural networks use advanced, recurrent hidden units. Two widely used types of these hidden units are the Long Short-Term Memory (LSTM) and the Gated Recurrent Unit (GRU). These specialized units, created for handling time-series data, have greatly simplified the development and training of recurrent networks. Recently, however, transformer-based [14] networks started to prevail also because they are faster to train [16].

One particular application of data-driven deep learning is deep anomaly detection, which involves using deep neural networks to obtain feature representations or anomaly scores. Anomaly detection focuses on identifying data instances that deviate significantly from the norm [2]. In the context of anomaly detection for multivariate time-series, Tian identifies three major challenges [4]. First, the scarcity of labeled data arising from the rarity of outlier instances. Second, identifying complex interactions and relationships among features proves to be a challenging task. Last, detecting hidden and inconspicuous anomalies in high-dimensional data presents a formidable obstacle. These challenges severely limit our ability to extract meaningful insights from the available data.

3. Deep Fault-Detection Models for Time-Series Data

Data-based fault detection using machine learning can go two ways. The first approach involves constructing a classifier using supervised learning techniques. This classifier is trained on labeled data and learns to classify a given data sample as either normal operating conditions (NOC) or a potential fault. Predicting faults in the (near) future is even more advantageous than simply detecting existing faults, and classification models can be trained accordingly. However, supervised learning relies on high-quality labeled data representing all possible system states. Obtaining such data in large quantities can be challenging, especially in many industrial environments where faults are infrequent and come at a high cost. Nevertheless, supervised deep-learning approaches for fault detection have been successfully applied in various areas, including chemical production systems [17], semiconductor manufacturing processes [18], and high-performance computing [19].

On the other hand, unsupervised learning provides a more suitable alternative for fault detection, particularly in scenarios with few or no faulty samples available for training. In this approach, autoencoders (AE) are widely used as a technique for deep fault detection [20,21]. Autoencoders are neural network architectures that encode the input signal into a latent representation and then attempt to reconstruct the original signal from this compressed information. A level of successful reconstruction of the input signal is a measure of similarity between the test signal and the pre-learned normal signals.

By training autoencoders exclusively with normal operating condition data, they learn the underlying structure or principal components of the signals that describe the normal operation of a plant. When presented with an anomalous signal, their ability to accurately recreate the input will be lower than with non-anomalous signals used in training. This difference in reconstruction performance enables us to distinguish anomalous samples from the NOC samples based on the reconstruction error alone.

Consequently, the performance of autoencoders heavily relies on selecting an appropriate error threshold, which leads researchers to employ Receiver Operating Characteristic (ROC) analysis by varying these thresholds. Unlike classifiers that can only distinguish between normal operating conditions and expected faults, autoencoders can detect even unanticipated states of operation.

3.1. Performance Metrics

Machine learning (ML) strongly emphasizes accuracy, primarily due to the generalization challenges that artificial neural networks face when confronted with unseen data. The main concern in ML is to mitigate incorrect outputs caused by the unstable propagation of features through ANNs, rendering them ineffective in the presence of minor input perturbations [22,23].

Several studies have exclusively concentrated on established machine learning evaluation metrics, such as accuracy, while neglecting the inherent sequential nature of the data and failing to consider fault-detection delays [24–26].

3.2. The Data

The time-series data are a sequence of data samples denoted by $S = [X^{(1)}, \dots, X^{(T)}]$, where each sample $X^{(t)}$ represents the input signals at time t, and T is the total number of time ticks. Specifically, the sample $X^{(t)} = [x_1^{(t)}; \dots; x_N^{(t)}], X^{(t)} \in \mathbb{R}^N$, represents the signal values of the N features at time tick t. The fault-detection model takes an input sample and generates the output $y = f(X), y \in \mathbb{R}$. Each input sample corresponds to one fault-detection case. Finally, a dataset, which consists of d sequences, can be denoted as $D = [S_1; S_2; \dots; S_d]$.

Let us define a sliding window function that selects the last w samples from a sequence S at time t:

$$W_w^{(t)}(S) := [X^{(t-w+1)}, \dots, X^{(t-1)}; X^{(t)}], \quad w \le t \le T. \tag{1}$$

This allows us to denote $S_w^{(t)} = W_w^{(t)}(S)$. In a sequence consisting of T samples, the window $W_T(S)^{(T)}$ selects the entire sequence: $S = W_T(S)^{(T)}$, and $W_1(S)^{(T)}$ selects only the last sample: $X^{(T)} = W_1^{(T)}(S)$. The sliding window utilized for sample selection is similar to, but should not be confused with, the fault-absorbing sliding windows [27].

3.3. The Context

All deep-learning models rely on a context that serves as the reference frame for the inputs they process. Samples preceding the most recent sample $X^{(T)}$ form the simplest context. Specifically, the context includes the w samples visible through the window $W_w^{(T-1)}$.

In the case of feed-forward (FF) models, the context is external and must be provided at each time step. One way to incorporate it is by introducing it as a second parameter to the fault-detection function, such as $y = f(S_1^{(T)}, S_w^{(T-1)})$. However, for simpler implementation, machine learning flattens the context and appends it to the current sample, resulting in $y = f(S_{w+1}^{(T)})$, or even more simply $y = f(S_w^{(T)})$. It is important to note that flattening the external context removes the temporal axis from the data.

In contrast, recurrent models utilize a hidden state H, eliminating the need for an external context. The operation of recurrent models can be represented as $(y^{(T)}, H^{(T)}) = f(S_1^{(T)}, H^{(T-1)})$. As H is an internal state, we can omit it from the notation, resulting in $f(S_1^{(T)}) = f(S_1^{(T)}, H^{(T-1)})$. Although recurrent models process time-series data and update their state by considering one sample $X^{(T)}$ at a time, they still require the processing of several consecutive samples to detect a fault because the state $H^{(t)}$ depends on $H^{(t-1)}$. Considering that all the previous states influence the internal state, we can express the entire history of processing as $y = y^{(T)} = f(S_1^{(1)}) \circ \dots \circ f(S_1^{(T)})$. Random initialization of $H^{(0)}$ makes $H^{(T-w)}$ a possible starting point for sequentially processing the sequence $S_w^{(T)}$, leading (again) to $y \approx f(S_w^{(T)})$. Unlike feed-forward networks, which require flattening consecutive samples into one wide input, recurrent models retain the temporal organization of the data.

The 'context data' size, determined by the hyperparameter w, limits the model's ability to capture long relationships. Feed-forward models have a limitation in that they can only capture correlations within the constrained context ($w << T$) and are unable to detect correlations that extend beyond it. It is important to note that the implementation of the model may impose restrictions on the context size. The context size limitation is observed in popular models like ChatGPT as well [28].

3.4. Fault-Detection Delay

Artificial neural networks are extremely quick at generating output. Unless a highly responsive system is being monitored, the time required for this transformation can be ignored, if we compare it to the duration of a single time step.

To quantify the fault-detection delay δ, which refers to the time elapsed between the actual onset of a fault and its detection [5], it is necessary to possess accurate information regarding the fault's exact occurrence time τ within the system. Unless an external source or an oracle provides this temporal data, determining the exact fault occurrence time becomes extremely challenging. Faults typically require a certain amount of time to be propagated through the system and are seldom detectable immediately upon initiation. Furthermore, there are instances when the process control system actively masks the fault by compensating for its adverse effects before the system enters a visibly anomalous state that can be detected.

In machine learning, there is a common assumption that the associations within a system can be acquired by recording its features and that the comprehensive data captures all relevant relationships. Consequently, utilizing *all* available data to make informed decisions through the execution of $f(S_T^{(T)})$ establishes the performance baseline for fault detection, with the fault-detection delay $\delta = T - \tau$. It is important to note that the baseline model exhibits the maximum delay when applied to pre-recorded data. The true fault-detection delay occurs only when the model is employed live on a data stream.

To determine the model's fault-detection delay when the fault time is unknown, we must identify the minimum number of samples required to provide sufficient information for accurate enough fault detection at any time step:

$$f(S_\delta^{(t)}) = f(S_{\delta+i}^{(t)}), \quad \forall (t,i) \in [\delta, T] \times [0, T-\delta] \tag{2}$$

Unfortunately, the brute force approach to determine δ using Equation (2) is very slow, because we must determine δ for all possible training inputs:

$$\delta = \max_K \delta(D), \tag{3}$$

where K is the set of all possible inputs of size w obtainable from the T time steps of long sequences from D. Using the sampling stride of 1 gives $|K| = |D| \cdot (T - w + 1)$ possible inputs. However, if one has knowledge of τ, one can determine δ much simpler, because the model requires δ time steps to detect a fault:

$$\begin{aligned} f(S_\delta^{(\tau+i)}) &= NOC \quad \forall i \in [0, \delta[\\ f(S_\delta^{(\tau+\delta)}) &\neq NOC \end{aligned} \tag{4}$$

If we do not have τ, we should try to put a lower bound on δ by measuring the delay at time step T. This is carried out by finding the smallest input that still produces the same output as the baseline decision $f(S_T^{(T)})$; we shall denote this statistic as λ:

$$
\begin{aligned}
f(S_{\lambda}^{(T)}) &= f(S_{\lambda+i}^{(T)}), \quad \forall i \in [0, T-\lambda] \\
&\neq f(S_{\lambda-1}^{(T)}).
\end{aligned}
\tag{5}
$$

High λ suggests that the model is unstable, while a lower λ value is a sign of a simple problem. λ is not $\delta^{(T)}$—the fault-detection delay at time T—but a lower bound (If the model performs fault identification, the lower bound corresponds to the highest λ of all faults) for fault-detection delay at time T. Although the delays for other inputs are probably different, the worst-case fault-detection delay will be at least λ:

$$
\lambda \leq \delta. \tag{6}
$$

Because no (deep) model is perfect, the decision regarding a fault can change with additional input(s). Raising premature alarms is bad but can only be mitigated by waiting for more data that would confirm the alarm but delay the decision. We need a measure of how fast the model's output stabilizes. A simple boundary can be determined by testing the model using inputs $S_t^{(t)}, t \in [1, T]$, which include the first t samples. Let us denote with μ the time step when the output becomes *stable*–subsequent samples do not change the outcome of the fault-detection process:

$$
\begin{aligned}
f(S_{\mu}^{(\mu)}) &= f(S_{\mu+i}^{(\mu+i)}), \quad \forall i \in [0, T-\mu] \\
&\neq f(S_{\mu-1}^{(\mu-1)}).
\end{aligned}
\tag{7}
$$

In contrast to λ, μ retains older samples and discards more recent ones from the input. When the precise time of fault initiation τ is known (e.g., provided by an oracle), the fault-detection delay can be calculated by straightforward subtraction:

$$
\delta = \mu - \tau. \tag{8}
$$

The delay estimation strategy applies when the fault occurrence time is unknown (Figure 2a). After determining the λ and μ statistics, we need $\lambda \leq \mu$ to interpret the results. Because λ and μ represent the delay's lower and upper bound ($\lambda \leq \delta \leq \mu$), a situation with $\lambda > \mu$ indicates problems with fault detection in the underlying model. These problems could be due to overfitting [29], instability [23], generalization problems [30], or other issues we must address. When we know the fault time τ, we can measure the detection time and directly compute the delay (Figure 2b).

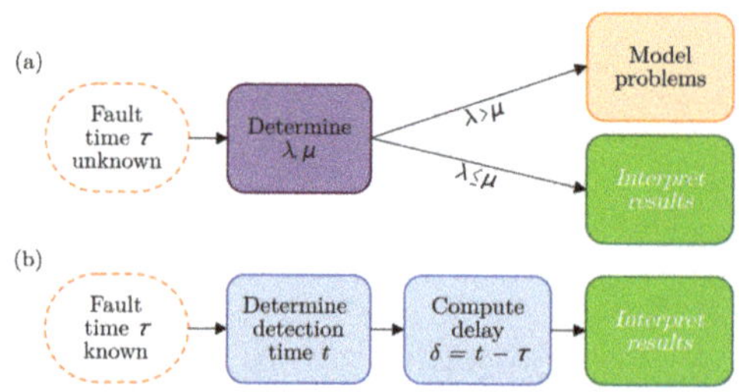

Figure 2. The approach to fault-detection delay analysis depends on the availability of the fault occurrence time. (**a**) Strategy if fault time is unknown; (**b**) procedure when the fault time is known.

4. Pseudo-Multi-Objective Optimization

In multi-objective optimization, a single model cannot simultaneously achieve the best performance in all dimensions [31]. Optimizing for accuracy and low delay in fault detection involves a trade-off, as these objectives are inherently conflicting. Consequently, exploring multiple Pareto optimal solutions that offer a balanced trade-off between accuracy and delay becomes crucial.

Various universal techniques for tackling multi-objective optimization exist. One common approach involves using weighting methods, such as adaptive weighting techniques proposed by Xie et al. [32], or using multi-objective instance weights as discussed by Lee et al. [33]. By incorporating such techniques, solutions that balance competing objectives form the Pareto front of candidate solutions to the optimization problem. Figure 3 positions various models according to their accuracy and fault-detection delay performance. If the trivial model solution, which never signals a fault, has no fault-detection delay, the ideal model would detect all faults instantly. Learning increases the models' accuracy because explicit ML loss optimization pushes models horizontally toward higher accuracy. Only an orthogonal incentive (explicit or implicit) would push the models towards short fault-detection delays.

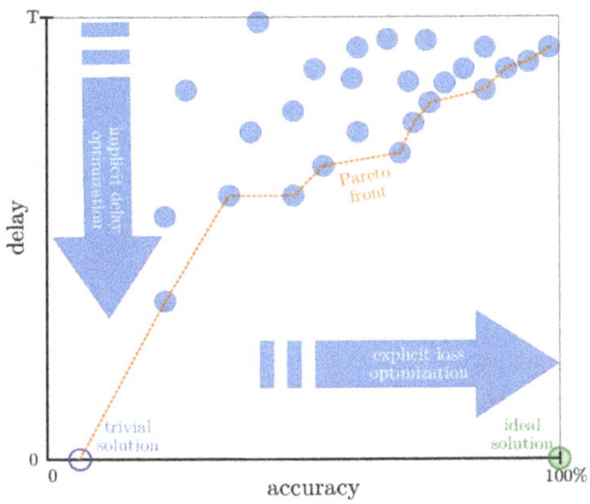

Figure 3. Pareto front connects non-dominating models on the accuracy and fault-detection delay plane.

In this context, we adopt the implicit approach. We prioritize utilizing established deep optimization techniques to maximize fault-detection accuracy while aiming for a short delay as an implicit objective. This implicit optimization for short delays aligns harmoniously with the accuracy-optimizing objectives of existing ML libraries without necessitating any modifications to the existing ML code.

When training a fault-detection model with recordings of historical data that stretch over many time steps, the conventional ML approach poses the question, "Do these historical data contain any faults?" However, in real-time fault detection, it is important to rephrase the question: "Do these historical data indicate an imminent or a recently occurred fault?" This shift in emphasis redirects the focus from analyzing the distant past to the near future or present.

When training the model with historical data with the fault introduced relatively early compared to the overall length of the sequence ($\tau << T$), we effectively ask the first question. To ask the second question, we would ideally need training data with the fault occurring in the last time step ($\tau = T$) or, even better, in the future ($\tau > T$). The acquisition of such data, especially in sufficient quantities for deep learning, can be very challenging, however.

However, when working with a large volume of historical data, it is important to exercise caution in its utilization. Instead of treating a single sequence as a single learning case, where the input $S = S_T^{(T)}$ includes all T samples, one can reorganize data into multiple smaller inputs [34]. Figure 4 shows a sliding window that samples at every time step and produces $T - w + 1$ distinct yet overlapping training cases $S_w^{(t)}$ of size w, where $t \in [w, T]$. We denote models trained on inputs of size w as M_w.

Strictly speaking, utilizing shorter inputs only partially falls under the umbrella of multi-objective optimization. Nevertheless, training with shorter inputs implicitly encourages machine learning algorithms to uncover short correlations for rapid fault detection.

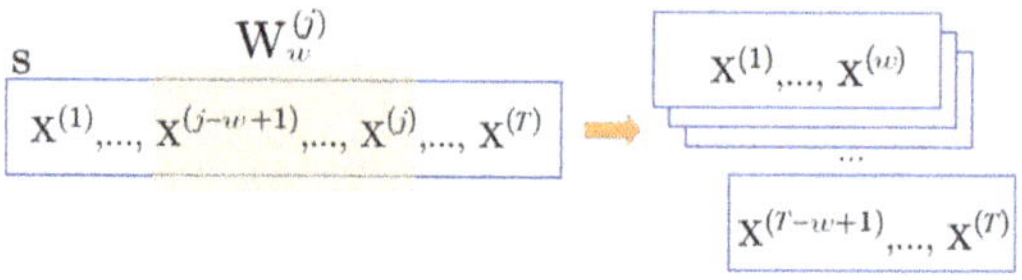

Figure 4. Sliding a window of size w over a long sequence with T samples produces $T-w+1$ sequences.

5. Case Study

The data used in our study are obtained from the Tennessee Eastman Process, originally introduced by Downs and Vogel [7] and extensively described by Chiang [35]. TEP is a widely recognized benchmark for researching process monitoring and control. It replicates natural processes by incorporating modified components, kinetics, and operating conditions. TEP is a synthetic dataset where all dynamic behavior arises from software-based simulations. Since its inception, the simulation code has undergone several enhancements, solidifying TEP as one of the most frequently employed benchmarks for studying highly nonlinear and strongly coupled data.

Our decision to utilize the Tennessee Eastman Process dataset in our study is based on several factors. First, TEP has been widely adopted by many researchers, as evident from the works of Heo et al. [36,37], Sun et al. [38], and Park et al. [39]. Second, the published papers we reviewed did not adequately address or fulfill the specific objectives of our research. Lastly, acquiring high-quality datasets is often a challenging endeavor. To ensure repeatability and facilitate transparency, we opted to employ an extensive recording of TEP simulation data provided by Dataverse [40]. Notably, this dataset is also employed in the MATLAB Help Center as an illustrative example for demonstrating the application of deep learning with time series and sequences using the Deep-Learning Toolbox [24].

The TEP dataset represents a chemical plant, where the overarching control strategy, as outlined in Downs and Vogel [7], aims to optimize overall performance. The plant's control system diligently monitors and logs 52 distinct features, comprised of 41 sensor measurements and 11 manipulated variables at 3-minute intervals. Within the TEP environment, the plant can operate under normal operating conditions, denoted as fault 0, or encounter any of the 20 preprogrammed faults (faults 1–20). Upon the occurrence of a fault, the control system attempts to mitigate the disturbance, by either successfully restoring the system to the NOC state or allowing the fault to escalate beyond the NOC boundaries.

The dataset includes a substantial amount of training and test data. Specifically, the training phase consists of 500 simulated plant runs for each combination of normal operating conditions and 20 fault scenarios, resulting in a total of 10,500 simulation runs. Each run spans 25 h, providing 500 samples per training sequence. In the case of a faulty run, the fault is intentionally triggered at $\tau = 20$ time steps into the normal plant operation.

The test data follow a similar structure, with 500 independent simulations conducted for each NOC/fault scenario. However, these simulations have a longer duration, consisting of 960 samples, and faults are introduced at a later stage, precisely after $\tau = 160$ time steps of normal operation.

The training data were divided into 400 training samples and 100 validation samples for effective model development and evaluation. Each simulation run was an individual classification case throughout all study phases, including training, validation, and testing.

The Tennessee Eastman Process has been the subject of extensive study by numerous researchers. Several authors excluded faults 3, 9, and 15 from their research [24,39]. The rationale behind this decision stems from the observation that the plant's control system can effectively handle the disturbances caused by these faults. Consequently, distinguishing these faults from the plant's normal operation proves to be a challenging task. We also removed faults 3, 9, and 15 from our dataset in light of these findings. Consequently, the training and test dataset consisted of 18 distinct plant states, resulting in 9000 recorded sequences for each dataset. Since the TEP data includes information about the faults and their occurrence times, the task goes beyond simple fault detection and involves fault identification through classification.

5.1. Setup

In developing and training our deep fault-detection models, we strictly adhered to the setup and procedure outlined in the tutorial [24], except that we employed Python in conjunction with the Keras/TensorFlow framework. The code snippet below illustrates the model creation process, faithfully reflecting the prescribed methodology. Each model had three layers of LSTM cells and 43,788 trainable parameters.

$$
\begin{aligned}
&model = tf.keras.Sequential([\\
&\quad LSTM(units = 52, return\_sequences = True),\\
&\quad Dropout(rate = 0.2),\\
&\quad LSTM(units = 40, return\_sequences = True),\\
&\quad Dropout(rate = 0.2),\\
&\quad LSTM(units = 25, return\_sequences = False),\\
&\quad Dropout(rate = 0.2),\\
&\quad Dense(units = 18, activation = tf.nn.softmax),\\
&])
\end{aligned}
$$

During the training phase, the simulation records were processed in batches of 32. Like in tutorial [24], we employed the mean squared error loss function and the Adam optimizer to optimize the model's parameters.

5.2. Fault-Detection Performance

The results presented in Table 1 are the average values obtained from 30 trained networks. At first glance, the selected model exhibited remarkable learning capabilities on the TEP data, yielding outstanding accuracy. This was confirmed by Matthew's Correlation Coefficient (MCC) score, which is known to be more effective in describing performance on multiclass and unbalanced datasets compared to traditional metrics like the F1 score [41].

The limitation of training the model within 30 epochs was sufficient in discovering a solution that appears to be close to the global optimum. The model achieved a validation loss of 2×10^{-5} and a training loss of 0.00027. The test results for this model are summarized in Table 2. We will designate this specific model as Model #1, representing the baseline M_{500} family, where all members are trained on cases of 500 samples.

Although the MATLAB tutorial [24] focuses exclusively on classification accuracy by employing all samples per sequence for a single fault classification, it ignores the fault-detection delay. The important question to answer is when deep models begin detecting faults.

Table 1. Training, validation, and test results.

Metric	Min	Max	Avg	Median	StDev
Training: 7200 simulations, 500 time steps each					
MCC:	0.7248	0.9999	0.9446	0.9569	0.0581
Acc:	0.7324	0.9999	0.9464	0.9590	0.0565
Validation: 1800 simulations, 500 time steps each					
MCC:	0.7257	1.0000	0.9416	0.9575	0.0575
Acc:	0.7333	1.0000	0.9435	0.9597	0.0559
Test: 9000 simulations, 960 time steps each					
MCC:	0.7214	0.9979	0.9395	0.9503	0.0594
Acc:	0.7289	0.9980	0.9415	0.9529	0.0578

Table 2. The confusion matrix of the reference Model #1 on the test data; 99.733% accuracy, MCC 0.99718, asterisk denotes NOC and fault categories 1, 2, 4, 5, 7, 8, 11, 14, 17, 19, and 20.

		ACTUAL						
	Fault	**6**	**10**	**12**	**13**	**16**	**18**	*
PREDICTED	**6**	498	0	0	0	0	0	0
	10	0	500	0	0	1	0	0
	12	0	0	496	0	0	0	0
	13	2	0	0	483	0	0	0
	16	0	0	0	0	499	0	0
	18	0	0	4	17	0	500	0
	*	0	0	0	0	0	0	6000

5.3. Fault-Detection Delay Analysis

During the training and validation phase, faults were introduced in the TEP dataset at time step $\tau = 20$. However, detecting these faults was delayed until step 500, when the last training record became accessible. We conducted the λ and μ analyses on the training, validation, and test data to investigate the behavior of the taught Model #1.

To demonstrate the λ score, Figure 5 depicts the performance of the reference classifier on a single test sequence labeled as 'fault 1'. The sequence was divided into 960 subsequences, denoted as $S^{(960)}_{960-t}$, $t \in [1, 960]$, and subsequently classified using the reference Model #1. Inputs with $\lambda = 16$ or more samples accurately supported the baseline 'fault 1' classification.

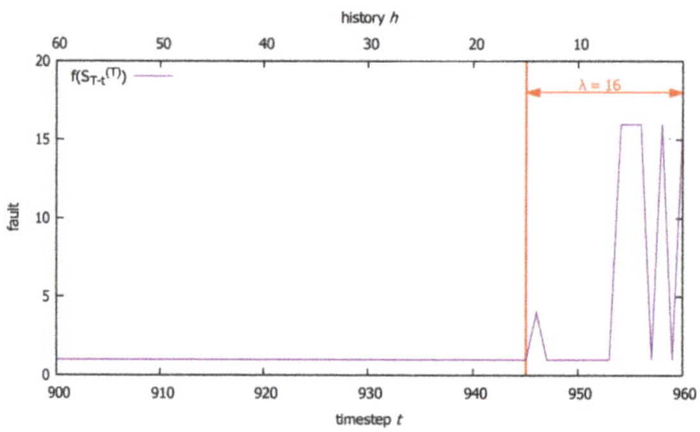

Figure 5. Fault detection using $S^{(T)}_{T-t}$ with windows of size $h = T - t$; fault 1 test case, $\lambda = 16$.

Table 3 presents the λ scores of the reference model for different faults on the validation data, which was otherwise perfectly classified. Surprisingly, the maximum λ score of 500 was observed for 'fault 12', indicating that the network required at least 500 steps to correctly classify a sample belonging to the 'fault 12' category. This finding is unexpected because the training/validation data encompass 20 steps of NOC data at the beginning of every 500-step sample. These initial 20 steps should not have influenced fault categorization, meaning that the network is overfitting the training data.

For completeness, Table 4 displays the λ values for the reference model on the test data, including a few incorrect baseline predictions.

Figure 6 shows our reference classifier's μ performance on the 'fault 1' test sample. Slices with less than 425 records were insufficient to recognize 'fault 1'; however, if at least $\mu = 425$ or more time steps were available, the network could predict 'fault 1' correctly.

Table 3. Reference classifier's λ results on the validation data with 100 sequences per fault.

Fault	#	Min	Max	Avg	Median	StDev
NOC	100	11	392	135.0	127.0	83.3
1	100	1	25	3.0	2.0	5.3
2	100	1	1	1.0	1.0	0.0
4	100	1	23	2.0	2.0	3.1
5	100	1	73	8.0	4.0	11.7
6	100	1	467	102.0	3.0	148.2
7	100	2	17	2.0	2.5	1.8
8	100	1	279	59.0	42.0	63.0
10	100	33	471	190.0	148.5	123.0
11	100	12	307	84.0	75.5	47.8
12	100	178	500	406.0	412.0	51.9
13	100	1	291	38.0	26.0	46.2
14	100	2	35	4.0	3.0	4.5
16	100	41	471	210.0	195.5	107.8
17	100	26	453	131.0	83.5	109.6
18	100	1	275	58.0	2.0	77.6
19	100	12	385	116.0	94.5	84.4
20	100	14	140	53.0	49.5	26.2

Table 4. Reference classifier's λ results on the test data with 500 samples per fault.

Fault	#	Min	Max	Avg	Median	StDev
NOC	500	11	570	157.0	137.0	97.7
1	500	1	53	3.0	2.0	6.8
2	500	1	1	1.0	1.0	0.0
4	500	1	89	3.0	2.0	8.0
5	500	1	131	9.0	4.0	14.4
6	498	1	835	246.0	3.5	298.8
7	500	2	19	2.0	2.0	1.3
8	500	1	367	65.0	47.0	67.0
10	501	7	783	194.0	140.0	152.0
11	500	2	261	91.0	83.5	52.0
12	496	88	857	724.0	749.0	93.8
13	485	1	476	46.0	24.0	64.7
14	500	2	41	4.0	3.0	4.2
16	499	16	810	228.0	178.0	161.2
17	500	17	750	141.0	90.0	140.1
18	521	1	650	51.0	2.0	128.1
19	500	5	663	159.0	124.5	127.0
20	500	2	237	55.0	50.0	31.2

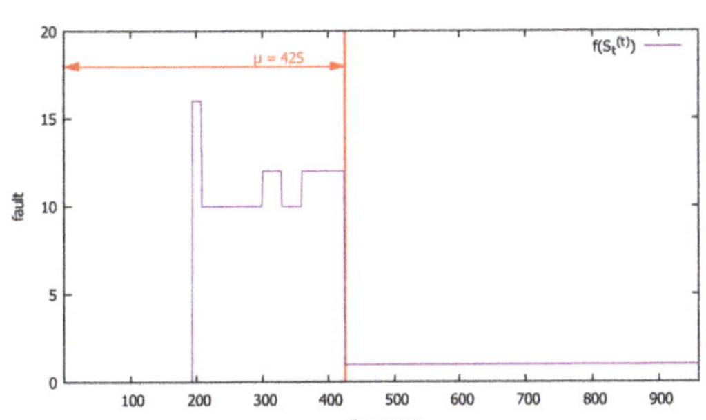

Figure 6. Reference classifier's decisions for inputs $S_t^{(t)}$; fault 1 test case, $\mu = 425$.

Table 5 presents the μ results obtained from the test data. It is important to note that the μ metric does not assess classification accuracy but focuses on its consistency over time. Similar to the observations with λ, we can again identify unexpected behavior. Despite training the network on 500 time step sequences, the average stability of classification can only be achieved well beyond 500 steps, as indicated by the value of $Avg(Max(\mu)) = 636.7$. This counterintuitive behavior further suggests that the network is not aligning with our initial expectations.

Given that we are aware of the fault introduction time of $\tau = 160$ in the TEP test data, we can calculate the average fault-detection delay for each fault by subtracting 160 from the highest μ score achieved by the classifier, as shown in Equation (8). On average, our best classifier would require $Avg(Max(\mu) - 160) = 476.7$ time steps to detect a fault. It is worth noting that only the NOC data slices were detectable before the 160th time step, with an average detection occurring after just 15 samples. One NOC sample, however, required at least 939 records to be correctly classified.

Table 5. Reference classifier's μ results on the test set.

Fault	#	Min	Max	Avg	Median	StDev
NOC	500	1	939	15.0	6.0	67.6
1	500	337	535	411.0	409.0	29.9
2	500	262	342	303.0	304.0	7.2
4	500	238	335	284.0	284.0	17.2
5	500	356	511	411.0	412.0	16.0
6	498	213	437	250.0	236.0	36.7
7	500	359	542	437.0	442.0	30.7
8	500	200	944	291.0	278.5	76.7
10	501	206	942	305.0	284.0	80.3
11	500	244	579	295.0	288.0	35.9
12	496	311	916	659.0	651.0	106.9
13	485	218	900	279.0	268.0	54.2
14	500	204	308	225.0	225.0	8.7
16	499	203	954	312.0	284.0	96.3
17	500	217	416	273.0	269.5	28.2
18	521	315	924	437.0	424.0	82.6
19	500	221	509	272.0	266.0	34.3
20	500	258	427	342.0	340.5	31.2

5.4. Comparison with Other Studies

There is a need for more directly comparable studies on fault-detection delay. For instance, the study by Heo et al. [37] mentions that linear PCA and p-NLPCA detected fault 5 as early as at time step 162, which corresponds to only two samples (equivalent to 6 min) after its introduction into the system. In contrast, our reference Model #1 needed 196 additional samples to detect the fault correctly.

Providing more insightful results are the findings from Park et al. [39], where a combined autoencoder and LSTM network was employed. According to their report, the average detection delay for faults 01, 02, 05, 06, 07, 12, and 14 was less than 30 min, showcasing superior performance compared to our baseline. However, it is worth noting that their model exhibited lower accuracy at 91.9%, which likely accounts for the disparities in the achieved detection delays. Our network, on the other hand, required more information to ensure higher classification accuracy. The question is, would shorter training cases make a difference?

5.5. Using Smaller Windows

The baseline Model #1 exhibited a notable fault-detection delay, highlighting the inadequacy of training on long sequences with faults embedded early in the process. Conversely, training on an individual sample per case fails to capture autocorrelations.

Given that our objective is not to find the optimal model but to illustrate the impact of shorter training cases, we chose to utilize the W_5 window to create models in the M_5 category. In the TEP dataset, a training case spanning 5 time steps represents 15 min of plant operation.

Generating training cases from a single sequence allowed us to augment the training dataset to include 3,571,200 cases. Similarly, the validation and test sets increased to 892,800 and 8,604,000 cases, respectively, resulting in a dataset with over 13 million fault-describing sequences. To create a representative Model #2 for the M_5 category of models, we followed the same procedure as when generating the baseline models of the M_{500} family. The final representative Model #2 models achieved a training loss of 0.00294 and a validation loss of 0.00293. With an accuracy of 97.88% and an MCC score of 0.8955, the test performance of Model #2 was lower than that of the reference Model #1.

To facilitate a more thorough comparison between the two models, we must assess their usability for fault detection. This evaluation should consider accuracy and delay based on the consecutive input samples that describe the operation of the plant.

In Figure 7, we can observe the variations in accuracy over time for the models. Figure 7a illustrates the models' performance on 500 steps of the training and validation data, while Figure 7b depicts the corresponding analysis for the test data, encompassing 960 steps. The accuracy at each time step is calculated based on 7200, 1800, and 9000 sample recordings from the training, validation, and test datasets, respectively.

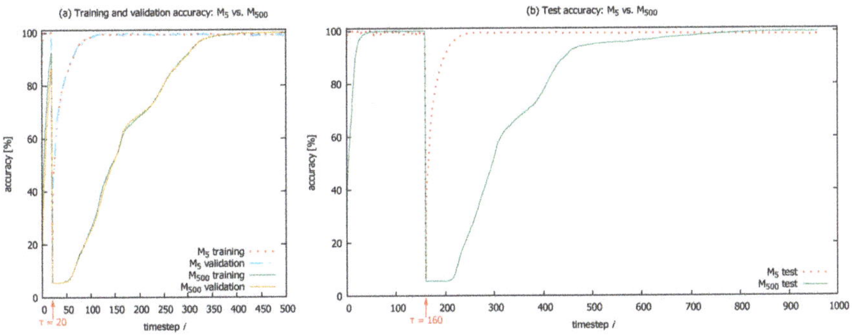

Figure 7. Running overall accuracy scores for the models #1 and #2 representing the respective M_{500} and M_5 category at each time step. (**a**) Results on training and validation data; (**b**) test data results.

The training and validation datasets were structured to include an initial period of 20 steps representing a faultless operation. For the baseline Model #1, the accuracy in identifying normal operating conditions started at 20% for the first time step and improved to 86% after 20 time steps. In contrast, Model #2 achieved 92% accuracy at the first time step and reached 100% accuracy after three samples. On the test data, it took the baseline Model #1 58 time steps to achieve a perfect (100%) accuracy score, while the accuracy of Model #2 had already started to decline by then.

The introduction of faults (indicated by arrows in Figure 7) resulted in a significant decrease in the accuracy of both models. Model #1 kept classifying all inputs as NOC for a while, whereas Model #2 started to improve immediately. On the validation data, it re-reached the 95% accuracy level with a delay of 55 time steps, whereas the baseline model's delay was 298 steps to reach the same level of performance.

5.6. Discussion

The subpar performance of the baseline model during the initial time steps can be caused by the inability of the S_{500} window to specify the first $X^{(i<\tau)}$ samples as belonging to the NOC category when the whole sequence was faulty. Per design, all samples, including the normal ones, were categorized as faulty. This combination of data could have caused the model to mistakenly associate the NOC state with a faulty condition, resulting in inferior start-up performance.

In all three datasets, there was a point where the baseline model started outperforming the M_5 representing model, reaching its peak accuracy at the final time step. This outcome aligns with the primary objective of machine learning, which aims to achieve high overall accuracy based on all available data. However, these graphs clearly illustrate that the standard ML loss criterion is inadequate for effective fault detection. If a model is not penalized for delays, it will prioritize marginal accuracy increases over significant delay improvements.

Recognizing faults becomes progressively easier the longer they persist in the system. However, training machine learning models to identify long-standing faults tends to result in slower detection. To address the detrimental effects of long-standing faults, we can employ data windowing and restrict the model's access to information during training and operation. Windowing creates multiple smaller fault-detection cases with reduced information, which may not capture long autocorrelations but encourage the model to focus on learning and leveraging short-term correlations. The "less means more" principle holds, as less data can lead to shorter fault-detection delays.

All models in this study utilize LSTMs with recurrent architecture, allowing them to generate outputs starting from the first sample. However, it is important to note that their internal contexts still require a warm-up period. Interestingly, the warm-up periods for both models differ significantly. The baseline model exhibits a much slower warm-up process, requiring a larger number of samples to achieve comparable levels of accuracy.

A pseudo-multi-objective optimization can improve delay and accuracy simultaneously. It uses the data window size as a hyperparameter that significantly influences the temporal behavior of the model. Tweaking other deep-learning hyperparameters, such as the number of training epochs or the size of the neural network, can improve accuracy [36] but can also negatively affect the delay. However, as our objective did not involve finding the optimal TEP fault-detection model, we refrained from conducting an extensive analysis of various window settings.

6. Conclusions

Although a control system can handle various disturbances, developing a dedicated monitoring system specifically designed for fault detection and identification is crucial. When applying deep-learning approaches to solve fault-detection problems, it is important to consider an additional objective other than accuracy. Standard metrics are inadequate and, as a result, misleading. They primarily focus on the correctness of results but neglect the importance of delays in fault detection. Furthermore, it is unreasonable to expect machine learning toolkits to excel in all domains universally; their effectiveness can vary significantly.

The monitoring component must recognize a fault from data samples collected during the fault-detection delay. The MC receives less information in the short period of time after a recently occurred fault than in the longer period of time after an old fault. Moreover, recent faults manifest less detectable anomalous traits than the older ones. Consequently, long delays support better detection of older faults. Fault detection is inherently a bicriteria optimization problem, where the fault-detection delay objective conflicts with the fault-detection accuracy objective.

The comparison of two deep neural network models, which were trained differently in some and identically in other aspects, highlights the need to understand the fundamental limitations of the machine learning approach for optimization. In this context, we described a simple alternative to a more complex multi-objective methodology that would have been required otherwise. Use of shorter training cases implicitly encourages deep-learning models to detect and leverage shorter correlations. Additionally, this approach aligns well with readily available machine learning frameworks.

Although we were able to replicate the high-accuracy results on the TEP dataset reported elsewhere, it is important to acknowledge that the baseline solution is not suitable for real-life applications. This becomes evident when observing the accuracy scores over time. The case study illustrates the flaw of the baseline deep fault-detection concept. We can produce better models only by circumventing the issue or applying multi-objective optimization. Following the No Free Lunch theorem [42], however, it is important to recognize that there is no universally best approach. We aim to highlight why fault detection and identification warrant special attention.

Author Contributions: Conceptualization, M.Š.; methodology, M.Š.; software, M.Š.; validation, M.Š. and D.V.; formal analysis, M.Š.; investigation, M.Š. and D.V.; resources, M.Š. and D.V.; data curation, M.Š.; writing—original draft preparation, M.Š.; writing—review and editing, M.Š. and D.V.; visualization, M.Š.; supervision, D.V. All authors have read and agreed to the published version of the manuscript.

Funding: This research was funded by the Slovenian Research Agency (research core funding No. P2-0057).

Data Availability Statement: The data presented in this study are openly available in Dataverse at https://doi.org/10.7910/DVN/6C3JR1, reference number [40].

Acknowledgments: The authors acknowledge the financial support from the Slovenian Research Agency.

Conflicts of Interest: The authors declare no conflict of interest.

Abbreviations

The following abbreviations are used in this manuscript:

AE	Autoencoder
ANN	Artificial Neural Network
FF	Feed-Forward
GRU	Gated Recurrent Unit
LSTM	Long Short-Term Memory
MC	Monitoring Component
MCC	Matthew's Correlation Coefficient
ML	Machine Learning
NOC	Normal Operating Conditions
ROC	Receiver Operating Characteristic
RNN	Recurrent Neural Network
TEP	Tennessee Eastman Process

References

1. Abid, A.; Khan, M.T.; Iqbal, J. A Review on Fault Detection and Diagnosis Techniques: Basics and Beyond. *Artif. Intell. Rev.* **2021**, *54*, 3639–3664. [CrossRef]
2. Pang, G.; Shen, C.; Cao, L.; Hengel, A.V.D. Deep learning for anomaly detection: A review. *Acm Comput. Surv. (CSUR)* **2021**, *54*, 1–38. [CrossRef]
3. Qiu, S.; Cui, X.; Ping, Z.; Shan, N.; Li, Z.; Bao, X.; Xu, X. Deep Learning Techniques in Intelligent Fault Diagnosis and Prognosis for Industrial Systems: A Review. *Sensors* **2023**, *23*, 1305. [CrossRef]
4. Tian, Z.; Zhuo, M.; Liu, L.; Chen, J.; Zhou, S. Anomaly detection using spatial and temporal information in multivariate time series. *Sci. Rep.* **2023**, *13*, 4400. [CrossRef]
5. Stoorvogel, A.; Niemann, H.; Saberi, A. Delays in fault detection and isolation. In Proceedings of the 2001 American Control Conference, (Cat. No.01CH37148), Arlington, VA, USA, 25–27 June 2001; Volume 1, pp. 459–463. [CrossRef]
6. Yin, S.; Ding, S.X.; Haghani, A.; Hao, H.; Zhang, P. A comparison study of basic data-driven fault diagnosis and process monitoring methods on the benchmark Tennessee Eastman process. *J. Process. Control* **2012**, *22*, 1567–1581. [CrossRef]
7. Downs, J.J.; Vogel, E.F. A plant-wide industrial process control problem. *Comput. Chem. Eng.* **1993**, *17*, 245–255. [CrossRef]

8. Ge, Z. Review on data-driven modeling and monitoring for plant-wide industrial processes. *Chemom. Intell. Lab. Syst.* **2017**, *171*, 16–25. [CrossRef]
9. Webert, H.; Döß, T.; Kaupp, L.; Simons, S. Fault Handling in Industry 4.0: Definition, Process and Applications. *Sensors* **2022**, *22*, 2205. [CrossRef] [PubMed]
10. Goodfellow, I.; Bengio, Y.; Courville, A. *Deep Learning*; MIT Press: Cambridge, MA, USA, 2016. Available online: https://www.deeplearningbook.org/ (accessed on 12 July 2023).
11. Saufi, S.R.; Ahmad, Z.A.B.; Leong, M.S.; Lim, M.H. Challenges and Opportunities of Deep Learning Models for Machinery Fault Detection and Diagnosis: A Review. *IEEE Access* **2019**, *7*, 122644–122662. [CrossRef]
12. Ganaie, M.; Hu, M.; Malik, A.; Tanveer, M.; Suganthan, P. Ensemble deep learning: A review. *Eng. Appl. Artif. Intell.* **2022**, *115*, 105151. [CrossRef]
13. Krizhevsky, A.; Sutskever, I.; Hinton, G.E. ImageNet Classification with Deep Convolutional Neural Networks. *Commun. ACM* **2017**, *60*, 84–90. [CrossRef]
14. Vaswani, A.; Shazeer, N.; Parmar, N.; Uszkoreit, J.; Jones, L.; Gomez, A.N.; Kaiser, Ł.; Polosukhin, I. Attention is all you need. In Proceedings of the Advances in Neural Information Processing Systems, Long Beach, CA, USA, 4–9 December 2017; pp. 5998–6008.
15. Chung, J.; Gulcehre, C.; Cho, K.; Bengio, Y. Empirical evaluation of gated recurrent neural networks on sequence modeling. In Proceedings of the NIPS 2014 Workshop on Deep Learning, Montreal, QC, Canada, 8–13 December 2014.
16. Zeyer, A.; Bahar, P.; Irie, K.; Schlüter, R.; Ney, H. A comparison of transformer and lstm encoder decoder models for asr. In Proceedings of the 2019 IEEE Automatic Speech Recognition and Understanding Workshop (ASRU), Singapore, 14–18 December 2019; pp. 8–15. [CrossRef]
17. Lv, F.; Wen, C.; Bao, Z.; Liu, M. Fault diagnosis based on deep learning. In Proceedings of the 2016 American Control Conference (ACC), Boston, MA, USA, 6–8 July 2016; pp. 6851–6856.
18. Lee, K.; Cheon, S.; Kim, C. A convolutional neural network for fault classification and diagnosis in semiconductor manufacturing processes. *IEEE Trans. Semicond. Manuf.* **2017**, *30*, 135–142. [CrossRef]
19. Borghesi, A.; Bartolini, A.; Lombardi, M.; Milano, M.; Benini, L. Anomaly Detection Using Autoencoders in High Performance Computing Systems. *Proc. AAAI Conf. Artif. Intell.* **2019**, *33*, 9428–9433. [CrossRef]
20. Qian, J.; Song, Z.; Yao, Y.; Zhu, Z.; Zhang, X. A review on autoencoder based representation learning for fault detection and diagnosis in industrial processes. *Chemom. Intell. Lab. Syst.* **2022**, *231*, 104711. [CrossRef]
21. Han, P.; Ellefsen, A.L.; Li, G.; Holmeset, F.T.; Zhang, H. Fault Detection With LSTM-Based Variational Autoencoder for Maritime Components. *IEEE Sens. J.* **2021**, *21*, 21903–21912. [CrossRef]
22. Colbrook, M.J.; Antun, V.; Hansen, A.C. The difficulty of computing stable and accurate neural networks: On the barriers of deep learning and Smale's 18th problem. *Proc. Natl. Acad. Sci. USA* **2022**, *119*, e2107151119. [CrossRef]
23. Akai, N.; Hirayama, T.; Murase, H. Experimental stability analysis of neural networks in classification problems with confidence sets for persistence diagrams. *Neural Netw.* **2021**, *143*, 42–51. [CrossRef]
24. MathWorks. Chemical Process Fault Detection Using Deep Learning. 2023. Available online: https://www.mathworks.com/help/deeplearning/ug/chemical-process-fault-detection-using-deep-learning.html (accessed on 12 July 2023).
25. Yan, W.; Guo, P.; Gong, L.; Li, Z. Nonlinear and robust statistical process monitoring based on variant autoencoders. *Chemom. Intell. Lab. Syst.* **2016**, *158*, 31–40. [CrossRef]
26. Torabi, H.; Mirtaheri, S.L.; Greco, S. Practical autoencoder based anomaly detection by using vector reconstruction error. *Cybersecurity* **2023**, *6*, 1. [CrossRef]
27. Barrera, J.M.; Reina, A.R.; Maté, A.; Trujillo, J.C. Fault detection and diagnosis for industrial processes based on clustering and autoencoders: A case of gas turbines. *Int. J. Mach. Learn. Cybern.* **2022**, *13*, 3113–3129. [CrossRef]
28. Bulatov, A.; Kuratov, Y.; Burtsev, M.S. Scaling Transformer to 1M tokens and beyond with RMT. *arXiv* **2023**, arXiv:2304.11062.
29. Rice, L.; Wong, E.; Kolter, Z. Overfitting in adversarially robust deep learning. In Proceedings of the International Conference on Machine Learning, Virtual Event, 13–18 July 2020; pp. 8093–8104.
30. Kawaguchi, K.; Bengio, Y.; Kaelbling, L. Generalization in Deep Learning. In *Mathematical Aspects of Deep Learning*; Grohs, P., Kutyniok, G., Eds.; Cambridge University Press: Cambridge, UK, 2022; pp. 112–148. [CrossRef]
31. Deb, K. *Multi-Objective Optimization Using Evolutionary Algorithms*; John Wiley & Sons, Inc.: Hoboken, NJ, USA, 2001.
32. Xie, Z.; Chen, J.; Feng, Y.; Zhang, K.; Zhou, Z. End to end multi-task learning with attention for multi-objective fault diagnosis under small sample. *J. Manuf. Syst.* **2022**, *62*, 301–316. [CrossRef]
33. Lee, K.; Han, S.; Pham, V.H.; Cho, S.; Choi, H.J.; Lee, J.; Noh, I.; Lee, S.W. Multi-Objective Instance Weighting-Based Deep Transfer Learning Network for Intelligent Fault Diagnosis. *Appl. Sci.* **2021**, *11*, 2370. [CrossRef]
34. TensorFlow. timeseries_dataset_from_array. 2022. Available online: https://www.tensorflow.org/api_docs/python/tf/keras/utils/timeseries_dataset_from_array (accessed on 12 July 2023).
35. Chiang, L.; Russell, E.; Braatz, R. *Fault Detection and Diagnosis in Industrial Systems*; Springer: London, UK, 2001.
36. Heo, S.; Lee, J.H. Fault detection and classification using artificial neural networks. *IFAC-PapersOnLine* **2018**, *51*, 470–475. [CrossRef]
37. Heo, S.; Lee, J. Statistical process monitoring of the Tennessee Eastman Process using parallel autoassociative neural networks and a large dataset. *Processes* **2019**, *7*, 411. [CrossRef]

38. Sun, W.; Paiva, A.R.; Xu, P.; Sundaram, A.; Braatz, R.D. Fault detection and identification using Bayesian recurrent neural networks. *Comput. Chem. Eng.* **2020**, *141*, 106991. [CrossRef]
39. Park, P.; Marco, P.; Shin, H.; Bang, J. Fault Detection and Diagnosis Using Combined Autoencoder and Long Short-Term Memory Network. *Sensors* **2019**, *19*, 4612. [CrossRef]
40. Rieth, C.; Amsel, B.; Tran, R.; Cook, M. Additional Tennessee Eastman Process Simulation Data for Anomaly Detection Evaluation, Harvard Dataverse, 2017. Available online: https://dataverse.harvard.edu/dataset.xhtml?persistentId=doi:10.7910/DVN/6C3JR1 (accessed on 12 July 2023).
41. Jurman, G.; Riccadonna, S.; Furlanello, C. A Comparison of MCC and CEN error measures in multi-class prediction. *PLoS ONE* **2012**, *7*, e41882. [CrossRef]
42. Wolpert, D.; Macready, W. No free lunch theorems for optimization. *IEEE Trans. Evol. Comput.* **1997**, *1*, 67–82. [CrossRef]

mathematics

Article

Anomaly Detection of Underground Transmission-Line through Multiscale Mask DCNN and Image Strengthening

Min-Gwan Kim [1], Siheon Jeong [1], Seok-Tae Kim [2] and Ki-Yong Oh [1,*]

[1] Department of Mechanical Convergence Engineering, Hanyang University, 222 Wangsimni-ro, Seondong-gu, Seoul 04763, Republic of Korea; kmg9752@hanyang.ac.kr (M.-G.K.); junction@hanyang.ac.kr (S.J.)
[2] KEPCO Research Institute, Korea Electric Power Corporation, 105 Munji-ro, Yuseong-gu, Daejeon 34056, Republic of Korea; stkim7604@naver.com
* Correspondence: kiyongoh@hanyang.ac.kr

Abstract: This study proposes an integrated framework to automatically detect anomalies and faults in underground transmission-line connectors (UTLCs) with thermal images because anomaly detection of underground transmission-line connectors (UTLCs) plays a critical role in power line risk management. The proposed framework features three key characteristics. First, the measured thermal images were preprocessed through z-score normalization and image strengthening. Z-score normalization improves the robustness of feature extraction for UTLCs even though noise exists in a thermal image, and image strengthening improves the accuracy of segmentation for UTLCs. Second, a preprocessed thermal image is segmented to detect UTLCs by addressing a multiscale mask deep convolutional neural network (MS mask DCNN). The MS mask DCNN effectively detects UTLCs, enabling anomaly detection only for pixels of UTLCs. Specifically, the multiscale feature extraction module enables the extraction of distinct features of UTLCs and environments, and the skip-layer fusion module concatenates distinct features from the feature extraction module. Furthermore, a half tensor is used to reduce computational resources but maintain the same segmentation accuracy, enhancing the feasibility of the proposed framework in field applications. Third, anomaly detection is performed by addressing the contour method and unsupervised clustering method of DBSCAN. The contour method compensates for the limits of the MS mask DCNN for real-world applications because the neural networks cannot secure perfect accuracy of 100% owing to a lack of sufficient training images and low computational resources. DBSCAN improves the accuracy of diagnosis and ensures robustness to eliminate noise from thermal reflection caused by low-emissivity objects. Field experiments with high-voltage UTLCs demonstrated the effectiveness of the proposed framework. Ablation studies also confirmed that the methods addressed in this study outperform other methods. The proposed framework with a novel automatic non-destructive patrol inspection system would decrease the risks of human casualties during the periodic operation and maintenance of UTLCs, which are currently the most critical concerns.

Keywords: anomaly detection; underground transmission lines; infrared camera; z-score normalization; statistical image strengthening; MS mask DCNN; segmentation; unsupervised clustering

MSC: 68T45

1. Introduction

Underground transmission lines (UTLs) have been introduced in urban areas because they are safe and robust to degradation originating from external environments compared with overhead transmission lines [1–3]. UTLs are also free from the limitations of installation spaces and concerns regarding the negative effects of magnetic fields on citizens in concentrated urban areas [4]. These advantages offered by UTLs have made them an indispensable option, actively replacing overhead transmission lines worldwide in urban areas despite the higher installation cost [5]. UTLs are installed with connectors that include insulators and various auxiliary components because the manufacturing process might have a limitation on the maximum length of the UTLs. Incorrect installation or poor jointing during repeated electrical loading can accelerate the degradation of connectors, and the faults of UTLs could affect the entire UTLs system, resulting in significant economic losses and human casualties [6]. In addition, UTLs are designed to have an expected lifetime of over 30 years with appropriate operation and maintenance [7]. Therefore, inspection of UTLs should be real-time, reliable, and automatic because it plays a critical role in ensuring the reliable operation and safety of UTLs.

Various studies have been conducted to ensure the reliability and safety of UTLs, focusing on UTLCs in which most faults and accidents have occurred in connectors [8]. Faults in UTLCs can be detected using non-destructive sensors, including magnetic sensors [9], current-voltage sensors [10,11] and electro-magnetic sensors [12–14]. Specifically, a set of measurements from a magnetic field sensor was used to reconstruct the current source of underground power cables for inspection by addressing the stochastic optimization technique and an artificial immune algorithm [9]. Fault detection of UTLs was also proposed by addressing an algorithm that considers the fault arc voltage with power quality monitoring data in the time domain [10] and by combining two methods of wavelet and time-domain analyses [11]. PD measurements have been proposed for anomaly detection of UTLs [12] because these measurements have several advantages, including accurate detection of anomalies and localization [13] and immunity to noise [14]. However, these methods involve installing contact-type sensors in the entire region of UTLs for accurate condition monitoring, suggesting that these methods are inefficient from an economic perspective because this approach requires a significant installation cost.

Fault detection with a non-contact type of sensor is promising because many sensors do not need to be installed for UTLs. In particular, infrared (IR) cameras have received considerable attention for health monitoring in the application field of electric and mechanical facilities because they provide meaningful information on the thermal energy emitted from an object of interest when a fault occurs. Intensive studies have been conducted to detect anomalies using IR cameras [15–19]. Fault detection using an aerial system deploying an IR camera was proposed for anomaly detection in photovoltaic farms [15,16] and overhead transmission lines [17]. A patrol inspection robot was proposed by deploying an IR camera to monitor the temperature of underground power facilities (UPF) with 2-D simultaneous localization and mapping [18]. Object detection through a customized neural network has also been proposed to identify defects in a thermal image [19]. These studies have improved the accuracy and efficiency of infrastructure health monitoring by deploying IR cameras. However, these methods are addressed by thresholding the intensity of pixels in the measured thermal images to detect anomalies in an autonomous manner, suggesting that these methods are difficult to apply in field applications because defining an appropriate threshold of intensity in thermal images is difficult and depends on the operational conditions of inspection.

The automatic separation of UTLs from environments could be achieved through deep learning because deep learning has witnessed significant advancements in recent years, revolutionizing various domains with its remarkable capabilities with complex data and extracting high-level representations. In particular, image segmentation has been improved by addressing mask-based deep convolutional networks (CNNs). CNNs are specialized in extracting hierarchical features from images, allowing them to recognize complex patterns and structures in images. Moreover, the spatial invariance of CNNs enables them to recognize patterns regardless of their location in an image. Parameter sharing and local connectivity enable reducing the computational cost, overcoming the limitations related to memory constraints. Specifically, image segmentation can be categorized into semantic segmentation and instance segmentation. Semantic segmentation assigns a label to each pixel in an image, providing a pixel-wise classification map, where each pixel is assigned a specific class. It offers a more comprehensive understanding of the entire image, enabling efficient image classification, object detection, and contextual comprehension. Moreover, semantic segmentation requires fewer computational resources compared with instance segmentation, whereas this method could not differentiate between instances of the same class; all pixels belonging to the same class are labeled identically. Instance segmentation provides an accurate description of object boundaries and enables object-level analysis, but this method is a more complex task that requires higher computational resources and slower inference times. Hence, the choice between the two methods depends on the specific application and the desired level of detail.

Various studies have been conducted on image segmentation through mask-based DCNNs to improve accuracy and robustness using models such as Fully Convolutional Network (FCN) [20], Residual U-Net (ResUNet) [21], and Mask-Region-based Convolutional Neural Network (Mask R-CNN) [22]. Specifically, FCN was proposed for the semantic segmentation of arbitrary-sized images through fully convolutional and deconvolutional layers, without relying on predefined fully connected layers, and employed end-to-end learning to optimize the network's performance across the entire architecture [20]. ResUNet employed the U-Net autoencoder architecture with residual and skip connections to enhance information flow, the ability to capture fine details and the spatial context of the image, and address the problem of gradient vanishing, even in deeper networks [21]. Mask-RCNN was proposed for the instance segmentation, combining object detection and semantic segmentation through the integration of a region proposal network and RoIAlign for accurate feature extraction of the images. Furthermore, a mask branch is employed to predict pixel-level object masks for image segmentation [22]. Note that it is challenging to detect anomalies in UPF using semantic segmentation with IR measurements, even though several architectures have been proposed to effectively extract features of objects of interest. This limitation would originate from the inherent characteristics of UTLCs, which are the major location of failures in UPF because UTLCs are covered by several auxiliary components, which significantly disturb the extraction of features of UTLCs for separating UTLCs from environments.

To overcome these limitations, this study proposes an integrated framework for the automatic anomaly detection of UTLCs using IR measurements. The proposed framework is simple yet accurate for fault detection in field applications; it includes a preprocessing phase with statistical image strengthening, separation of UTLC from environments based on the features extracted through the MS mask DCNN, and anomaly detection with unsupervised clustering. Note that this complete framework compensates for the limitations of deep learning approaches, thereby securing high accuracy and robustness for field applications. The contributions of this study are summarized as follows:

- The preprocessing phase improves the performance of the segmentation of UTLCs in a thermal image statistical image strengthening by employing two key features. Specifically, z-score normalization improves the robustness of feature extraction for UTLCs and reduces the noise in a thermal image. BHEPL improves the accuracy of segmentation for UTLCs.
- Automatic separation was achieved through the MS mask DCNN, which incorporates two key characteristics: a multiscale feature extraction module and a skip-layer fusion module. The multiscale feature extraction module enables the extraction of distinctive features from UTLCs and their environments, whereas the skip-layer fusion module combines these features extracted from the multiscale feature extraction module.
- The anomaly detection phase addressed the problem of false segmentation of UTLCs when detecting anomalies with fast yet accurate post-processing methods. Specifically, the contour method can eliminate false segmentation of UTLCs with low computational cost, whereas the unsupervised clustering method of DBSCAN eliminates noise from thermal reflection, securing high accuracy and robustness in field applications.
- Intensive field tests demonstrate the effectiveness of the proposed framework in real-world applications. Moreover, implementation of the half tensor during testing

noticeably improved the framework's inference time, demonstrating its suitability for practical field applications.

The remainder of this paper is organized as follows. Section 2 proposes an integrated framework for anomaly detection in the UTLCs. This section includes a detailed statistical image-strengthening method and the architecture of the MS-mask DCNN. Section 3 describes experiments for the calibration of the IR camera, dataset measurements from field experiments, and the construction of the MS mask DCNN. Section 4 presents the results, an ablation study of the proposed framework, and an in-depth discussion. Section 5 concludes the paper with both quantitative and qualitative highlights.

2. An Integrated Framework of Anomaly Detection

This section presents an integrated framework for the anomaly detection of UTLCs with thermal images measured using an IR camera. The proposed method comprises three phases (Figure 1). First, the visualized thermal energy of the UTLCs overlaid on a visible spectrum image was normalized and statistically strengthened in phase A. This phase aims to help the proposed neural network extract features of UTLCs by distinguishing their features from those of the environment. Second, semantic segmentation is executed through the MS mask DCNN in Phase B to separate the UTLC from the environments in the thermal image. Hence, the MS mask DCNN plays a filtering role in detecting a UTLC in the proposed method. Third, anomalies in UTLCs are detected in phase C based on the KEPCO inspection regulation [23] using a contour method and an unsupervised clustering method. The contour method aims to eliminate false-segmented inference from MS mask DCNN because artificial intelligence cannot secure complete accuracy of 100% owing to a lack of sufficient training images. An unsupervised clustering method of DBSCAN is also employed to improve the robustness of the proposed method by decreasing the false alarms caused by noise from thermal reflection. The proposed method can detect anomalies for single and multiple phases of UTLCs in the sense that UTLCs are composed of multiple phases. Details of each phase are described in the following subsections.

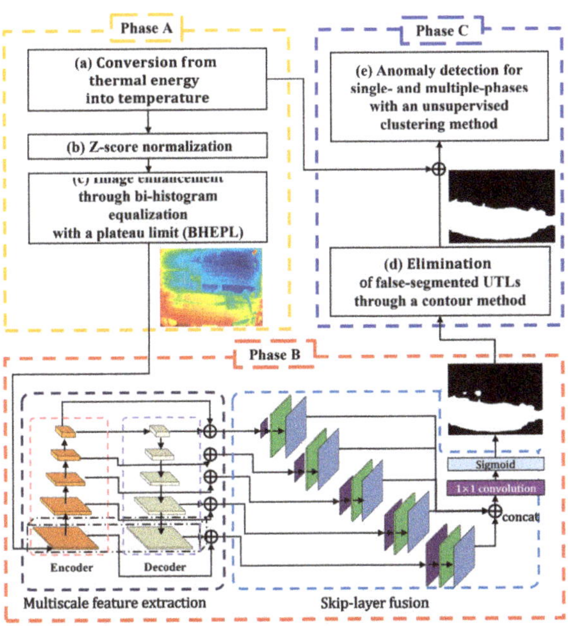

Figure 1. The proposed framework for anomaly detection of underground transmission-line connectors (UTLCs).

2.1. Phase A Image Preprocessing and Statistical Image Strengthening

This subsection presents detailed methods of image preprocessing and statistical strengthening (Phase A in Figure 1), which aim to improve the performance of semantic segmentation and thereby help effectively train a neural network in the next phase. The proposed method comprises three procedures: conversion of thermal energy into a temperature image (Figure 1a), z-score normalization (Figure 1b), and image strengthening through bi-histogram equalization with a plateau limit (BHEPL, Figure 1c) [24].

First, thermal energy measured from an IR camera is converted to a representative temperature because inspection regulation defines anomaly detection based on the temperature variation of UTLCs [23]. Hence, the accurate conversion of thermal energy into a representative temperature plays an important role in ensuring the accuracy and reliability of inspection. The IR camera is a non-contact sensor for measuring thermal energy through the infrared wavelength band radiated from objects with an absolute temperature above 0 K. An IR camera of the TE-EV1 (I3systems, Daejeon, Republic of Korea) was used for anomaly detection of UTLCs because this camera features a low noise-equivalent temperature difference of 30 mK (@ 300 K), a wide-range field of view (FOV) of 76° and 59.5° and a high resolution of 640 × 480 pixels. The calibration sheet was provided with specifications from the manufacturer, i.e., I3 systems. This sheet provides a conversion formula from the thermal energy of the thermal data measured from the IR camera to temperature as follows:

$$T_{ij} = \frac{(W_{ij} - 5000)}{100}, \tag{1}$$

where W_{ij} and T_{ij} denote the measured thermal energy and converted temperature at the ith row and jth column of the image. However, preliminary experiments revealed that this calibration formula has a large uncertainty, suggesting that independent calibration should be executed to ensure the accuracy of conversion with a governing equation as follows:

$$T^*_{ij} = a_1 T_{ij} + b_1, \tag{2}$$

where T^*_{ij} denotes the calibrated temperature at the ith row and jth column of a pixel in the temperature image of interest, and a_1 and b_1 denote the coefficients in the first-order polynomial regression. Note that the detailed process of the calibration is described in Section 3.1.

Next, a calibrated temperature image was z-score-normalized. This method aims to help the proposed framework detect UTLCs regardless of several existing heat sources, such as ceiling lights and hot spots in the UTLCs. These heat sources are located in the UPF and disturb the ability to distinguish UTLCs from the environment because these objects also emit thermal energy. In other words, UTLCs and other environments are difficult to distinguish without z-score normalization when these heat sources exist in a measured thermal image because the heats emitted from these heat sources are higher than those emitted from UTLCs, as exemplified in Figure 2a,b. The proposed method would be effective in this situation because z-score normalization can statistically mitigate outliers exceeding three-sigma, as follows:

$$Z_{ij} = \begin{cases} \mu_T + 3\sigma_T & \left(T^*_{ij} \geq \mu_T + 3\sigma_T\right) \\ \mu_T - 3\sigma_T & \left(T^*_{ij} \leq \mu_T - 3\sigma_T\right) \\ T^*_{ij} & else \end{cases}, \tag{3}$$

where Z_{ij} denotes the z-scored temperature in the ith row and jth column of a pixel in an image, and μ_T and σ_T denote the mean temperature and standard deviation of the converted temperature. Specifically, temperatures exceeding $\pm 3\sigma_T$ are changed to values of $\mu_T \pm 3\sigma_T$ (blue and red line in Figure 2b), whereas temperatures within $\pm 3\sigma_T$ hold the same values because excessive temperature is measured, that is, outliers exceeding $3\sigma_T$, resulting in a small variation in UTLCs compared with environments in a thermal image (Figure 2a).

In other words, this process helps to suppress excessive temperatures exceeding $\mu_T \pm 3\sigma_T$. Furthermore, a thermal image, where outliers are calibrated to $\mu_T \pm 3\sigma_T$, is normalized as:

$$X_{ij} = \frac{Z_{ij} - (\mu_T - 3\sigma_T)}{((\mu_T + 3\sigma_T) - (\mu_T - 3\sigma_T))} = \frac{Z_{ij} - (\mu_T - 3\sigma_T)}{6\sigma_T}, \quad (4)$$

where X_{ij} denotes the z-score normalized thermal energy in the ith row and jth column of a pixel in an image. Note that z-scored temperatures corresponding to $\mu_T - 3\sigma_T$ and $\mu_T + 3\sigma_T$ are changed to zero and unity, whereas z-score temperatures within $\mu_T + 3\sigma_T$ are normalized in the range between zero and unity. Hence, these processes clearly distinguish UTLCs and other auxiliary facilities in a calibrated thermal image, even though some heat sources exist in the image, as shown in Figure 2c, suggesting that the MS mask DCNN easily detects and separates a UTLC from the environment. Note that this procedure does not eliminate statistical outliers during the final inspection. This preprocessing aims to clearly distinguish UTLCs from environments in spite of existing unexpected anomalies, including hot spots in UTLCs and ceiling lights, through MS mask DCNN in thermal images in phase C.

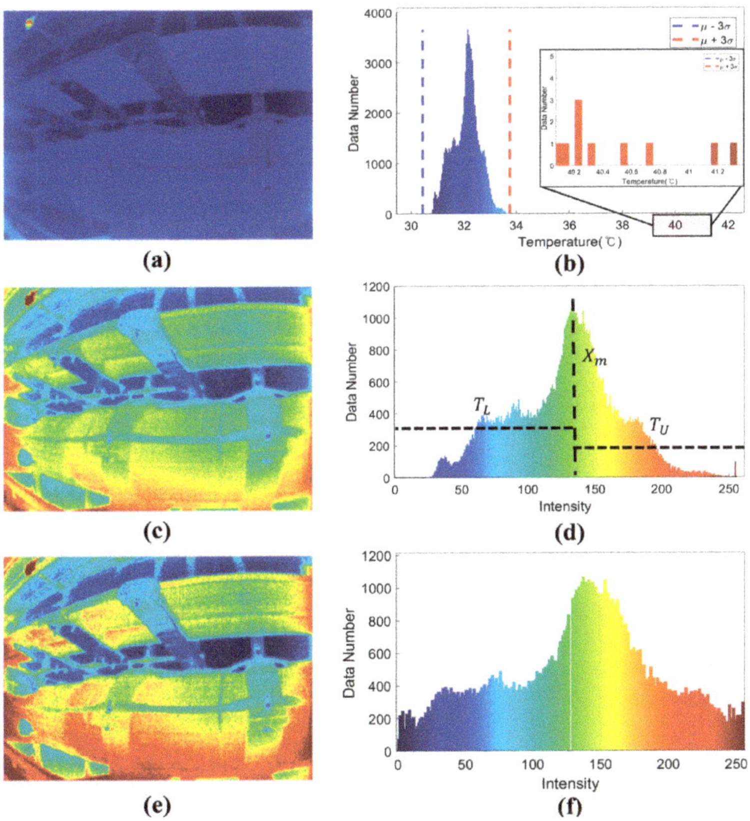

Figure 2. Resulting images of each process in phase A: (**a**) original thermal image and (**b**) its histogram; (**c**) z-score normalized thermal image and (**d**) its histogram; (**e**) BHEPL enhanced thermal image with z-score normalization and (**f**) its histogram.

Finally, a z-score normalized image was statistically strengthened by addressing the BHEPL (Figure 3) [24]. This process comprises seven steps. First, the average intensity X_m

is calculated for each z-score-normalized thermal image (Figure 3a). Second, a thermal image is decomposed into two sub-images by X_m to maintain the mean brightness of the thermal image (Figure 3b) as follows:

$$X = X_L \cup X_U, \tag{5}$$

where X_L and X_U denote two sub-images divided by X_m defined as

$$X_L = \{X(i,j)|X(i,j) \leq X_m, \forall X(i,j) \in X\}, \tag{6}$$

$$X_U = \{X(i,j)|X(i,j) > X_m, \forall X(i,j) \in X\}. \tag{7}$$

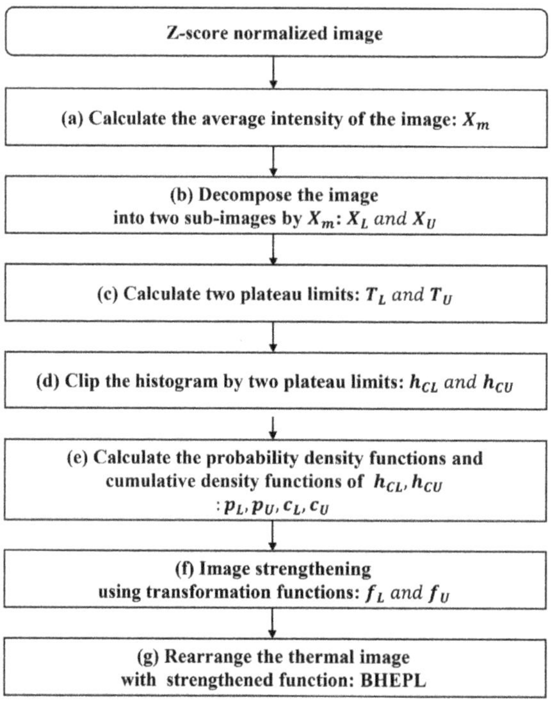

Figure 3. A flow chart of image strengthening through bi-histogram with a plateau limit (BHEPL).

Note that the sub-image X_L is composed of $\{X_0, X_1, \ldots, X_m\}$, and the other sub-image X_U is composed of $\{X_{m+1}, X_{m+2}, \ldots, X_{L-1}\}$ based on the calculated average intensity X_m as shown in Figure 2d. Third, two plateau limits T_L and T_U are set calculated to clip each sub-histogram (Figure 3c) as follows:

$$T_L = \frac{1}{X_m + 1} \sum_{k=0}^{X_m} h_L(k), \tag{8}$$

$$T_U = \frac{1}{(L-1) - X_m} \sum_{k=X_m+1}^{X_{L-1}} h_U(k), \tag{9}$$

where h_L and h_U denote two sub-histograms of the divided sub-images, X_L and X_U. Furthermore, T_L and T_U is calculated to the average of h_L and h_U as shown in Figure 2d.

Fourth, each sub-histogram is clipped by two plateau limits to prevent a level saturation effect (Figure 3d), which pushes the intensities toward the right or left side of the histogram. The clipped histograms through the two plateau limits T_L and T_U are denoted as h_{CL} and h_{CU}, which are given as

$$h_{CL}(x) = \begin{cases} h_L(x) & if\ h_L(x) \leq T_L \\ T_L & elsewhere \end{cases}, \tag{10}$$

$$h_{UL}(x) = \begin{cases} h_U(x) & if\ h_U(x) \leq T_U \\ T_U & elsewhere \end{cases}. \tag{11}$$

Fifth, the probability density functions, and cumulative density functions of each clipped histogram were calculated to obtain the robustness transformation functions (Figure 3e) as

$$p_L(x) = \frac{h_L(X_K)}{M_L}, \quad \text{for } k = 0, 1, \ldots, m, \tag{12}$$

$$p_U(x) = \frac{h_U(X_k)}{M_U}, \quad \text{for } k = m+1, m+2, \ldots, L-1, \tag{13}$$

where p_L and p_U denote the probability density functions of h_{CL} and h_{CU}, respectively, and M_L and M_U denote the total number of pixels in h_{CL} and h_{CU}, respectively. These probability density functions are used to calculate the cumulative density functions c_L and c_U of X_L and X_U, respectively, as follows:

$$c_L(x) = \sum_{k=0}^{m} p_L(X_k), \tag{14}$$

$$c_U(x) = \sum_{k=k+1}^{L-1} p_U(X_k). \tag{15}$$

Sixth, the robustness transformation functions $f_L(x)$ and $f_U(x)$ are addressed with two sub-images for executing histogram equalization and inversion histogram equalization processes (Figure 3f) as

$$f_L(x) = X_0 + (X_m - X_0)[c_L(x) - 0.5p_L(x)], \tag{16}$$

$$f_U(x) = X_{m+1} + (X_{L-1} - X_{m+1})[c_U(x) - 0.5p_U(x)]. \tag{17}$$

Note that the two decomposed sub-images are strengthened independently based on their transformation functions. Finally, the output image is expressed (Figure 3g) as follows:

$$Y = \{Y(i,j)\} = f_L(X_L) \cup f_U(X_U), \tag{18}$$

where $f_L(X_L)$ and $f_U(X_U)$ denote the sub-set images defined, respectively, as

$$f_L(X_L) = \{f_L(X(i,j)) | \forall X(i,j) \in X_L, \tag{19}$$

$$f_U(X_U) = \{f_U(X(i,j)) | \forall X(i,j) \in X_U. \tag{20}$$

The strengthened image Y from BHEPL is shown in Figure 2e, and the intensity histogram of image Y is shown in Figure 2f. A comparison between Figure 2c,e suggests that enhanced thermal image through BHEPL (Figure 2e) would be more effective in training the MS mask DCNN when other heat sources exist in a representative temperature image, implying that the proposed method helps distinguish features of UTLCs from those of environments in a thermal image for training the mask-based neural network, even though several heat sources exist in the thermal images.

2.2. Phase B Multi-Scale Mask Deep Convolution Neural Network

This subsection presents a method for detecting a UTLC through an MS mask DCNN (phase B in Figure 1) from a thermal image preprocessed in phase A. The MS mask DCNN is designed to separate a UTLC from the background of the thermal image because the MS mask DCNN ensures high accuracy and robustness [25]. The architecture of the proposed MS mask DCNN is designed for pixel-wise semantic segmentation, as shown in Figure 4, featuring two characteristics: a multiscale feature extraction module (① in Figure 4) and a skip-layer fusion module (② in Figure 4).

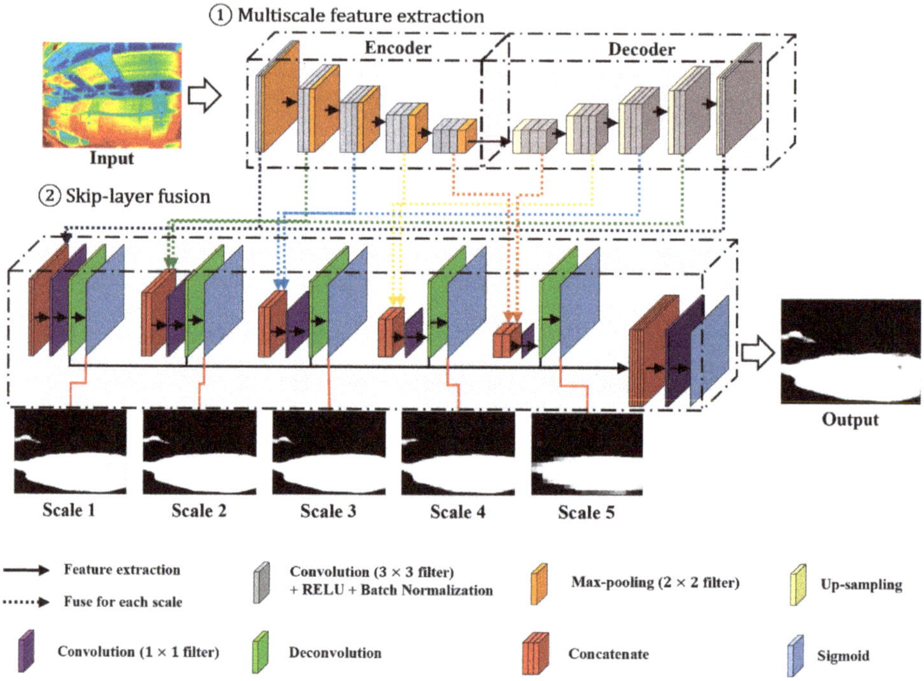

Figure 4. Architecture of the proposed multiscale mask deep convolutional neural network (MS mask DCNN).

The multiscale feature extraction module is constructed using a symmetric autoencoder architecture. Specifically, the encoder and decoder construct multiscale layers to effectively extract both local and global semantic features from an input thermal image. Each layer in the encoder comprises several ConvReLU layers (gray blocks at ① in Figure 4) that combine a convolution layer, activation function layer, batch normalization layer, and max-pooling layer. First, different scales of convolution layers are used to extract low- and high-scale features and construct multiscale feature maps. Low-scale layers extract high-frequency details, including complex temperature gradients and the edges of facilities, with high resolution. Hence, complex local features of UTLCs and the background are extracted at low scales because they are similar in size to an input image. In contrast, the high-scale layers extract low-frequency details, including the global temperature gradient and overall shapes of the UTLCs and the background with low resolution. In other words, the global features of the UTLCs and the background are extracted at the high-scale layers because they retain the implicated features at a small size. Hence, the proposed architecture effectively extracts both local and global features from a thermal image. Second, the activation function layer executes a nonlinear space transformation to easily identify and extract features. This layer addresses the ReLU function as an activation function because it helps train the feature maps effectively through nonlinear space transformation with efficient gradient propagation [26]. Third, a batch normalization layer plays a regulatory role, preventing the gradient vanishing problem. Finally, a max pooling layer (orange blocks at

① in Figure 4) is added at the end of the encoder layers in each scale. This layer consists of a stride larger than one and helps train the input thermal images effectively because these networks reduce the size of the parameters and extract important features from an input thermal image. Similarly, each layer in the decoder comprises several up-sampling and ConvReLU layers symmetric to those in the encoder. The up-sampling layers (yellow blocks at ① in Figure 4) in front of each decoder layer match the extracted feature maps corresponding to the size of the encoder layers. This layer uses a bilinear interpolation method to improve the inference time [27]. However, this might result in a loss of spatial resolution and boundary bias. Hence, max-pooling indices are recorded and used for up-sampling to compensate for the absence of representative information. The ConvReLU layers in the decoder play the same role as those in the encoder. However, several nonlinear space transformations at the activation layers of each scale enable feature extraction at different hyperplanes, strengthening the features for accurate separation of UTLCs.

The skip-layer fusion module is introduced at each scale to mitigate concerns regarding spatial loss from the convolution layers of the encoder and decoder. This module comprises a concatenate layer (red blocks at ② in Figure 4), a convolution layer (purple blocks at ② in Figure 4), a deconvolution layer (green blocks at ② in Figure 4), and a sigmoid activation function layer (sky blue blocks at ② in Figure 4). First, the same scales of the feature maps in the encoder and decoder are concatenated to reduce the spatial loss in the concatenated layer. Second, each concatenated feature map is fed into a 1×1 convolution layer, changing the size of the feature maps from multi-channel to one-channel. This layer helps train a neural network effectively because it reduces the size of the parameters. Subsequently, one-channel feature map passes through the deconvolution layers to resize the feature maps the same as the input image. Finally, these feature maps are concatenated and then passed through 1×1 convolution and sigmoid layers to separate the UTLCs from the environment, as shown in Figure 5a. Therefore, the MS mask DCNN results in a binary filter image to separate the UTLC from the environment.

2.3. Phase C Anomaly Detection of Transmission Line

This subsection presents a detailed method for anomaly detection in UTLCs (Figure 5) The proposed method combines the contour method and the unsupervised clustering method to improve the accuracy of semantic segmentation of UTLCs, thereby decreasing the false-alarm rate. The contour method effectively eliminates the false-segmented pixels of UTLCs with a low computational cost. The proposed method comprises three procedures: elimination of false-segmented UTLCs, anomaly detection for single-phase UTLCs, and anomaly detection for multiple phases of UTLC.

First, false-segmented pixels of the UTLCs are eliminated through a contour method (Figure 1d) because a segmented UTLC through the MS-mask DCNN included false-segmented pixels (red circles in Figure 5a). Note that neural networks cannot secure the perfect accuracy of 100% because of insufficient training data and thermal reflection, which are inherent characteristics of IR cameras [28]. Additionally, this study predefined a value of 1 for the number of segmented UTLCs in an image. These concerns were mitigated by employing a contour method [29] comprising four steps. First, contours were detected by extracting pixels corresponding to the same value in a binary image. Second, the areas of each contour were calculated, and the detected contours were sorted by area. Third, all the pixels were eliminated, excluding the contour with the largest area. The contour method eliminates all false-segmented regions predicted from the MS mask DCNN because prediction from the MS mask DCNN secures an accuracy of over 90%, and thus, the largest region represents the connector region of interest. Finally, the retained contours are filled to refine the segmented UTLC (Figure 5b), demonstrating that the contour method effectively eliminates false-segmented regions. Note that this binary image is used as a filter to extract only the temperature distribution of a UTLC, implying that this method does not affect the detection accuracy of an anomalous UTLC. Subsequently, the UTLC regions are extracted from a thermal image. Specifically, the binary filter (Figure 5b) refined from the contour method is multiplied by the original thermal image, resulting in the temperature distribution of the UTLC regions (Figure 5c).

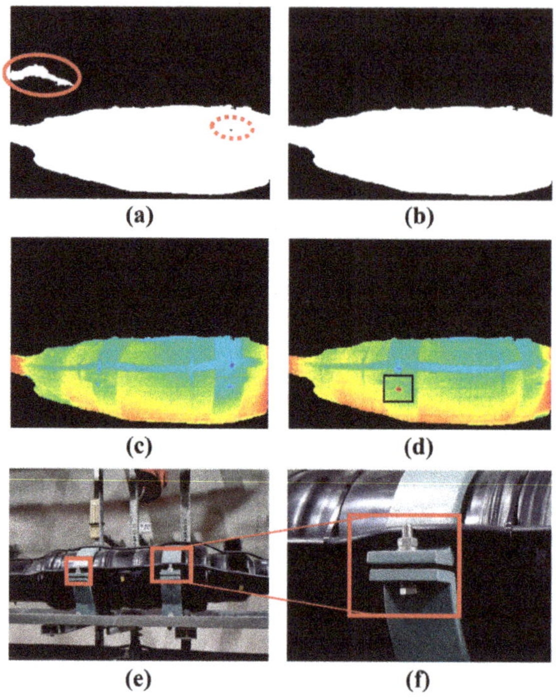

Figure 5. A binary image (**a**) through MS mask DCNN and (**b**) refined by the contour method from a thermal image; temperature distribution of a connector passing through the refined filter (**c**) without and (**d**) with thermal reflection; (**e**,**f**) an optical image of a connector, where the red box denotes bolts and nuts resulting in thermal reflection.

Second, an anomaly was detected for the single- and multi-phase UTLCs. The criteria for anomaly detection are defined by regulations from KEPCO [23]. Specifically, the regulations given by KEPCO classify the conditions of UTLCs into three categories: normal, caution, and warning. Caution and warning are defined as regions with temperatures exceeding 2 °C and 4 °C from the mean temperature of the UTLCs, respectively; otherwise, the UTLCs are normal. Interestingly, a filtered thermal image of a UTLC includes a small region of high-temperature pixels (the black box in Figure 5d) in some cases, which could be considered an anomaly. An expert system reveals that these regions clustered below 10 pixels are not overheated regions but regions of thermal reflection because overheating leads to large pixels clustered because of thermal conduction in UTLs. Thermal reflection is an inherent characteristic of IR cameras, which occurs when recording a highly reflective object [28]. Underground transmission facilities include highly reflective metallic components such as supporting structures, bolts, and nuts. Bolts and nuts fixing the supporting structures are orthogonal to the IR camera in some cases, resulting in thermal reflection (the red boxes in Figure 5e,f). Hence, the anomaly is determined by an unsupervised clustering method of the DBSAN among several outlier pixels [30] because this method is effective in eliminating small numbers of noisy pixels (Figure 1e). The proposed anomaly-detection method comprises four steps. First, the mean temperature is calculated for the pixels of a UTLC, which corresponds to a segmented UTLC in a thermal image (Figure 5d). Second, overheated pixels exceeding 2 °C are identified because these pixels are anomaly candidates in the KEPCO regulation [23]. Third, these pixels are clustered through DBSCAN to separate anomalies from noise from thermal reflection with two parameters, radius and number of minimum points, where radius and number of minimum points denote the maximum distance between pixels and the minimum number of pixels within the radius in a cluster, respectively. This study uses predefined values of 100 and 10 for the radius and number of minimum points, respectively, based on experiments. Hence, clustered pixels exceeding the predefined threshold are overheated regions, whereas other clusters are noise from thermal reflection. Specifically, overheated regions are classified as caution and warnings when they exceed 2 °C and 4 °C, respectively. Anomalies were further analyzed (Figure 1e) for the three phases of UTLCs because UTLCs comprise three phases of UTLCs. Specifically, the mean temperatures for the three phases of the UTLCs were compared. A UTLC with a high mean temperature exceeding 2 °C and 4 °C is classified as an anomaly UTLC with a class of caution and warning. Moreover, the proposed method is capable of handling various types of UTLC anomalies because anomalies in UTLCs are caused by mechanical and electrical defects, which result in localized temperature increases at the faulty components, and temperature distributions could exhibit similar patterns.

3. Experiments

3.1. Calibration of IR Camera

This subsection presents a detailed calibration process for an IR camera to accurately convert thermal energy to the temperature of the UTLCs. Note that the inherent characteristics of an IR camera make it difficult to obtain accurate measurements of the UTLCs. Specifically, an IR camera is a non-contact sensor that measures thermal energy rather than temperature from the radiant wavelength of objects. Hence, the conversion of thermal energy into temperature results in errors when the parameters correlated to the conversion are affected by the environment, including thermal reflection. Hence, the conversion equation from the thermal energy to the representative temperature (Equation (1)) of TE-EV1 should be calibrated to accurately estimate the temperature of the UTLCs and their environments.

Calibration was performed by comparing the temperature estimated from the IR camera with that from the T-type thermocouple (OMEGA, Norwalk, CT, USA) with a cup covered with black insulating tape made of polylactic acid (PVC, orange box in Figure 6a). A cup covered by PVC was used in this experiment to match the emissivity of the surface of the UTLCs because the surface of the UTLCs is covered by an insulator made of PVC (Figure 5e). Note that matching emissivity is important for the accurate calibration of measurements from an IR camera [31]. Experiments were conducted with several working distances (WD) from 1.0 to 2.5 m with 0.5 m intervals between UTLCs and an IR camera under heated water inside a cup at a natural convection condition. Hence, the temperature of the cup filled with water decreased over time because of the thermal convection between the cup and the environment. Measurements with a period of 3000 s were used for calibration.

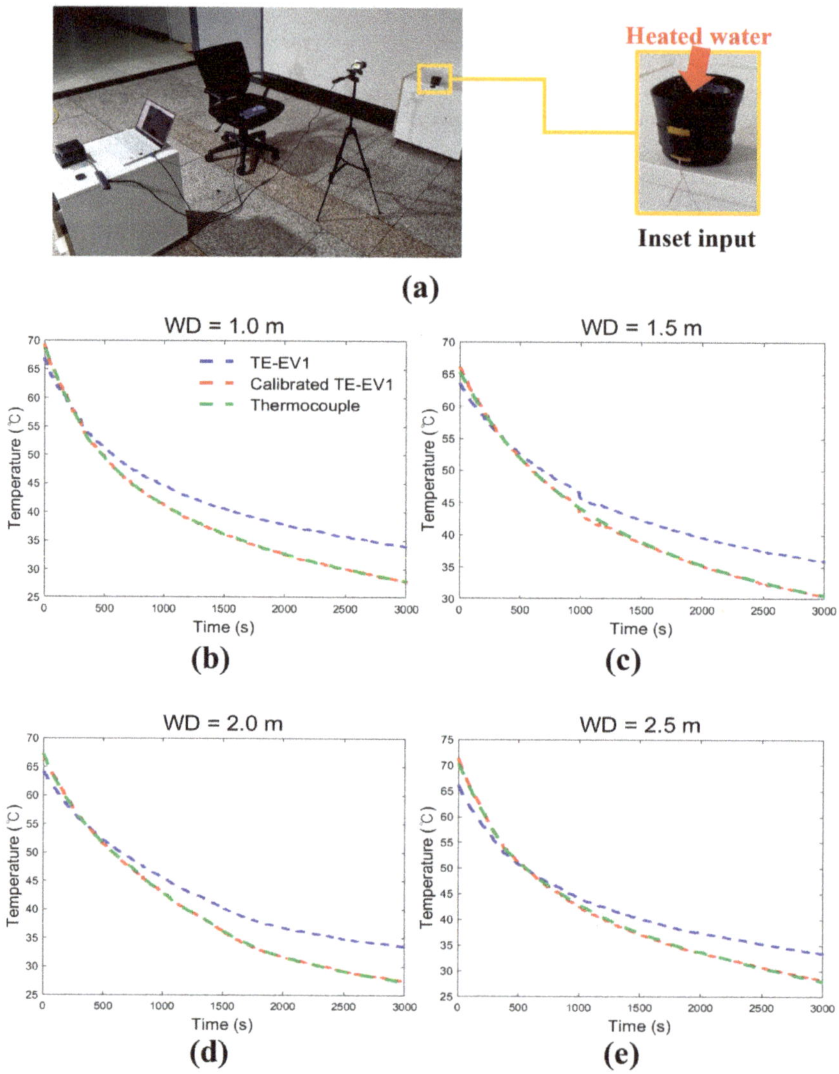

Figure 6. Experimental (**a**) setup and (**b–e**) results for calibration of an IR camera.

The coefficients a and b in the first-order polynomial regression are identified as 1.29 and -15.53, respectively, using Equation (2) based on the least square method, minimizing the root mean square errors (RMSEs) between the converted temperature from the IR camera and the temperature measured by the thermocouple (Figure 6b–e). The RMSEs of the calibrated temperature were 0.63, 0.35, 0.20, and 1.07 °C (the red lines in Figure 6) when executing calibration at WDs of 1.0, 1.5, 2.0, and 2.5 m, respectively, whereas the RMSEs of temperature were 4.96, 4.62, 4.17, and 3.55 °C without calibration for the corresponding WDs (the blue lines in Figure 6). The mean RMSE for all cases was reduced from 4.325 to 0.56 °C after calibration, implying that errors in estimating temperature significantly decreased over seven times through the proposed calibration process. These results confirm that the calibrated temperature of an IR camera is accurate for measuring the surface temperature of PVC UTLCs.

3.2. Thermal Diagnosis System

A thermal diagnosis system (TDS) was designed and mounted on a mobile robot (Rover Zero 2, Rover Robotics, Wayzata, MN, USA) for the patrol inspection of UTLCs (Figure 7). This system can also be used to measure sufficient image sets of UTLCs because deep learning approaches require significant images for model construction. The weight reduction of the TDS was a major consideration when designing the TDS because the weight of the payload equipped in the mobile robot significantly affects the operating time (i.e., inspection time). The TDS comprises an IR camera of TE-EV1 (I3systems, Daejeon, Republic of Korea), a 3D Lidar (Velodyne VLP-16, USA), a Jetson Xavier AGX (NVIDIA, Santa Clara, CA, USA), five gas sensors, and a customized gimbal. Specifically, the IR camera was mounted on a customized gimbal printed with polylactic acid using a three-dimensional printer from S5 (Ultimaker, Utrecht, The Netherlands). The FOV of TE-EV1 was 76° and 59.5° in the horizontal and vertical directions, respectively, and a vibration isolator with a soft sponge was designed in the gimbal to isolate vibration from the motors and ground during operation (red box in Figure 7). A 3D Lidar was used for the autonomous driving of a mobile robot, and the five gas sensors monitored the air conditions of the UPF. However, detailed descriptions of these sensors are omitted because their measurements were beyond the scope of this study. A Jetson AGX featuring a 512-core Volta graphical processing unit and an octa-core ARM 64-bit central processing unit was also mounted on a customized gimbal printed of carbon fiber to secure high stiffness because the Jetson AGX is heavier than the TE-EV1. The power was supplied by a series of six-cell 18650 Li-ion batteries with 3.7 a of normal voltage and 3500 mAh capacity. The total weight of the TDS was only 2.7 kg, resulting in an operating time of 4 h, ensuring sufficient inspection time.

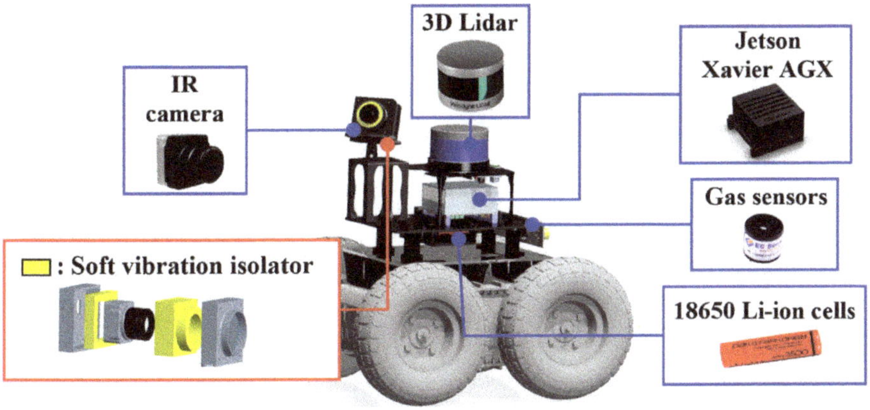

Figure 7. Hardware configuration of the thermal diagnosis mobile robot.

3.3. Field Experiments

A mobile robot equipped with TDS was used to record thermal images of connectors in UTLCs at 345 kV (Shingwangmyeong-Yeongdeungpo (SY) UPF, Seoul, Republic of Korea). The robot was positioned at the center of the sidewalk in the UPF (Figure 8a), and the thermal images were measured using an IR camera with a resolution of 640 × 480 pixels that faced the UTLCs perpendicularly. The IR camera was panned from side to side to measure the entire connector of the UTLCs because it could not record the thermal images of the connectors of interest in one frame. Note that this limit occurred because of the short distance between the IR camera located on the sidewalk and the connectors, even though the IR camera with the widest FOV was selected and used. Thermal images were measured from five junction boxes (JB) #1 to #5 of two 345 kV UTLCs, SY #1 and SY #2 (the red and blue boxes in Figure 8a), under normal and replicated anomalous conditions (Table 1). Repeated frames of the thermal images were removed from the recorded images because they were not useful for training the proposed neural network. A hot pack was randomly located at one phase of each connector from JB #1 to #5 to replicate anomalous conditions because it is difficult to measure thermal images of anomalous connectors in actual field experiments. Hence, some thermal images measured under normal conditions were used to construct the MS mask DCNN, and several thermal images measured under normal and replicated anomalous conditions were used to test the effectiveness and robustness of the entire framework of the proposed anomaly detection method.

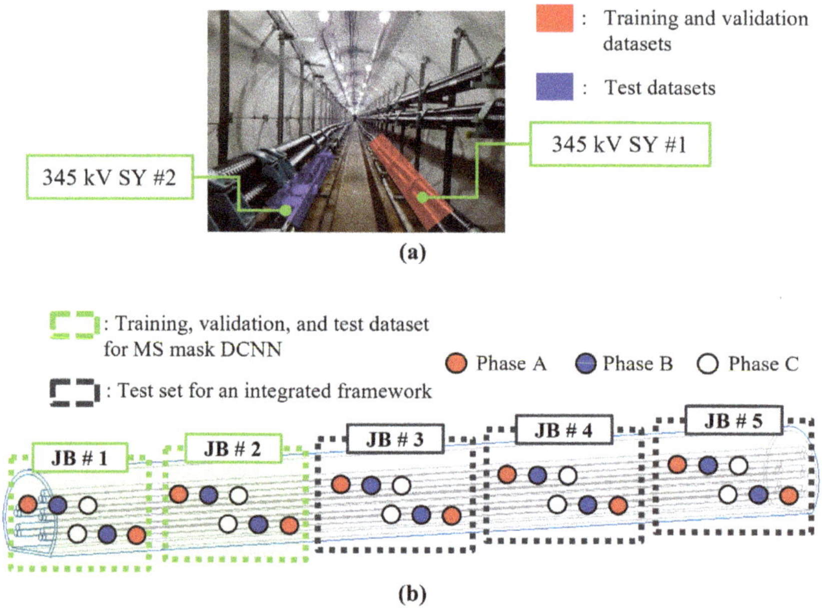

Figure 8. (**a**) Configuration of UPF for image acquisition from SY UPF and (**b**) detailed construction of a dataset for MS mask DCNN and an integrated framework.

Table 1. Detailed information on the acquired thermal images.

Dataset #	UTLC #	JB #	Images-Sets	
			Normal	Abnormal
DS #1	SY #1	1–2	515	-
DS #1	SY #2	1–2	97	32
DS #2	SY #1	3–5	2500	625
DS #2	SY #2	3–5	2500	625

Total thermal images of 6894 were measured from SY #1 to #2. These images were divided into two datasets (DS), DS #1 and #2. DS #1 comprises 644 thermal images recorded from JB #1 and #2 of SY #1 and #2 in two different frames. Images in the first frame included thermal reflection from the supporting structures, whereas those in the second frame minimized thermal reflection from the supporting structures. Note that images from different views can improve the robustness of the trained MS mask DCNN. In contrast, the images of DS #2 were only measured at the frame to minimally locate the metal supporting structures in the recorded thermal images. This frame was selected from the expert system of KEPCO to minimize errors from thermal reflection because the high thermal reflectivity of metal frames distorts the measured thermal images, resulting in inaccurate thermal images. Note that thermal images of metal frames with relatively low emissivity are predominantly influenced by the environment [32]. DS #2 comprises thermal images of 6250 recorded from JB #3 to #5 of SY #1 and #2 to test the proposed anomaly detection method for real-world applications. The total thermal images included 5000 and 1250 normal and replicated abnormal images, respectively (Figure 8b).

3.4. Construction of MS Mask DCNN

This subsection describes the construction of the MS-mask DCNN. Two Tesla V100 (32GB) processing units (GPU) with two Intel Xeon Gold 5220R central processing units (CPUs) were used for training, validation, and testing of the proposed MS mask DCNN with the image sets described in Section 3.3.

Original input images with a resolution of 640 × 480 pixels and downsized images with a resolution of 320 × 240 pixels were prepared to quantitatively analyze the accuracy and inference time of the proposed MS mask DCNN with different scales. All the thermal images were used to construct the ground truth of binary images through the open-source labeling tool, labelimg [33]. Thermal images of DS #1 were separated into thermal images of 386 (60%), 129 (20%), and 129 (20%) for model construction. The proposed architecture was trained with the 3-channel RGB thermal images and masked binary images denoting ground truth through the format of an autoencoder combining four to six scales of encoders and decoders (Figure 4). Notably, combining features extracted from deep and wide neural networks enhances the accuracy and robustness of the model. The larger the scale of the multiscale neural network, the more accurate the estimation, but the greater the inference time, suggesting that trade-offs exist in the construction of neural networks. Therefore, the optimal architecture of the MS mask DCNN was selected by comparing the performances of the MS-mask DCNN with three different scales because both accuracy and inference time are important for real-time applications. Specifically, the encoder comprised 10, 13, and 16 convolutional layers when four, five, and six scaled layers were used, respectively, and the decoder was a symmetrical network corresponding to the encoder. In the encoder, the feature maps were extracted by a factor of 1/2 of the size of the input feature map using the max-pooling layer after the convolutional layers until the number of scale feature maps was generated. In the decoder, convolution layers were used to extract features, and up-sampling layers were then used to increase the size of the feature maps by a factor of two, resulting in prediction maps that were the same as the ground truth feature maps. The convolutional kernel size is chosen to be 3 × 3 and the max-pooling kernel size is chosen to be 2 × 2 to build a deeper network effectively.

A balanced binary cross-entropy loss function was used in the training because this loss function ensures high accuracy of the segmented unbalanced UTLCs [34]. Thermal images with statistical image strengthening were used to decrease the losses between the ground truth of the UTLCs and the prediction of the MS mask DCNN using the Adam optimizer. The hyperparameters of the Adam optimizer were optimized using Bayesian optimization (BO) [35] because BO secures the global minimum with fast convergence compared with other optimization methods, including grid search and genetic algorithms. Note that the scales of the MS mask DCNN were manually changed during training to quantitatively analyze the accuracy and inference time of the proposed neural network from four to six scales, whereas the other hyperparameters were optimized from BO. In addition, the hyperparameters of the Adam optimizer for other mask-based neural networks were optimized using BO for a fair comparison of the performance of the neural networks (Table 2). Hence, this optimization procedure can guarantee the best performance of each neural network, demonstrating the superiority of the proposed method. The training and validation image sets were used to optimize the hyperparameters, whereas the test image sets were used to evaluate the final accuracy and robustness of the proposed method.

Table 2. Initial ranges and optimal hyperparameters of the mask-based CNNs with Z-score normalization and BHEPL image strengthening.

Initial Ranges of the Hyperparameters						
Networks	Hyperparameters					
	Batch Size	Learning Rate	First Momentum	Second Momentum	Weight Decay	Epsilon
All	4–20 w/2 interval	1×10^{-6} -1×10^{-4}	0.9–0.999	0.9–0.999	0.01 –0.3	1×10^{-8} -1×10^{-6}
Optimized Hyperparameters						
Networks	Hyperparameters					
	Batch Size	Learning Rate	First Momentum	Second Momentum	Weight Decay	Epsilon
Mask R-CNN	12	9.41×10^{-5}	0.929	0.958	0.129	2.41×10^{-8}
ResUNet	20	9.63×10^{-5}	0.955	0.985	0.143	5.80×10^{-7}
MS mask DCNN (s4)	18	5.74×10^{-5}	0.923	0.951	0.113	9.69×10^{-6}
MS mask DCNN (s5)	20	2.67×10^{-5}	0.944	0.983	0.017	2.42×10^{-6}
MS mask DCNN (s6)	4	5.21×10^{-5}	0.959	0.961	0.269	5.27×10^{-8}

A half tensor was employed to test the proposed method to increase the FPS for real-time applications because most deep neural networks do not require a large number of bits during the testing phase in the absence of any vanishing or exploding concerns [36]. In other words, the proposed network employs a float tensor during the training and validation phases, whereas the half-tensor is used to enhance the inference time during the test, suggesting that the efficiency of our approach does not come at the expense of accuracy. The mean intersection over union (MIoU) was used to evaluate the semantic segmentation performance of mask-based neural networks as

$$MIoU = \frac{TP}{TP + FP + FN}, \tag{21}$$

where TP, FP, and FN denote the intersection area between ground truth and prediction.

4. Results and Discussion

4.1. Results of Each Phase from the Proposed Integrated Framework

This subsection describes the results from each phase of the proposed method, including statistical image strengthening, segmentation of the UTLC through the MS mask DCNN, and the contour method. This demonstration executes all the procedures with two samples from the test dataset of SY #2 under normal (Figure 9a–e) and abnormal (Figure 9f–j) conditions. Note that training of the MS mask DCNN was executed with the dataset of SY #1; thus, the demonstration of the proposed method should be conducted with different images from the training images.

First, a measured thermal image (Figure 9a,f) was passed through statistical image strengthening, including z-score normalization and BHEPL. This process results in a significant thermal gradient of pixels corresponding to a UTLC and environments in a thermal image using clipped plateaus and statistical limits (Figure 9b,g), enabling the neural network to easily extract features of the UTLC for separating connectors from environments. Notably, this process also effectively eliminates environments when a strong heat source or anomaly exists in the environment or a UTLC exists in a recorded thermal image. The preprocessed thermal images are then passed through the MS mask

DCNN, separating the UTLC of interest from the environment as a binary classification (Figure 9c,h) with a predefined threshold of 0.5. However, false segmentations would be included in the predicted result (Figure 9h) because the neural network cannot secure a perfect accuracy of 100% owing to insufficient training datasets. This limitation can be compensated for by employing a simple yet effective image-processing method. Specifically, the contour method eliminates false segmentations of the UTLC (Figure 9d,i) because it effectively detects the corners and edges of the UTLC from the predicted binary information. The proposed framework then selects pixels corresponding to the largest region of the contour representing the UTLC in a thermal image and eliminates other regions, thereby improving the accuracy of semantic segmentation of the UTLC with a low computational cost. Finally, anomalies are detected by comparing the temperature of pixels in the UTLC region with the mean temperature of the UTLC through DBSCAN, resulting in an orange box within the thermal image (Figure 9j). Note that the anomaly is detected by analyzing the temperature of the UTLC using only the corresponding pixels in the refined segmented UTLC. Hence, a strong heat source in the environment was excluded from this process. DBSCAN also effectively removes a small portion of the relatively high temperature due to thermal reflection from metal structures in connectors, such as bolts and nuts (Figure 5e,f), improving the accuracy of anomaly detection.

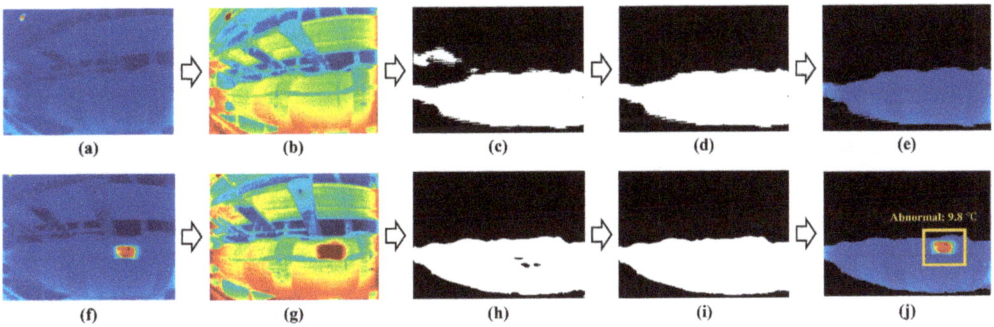

Figure 9. Results of the proposed integrated framework for underground transmission connectors under (**a**–**e**) normal; (**f**–**j**) replicated anomaly conditions.

4.2. Ablation Study for the Proposed Framework

This subsection demonstrates the effectiveness of z-score normalization, BHEPL methods, and MS mask DCNN compared with min-max normalization, other histogram-based image strengthening (HBIS) [37–39], and other mask-based DCNNs to extract distinct features of a UTLC from a thermal image (Figure 10). Table 3 lists the MIoUs obtained from three different factors using the SY #2 dataset. The min-max normalization was executed using the minimum and maximum temperatures from each thermal image. "None" in the HBIS methods in Table 3 denotes that an original thermal image was used for separating a UTLC from an environment through mask-based DCNNs.

First, MIoUs obtained with z-score normalization are generally higher than those obtained with min-max normalization, regardless of HBIS and mask-based DCNNs. Specifically, z-score normalization enhances MIoUs from 0.23 to 18.72% under normal conditions and from 1.78 to 63.64% under abnormal conditions compared with those of min-max normalization (bold values in Table 3). This quantitative analysis implies that z-score normalization is more effective than min-max normalization for extracting features of thermal images because a statistical threshold secures high accuracy compared with min-max normalization in this situation. Statistical normalization also ensures high robustness because field measurements include several unexpected anomalies, such as ceiling light and hot spots in UTLCs, that distort the estimated results from the neural network. Similar results have been reported in the literature when using field measurements [40,41], confirming that z-score normalization is effective for inferences from neural networks with field measurements. Note that HBIS methods cannot secure the accuracy of MIoU under abnormal conditions when min-max normalization is used because min-max normalization cannot separate the environments and UTLs effectively in cases in which unexpected anomalies exist, including ceiling lights and hot spots in UTLCs.

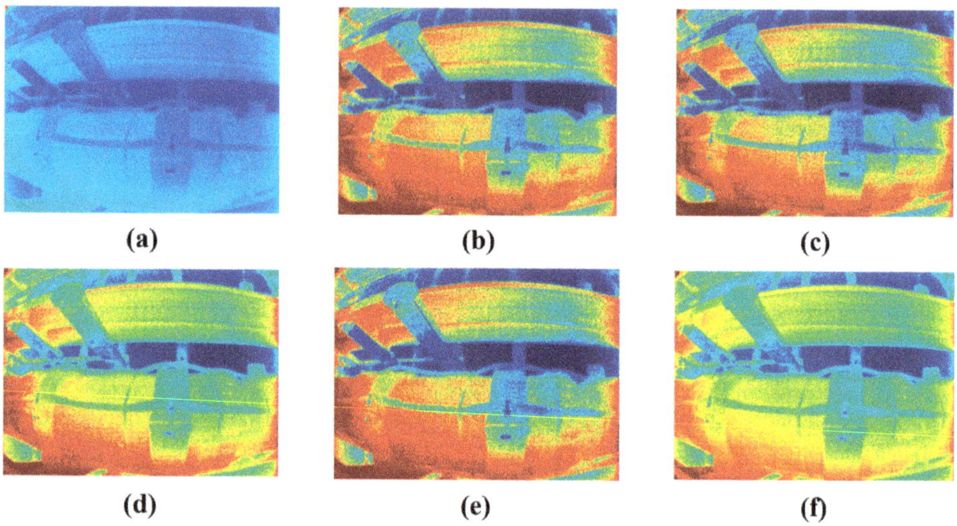

Figure 10. (**a**) A measured thermal image and strengthened image for an underground transmission connector using (**b**) HE; (**c**) BBHE; (**d**) RMSHE; (**e**) MMBEBHE; (**f**) BHEPL.

Table 3. Comparative analysis of MIoU with the dataset of DS #1 @ SY #2.

Mask-Based CNNs	Normalization	Histogram-Based Image Strengthening						FPS
		None	HE	BBHE	RMSHE	MMBEBHE	BHEPL (Proposed)	
MIoU (%) @ Normal Data								
Mask R-CNN	Min-Max	68.45	74.80	77.66	76.70	78.04	81.92	16.4
	Z-score	82.69	77.82	79.15	79.94	78.42	84.42	
ResUNet	Min-Max	79.37	77.90	82.40	82.15	81.40	86.34	44.2
	Z-score	82.18	82.89	84.14	85.86	86.81	87.43	
MS mask DCNN (s4)	Min-Max	70.86	85.53	85.63	78.46	76.50	70.85	63.1
	Z-score	63.45	85.77	89.11	87.96	84.34	**89.57**	
MS mask DCNN (s5)	Min-Max	87.16	80.64	81.65	85.26	82.88	88.65	46.7
	Z-score	90.48	86.02	84.67	88.00	83.19	**90.59**	
MS mask DCNN (s6)	Min-Max	88.18	87.08	87.59	83.08	83.02	90.78	30.0
	Z-score	89.27	89.25	89.41	87.19	89.66	**90.95**	
MIoU (%) @ Anomaly Data								
Mask R-CNN	Min-Max	27.13	74.93	64.56	18.79	49.00	24.62	16.4
	Z-score	73.46	77.22	77.19	79.43	78.74	80.38	
ResUNet	Min-Max	25.98	77.90	40.04	17.22	48.72	45.93	44.2
	Z-score	77.50	84.06	83.72	80.86	85.24	86.95	

Table 3. *Cont.*

		MIoU (%) @ Normal Data						
		Histogram-Based Image Strengthening						
Mask-Based CNNs	**Normalization**	**None**	**HE**	**BBHE**	**RMSHE**	**MMBEBHE**	**BHEPL (Proposed)**	**FPS**
MS mask DCNN (s4)	Min-Max	32.97	75.97	64.52	30.38	60.87	43.35	63.1
	Z-score	62.14	87.52	82.00	83.81	86.43	**91.57**	
MS mask DCNN (s5)	Min-Max	68.93	80.12	79.02	71.62	70.16	60.62	46.7
	Z-score	70.71	88.71	87.02	80.71	82.58	**92.92**	
MS mask DCNN (s6)	Min-Max	76.81	87.44	75.03	58.80	71.94	74.49	30.0
	Z-score	82.68	91.40	85.03	71.78	90.33	**91.86**	

Second, the BHEPL method enhances MIoUs when z-score normalization is employed, regardless of the mask-based DCNNS. Specifically, BHEPL enhances the MIoUs from 0.11 to 26.12% under normal conditions and from 0.46 to 29.43% under abnormal conditions compared with those from other HBIS methods. This quantitative analysis implies that the BHEPL is appropriate when z-score normalization is used because the BHEPL emphasizes numerous pixels, including environments and UTLC, with two sub-histograms using the clipped plateau limit. Note that BHEPL effectively preserves the bias of the intensity using two sub-histograms and the level saturation using the clipped plateau limit, thereby strengthening the features of the UTLCs.

Third, the MS mask DCNNs show the highest MIoUs, regardless of the number of latent layers, for both normal and abnormal conditions when the z-score normalization method and BHEPL are addressed. Specifically, the MS mask DCNNs secure high MIoUs of around 90% regardless of the number of latent layers. Quantitatively, the lowest accuracy of the MS mask DCNN is 2% higher than the highest accuracy of other networks. This observation suggests that a multiscale feature extraction module in the MS mask DCNN secures high accuracy because it effectively extracts distinct and semantic features to separate UTLC from the environments in the prediction layers. In contrast, Mask R-CNN requires both segmented mask and bounding box information to calculate the loss, including the classification and regression of masks and bounding boxes, for instance, for segmentation of the images [22]. However, the training dataset of DS #1 may include different environments adjacent to UTLCs, characterized by irregular and diverse shapes and complex thermal gradients in the bounding boxes. These irregular and diverse shapes in the surrounding environment pose challenges for extracting distinct features from thermal images in the Mask R-CNN architecture, resulting in low accuracy. Furthermore, Mask R-CNN shows lower FPS compared with both ResUNet and MS mask DCNN, two semantic segmentation models. Specifically, FPS from Mask R-CNN is 2.8 times lower than ResUNet and 1.8 to 3.8 times lower than MS mask DCNN. The architecture of ResUNet is similar to that of the MS mask DCNN because ResUNet also employs the architecture of the autoencoder. However, MIoUs from ResUNet are lower than those from the MS mask DCNN because the architecture of ResUNet is less effective than that of the MS mask DCNN. Specifically, ResUNet [21] concatenates feature maps from both the encoder and decoder and then estimates the mask at the last layer after passing through several convolution layers, whereas the MS mask DCNN generates multiscale feature maps from the autoencoder and directly estimates the mask of the UTLC. In other words, feature maps extracted from ResUNet faded out when passing through several convolution layers, whereas the MS mask DCNN preserved the semantic information of UTLCs, which were extracted from different scales, resulting in enhanced performances for separating UTLCs from the background. Among the MS mask DCNNs with different numbers of latent layers, the MS mask DCNN (S6) showed the highest accuracy for normal data, whereas the MS mask DCNN (S5) showed the highest accuracy for abnormal data. These results can be explained by the fact that the neural network was trained using the SY #1 dataset, which only included normal data. Therefore, the MS mask DCNN (S6) is overfitted to the normal condition because of its deep architecture. In this study, the MS mask DCNN (S5) is deployed on TDS because it aims to accurately detect anomalies in UTLCs. Note that the FPS of the MS mask DCNN (S5) is also higher than that of the MS mask DCNN (S6), suggesting that the MS mask DCNN (S5) is more effective for field applications.

In summary, a combination of the z-score normalization, BHEPL method, and MS mask DCNN (S5) outperformed min-max normalization, other HBIS methods, and other mask-based DCNNs in terms of both accuracy and robustness. Moreover, the MS mask DCNN (S5) is accurate and fast for deploying this method in TDS.

4.3. Contribution of the Contour Method and Half Tensor

This subsection describes the contribution of the contour method and half tensor to the improvements in MIoU and FPS (Table 4). The MS mask DCNN (S5) is used for this analysis because this architecture shows the best performance, as described in Section 4.2.

Table 4. Contribution of the contour method and half tensor on the accuracy and inference time of the proposed framework.

Dataset	Data Type	w/o the Contour Method		w/the Contour Method	
		MIoU (%)	FPS	MIoU (%)	FPS
Normal	Single tensor	90.59	42.0	92.49	41.6
Normal	Half tensor	90.60	64.4	92.49	62.7
Abnormal	Single tensor	92.92	34.6	92.92	34.0
Abnormal	Half tensor	92.92	48.2	92.92	47.5

The contour method improves the MIoU by 1.9% under normal conditions and the same under abnormal conditions, effectively eliminating false segmentation of UTLCs. Note that the contour method improves the MIoU under normal conditions because it eliminates the false segmentation of UTL, which has a similar temperature distribution as UTLC under normal conditions. In contrast, there is no false segmentation of UTLC in the abnormal condition because anomalies in the UTLC make the intensity of the pixels higher than that in the normal condition (Figure 9b,g), resulting in no error in estimating the segmentation of UTLC. Moreover, the FPS is approximately equivalent to that of anomaly detection when addressing the contour method, leaving out consideration for the contour method. Specifically, the contour method increases the framework slowly from 42.0 to 41.6 FPS, implying that the contour method effectively eliminates falsely segmented UTLCs with low computational cost. Remarkably, the FPS of the proposed framework was significantly enhanced by addressing the half-tensor with the same accuracy. The half tensor reduces the inference time from 41.6 to 62.7 FPS when the contour method is addressed, whereas the MIoUs are the same. This observation suggests that the half tensor can allocate the weights of the trained neural networks with lower GPU resources than the single tensor because the half tensor comprises 1, 5, and 10 bits for the sign, exponent, and fraction, respectively, whereas the single tensor comprises 1, 8, and 23 bits for the sign, exponent, and fraction, respectively. Moreover, inference in the final application does not require large digits of 32 because it is performed by forward propagation, whereas training is performed by back propagation, which might cause gradient vanishing or exploding problems. Therefore, the segmented UTLCs from the proposed framework can be used for anomaly detection by analyzing the corresponding temperature.

4.4. Anomaly Detection

This subsection describes the anomaly detection for single- and multi-phase connectors. The detection performances of anomalies for single and three phases were analyzed with the DS #2 dataset. An anomaly randomly located at the phase of UTLCs was inspected through the proposed framework (Figure 9i) based on the regulations of KEPCO [23]. Specifically, inspection of UTLCs was conducted by analyzing sequential thermal images because detection of anomalies should be considered for both single and three phases.

First, DBSCAN eliminates noise exceeding 2 °C over the mean temperature in segmented pixels of the UTLC because noise from highly reflective objects, including supporting structures, bolts, and nuts, should be eliminated. Note that the number of pixels for noise was less than 10, within a radius of 100 pixels. Hence, noise elimination does not affect the accuracy of anomaly detection in UTLCs. Furthermore, the temperature of each pixel was compared with the mean temperature of the UTLC to detect pixels exceeding 2 °C and 4 °C, which are classified as a caution and an anomaly in the regulation of KEPCO, respectively. Finally, the centers of caution and anomalies were calculated using a thermal image. Hence, the detected anomaly for a single phase is noted with the temperature difference from the mean temperature demonstrated as 9.8 °C in Figure 9j. Remarkably, the proposed framework achieves a precision of 99.25% and a recall of 100% with a correct direction of 6203 from a total of 6250 images, confirming that the proposed framework is effective for real-world applications.

Second, an anomaly was detected for the three phases of the UTLC. Specifically, the maximum temperature of the UTLCs ($\overline{T_{max}}$) was calculated from the measured sequential thermal images for all three phases, excluding the pixels under abnormal conditions because abnormal pixels are used to detect anomalies by comparison with the maximum temperature of each phase of the UTLCs. Furthermore, the maximum temperature of each phase $T_{max}^{@phase}$ was calculated, and the maximum temperature of each phase $T_{max}^{@phase}$ was compared with $\overline{T_{max}}$ to detect anomalies of the UTLCs. Finally, the maximum temperature difference (ΔT) exceeding 2 °C and 4 °C was classified as a caution and an anomaly, respectively. Note that a hot pack was randomly installed in one of the three phases. Table 5 lists the detected anomalies for the three phases of the UTLCs. For example, the anomaly is detected only in phase B with a ΔT of 9.2 °C at JB #5 because $\overline{T_{max}}$ is 32.7 °C, whereas T_{max}^{A}, T_{max}^{B}, and T_{max}^{C} are 32.6, 41.9, and 32.7 °C, respectively. Similar results were observed for the other JBs. Hence, randomly located abnormal phases of the UTLCs were detected. Future work will include long-term monitoring of UTLCs with the proposed framework by deploying TDS and quantifying the accuracy of the proposed framework for real anomalies occurring at UTLCs.

Table 5. Detected anomalies from three-phases of UTLCs at the dataset of DS #2.

UTLC #	JB #	$\overline{T_{max}}$ (°C) *	T_{max}^{A} (°C) **	T_{max}^{B} (°C) **	T_{max}^{C} (°C) **	ΔT (°C) ***	Anomaly Phase #
SY #1	# 3	32.6	32.6	41.3	32.7	8.7	B
	# 4	32.7	43.3	32.9	32.6	10.6	A
	# 5	31.7	31.9	31.9	43.1	11.5	C
SY #2	# 3	31.6	31.6	41.1	31.4	9.5	B
	# 4	32.5	45.0	32.5	31.9	12.6	A
	# 5	32.7	32.6	41.9	32.7	9.2	B

* $\overline{T_{max}}$: mean temperature of the maximum temperature in the UTLCs for three phases, excluding pixels under abnormal conditions. ** $T_{max}^{@}$: maximum temperature of each phase. *** ΔT: maximum temperature difference between $\overline{T_{max}}$ and $T_{max}^{@}$.

5. Conclusions

This study proposes an integrated framework for anomaly detection of UTLCs in automatic manner based on three crucial characteristics. First, statistical image strengthening is addressed to improve the performance of segmentation for UTLCs through mask-based CNNs through z-score normalization and BHEPL. Specifically, z-score normalization improves the robustness of feature extraction for UTLCs even if a hot spot exists in the thermal image, and BHEPL improves the accuracy of segmentation to separate UTLCs from environments. Second, semantic segmentation of the MS mask DCNN is employed to detect the UTLC domain from a thermal image. The MS mask DCNN has two key characteristics: a multiscale feature extraction module enables the extraction of distinct features of UTLCs and environments, and the skip layer fusion module concatenates distinct features from the multiscale feature extraction module, effectively separating the ULCs from the environment. Third, anomaly detection based on temperature differences is addressed to improve the accuracy of diagnosis for anomaly detection by the contour method and unsupervised clustering of DBSCAN. Specifically, the contour method is addressed to eliminate the false segmentation of UTLCs by considering the largest domain of UTLCs, and DBSCAN improves the robustness and accuracy of diagnosis by eliminating noise from thermal reflection, which is caused by low-emissivity objects within thermal images. In addition, intensive field tests and ablation studies confirmed the effectiveness of the proposed framework in real-world applications. The simple yet accurate framework proposed would open a new era of automatic inspection for tunnel facilities. The proposed method could also be deployed on mobile robots that inspect for various field applications, including power lines, facilities, military, medicine, and security. Note that it is important to carefully evaluate the specific characteristics and requirements of the target domain when applying the proposed framework. The future work includes validating the robustness and efficiency of the proposed method in UPFs constructed in different environments. Furthermore, efforts should be focused on gathering real anomalous thermal images through long-term monitoring with a mobile robot equipped with an infrared camera to validate the proposed method. Alternative clustering methods will also be explored with other applications.

Author Contributions: Conceptualization, M.-G.K., S.-T.K. and K.-Y.O.; methodology, M.-G.K.; software, S.J. and M.-G.K.; data curation, M.-G.K. and S.J.; validation, S.-T.K. and M.-G.K.; formal analysis, M.-G.K.; investigation, S.-T.K.; resources, S.J.; writing-original draft preparation, M.-G.K.; writing-review and editing, K.-Y.O.; visualization, S.-T.K.; supervision, K.-Y.O.; project administration, K.-Y.O. All authors have read and agreed to the published version of the manuscript.

Funding: This research was supported by the Korea Electric Power Corporation through the KEPCO Research Institute (gran no. R19TA10) and the Research and Development on Fire Safety Technology for ESS Hydrogen Facilities, 20011568, Development of Automatic Extinguishing System for ESS Fire, funded by the National Fire Agency (NFA, Korea) and Korea Institute of Energy Technology Evaluation and Planning (KETEP) grant funded by the Korea government (MOTIE) (20213030020260, Development of Fire detection and protection system for wind turbine).

Data Availability Statement: The datasets generated and analyzed during the current study are not publicly available due they contain confidential national information but are available from the corresponding author on reasonable request.

Conflicts of Interest: The authors declare no conflict of interest.

References

1. Aras, F.; Alekperov, V.; Can, N.; Kirkici, H. Aging of 154 kV underground power cable insulation under combined thermal and electrical stresses. *IEEE Electr. Insul. Mag.* **2007**, *23*, 25–33. [CrossRef]
2. Yang, X.; Choi, M.S.; Lee, S.J.; Ten, C.W.; Lim, S.I. Fault location for underground power cable using distributed parameter approach. *IEEE Trans. Power Syst.* **2008**, *23*, 1809–1816. [CrossRef]
3. Bicen, Y. Trend adjusted lifetime monitoring of underground power cable. *Electr. Power Syst. Res.* **2017**, *143*, 189–196. [CrossRef]
4. Bascom, E.C.R.; Antonello, V.D. Underground power cable consideration: Alternatives to overhead. In Proceedings of the Conference Minnesota Power Systems, Brooklyn Center, MN, USA, 1–3 November 2011.
5. Shafiq, M.; Kiitam, I.; Taklaja, P.; Kutt, L.; Kauhaniemi, K.; Palu, I. Identification and location of PD defects in medium voltage underground power cables using high frequency current transformer. *IEEE Access* **2019**, *7*, 103608–103618. [CrossRef]
6. Densley, J. Ageing mechanisms and diagnostics for power cables—An overview. *IEEE Electr. Insul. Mag.* **2001**, *17*, 14–22. [CrossRef]
7. Kaminaga, K.; Ichihara, M.; Jinno, M.; Fujii, O.; Fukunaga, S.; Kobayashi, M. Development of 500-kV XLPE cables and accessories for long-distance underground transmission line V. Long-term performance for 5000-kV XLPE cables and joints. *IEEE Trans. Power Deliv.* **1996**, *11*, 1185–1194. [CrossRef]

8. Peter, C.J.M.; der Wielen, V.; Steennis, E.F. On-line PD monitoring system for MV cable connections with weak spot location. In Proceedings of the 2008 IEEE Power and Energy Society General Meeting—Conversion and Delivery of Electrical Energy in the 21st Century, Pittsburgh, PA, USA, 20–24 July 2008. [CrossRef]
9. Sun, X.; Lee, W.K.; Hou, Y.; Pong, P.W.T. Underground power cable detection and inspection technology based on magnetic field sensing at ground surface level. *IEEE Trans. Magn.* **2014**, *50*, 6200605. [CrossRef]
10. Kulkarni, S.; Santoso, S.; Thomas, A. Incipient fault location algorithm for underground cables. *IEEE Trans. Smart Grid* **2014**, *5*, 1165–1174. [CrossRef]
11. Sidhu, T.S.; Xu, Z. Detection of incipient faults in distribution underground cables. *IEEE Trans. Power Deliv.* **2010**, *25*, 1363–1371. [CrossRef]
12. Boggs, S.A. Partial Discharge: Overview and signal generation. *IEEE Electr. Insul. Mag.* **1990**, *6*, 33–39. [CrossRef]
13. Satish, L.; Nazneen, B. Wavelet-based denoising of partial discharge signals buried in excessive noise and interference. *IEEE Trans. Dielectr. Electr. Insul.* **2003**, *10*, 354–367. [CrossRef]
14. Wu, R.N.; Chang, C.K. The use of partial discharge as an online monitoring system for underground cable joints. *IEEE Trans. Power Deliv.* **2011**, *26*, 1585–1591. [CrossRef]
15. Kirsten, V.O.A.; Aghaej, M.; Rüther, R. Aerial infrared thermography for low-cost and fast fault detection in utility-scale PV power plants. *Sol. Energy* **2020**, *211*, 721–724. [CrossRef]
16. Alsafasfeh, M.; Abdel-Qader, I.; Bazuin, B.; Alsafasfeh, Q.; Su, W. Unsupervised fault detection and analysis for large photovoltaic systems using drones and machine vision. *Energies* **2018**, *11*, 2252. [CrossRef]
17. Jalil, B.; Leone, G.R.; Martinelli, M.; Moroni, D.; Pascali, M.A.; Merton, A. Fault detection in power equipment via an unmanned aerial system using multi modal data. *Sensors* **2019**, *19*, 3014. [CrossRef] [PubMed]
18. Jia, Z.; Liu, H.; Zheng, H.; Fan, S.; Liu, Z. An intelligent inspection robot for underground cable trenches based on adaptive 2d-slam. *Machines* **2022**, *10*, 1011. [CrossRef]
19. Kim, J.S.; Choi, K.N.; Kang, S.W. Infrared thermal image-based sustainable fault detection for electrical facilities. *Sustainability* **2020**, *13*, 557. [CrossRef]
20. Long, J.; Shelhamer, E.; Darrell, T. Fully convolutional networks for semantic segmentation. In Proceedings of the 2015 IEEE Computer Vision and Pattern Recognition (CVPR), Boston, MA, USA, 7–12 June 2015; pp. 3431–3440. [CrossRef]
21. Zhang, Z.; Liu, Q.; Wang, Y. Road extraction by deep residual u-net. *IEEE Geosci. Remote Sens. Lett.* **2018**, *15*, 2961–2969. [CrossRef]
22. He, K.; Gkioxari, G.; Dollar, P.; Girshick, R. Mask R-CNN. In Proceedings of the 2017 IEEE International Conference on Computer Vision (ICCV), Venice, Italy, 22–29 October 2017. [CrossRef]
23. KEPCO. *Underground Transmission Operation Standards*; KEPCO: Naju-si, Republic of Korea, 2016.
24. Ooi, C.H.; Kong, N.S.P.; Ibrahim, H. Bi-histogram equalization with a plateau limit for digital image enhancement. *IEEE Trans. Consum. Electron.* **2009**, *55*, 2072–2080. [CrossRef]
25. Zou, Q.; Zhang, Z.; Li, Q.; Qi, X.; Wang, Q.; Wang, S. DeepCrack: Learning hierarchical convolutional features for crack detection. *IEEE Trans. Image Process.* **2018**, *28*, 1498–1512. [CrossRef]
26. Nair, V.; Hinton, G.E. Rectified linear units improve restricted Boltzmann machines. In Proceedings of the 27th International Conference on International Conference on Machine Learning, Haifa, Israel, 21–24 June 2010.
27. Noh, H.; Hong, S.H.; Han, B.Y. Learning deconvolution network for semantic segmentation. In Proceedings of the 2015 IEEE International Conference Computer Vision (ICCV), Santiago, Chile, 17 May 2015. [CrossRef]
28. Henke, S.; Karstadt, D.; Mollmann, K.P.; Pinno, F.; Volmmer, M. Identification and suppression of thermal reflection in infrared thermal imaging. *InfraMation* **2004**, *5*, 287–298.
29. Suuzuki, S.; Be, K. Topological structural analysis of digitized binary images by border following. *Comput. Vis. Graph. Image Process.* **1985**, *30*, 32–46. [CrossRef]
30. Ester, M.; Kriegel, H.P.; Sander, J.; Xu, X. A density-based algorithm for discovering clusters in large spatial databases with noise. In Proceedings of the Second International Conference on Knowledge Discovery and Data Mining, Portland, OR, USA, 2–4 August 1996; pp. 226–231.
31. Bernard, V.; Staffa, E.; Mornstein, V.; Bourek, A. Infrared camera assessment of skin surface temperature-effect of emissivity. *Phys. Medica* **2013**, *29*, 583–591. [CrossRef] [PubMed]
32. Barreira, E.; Almeida, R.M.S.F.; Simões, M.L. Emissivity of building materials for infrared measurements. *Sensors* **2021**, *21*, 1961. [CrossRef] [PubMed]
33. Russell, B.C.; Torralba, A.; Murphy, K.P.; Freeman, W.T. LabelMe: A Database and web-based tool for image annotation. *Int. J. Comput. Vis.* **2008**, *77*, 157–173. [CrossRef]
34. Jardon, S. A survey of loss functions for semantic segmentation. In Proceedings of the 2020 IEEE Conference on Computational Intelligence in Bioinformatics and Computational Biology (CIBCB), Via del Mar, Chile, 27–29 October 2020. [CrossRef]
35. Frazier, P.I. A tutorial on Bayesian optimization. *arXiv* **2018**, arXiv:1807.02811. [CrossRef]
36. Micikevicius, P.; Narang, S.; Alben, J.; Diamos, G.; Elsen, E.; Garcia, D.; Ginsburg, B.; Houston, M.; Kuchaiev, O.; Venkatesh, G.; et al. Mixed precision training. *arXiv* **2018**, arXiv:1710.03740. [CrossRef]
37. Kim, Y.T. Contrast enhancement using brightness preserving bi—Histogram equalization. *IEEE Trans Consum. Electron.* **1997**, *43*, 1–8. [CrossRef]

38. Chen, S.D.; Ramli, A.R. Contrast enhancement using recursive mean-sperate histogram equalization for scalable brightness preservation. *IEEE Trans Consum. Electron.* **2003**, *49*, 1301–1309. [CrossRef]
39. Chen, S.D.; Ramli, A.R. Minimum mean brightness error bi-histogram equalization in contrast enhancement. *IEEE Trans Consum. Electron.* **2003**, *49*, 1310–1319. [CrossRef]
40. Fei, N.; Gao, Y.; Lu, Z.; Xiang, T. Z-score normalization, hubness, and few-shot learning. In Proceedings of the 2021 IEEE/CVF International Conference on Computer Vision (ICCV), Montreal, QC, Canada, 10–17 October 2021. [CrossRef]
41. Singh, D.; Singh, B. Feature wise normalization: An effective way of normalizing data. *Pattern Recognit.* **2022**, *122*, 108307. [CrossRef]

mathematics

Article

Gearbox Fault Diagnosis Based on Multi-Sensor Deep Spatiotemporal Feature Representation

Fengyun Xie [1,2,3,*], Gan Wang [1], Jiandong Shang [1], Enguang Sun [1] and Sanmao Xie [1,2,3]

1 School of Mechanical Electrical and Vehicle Engineering, East China Jiaotong University, Nanchang 330013, China
2 State Key Laboratory of Performance Monitoring Protecting of Rail Transit Infrastructure, East China Jiaotong University, Nanchang 330013, China
3 Life-Cycle Technology Innovation Center of Intelligent Transportation Equipment, Nanchang 330013, China
* Correspondence: xiefyun@163.com

Abstract: The vibration signal acquired by a single sensor contains limited information and is easily interfered by noise signals, resulting in the inability to fully express the operating characteristics and state of a gearbox. To address this problem, our study proposes a gearbox fault diagnosis method based on multi-sensor deep spatiotemporal feature representation. This method utilizes two vibration sensors to obtain the vibration information of the gearbox. A fault diagnosis model (PCNN–GRU) combined with a parallel convolutional neural network (PCNN) and gated recurrent unit (GRU) was used to fuse the gearbox vibration information. The parallel convolutional neural network was used to extract the spatial information of the vibration signals collected by different position sensors, and the timing information was mined through the gated recurrent unit. The deep spatiotemporal features that fuse the multi-sensor spatial and temporal information were composed. The collected multi-sensor vibration signals were directly input into the PCNN–GRU model, and an end-to-end intelligent diagnosis of the gearbox faults was realized. Finally, through experimental verification, the accuracy rate of this model can reach up to 99.92%. Compared with other models, this model has a higher diagnostic accuracy and stability.

Keywords: gearbox; multi-sensor fusion; convolutional neural network; gated recurrent unit; spatiotemporal features

MSC: 68T01

1. Introduction

The gearbox is a common rotating mechanical device used to transmit power, and it is widely used in various fields. Once the gear box breaks down, it will directly affect industrial production and daily life [1,2]. Severe cases may even cause personal injury and serious economic losses [3]. Therefore, carrying out a fault diagnosis on—as well as the timely detection and troubleshooting of—a gearbox and its key components plays a key role in ensuring the healthy operation of mechanical equipment and reducing equipment maintenance costs. The gearbox has a complex structure, and the interaction between its various parts during operation is accompanied by the interference of environmental noise [4]. The means with which to extract useful information from vibration signals containing complex information and interference components, along with realizing the intelligent diagnosis of gearboxes and its key component failures have particularly important practical significance for the normal operation of mechanical equipment and the improvement of production efficiencies.

Methods for the fault diagnosis of gearboxes can generally be divided into three categories: signal-processing-based methods [5], traditional machine learning-based methods [6], and deep learning-based methods [7]. The signal-processing method mainly completes the fault diagnosis of the gearbox by analyzing the acquired vibration signal and extracting the characteristic information that can reflect the health condition [8]. The methods based on signal processing are usually diagnosed and analyzed from the time domain, frequency domain, and time–frequency domain. Although the methods based on signal processing have made some achievements in the fault diagnosis of rotating equipment such as gearboxes, they require strong manual experience and theoretical knowledge reserves in the process of diagnosis [9,10]. Especially in the face of massive data collection in engineering, it is difficult to realize automatic and intelligent fault diagnosis.

The fault diagnosis method based on traditional machine learning methods mainly extracts useful feature indexes that can represent vibration signals through signal processing methods [11]. Additionally, a shallow machine learning method to perform pattern recognition and to complete the intelligent diagnosis of gearbox faults can be conducted [12]. The commonly used shallow machine learning methods mainly include the BP neural network [13], the support vector machine (SVM) [14], the extreme learning machine (ELM) [15], and other models. Although the traditional machine learning algorithm can realize the intelligent diagnosis of faults, it improves the efficiency and accuracy of a fault diagnosis to a certain extent [16]. However, there is still the limitation that the manual feature extraction of vibration signals is required, and existing feature-extraction methods still rely on signal-processing methods. At the same time, whether the feature extraction is good or not will have a direct impact on the subsequent pattern recognition and classification accuracy [17,18].

The concept of deep learning was first proposed by scholars such as Hinton [19], and it has been widely used in image processing and in other directions. In recent years, more and more scholars have applied deep learning models to conduct a fault diagnosis of mechanical equipment. Compared with the traditional fault diagnosis method of the machine learning model, the fault diagnosis method based on a deep learning model does not need manual feature extraction. Using the stacked multi-layer nonlinear layers in the deep learning model can automatically complete the mining of latent features inside the signal [20]. The dependence on signal-processing-based feature-extraction methods and the influence of human experience on feature extraction are reduced. The generalization performance and adaptability of the fault diagnosis method are improved [21]. Huang et al. [22] input the vibration signal of the gearbox that was decomposed by the wavelet packet into the multi-scale CNN and realized the effective classification of the faults. This method combines the multi-scale characteristics of WPD and the powerful classification ability of CNN, without the complicated manual feature-extraction steps adopted. This end-to-end intelligent fault diagnosis is worth learning. Jin et al. [23] proposed a light neural network based on CNN that can realize the effective diagnosis of rotating machinery faults, such as gearboxes, with fewer parameters, and it maintains a good diagnostic performance under different working conditions. However, the scale of this light neural network is small and the number of parameters is limited, which is prone to overfitting problems in the training process. Yin et al. [24] used LSTM with cosine loss to improve the classification ability of wind turbine gearbox faults. By introducing memory units and gating mechanisms, LSTM can effectively capture and maintain long-term dependencies of information, making it perform well in processing long sequence data. Miao et al. [25] used GRU for the real-time status monitoring of planetary gearboxes and introduced dropout technology to reduce the requirements for training data, which has good real-time diagnostic capabilities. GRU has a more compact structure than LSTM, reducing the number of required parameters. Thus, the GRU model is relatively light and is easier to train and compute. If CNN and GRU can be combined to obtain the deep spatiotemporal features of spatial information and temporal information, good results may be obtained.

With the continuous improvement of sensor technology, sensors are used to obtain various signals that can effectively characterize the operating status of equipment. Additionally, the use of the acquired signal to analyze the health status of mechanical equipment has been widely studied by, and has been of interest for, many scholars in recent years [26]. In fault diagnoses, signals such as vibration, acoustic emission, oil, and temperature are commonly used for analysis. Compared with other signals, vibration signal detection technology is more mature and is easy to operate; it also contains a wealth of useful information, such that it is often used to analyze the health status of rotating machinery. At the same time, thanks to the advancement of artificial intelligence technology, fault diagnosis methods have also developed rapidly. In particular, the advancement of machine learning and deep learning methods has gradually reduced the dependence on expert experience and human judgment for fault diagnoses [27]. Intelligent fault diagnosis has gradually become an important direction for gearbox fault diagnosis.

In summary, this paper proposes a gearbox fault diagnosis method based on multi-sensor deep spatiotemporal feature representation. The contributions of this paper are as follows:

(1) The vibration signal obtained by a single sensor is susceptible to noise interference and cannot effectively characterize the operating state and fault characteristics of the gearbox. At the same time, it is also necessary to obtain a more effective and stable gearbox fault diagnosis model. A fault diagnosis model based on the PCNN–GRU fusion of multi-sensor information is proposed.

(2) On the basis of CNN–GRU, a parallel CNN combined with the GRU fault diagnosis model is proposed to fuse the vibration signal information acquired by the multiple sensors. Additionally, SoftMax was used to identify and complete the intelligent diagnosis of gearbox "end" to "end".

(3) A fault diagnosis experiment platform was designed and built, and the validity and stability of the model proposed in this paper were verified by comparing it against other related models.

The remainder of this paper is organized as follows: Section 2 introduces the relevant background of this paper, including the CNN, GRU, and multi-sensor information fusion technology; Section 3 introduces the construction of the relevant fault diagnosis model in this paper; Section 4 introduces the construction of the gearbox fault diagnosis experiment platform and the data collection and division; Section 5 is the experimental analysis and verification section; and, lastly, Section 6 contains the conclusion of this paper.

2. Principle Introduction

2.1. CNN

Convolutional neural networks (CNNs) are feedforward neural networks with a deep structure. They have been widely used in the field of fault diagnosis, and their main structures include convolutional layers, pooling layers, and fully connected layers [28]. CNNs extract features through multiple-stacked convolutional layers and pooling layers, and they complete the output of features through fully connected layers [29].

2.1.1. Convolutional Layer

The convolutional layer is the core component of CNNs and is the basic unit of a CNN. The convolutional layer has the characteristics of weight sharing, which can effectively reduce the parameters of the deep network during the training process. It reduces the complexity of the model and improves the training speed [30]. In CNN, each convolutional layer contains multiple convolutional kernels, and the optimal parameters of these convolutional kernels are obtained through the backpropagation algorithm. At the same time, the convolution kernel is used as a filter to effectively extract the key features of the input information. The inner product operation is performed between the input information and the convolution kernel [31]. Usually, after the convolution operation between the input data and the convolution kernel, a bias item needs to be added to the result to obtain the final output result. Its calculation formula is shown in Formula (1):

$$x_j^l = f\left(\sum_{i\in M_j}^{n} x_i^{l-1} * k_{i,j}^l + b_j^l\right) \tag{1}$$

In Formula (1), l is the number of convolutional layers and x_j^l is the output result of the l-th convolutional layer. x_i^{l-1} is the input information of the l-th convolutional layer. $k_{i,j}^l$ is the convolution kernel of the l-th convolutional layer and b_j^l is the bias item. $f(\bullet)$ is the activation function. M_j denotes input data.

In the calculation process of the convolutional layer, the size of the output information is mainly expressed by Formula (2):

$$O_1 = \frac{H_1 - W_1 + 2 \times P}{S} + 1 \tag{2}$$

In Formula (2), O_1 is the size of the output information. H_1 is the size of the input information. W_1 is the size of the convolution kernel. P is the zero complement operation in the convolution process. S is the step size of the convolution operation.

2.1.2. Pooling Layer

In CNNs, a pooling layer is usually added after the convolutional layer. The pooling layer can select features and can effectively reduce the output feature dimension. While retaining useful features, the calculation amount and parameters of the network are effectively reduced, and the calculation efficiency is improved [32]. Therefore, this is also called the downsampling layer, and it can also prevent overfitting from occurring. The pooling layer is mainly divided into two types: average pooling and maximum pooling. Average pooling averages the values within a range. Max pooling is to keep the maximum value in the range [33]. Formula (3) is the calculation formula for the output size of the pooling layer:

$$O_2 = \frac{H_2 - W_2}{S} + 1 \tag{3}$$

In Formula (3), O_2 is the output size of the pooling layer; H_2 is the size of the input information; and W_2 is the size of the pooling window.

2.1.3. Activation Function

In practical problems, most of the problems are nonlinear problems. The activation function can map the output linear results to a nonlinear space such that the neural network can learn and train nonlinear models as well as improve the ability of the neural network to deal with nonlinear problems. Sigmoid, Tanh, and ReLU are commonly used activation functions [34].

2.1.4. Fully Connected Layer

The role of the fully connected layer is that it is mainly used for classification. The fully connected layer is often set after multi-layer convolution and pooling. It can effectively integrate the feature information obtained by multi-layer convolution kernel pooling. The SoftMax logistic regression function is often used for classification. The SoftMax function can map the input to a real number between 0 and 1. All neurons in the previous layer of the fully connected layer are connected to neurons in the fully connected layer [35]. Therefore, the parameters and calculation amount in this layer are often relatively large. The calculation expression for the forward propagation of the fully connected layer is shown in Formula (4):

$$Z_j^l = f\left(\sum_{k=i}^{n} w_i^l x_i^l + b_j^l\right) \tag{4}$$

In Formula (4), i represents the number and l represents the number of layers. w_i^l represents the connection weight between the i-th neuron of the l-th layer and the i-th neuron of the neurons of the previous layer. b_j^l is the bias item of the j-th neuron in the l-th layer. $f(\bullet)$ is the activation function.

2.2. GRU

A gated recurrent unit (GRU) is a simplified form of a long short-term memory (LSTM) model. Compared with LSTM, GRU has a simpler structure that can efficiently mine the inner connection and long-term information of a time series [36]. Compared with the traditional RNN, GRU not only has smaller training parameters, but it can also effectively solve the problem of gradient disappearance. Structurally, only two gates are included in the GRU—the update gate and the reset gate—both of which belong to the gating mechanism [37]. The GRU gating mechanism is crucial for the correct operation of the model. Specifically, resetting the part and previous hidden states play an important role in determining candidate hidden states. The structure of the GRU in this study is shown in Figure 1:

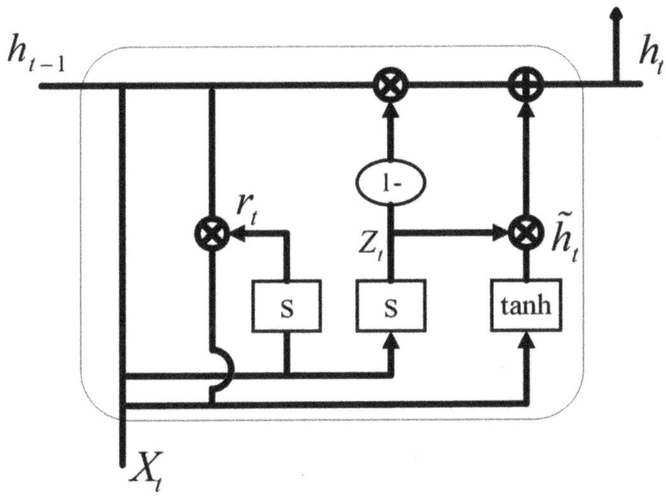

Figure 1. GRU structure diagram.

In a GRU, the reset gate helps the model decide how much of the previous hidden state should be forgotten or reset. It determines which parts of the previous hidden state are relevant to the current step of the model. The reset gate is usually a sigmoid function that takes as input the concatenation of the current input and the previous hidden state. Candidate hidden states are intermediate states computed using the reset gate and the current input. It is combined with the previous hidden state, considering the update gate, to produce the final hidden state of the GRU.

The states of the update gate z_t and the reset gate r_t are obtained by the output state h_{t-1} at the previous moment and the input data x_t at this time. Among them, the update gate is used to evaluate the importance of the information at the last moment to determine the size of the information transmitted to the current hidden layer. Its calculation formula is shown in Formula (5):

$$z_t = \sigma(w_z x_t + w_z h_{t-1} + b_z) \tag{5}$$

In Formula (5), σ represents the sigmoid function, such that the result is distributed between 0 and 1. Thus, 1 means it retains information completely, and 0 means it ignores information completely. w_z and w_z are denoted as weights and biases, respectively. The reset gate is used to determine the information size of the previous moment that needs to be ignored. Its calculation formula is shown in Formula (6):

$$r_t = \sigma(w_r x_t + w_r h_{t-1} + b_r) \tag{6}$$

In Formula (6), σ represents the sigmoid function; w_r and b_r represent the weight and bias, respectively. The information $\widetilde{h}_t$ at the current moment can be obtained by Formula (7):

$$\widetilde{h}_t = \tanh(w_h x_t + r_t \otimes w_h h_{t-1}) \tag{7}$$

In Formula (7), $\otimes$ is the Hadamard product. Tanh is the hyperbolic tangent function used to distribute the result between -1 and 1. w_h is the weight. Then, the final output result Ht is obtained according to Formula (8):

$$h_t = z_t \otimes h_{t-1} + (1 - z_t) \otimes \widetilde{h}_t \tag{8}$$

where h_t is the final output result, z_t is the update gate, and $\widetilde{h}_t$ is obtained by Formula (7).

2.3. *Multi-Sensor Information Fusion*

Multi-sensor information fusion can effectively reduce the information loss caused by a single sensor, and it can improve the accuracy and stability of fault diagnosis [38]. The method of multi-sensor information fusion is mainly divided into three levels: the data level, feature level, and decision level [39].

2.3.1. Fusion at the Data Level

Fusion at the data level refers to the direct fusion of the information acquired by multiple sensors; then, feature-extraction and pattern-recognition operations on the fused information are performed. They belong to the most primitive of information fusion approaches.

2.3.2. Fusion at the Feature Level

The information is fused at the feature level. That is, the feature-extraction operation is performed separately on the information obtained by multiple sensors, and the features representing different sensor information are fused. Finally, a pattern recognition method is used to recognize the fusion features.

2.3.3. Fusion at the Decision-Making Level

Fusion at the decision-making level is a type of advanced fusion method. After the information of different sensors is preprocessed, separate decisions are made on the tested equipment. Finally, different decisions are fused to obtain a final decision with overall consistency.

The advantages and disadvantages of the different levels of the fusion methods are shown in Table 1:

Table 1. Advantages and disadvantages of the different integration methods.

Information Fusion Method	Advantages	Disadvantages
Data level	Less information loss, higher fusion accuracy	The amount of calculation is too large, and the information needs to come from the same type of sensor
Feature level	Can effectively compress and extract information	Recognition accuracy depends on whether the proposed features are valid
Decision-making level	Has strong anti-interference ability, no requirement for sensor type	Large amount of information loss and poor accuracy

Due to the information fusion at the feature level, different sensor information can be effectively compressed. Therefore, this paper proposes a fault diagnosis model combining a parallel convolutional neural network and gated recurrent unit (PCNN–GRU) to automatically mine the intrinsic characteristics of vibration signals acquired by the sensors at different positions; in addition, complete information fusion is used at the feature level.

3. Fault Diagnosis Model Construction

According to the complexity of the network model and the scale of the data obtained from the designed fault diagnosis experiment, as well as multiple experiments to adjust and optimize the model parameters, a fault diagnosis model is constructed. The structure of the fault diagnosis model proposed in this paper based on PCNN–GRU fusion of multi-sensor information is shown in Figure 2. The model structure parameters are shown in Table 2.

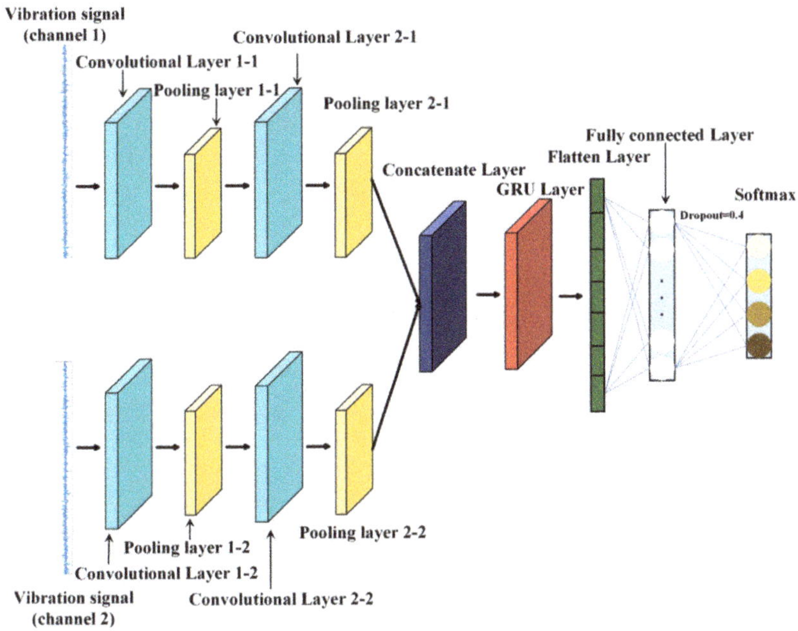

Figure 2. The PCNN–GRU model structure diagram.

Table 2. The parameters of each layer of the PCNN–GRU model.

Network Layer	Number of Convolution Kernels	Convolution Kernel Size	Step Length	Activation Function	Output Size
Convolutional layer 1–1	32	64	8	ReLU	256 × 32
Pooling layer 1–1	32	4	1	—	64 × 32
Convolutional layer 2–1	64	5	1	ReLU	64 × 64
Pooling layer 2–1	64	2	1	—	32 × 64
Convolutional layer 1–2	32	64	8	ReLU	256 × 32
Pooling layer 1–2	32	4	1	—	64 × 32
Convolutional layer 2–2	64	5	1	ReLU	64 × 64
Pooling layer 2–2	64	2	1	—	32 × 64
Fusion layer	—	—	—	—	32 × 128
GRU layer	16	—	—	Tanh	32 × 16
Fully connected layer	32	—	—	Tanh	32
SoftMax	4	—	—	SoftMax	4

From Figure 2 and Table 2, it can be seen that the model mainly consists of two parallel convolutional neural network layers, a fusion layer, a gated loop unit layer, and two fully connected layers (the last layer is the SoftMax layer for the final classification). Parallel convolutional neural networks are composed of two one-dimensional convolutional layers and two one-dimensional pooling layers. Additionally, the model structure parameters of the upper and lower channels are set as the same. The number of convolutional kernels, the kernel size, and the stride of convolutional layer 1–1 and convolutional layer 1–2 were all set to 32, 64, and 8, respectively. The number of convolution kernels, the kernel size, and the step size of convolution layer 2–1 and convolution layer 2–2 were all set to 64, 5, and 1, respectively. Among them, the padding mode and activation function of the convolutional layer were set to 'same' and 'ReLU', respectively. The size and stride of the pooling layers 1–1 and 1–2 were set to 4 and 1, respectively, and the size and stride of the pooling layers 2–1 and 2–2 were set to 2 and 1, respectively, both of which adopted maximum pooling. Through the joint action of the continuous convolutional layer and the pooling layer, the spatial characteristics of the vibration signals acquired by sensors at different positions were continuously mined and fused through the fusion layer. The spatial features obtained by merging the position information of different sensors were further mined for time series information; this was achieved via a GRU with 16 neurons to obtain the final multi-sensor deep spatiotemporal features. Finally, the expanded features are classified using a fully connected layer with thirty-two neurons and a SoftMax layer with four neurons, thus completing the end-to-end intelligent diagnosis of gearbox faults. That is, the effective identification of different fault states can be completed by directly inputting the vibration signal of the gearbox into the model. The overall flowchart of the fault diagnosis model is shown in Figure 3.

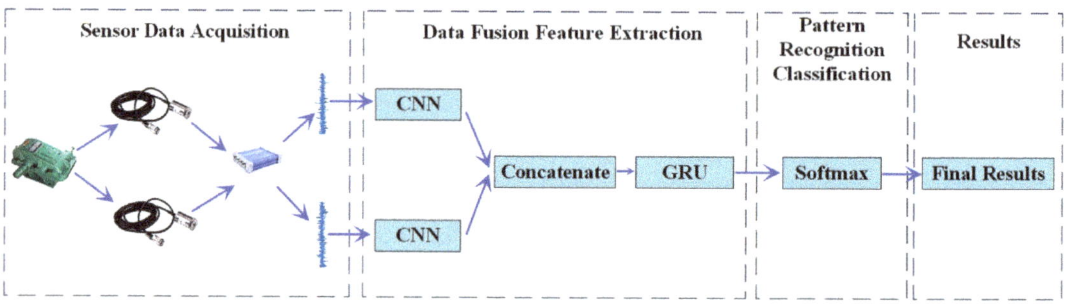

Figure 3. Overall flowchart of the fault diagnosis model.

It can be seen from Figure 3 that the overall process is divided into four parts. The first part is the sensor data-collection part. The vibration signals of the gearbox are collected separately by dual sensors and output to the computer through the acquisition card to obtain the vibration signals of the gearbox. The second part is the data feature-extraction part. The gearbox vibration signal is input into the parallel CNN to mine the spatial information of the vibration signal, the fusion layer is used to fuse the spatial information of the different sensors, and the GRU model was further used to extract the time series information to obtain the deep spatiotemporal features that integrate the spatial and temporal information of multiple sensors. The third part is the feature-extraction part. The SoftMax layer was used for pattern recognition and classification, and then the classification information was finally output to obtain the final result.

4. Gearbox Fault Diagnosis Experiment

4.1. Analysis of Typical Fault Forms of Gearboxes

The gearbox is a complex mechanical system composed of gears, rolling bearings, bearing end covers, transmission shafts, boxes, and other parts. Gearbox casing has a good sealing performance and rigidity, and it plays the role of supporting the rotating mechanism and isolating the external environment [40]. In actual production and life, the faults and failures of gearboxes usually occur on important transmission parts such as gears, transmission shafts, and bearings. The failures caused by the failure of these transmission components account for 89% of gearbox failures, and the highest probability of gear failure is 60%, which is followed by bearing failure at 19%. When a gear fails, it usually occurs at the tooth surface and tooth root of a pair of gears meshing with each other. Four failure modes of wear, pitting, binding, and tooth fracture account for 92% of the total failure modes of gears [41]. These failure modes are important causes of gear failure and are among the main failure modes of gears; in addition, the failure probability caused by tooth fracture is the highest at 41%. Followed by the fatigue pitting failure of gears at 31%, gear teeth gluing and wear account for 10%, respectively [42].

4.2. Construction of Gearbox Fault Experiment Platform

4.2.1. Experimental Platform Equipment Selection

The experimental devices used in this paper were the following: a G7R5/P011T4 frequency converter, a YE3-100L2-4 three-phase asynchronous motor, a JZQ250 gearbox, a CAYD051V piezoelectric acceleration sensor, a YE6231 data acquisition card, a FZ-A-12 magnetic powder brake, couplings, pulleys, and PCs.

4.2.2. Gear Failure Settings

From Section 4.1 (Analysis of Typical Fault Forms of Gearboxes), it can be seen that the faults caused by gears account for the largest proportion, followed by bearing faults. There are not enough gear samples in this experiment, and gear failures caused by tooth fracture, pitting, and wear account for 82% of gear failures. Therefore, this paper mainly sets three failure forms of broken teeth: both the pitting and wear with the highest proportion of gear failures, and the one normal form that has a total of four states of gear samples for subsequent experimental development, data collection, and intelligent diagnosis. These are shown in Figure 4.

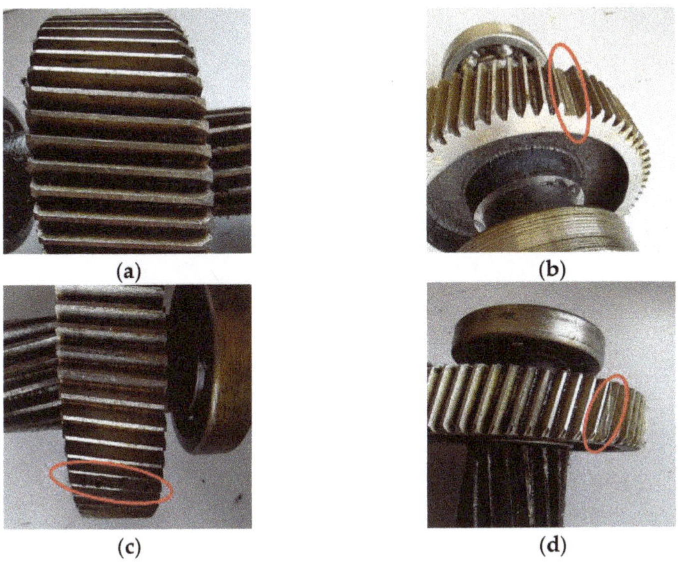

Figure 4. Gear fault setting: (**a**) normal; (**b**) broken; (**c**) pitting; and (**d**) wear.

In Figure 4a–d, the four gear states of normal, broken, pitting, and wear, respectively, are shown. The breakage shown in Figure 4b is a serious form of gear failure, where generally one or more teeth of the gear is broken. When the gear is overloaded, eccentrically loaded, or subjected to a large impact during work, the teeth may break. Figure 4c shows an example that is prone to pitting failure on the root surface near the pitch line. The occurrence of gear pitting makes the meshing performance of the gears worse, which easily generates large vibrations. The wear in Figure 4d is mainly a failure form caused by insufficient lubrication or the entry of hard abrasives such as metal particles, dust, and metal oxides onto the working surface of the gear during transmission, resulting in severe wear on the gear contact surface.

4.2.3. Experimental Platform Construction

In order to complete the construction of the gear box fault experiment platform, the relevant experimental schemes were set up based on the abovementioned fault forms and the selected experimental equipment. The connection relationship of the relevant experimental equipment is shown in Figure 5.

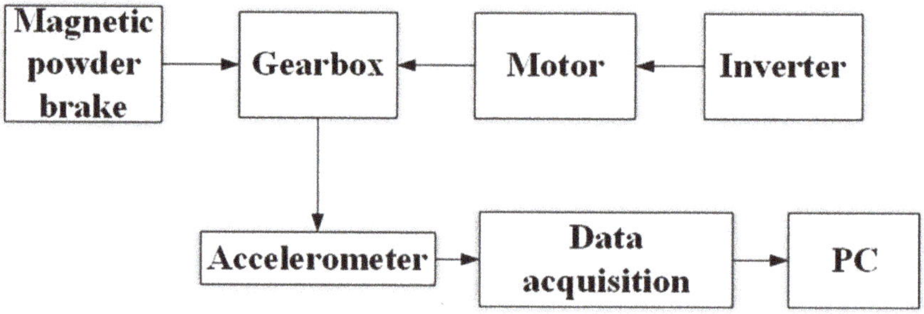

Figure 5. Experimental equipment connection diagram.

It can be seen from Figure 5 that, during the experiment, the three-phase asynchronous motor, gearbox, and magnetic powder brake were first fixed on the test bench. The three-phase asynchronous motor was connected to the power supply through the frequency converter. The motor and the gearbox were connected by a pulley. The magnetic powder brake was connected with the gearbox through a coupling. The acceleration sensor was fixed on the bearing seats at both ends of the high-speed shaft of the gearbox and connected to the data acquisition card to transmit the acquired vibration data to the PC for analysis. Figure 6 shows the physical map of the gear box fault test platform.

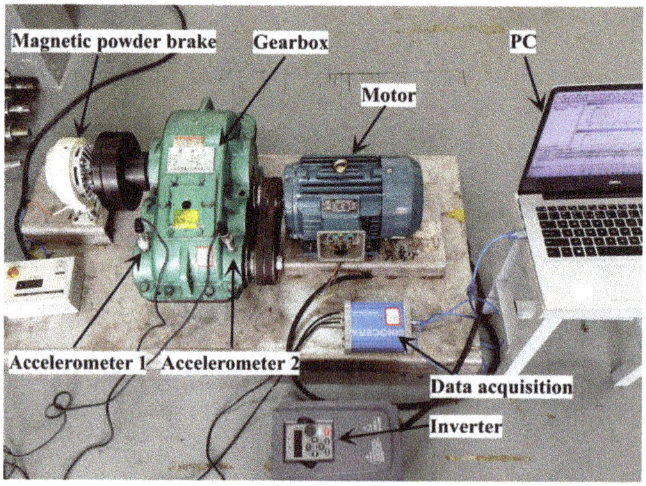

Figure 6. The physical picture of the gear box fault experiment platform.

In the experiment, the frequency converter was used to control and adjust the motor speed so as to realize the control and adjustment of the gearbox speed. The relationship between the motor speed and the output frequency of the inverter is shown in Formula (9):

$$v = \frac{1500f}{f_{\max}} \tag{9}$$

In Formula (9), v is the motor speed and f is the frequency adjusted by the inverter. The constant 1500 is the theoretical output maximum value of the motor selected in the experiment. $f_{\max}$ is the maximum value of the frequency converter output frequency, and $f_{\max}$ is taken as 50 Hz. The experimental information is shown in Table 3.

Table 3. Experimental information.

Type	Gearbox Status	Motor Speed/Hz	Brake Load/A	Data Length	Number of Datasets
1	Broken	30	0.5	2048	300 × 2
2	Pitting	30	0.5	2048	300 × 2
3	Normal	30	0.5	2048	300 × 2
4	Wear	30	0.5	2048	300 × 2

It can be seen from Table 3 that the sampling frequency was set to 6 k Hz in this paper. The experimental load was set to 0.5 A through the magnetic powder brake controller. The data acquisition card and sensor were used to collect the vibration data when the speed was 900 r/min—that is, when the output power of the frequency converter was 30 Hz as the analysis object. A total of 300 groups were collected for each state, and since there are two sensor channels, the number of groups for each state is 300 × 2. The sample length of each group is 2048, and the four states total 1200 × 2 groups.

4.2.4. Experimental Data Design

The vibration signals of different positions of the gearbox obtained by Sensor 1 (Channel 1) and Sensor 2 (Channel 2) in the abovementioned gearbox fault diagnosis experiment platform were designed. The data introduction is shown in Table 4.

Table 4. Data introduction.

Type	Gearbox Status	Number of Training Sets	Number of Validation Sets	Number of Test Sets	Label
1	Broken	180 × 2048 × 2	60 × 2048 × 2	60 × 2048 × 2	1 0 0 0
2	Pitting	180 × 2048 × 2	60 × 2048 × 2	60 × 2048 × 2	0 1 0 0
3	Normal	180 × 2048 × 2	60 × 2048 × 2	60 × 2048 × 2	0 0 1 0
4	Wear	180 × 2048 × 2	60 × 2048 × 2	60 × 2048 × 2	0 0 0 1

It can be seen from Table 4 that firstly, the vibration signals collected by the two acceleration sensors are constructed into a dual-channel sample. The training set, verification set, and test set were randomly divided according to a 6:2:2 ratio—that is, 180 sets of training, 60 sets of verification, and 60 sets of testing for each state of a single sensor. A total of 720 sets of training samples, 240 sets of verification samples, and 240 sets of test samples were obtained in the four states. There are 2048 points in each sample, thus the sample composition of each sensor channel is as follows: the training set structure is 720 × 2048; the validation set sample structure is 240 × 2048; and the test set sample structure is 240 × 2048. Two sensor samples of the same state of the gear are regarded as the same class. The labels of broken teeth, pitting, normal, and worn states as 1, 2, 3, and 4, respectively, were set. The labels were one-hot encoded—that is, the four labels 1, 2, 3, and 4 correspond to 1 0 0 0, 0 1 0 0, 0 0 1 0, and 0 0 0 1, respectively. Additionally, the dual-channel training samples were input into the model for training. The upper channel of PCNN receives samples from Sensor 1, and the lower channel receives samples from Sensor 2.

5. Experimental Analysis and Verification

5.1. Experimental Analysis

Through using the experimental data information in Tables 3 and 4, the time-domain and frequency-domain diagrams of the vibration signals of the two channels and four states of the gearbox were obtained. These are shown in Figures 7 and 8, respectively.

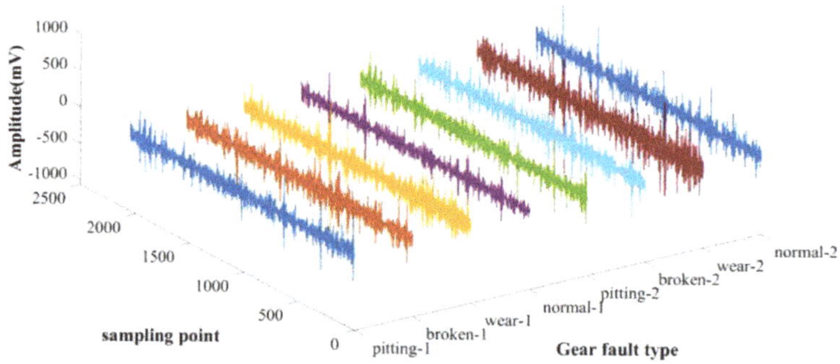

Figure 7. Gearbox data time-domain diagram.

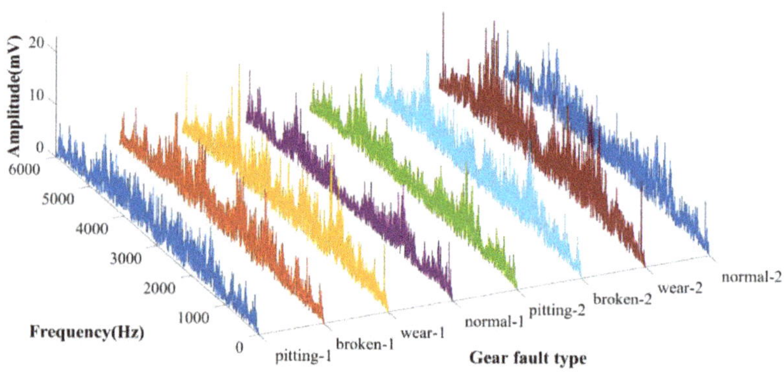

Figure 8. Gearbox data frequency-domain plot.

The time-domain plot of Figure 7 is a representation of a signal on a time axis, thus showing the amplitude of the signal as a function of time. The frequency-domain plot of Figure 8 is a representation of the signal on the frequency axis, showing the energy distribution of the signal at different frequencies. By decomposing a signal into its frequency components, it provides the frequency characteristics of the signal. From Figures 7 and 8, it can be seen intuitively that the time-domain signals and frequency-domain signals received by Sensor 1 and Sensor 2, respectively, in the four states of the gearbox are evidently different and both present periodic fluctuations.

This experiment was run on a Windows 11 64-bit operating system with 8 GB of running memory. The software and hardware configuration conditions were as follows: Python version 3.10.4; the Spyder version 5.2.2; and TensorFlow version 2.9.1. The model training parameter settings were as follows: number of iterations was set to 50; batch_size set to 32; an Adam optimizer was used; the initial learning rate was set to 0.001; the learning rate decay value was set to 0.02; and the dropout ratio was set to 0.4. To avoid the effects of chance, the experiment process was repeated ten times. During the training process of one experiment, the accuracy change curves and loss rate change curves of the training and verification sets are shown in Figures 9 and 10, respectively.

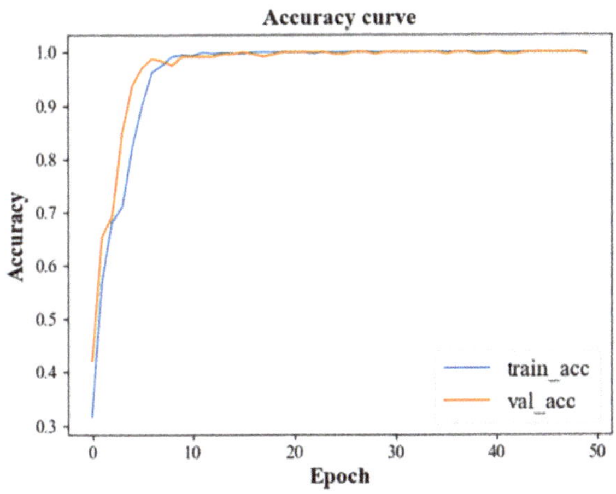

Figure 9. Accuracy change curve.

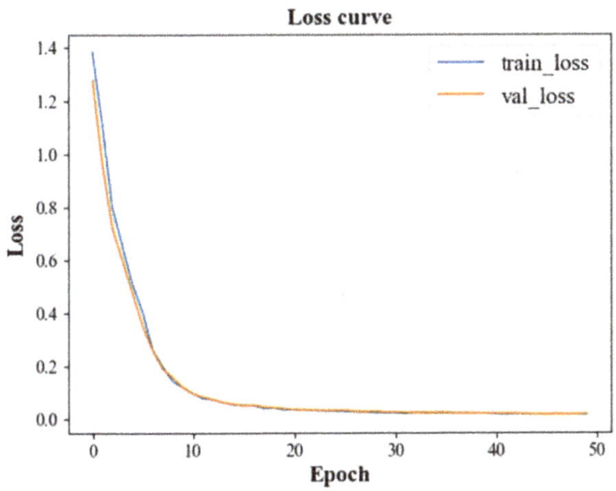

Figure 10. Loss rate change curve.

It can be seen from Figure 9 that, with the iterative process, the accuracy of the training set and the verification set were significantly improved. After the 20th iteration, it is essentially stable and tends to be flat. The accuracy curves of the training set and the verification set ultimately coincide after the 20th iteration, and the accuracy rates are both 1. It can be seen from the loss rate change curve in Figure 10 that the loss rate of the training set and the verification set gradually decreases with the increase in the number of iterations. Additionally, the values are essentially stabilized and leveled off after the 20th iteration. The loss rate curves of the training set and the verification set also essentially coincide after the 20th iteration, and the loss rate is close to 0. Through the analysis of the above two figures, the model is shown to converge well and that it has been fitted effectively.

The test set was input into the trained model and the obtained test results were visualized through the confusion matrix. The confusion matrix of the test set is shown in Figure 11.

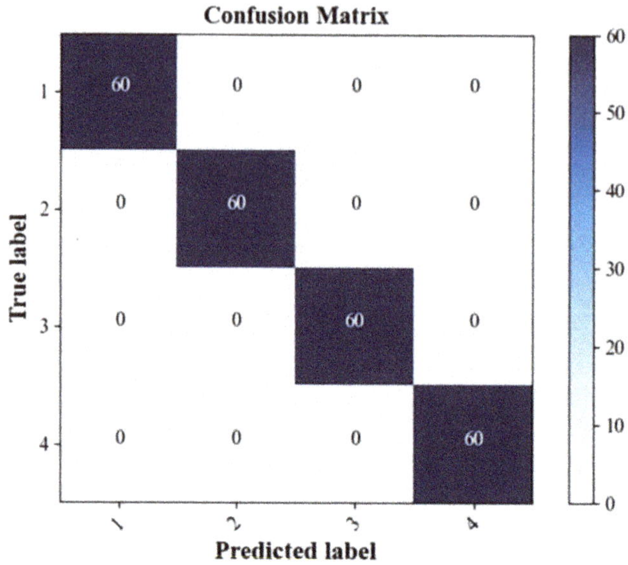

Figure 11. Confusion matrix of the test results.

It can be seen from Figure 11 that all of the samples in the test set were recognized correctly and the overall recognition rate is 100%. It shows that the PCNN–GRU fault diagnosis model fused with multi-sensor information can effectively identify different fault states of the gearbox. In order to prevent the randomness of the results, the test results of the 10 experiments of the model are shown in Table 5.

Table 5. Test results of ten experiments of PCNN–GRU

Number of Times	Loss Rate/%	Accuracy/%	Average Accuracy Rate/%	Average Loss Rate/%
1	0.06	100	99.92	0.09
2	0.11	99.58		
3	0.11	100		
4	0.18	100		
5	0.04	99.58		
6	0.13	100		
7	0.18	100		
8	0.03	100		
9	0.09	100		
10	0.01	100		

It can be seen from Table 5 that the highest recognition rate in the 10 experiments is 100%, the lowest is 99.58%, and the average recognition rate is 99.92%. This shows that the PCNN–GRU fusion sensor information gearbox fault diagnosis method proposed in this paper has a good recognition effect.

5.2. t-SNE Visualization

t-SNE was used to visualize the output features of each layer during the testing process of the first experiment of the model. Figure 12 shows the feature distribution of different layers of the model.

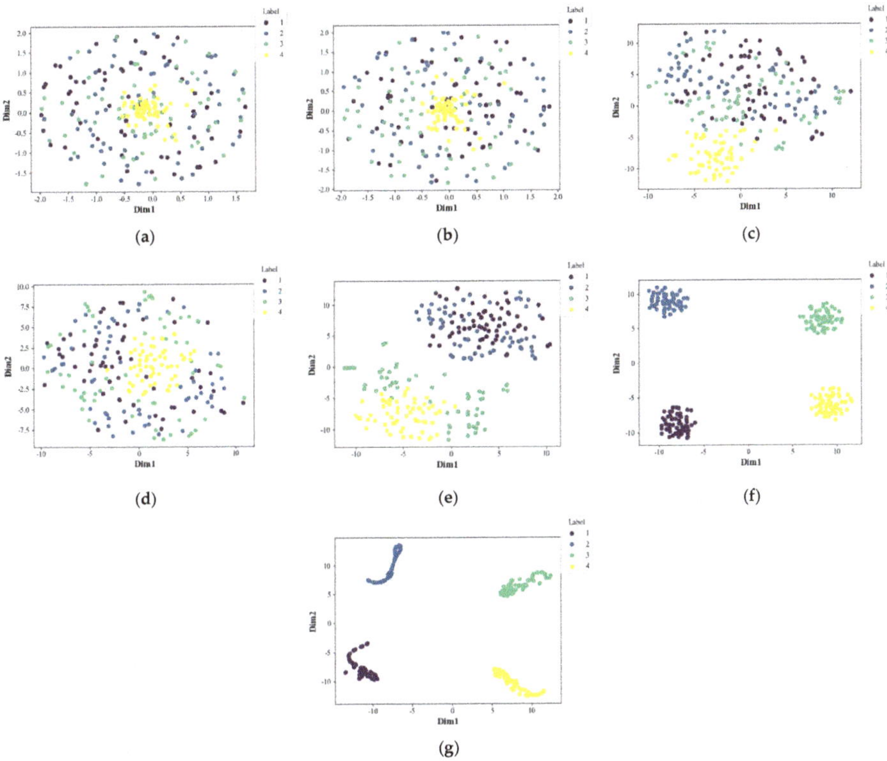

Figure 12. Distribution of the features in each layer of the PCNN−GRU model: (**a**) feature distribution of the upper channel raw data; (**b**) the lower channel raw data feature distribution; (**c**) the convolution layer 2–1 feature distribution; (**d**) the convolution layer 2−2 feature distribution; (**e**) the feature distribution of the fusion layer; (**f**) the feature distribution of GRU layers; and (**g**) the output layer feature distribution.

It can be seen from Figure 12a,b that the distribution of the four states of raw data from different sensors greatly overlaps, and that different states cannot be effectively distinguished. It can be seen from Figure 12c,d that after the second layer of convolution, the raw data of Sensor 1 and Sensor 2 begin to gather in the same categories, but it is still difficult to distinguish them. It can be seen from Figure 12e,f that after fusing the features of the upper and lower channels of the convolutional neural network, the distinction of different categories of features and the aggregation of the same category of features are significantly improved. Additionally, after passing through the GRU layer, the four states can be clearly distinguished. As shown in Figure 12g, the final fusion features are effectively recognized at the recognition layer, and the four states are clearly distinguished. This is consistent with the final recognition results and the display of the confusion matrix. It shows that the PCNN–GRU method can mine useful features that can characterize the different fault states of gearboxes from vibration signals.

5.3. Comparison of Methods

In order to illustrate the effectiveness and advantages of the method in this paper, the PCNN–GRU method in this chapter is compared with the following methods:

(1) PCNN: The vibration data of Sensor 1 and Sensor 2 were input into the PCNN;
(2) Upper channel (Sensor 1) + CNN–GRU: Only the upper channel (Sensor 1) vibration signal was used to input into the CNN–GRU;

(3) Lower channel (Sensor 2) + CNN–GRU: Only the lower channel (Sensor 2) vibration signal was used to input into the CNN–GRU;
(4) Upper channel (Sensor 1) + CNN: Only the upper channel (Sensor 1) vibration signal was used to input into the CNN;
(5) Lower channel (Sensor 2) + CNN: Only the vibration signal of the lower channel (Sensor 2) was used to input into the CNN.

Each method was independently trained and tested 10 times. The average recognition rate and average loss rate of the 10 diagnostic results by different methods are shown in Table 6.

Table 6. The average recognition rate and average loss rate of 10 diagnostic results by different methods.

Method	Average Loss Rate of 10 Tests/%	Average Recognition Rate of 10 Tests/%
PCNN–GRU	0.09	99.92
PCNN	5.67	99.42
Sensor 1-CNN–GRU	9.32	96.84
Sensor 2-CNN–GRU	11.12	96.38
Sensor 1-CNN	17.84	94.96
Sensor 2-CNN	24.79	92.92

It can be seen from Table 6 that the PCNN–GRU fusion multi-sensor information gearbox fault diagnosis model proposed in this paper has the highest recognition rate of 99.92%. Additionally, the loss rate is also the lowest at 0.09% (the loss rate refers to the cross-entropy value between the prediction result and the actual value; the lower the loss rate, the closer the prediction result is to the real value, which indicates that the prediction effect of the model is better). Compared with the multi-sensor information fusion method when using only PCNN, the accuracy rate is increased by 0.5% and the loss rate is reduced by 5.58%. This shows that after using GRU to further extract the timing features of multiple sensors, not only has the accuracy rate been improved, but also the obtained results are closer to the actual value. Compared with the method based on a single sensor, the recognition rate has been effectively improved to varying degrees. It is also compared with some models mentioned in the introduction, such as WPD–CNN and LSTM model with cosine loss. Many tests have shown that the PCNN–GRU fusion multi-sensor information gearbox fault diagnosis model proposed in this paper has the highest recognition rate and the lowest loss rate. This shows that multi-sensor information fusion can more comprehensively characterize the fault characteristics of a gearbox, and it can effectively identify different fault states. The box plot of 10 diagnostic results by different methods is shown in Figure 13.

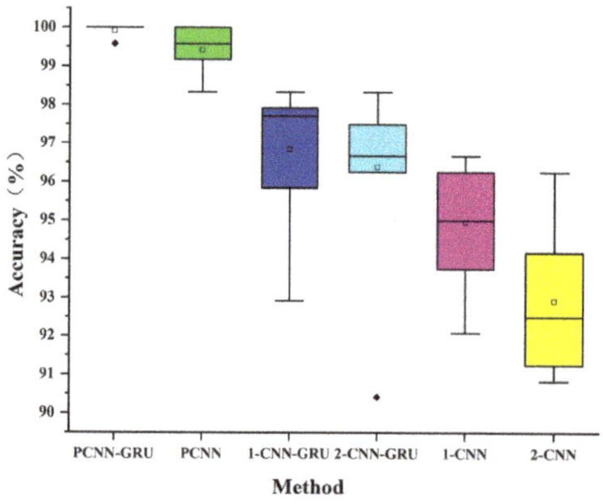

Figure 13. Box plot for the results of the 10 tests.

It can be seen from Figure 13 that the PCNN–GRU method in this chapter has a higher recognition rate than the other methods, and the results of the 10 tests are more concentrated. It also shows that the model recognition effect of the PCNN–GRU fusion multi-sensor information method is more stable, and that the fluctuation is smaller.

6. Conclusions

In this paper, a gearbox fault diagnosis method based on multi-sensor deep spatiotemporal feature representation is proposed. The vibration signals collected by the acceleration sensors at different positions in the gearbox fault test platform are input into the parallel CNN (PCNN) to mine the spatial information of the vibration signals. The fusion layer was used to fuse the spatial information of the different sensors. The GRU model was further used to extract the time series information in order to obtain the deep spatiotemporal features that fuse the spatial and temporal information of the multiple sensors. SoftMax was used for identification, and the intelligent diagnosis of the gearbox end-to-end was completed. The accuracy rate of the 10 tests was 99.92%, which is higher than those of the multi-sensor + parallel CNN and single-sensor-based diagnosis methods, and it also has a higher stability and lower loss rate. This proves that the PCNN–GRU fusion multi-sensor information fault diagnosis method is effective and superior.

Author Contributions: Conceptualization, F.X. and G.W.; methodology, F.X. and J.S.; validation, F.X. and G.W.; investigation, F.X. and E.S.; writing—original draft preparation, F.X. and G.W.; writing—review and editing, F.X. and S.X. All authors have read and agreed to the published version of the manuscript.

Funding: This research was funded by the National Natural Science Foundation of China (52265068), the Natural Science Foundation of Jiangxi Province (20224BAB204050), the Carrier and Equipment Key Laboratory Project of the Ministry of Education (KLCEZ2022-02), and the Project of Jiangxi Provincial Department of Education (GJJ2200627).

Institutional Review Board Statement: Not applicable.

Informed Consent Statement: Not applicable.

Data Availability Statement: The data used to support the findings of this study are available from the corresponding authors upon request.

Conflicts of Interest: The authors declare no conflict of interest.

References

1. Khan, A.; Hwang, H.; Kim, H.S. Synthetic Data Augmentation and Deep Learning for the Fault Diagnosis of Rotating Machines. *Mathematics* **2021**, *9*, 2336. [CrossRef]
2. Liang, X.; Zuo, M.J.; Feng, Z. Dynamic modeling of gearbox faults: A review. *Mech. Syst. Signal Process.* **2018**, *98*, 852–876. [CrossRef]
3. Khalid, S.; Hwang, H.; Kim, H.S. Real-World Data-Driven Machine-Learning-Based Optimal Sensor Selection Approach for Equipment Fault Detection in a Thermal Power Plant. *Mathematics* **2021**, *9*, 2814. [CrossRef]
4. Schmidt, S.; Heyns, P.S.; Gryllias, K.C. A methodology using the spectral coherence and healthy historical data to perform gearbox fault diagnosis under varying operating conditions. *Appl. Acoust.* **2020**, *158*, 107038. [CrossRef]
5. Jiang, Z.; Han, Q.; Xu, X. Fault diagnosis of planetary gearbox based on motor current signal analysis. *Shock Vib.* **2020**, *2020*, 8854776. [CrossRef]
6. Praveenkumar, T.; Saimurugan, M.; Krishnakumar, P.; Ramachandran, K.I. Fault diagnosis of automobile gearbox based on machine learning techniques. *Procedia Eng.* **2014**, *97*, 2092–2098. [CrossRef]
7. Saufi, S.R.; Ahmad, Z.A.B.; Leong, M.S.; Lim, M.H. Gearbox fault diagnosis using a deep learning model with limited data sample. *IEEE Trans. Ind. Inform.* **2020**, *16*, 6263–6271. [CrossRef]
8. Fan, X.; Zuo, M.J. Gearbox fault detection using Hilbert and wavelet packet transform. *Mech. Syst. Signal Process.* **2006**, *20*, 966–982. [CrossRef]
9. Feng, Z.; Zhu, W.; Zhang, D. Time-Frequency demodulation analysis via Vold-Kalman filter for wind turbine planetary gearbox fault diagnosis under nonstationary speeds. *Mech. Syst. Signal Process.* **2019**, *128*, 93–109. [CrossRef]
10. Yoon, J.; He, D.; Van Hecke, B. On the use of a single piezoelectric strain sensor for wind turbine planetary gearbox fault diagnosis. *IEEE Trans. Ind. Electron.* **2015**, *62*, 6585–6593. [CrossRef]

11. Singh, J.; Azamfar, M.; Ainapure, A.; Lee, J. Deep learning-based cross-domain adaptation for gearbox fault diagnosis under variable speed conditions. *Meas. Sci. Technol.* **2020**, *31*, 055601. [CrossRef]
12. Manikandan, S.; Duraivelu, K. Fault diagnosis of various rotating equipment using machine learning approaches–A review. *Proc. Inst. Mech. Eng. Part E J. Process Mech. Eng.* **2021**, *235*, 629–642. [CrossRef]
13. Xia, T.; Jiang, Y.; Zhuo, P.; Xi, L.; Wang, D. Dual-ensemble multi-feedback neural network for gearbox fault diagnosis. *IEEE Trans. Instrum. Meas.* **2021**, *70*, 3519610. [CrossRef]
14. Liao, Y.; Zhang, L.; Li, W. Regrouping particle swarm optimization based variable neural network for gearbox fault diagnosis. *J. Intell. Fuzzy Syst.* **2018**, *34*, 3671–3680. [CrossRef]
15. Zhang, X.; Han, P.; Xu, L.; Zhang, F.; Wang, Y.; Gao, L. Research on bearing fault diagnosis of wind turbine gearbox based on 1DCNN-PSO-SVM. *IEEE Access* **2020**, *8*, 192248–192258. [CrossRef]
16. Wang, Z.; Wang, J.; Wang, Y. An intelligent diagnosis scheme based on generative adversarial learning deep neural networks and its application to planetary gearbox fault pattern recognition. *Neurocomputing* **2018**, *310*, 213–222. [CrossRef]
17. Tong, S.; Li, J.; Cong, F.; Fu, Z.; Tong, Z. Vibration Separation Methodology Compensated by Time-Varying Transfer Function for Fault Diagnosis of Non-Hunting Tooth Planetary Gearbox. *Sensors* **2022**, *22*, 557. [CrossRef]
18. Jia, F.; Lei, Y.; Guo, L.; Lin, J.; Xing, S. A neural network constructed by deep learning technique and its application to intelligent fault diagnosis of machines. *Neurocomputing* **2018**, *272*, 619–628. [CrossRef]
19. Hinton, G.E.; Salakhutdinov, R.R. Reducing the dimensionality of data with neural networks. *Science* **2006**, *313*, 504–507. [CrossRef]
20. He, M.; He, D. Deep learning based approach for bearing fault diagnosis. *IEEE Trans. Ind. Appl.* **2017**, *53*, 3057–3065. [CrossRef]
21. Xu, Y.; Li, Z.; Wang, S.; Li, W.; Sarkodie-Gyan, T.; Feng, S. A hybrid deep-learning model for fault diagnosis of rolling bearings. *Measurement* **2021**, *169*, 108502. [CrossRef]
22. Huang, D.; Zhang, W.A.; Guo, F.; Liu, W.; Shi, X. Wavelet Packet Decomposition-Based Multiscale CNN for Fault Diagnosis of Wind Turbine Gearbox. *IEEE Trans. Cybern.* **2023**, *53*, 443–453. [CrossRef]
23. Jin, T.; Yan, C.; Chen, C.; Yang, Z.; Tian, H.; Wang, S. Light neural network with fewer parameters based on CNN for fault diagnosis of rotating machinery. *Measurement* **2021**, *181*, 109639. [CrossRef]
24. Yin, A.; Yan, Y.; Zhang, Z.; Li, C.; Sánchez, R.-V. Fault Diagnosis of Wind Turbine Gearbox Based on the Optimized LSTM Neural Network with Cosine Loss. *Sensors* **2020**, *20*, 2339. [CrossRef] [PubMed]
25. Miao, X.; Li, S.; Zhu, Y.; An, Z. A novel real-time fault diagnosis method for planetary gearbox using transferable hidden layer. *IEEE Sens. J.* **2020**, *20*, 8403–8412. [CrossRef]
26. Du, Z.; Fan, B.; Chi, J.; Jin, X. Sensor fault detection and its efficiency analysis in air handling unit using the combined neural networks. *Energy Build.* **2014**, *72*, 157–166. [CrossRef]
27. Hussain, S.; Mokhtar, M.; Howe, J.M. Sensor failure detection, identification, and accommodation using fully connected cascade neural network. *IEEE Trans. Ind. Electron.* **2014**, *62*, 1683–1692. [CrossRef]
28. Wang, H.; Xu, J.; Yan, R.; Sun, C.; Chen, X. Intelligent bearing fault diagnosis using multi-head attention-based CNN. *Procedia Manuf.* **2020**, *49*, 112–118. [CrossRef]
29. Chen, J.; Jiang, J.; Guo, X.; Tan, L. A self-Adaptive CNN with PSO for bearing fault diagnosis. *Syst. Sci. Control Eng.* **2021**, *9*, 11–22. [CrossRef]
30. Li, H.; Zhang, Q.; Qin, X.; Sun, Y. K-SVD-based WVD enhancement algorithm for planetary gearbox fault diagnosis under a CNN framework. *Meas. Sci. Technol.* **2019**, *31*, 025003. [CrossRef]
31. Jiang, J.; Bie, Y.; Li, J.; Yang, X.; Ma, G.; Lu, Y.; Zhang, C. Fault diagnosis of the bushing infrared images based on mask R-CNN and improved PCNN joint algorithm. *High Volt.* **2021**, *6*, 116–124. [CrossRef]
32. Ruan, D.; Song, X.; Gühmann, C.; Yan, J. Collaborative optimization of CNN and GAN for bearing fault diagnosis under unbalanced datasets. *Lubricants* **2021**, *9*, 105. [CrossRef]
33. Liu, Y.; Chen, C.; Wang, T.; Cheng, L. An attention enhanced dilated CNN approach for cross-axis industrial robotics fault diagnosis. *Auton. Intell. Syst.* **2022**, *2*, 11. [CrossRef]
34. Wang, J.; Yang, J.; Wang, Y.; Bai, Y.; Zhang, T.; Yao, D. Ensemble decision approach with dislocated time–frequency representation and pre-trained CNN for fault diagnosis of railway vehicle gearboxes under variable conditions. *Int. J. Rail Transp.* **2022**, *10*, 655–673. [CrossRef]
35. Ma, Y.; Jia, X.; Bai, H.; Liu, G.; Wang, G.; Guo, C.; Wang, S. A new fault diagnosis method based on convolutional neural network and compressive sensing. *J. Mech. Sci. Technol.* **2019**, *33*, 5177–5188. [CrossRef]
36. Liu, H.; Ma, R.; Li, D.; Yan, L.; Ma, Z. Machinery fault diagnosis based on deep learning for time series analysis and knowledge graphs. *J. Signal Process. Syst.* **2021**, *93*, 1433–1455. [CrossRef]
37. Tao, Y.; Wang, X.; Sánchez, R.V.; Yang, S.; Bai, Y. Spur gear fault diagnosis using a multilayer gated recurrent unit approach with vibration signal. *IEEE Access* **2019**, *7*, 56880–56889. [CrossRef]
38. Guo, S.; Zhang, B.; Yang, T.; Lyu, D.; Gao, W. Multitask convolutional neural network with information fusion for bearing fault diagnosis and localization. *IEEE Trans. Ind. Electron.* **2019**, *67*, 8005–8015. [CrossRef]
39. Xu, Z.; Bashir, M.; Zhang, W.; Yang, Y.; Wang, X.; Li, C. An intelligent fault diagnosis for machine maintenance using weighted soft-voting rule based multi-attention module with multi-scale information fusion. *Inf. Fusion* **2022**, *86*, 17–29. [CrossRef]

40. Aherwar, A. An investigation on gearbox fault detection using vibration analysis techniques: A review. *Aust. J. Mech. Eng.* **2012**, *10*, 169–183. [CrossRef]
41. Chen, J.P.; Wang, Y.L.; Zhao, C.X.; Li, X. Failure Analysis and Preventive Measures of Cooling Tower Fan Gearbox. *Adv. Mater. Res.* **2014**, *989*, 3302–3305. [CrossRef]
42. Fischer, K.; Besnard, F.; Bertling, L. Reliability-centered maintenance for wind turbines based on statistical analysis and practical experience. *IEEE Trans. Energy Convers.* **2011**, *27*, 184–195. [CrossRef]

mathematics

MDPI

Article

Application of Hybrid Model between the Technique for Order of Preference by Similarity to Ideal Solution and Feature Extractions for Bearing Defect Classification

Chun-Yao Lee [1,*], Truong-An Le [2] and Chung-Yao Chang [1]

1 Department of Electrical Engineering, Chung Yuan Christian University, Taoyuan 320314, Taiwan
2 Department of Electrical and Electronic Engineering, Thu Dau Mot University, Thu Dau Mot 75000, Vietnam
* Correspondence: cyl@cycu.edu.tw

Abstract: This paper describes a development that offers new opportunities for detecting faulty bearings. Prioritization is based on the technique for order of preference by similarity to the ideal solution (TOPSIS) for the most discriminative features in the faulty bearing dataset. The proposed model is divided into three steps: feature extraction, feature selection, and classification. In feature extraction, variational mode decomposition (VMD) and fast Fourier transform (FFT) are used to extract features from the measured signal of the test motors and use the symmetrical uncertainty (SU) value for calculation, reducing the redundancy of data. In terms of feature selection, the TOPSIS method is used instead of the traditional filtering method, which is applied to analysis and decision making, and important features are selected from seven filtering methods. Finally, in order to validate the classification ability of the proposed model, k-nearest neighbors (KNN), support vector machine (SVM), and artificial neural networks (ANN) are used as independent classifiers. The effectiveness of the proposed model is evaluated by applying two bearing datasets, namely the current dataset of motor vibration signals and the dataset of bearing motors provided by Case Western Reserve University (CWRU). The results show that the comparison of the proposed model with other models shows the feasibility of this study.

Keywords: bearing fault diagnosis; feature selection; TOPSIS; feature extraction

MSC: 68T07

1. Introduction

Rolling bearings are an important part of industrial machinery and equipment and have been widely used in this field. Rolling bearings need to bear the weight of rotating machines and ensure normal operation [1]. However, the bearing suffers vibration, wear, corrosion, fatigue, etc., during operation. When the bearing fails, the vibration will increase when it is fatigued, and its working efficiency will be reduced and even cause casualties. Therefore, bearing fault detection can sense the subtle vibration of the bearing, and the running state of the bearing can be judged through simple data, which can be seen at a glance [2–4]. Fault vibration of rolling bearings is caused by two kinds of faults: local faults and distributed faults. The ultimate goal of vibration monitoring is to know when the bearing needs to be replaced by tracking the state of the bearing. According to statistics, about 30% to 40% of mechanical failures in rotating equipment using rolling bearings are caused by rolling bearings [5,6]. Therefore, early fault diagnosis is an important topic in a wide range of applications to improve the safety and reliability of rotating electrical machines [7]. The purpose of this study is to propose an efficient method for bearing fault diagnosis based on machine learning. The bearing fault diagnosis model includes five steps: raw data acquisition, data preprocessing, feature extraction, feature selection, and fault mode recognition [8]. When the rolling bearing fails, it sends out vibration and impact signals, and the collection of vibration signals can directly reflect the operating status of the faulty mechanical equipment. With the technical improvement of feature extraction methods, the dimension or category of extracted feature vectors is increasing, and there are more and more irrelevant and redundant feature vectors in high-dimensional feature sets, which may affect the accuracy rate. Therefore, some dimensionality reduction strategies are used in feature extraction to select sensitive features, which will also affect the diagnosis results as computational efficiency. There are several feature extraction methods [9,10]: the more famous ones are envelope analysis, such as principal component analysis [11,12], distance estimation techniques, symmetric uncertainty (SU) methods [13], and empirical mode decomposition (EMD) [14]; variational mode decomposition (VMD) [15]; and fast Fourier transform (FFT) methods [16,17]. EMD technology has high precision in signal extraction and fast convergence speed, which is very suitable for bearing fault diagnosis. However, in extracting the signal, VMD can set the desired mode number and avoid the endpoint effect similar to EMD decomposition through mirror extension [18]. After the feature extraction step, the feature set has been preliminarily formed, but there are still many redundant features in the extracted datasets, especially in high-dimensional datasets. These redundant features lead to a decrease in the accuracy of the final classification. Therefore, a feature selection step is required, which is an intermediate step between data extraction and classification. What it does is preprocess the dataset to further select its features before sending it to the classifier. Feature selection has flourished, and algorithms have gained attention in solving dataset optimization problems. Regarding fault classification methods, some artificial intelligence methods [19] include support vector machine (SVM) [20,21], k-nearest neighbors (KNN) [22], fuzzy inference system [23], random forest (RF) [24], and artificial neural network (ANN) [25–30]. Ultimately, bearing health depends on these technologies.

Since a single feature selection method cannot provide excellent classification accuracy in the case of different faulty bearings, to improve the performance of a new method for bearing defect classification, the proposed method relies on an ideal solution with an order preference similar to the ideal technical solution (TOPSIS) [31]. The information in the original data can be fully utilized, and the results can accurately reflect the gap between evaluation schemes. The basic process is to use the cosine method to find the optimal solution and the worst solution in the finite solution based on the normalized original data matrix and then calculate the distances between each evaluation object and the optimal solution and the worst solution, respectively, and calculate the relative closeness of each evaluation object to the optimal solution as the basis for evaluating the advantages and disadvantages. Although TOPSIS avoids the subjectivity of data, has no strict requirements on data components and samples, and is more flexible in describing the comprehensive impact of multiple indicators, it needs the data of each indicator, and it is difficult to choose the corresponding quantitative weight. It needs to be determined in order to accurately describe the impact of weights. The purpose of this research is to try to apply the TOPSIS method to the feature selection of filters and try to improve the lack of filter classification accuracy. For the stability and accuracy of the final feature extraction, this study uses the SU method to delete redundant features and combines six feature selection methods for weight distribution. For specific research, six typical feature selection methods are considered, which are important for TOPSIS. The construction of the method is challenging, because not every filter method is suitable for different data, and these filter methods are combined by the TOPSIS method, which will lower the recognition rate. The number of indicators selected is appropriate, which can describe the influence of the indicators well and overcome the blind spots of the TOPSIS method. This study utilizes multiple methods, namely, RF [24], minimum redundancy maximum relevance (mRMR) [32], correlation-based feature selection (CFS) [33], F-score (FS) [34], Pearson correlation coefficient (PCC) [35], and item variance (TV) [33]; in addition, we also utilize three well-known classifications, the SVM [20,21], KNN [22], and ANN [26–30]. After extracting the original data by VMD-FFT, the correlation coefficient is calculated by the SU method to reduce the uncertainty characteristics. The selection filtering method is used as the selection weight because the calculation speed of this method is very fast and can be applied to various machine learning models.

In this paper, an optimal feature selection method in TOPSIS is proposed, which also removes redundant features to make the method more refined. The optimization trade-off between detection accuracy, processing speed, and flexibility is the main consideration of this method. The results through the classifier show that the best features can be selected quickly and provide stable and real-time performance.

The main contributions of this paper are summarized as follows:

(1) In the research of filtering methods, combining the advantages of different filtering methods makes the accuracy rate more stable and effectively removes irrelevant and redundant functions.
(2) We introduce a new orientation-adaptive feature extraction method. This paper proposes a fault diagnosis method based on TOPSIS. Compared with the traditional signal method, this method takes advantage of the combination of multiple feature extractions to fill in the order of the newly sorted features, thereby improving the stability of feature recognition.
(3) In this paper, a hybrid model for rolling bearing fault identification is established, and the model is tested using existing equipment and fault data under different conditions to achieve accurate fault diagnosis and compare the currently available algorithms. The proposed model has a lower computational cost.

The structure of this paper is as follows: Section 2 describes the basics and workflow involved in the TOPSIS hybrid model. Section 3 introduces the method for measuring motor signals in the bearing motor dataset and the Case Western Reserve University (CWRU) dataset. In Section 4, the results of three classifiers in four different models of the two faulty bearing datasets in Section 3 are discussed, and the information and performance are analyzed and evaluated in detail. Finally, the optimal model is determined based on these values.

2. Hybrid Models

2.1. Variational Mode Decomposition (VMD)

Variational pattern decomposition has previously been published (Dragomiretskiy, 2014). VMD is a novel adaptive nonrecursive signal decomposition methods for enhancing sequence stability [15]. In addition to VMD, it can specify the number of modes desired for the outcome. The IMF decomposed by its method has an independent center frequency and shows the characteristics of sparsity in the frequency domain, which has the characteristics of sparse research. In the process of solving the IMF, the endpoint effect similar to that in the EMD decomposition is avoided by means of mirror extension. Selecting an appropriate value of K can effectively avoid modal aliasing. This study used VMD to decompose the ball bearing test data series for normal and faulty bearings. The VMD structure is as follows: For VMD, the preset K value determines the number of IMF components. The sum of the IMFs is the original signal. The constraints are expressed by (1) and (2):

$$\min \sum_{k=1}^{K} \|\partial_t \left[\left(\delta(t) + \frac{j}{\pi t} \right) \times u_k(t) \right] e^{-\mathrm{j}wt} \|^2 \tag{1}$$

$$\text{s.t.} \sum_{k} u_k = f \tag{2}$$

where $\{u_k\} = \{u_{\text{IMF1}}, \cdots, u_{\text{IMFK}}\}$ contains local characteristic signals of different time scales of the original signal; $\{w_k\} = \{w_1, \cdots w_k\}$ represents the center frequency of each IMF component; $\sum_k u_k$ represents the sum of all modal components; and f represents the time series of ball bearing test data for decomposed normal and faulty bearings.

VMD solution: a secondary penalty factor α and the introduction of a Lagrangian penalty operator $\lambda(t)$ to transform the constrained variational problem given by (1) and (2) into an unconstrained variational problem where the extension of the Lagrangian expression is given in (3) below:

$$L\,\{u_k\}\{w_k\},\ \lambda(t)) = \alpha \sum_k \|\partial_t \left[\left(\delta(t) + \frac{j}{\pi t} \right) u_k(t) \right] e^{-jwt} \|_2^2 \quad (3)$$

The Alternating Direction Multiplier Algorithm [2] is used to solve the variational problem given by (3), above which produces the alternately updated $\overline{u_k^{n+1}}(w)$ and w_k^{n+1} expressions given in (4) and (5):

$$\overline{u_k^{n+1}}(w) = \frac{\overline{f}(w) \ - \ \sum_{i} \neq_k \overline{u_k}(w) + \overline{\lambda}(w)/2}{1 + 2\alpha(w - w_k)^2} \quad (4)$$

$$w_k^{n+1} = \frac{\int_0^\infty w|\overline{u_k}(w)|^2 dw}{\int_0^\infty |\overline{u_k}(w)|^2 dw} \quad (5)$$

where $\overline{u_k^{n+1}}(w)$ is the Wiener filter of $\overline{f}(w) - \sum \overline{u_i}(w)$ that yields w_k^{n+1}, the corresponding power spectrum of the centroid modal function.

The VMD model is as follows:

Step 1: Initialize u_k, w_k, λ and $n = 0$.

Step 2: $n = n + 1$ (number of iterations).

Step 3: Update u_k and w_k according to the VMD algorithm formula.

Step 4: Update the Lagrange multiplier λ according to the relevant algorithm.

Step 5: Know until a certain condition is met (judged by the similarity coefficient), stop the iteration; otherwise, go to Step 2.

Step 6: As $k = k + 1$, subtract the decomposed mode from the source signal and use it as the source signal for the next cycle; go to Step 1.

2.2. Fast Fourier Transform (FFT)

FFT [16,17] is based on the mathematics of discrete Fourier transform (DFT), which utilizes the symmetric properties of discrete Fourier transform complex multiplication on the complex plane, and multiple multiplications with symmetric properties are combined into one item, so it can effectively reduce the number of mathematical calculations and obtain more efficient calculations without changing the original mathematical model structure. This calculation method was proposed by Cooly and Tukey in 1965. In the field of digital signal processing, the data can be converted from the time domain waveform to the frequency spectrum through the Fourier transform. The fast Fourier transform model is defined as follows:

DFT is obtained by decomposing a series of values into components of different frequencies. The definition of DFT is expressed as (6):

$$X(k) \ \equiv \ X(e^{\frac{j2\pi k}{N}}) = \sum_{n=0}^{N-1} x(n) W_N^{kn},\ k = 0,\ 1,\ \ldots,\ N \ - \ 1 \quad (6)$$

It is further expressed as the sum of the following odd-numbered terms plus the sum of the even-numbered terms.

$$X(k) = \sum_{r=0}^{N/(2-1)} x(2r)(W_N^2)^{rk} + \sum_{r=0}^{N/(2-1)} X(2r+1)(W_N^2)^{rk}\cdot = G(k) + W_N^k \cdot H(k) \quad (7)$$

In $W_N^2 = e^{-\frac{j2\pi}{\frac{N}{2}}} = W_{N/2}$, $G(k)$ and $H(k)$ are, respectively, the DFT of the following two $N/2$ points:

$$G(k) = \sum_{n=0}^{N/(2-1)} x(2n) W_{N/2}^{kn} \tag{8}$$

$$H(k) = \sum_{n=0}^{\frac{N}{2-1}} x(2n+1) W_{\frac{N}{2}}^{kn} \tag{9}$$

For each pair of $X(k)$ and $X(k + N/2)$, as long as the even part is known, another even part is found. The odd part is the same.

2.3. Feature Extraction Process

VMD minimizes the sum of the estimated bandwidths of each mode, where each mode is assumed to be a finite bandwidth with a different center frequency. To solve this variational problem, an alternating direction multiplier method is used to continuously update each mode, and its center frequency is gradually demodulated to the corresponding baseband; finally, each mode, that is, the corresponding center frequency, is extracted together. We extract the max, min, mse, rsm, and mean values from each of the eight IMFs decomposed by VMD. The features extracted in VMD are F1~F40. The eight IMFs decomposed by VMD extract the maximum value, minimum value, and average value through FFT analysis. The features extracted in the FFT are F41~F80. Eighty features were extracted in feature extraction. Its calculation method is shown in Figure 1.

2.4. Symmetric Uncertainty (SU) Value Feature Selection

Information entropy is the average amount of information contained in each received message, proposed by Shannon in 1948 [36]. Messages represent events, samples, or features from a distribution or data stream. Another characteristic of the source is the probability distribution of the sample. The probability distribution of events and the amount of information for each event constitute a random variable, and the mean (i.e., expectation) of this random variable is the average (i.e., entropy) of the amount of information generated by this distribution. The calculation formula of entropy is shown in (10), and its information gain is shown in (11):

$$H(t) = -k \sum_{i}^{N} P(X_i) I(X_i) \tag{10}$$

$$I(X) = \sum_{i}^{N} InP(x_i) \tag{11}$$

where P is the probability mass function of x, k is a proportional constant corresponding to the chosen metric, and i is the information body of x.

For the decision-making system, the greater the probability of occurrence of each piece of information, the smaller $H(X)$ will be. This means that the greater the regularity that appears in the information, the smaller the degree of uncertainty, which means that the decision-making system has a high probability of presenting correct information; on the contrary, if the amount of information is too large, it means that the amount of information in the system is full of various information, so there will be a phenomenon of information overload. This is the most direct and fastest way to judge. By calculating the correlation coefficient, the correlation between them can be quickly obtained. However, if the correlation is used to select features, it often leads to the tendency to select features with larger values [4]. Therefore, this study uses the method of SU value to calculate the degree of correlation between the feature and the target, where SU is expressed as (12):

$$\mathrm{SU}(X,Y) = \frac{I(X)}{H(X)+H(Y)} \tag{12}$$

The above expression is interpreted as the form of normalized information gain by definition, and the nonlinear related information variable defined by information entropy is used to reconstruct the degree of correlation between nonlinear random variables. Among them, the SU value is used to calculate the symmetric uncertainty. Its concept is similar to information acquisition, but the value range is between 0 and 1 (0 means that X has nothing to do with Y, and 1 means that knowing Y can accurately predict X).

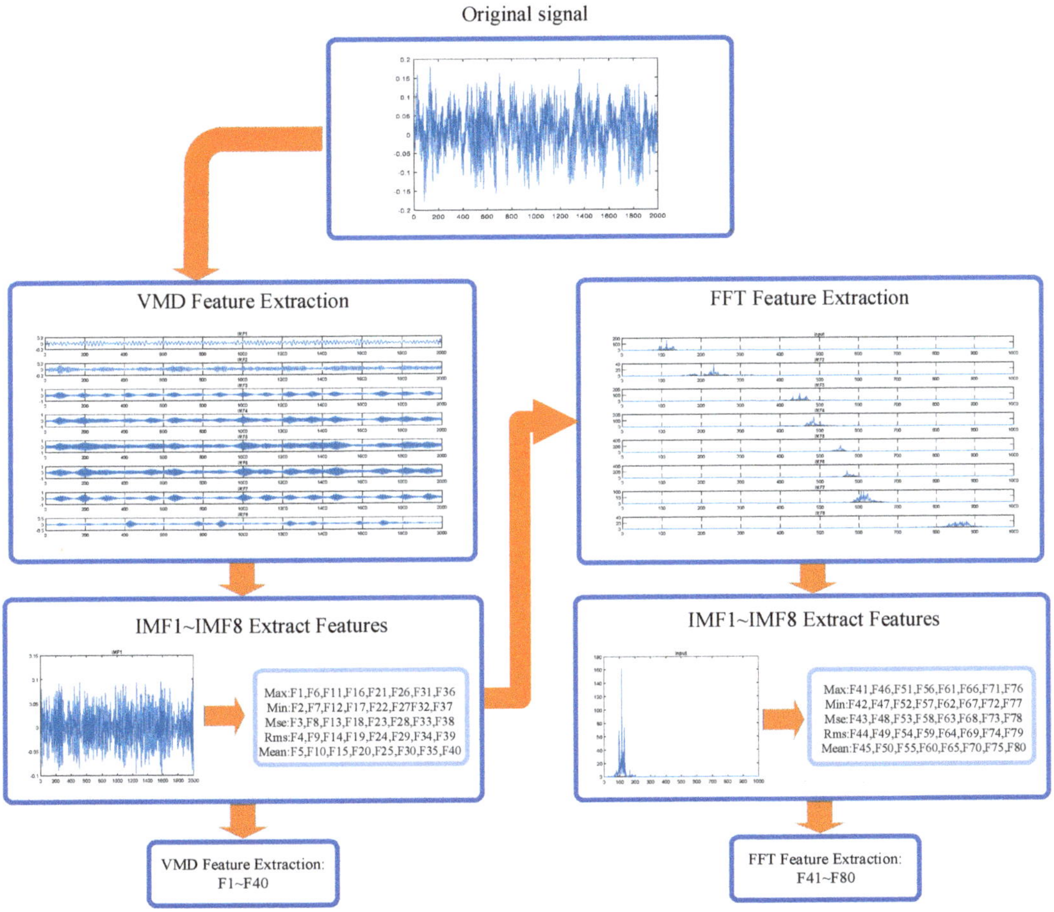

Figure 1. Feature extraction method flowchart.

2.5. Symmetric Uncertainty Method Feature Selection Process

Using the SU value of the fault type, the features (F1–F80) captured by VMD-FFT are sorted in descending order from the highest to the lowest correlation. During the screening process, the method compares the two features and retains the correlation with the target. Higher features use the features with higher correlation to complete the screening. The features with less influence are deleted by threshold setting, and the original 80 features are paired down to 60 features to obtain a feature subset and then feature comparison. This method will reduce the time complexity and realize the function of filtering while calculating to achieve the effect of speeding up the operation and improving the accuracy rate.

2.6. Feature Selection Method Process

In the filter feature selection method (FFS) [37], seven feature selection methods are used, as shown in Table 1 below. The FFS method is often used as a preprocessing step to rank the importance of variables in regression or classification problems. It selects features based on scores in various statistical tests and indicators of correlation. The algorithm of the FFS method has strong versatility, saves the training steps of the classifier, and has low algorithm complexity, so it is suitable for large-scale datasets and can quickly remove a large number of irrelevant features. It is very suitable as a prefilter for features. However, each type of method has a different calculation method to evaluate the weights of the features. This makes it difficult to make a final decision. Therefore, the main idea of this study is to apply TOPSIS to evaluate the priority order from the results of filter feature selection methods. SU is a preprocessor to remove redundant features before the remaining features are evaluated. In this study, a method with TOPSIS was proposed to improve the stability of the results of the FFS method (Table 2). Using the TOPSIS method to evaluate the current signals and select the best ranking of the signals for classification (Figure 2). The TOPSIS method is described in detail in the next section.

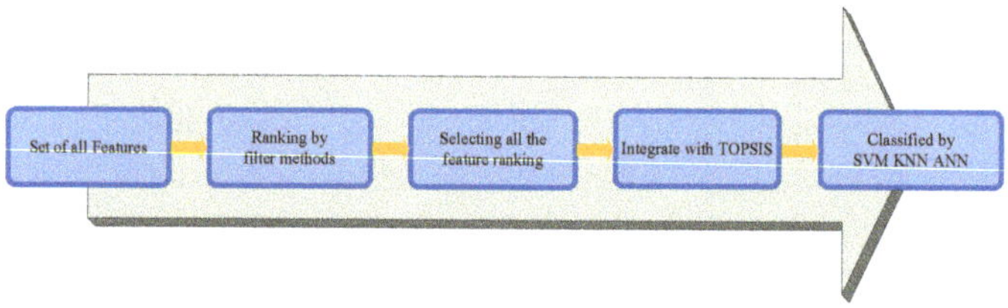

Figure 2. Schematic of the filter method proposed data analysis procedure.

Table 1. Filter methods for feature selection.

Methods	Advantages	Disadvantages	References
ReliefF (RF)	The algorithm is relatively simple High operating efficiency	The limitation of the algorithm is that it cannot effectively remove redundant features.	[24]
Minimum redundancy feature selection (mRMR)	Maximize the correlation between features and categorical variables Minimize the correlation between features and features	Does not take into account the correlation between features	[32]
Symmetrical uncertainty (SU)	Select a subset of features that are highly correlated with the category	A feature that has a high correlation with the target variable but little correlation with other features	[13]
Correlation-based feature selection (CFS)	Contains a subset of features that are highly correlated with the class but not correlated with each other	No interaction with classifiers, ignoring feature correlations	[33]
F-score (FS)	The accuracy rate can judge the total correct rate	In the case of unbalanced samples, it is not a good indicator to measure the results.	[34]
Pearson correlation coefficient (PCC)	The relationship of variables can be measured numerically and is directional	This method cannot be used to refine and solidify the relationship between variables to form a model.	[35]
Term variance (TV)	The method independently measures the relationship between each feature and the response variable.	The relationship between variables is not considered, so there will be redundant variables between numbers.	[33]

Table 2. Feature selection ranking collection.

Selected Type	Selected Methods
A	RF, mRMR, SU, CFS, FS, PCC, TV
B	RF, mRMR, CFS, FS, PCC, TV
C	RF, mRMR, CFS, FS, PCC
D	RF, CFS, FS, PCC, TV

2.7. The Feature Selection in TOPSIS

The TOPSIS method is a sequence optimization technique for ideal target similarity, and it is a very effective method in multiobjective decision analysis, proposed by Hwang and Yoon in 1981 [31]. Calculate the distance between each evaluation target and the ideal solution and anti-ideal solution, and use this as the basis for evaluating the target.

The workflow of the TOPSIS method consists of the following seven steps [38].

Step 1: Generating an *m-by-n* evaluation matrix contains m alternatives $A_1, A_2; \ldots, A_m$, with each evaluation matrix assessed by n local criteria $C_1, C_2; \ldots; C_n$.

Step 2: Normalizing the decision matrix:

$$u_{ij} = \frac{X_{ij}}{\sqrt{\sum_{k=1}^{m} x_{kj}^2}}\ ; i = 1, \ldots, m;\ j = 1, \ldots, n \tag{13}$$

where x_{ij} is the score of alternative A_i concerning criterion C_j.

Step 3: Calculating the weighted normalized decision matrix, for which its values V_{ij} are computed as (14):

$$V_{ij} = W_i \times u_{ij};\ j = 1, 2, \ldots, m;\ i = 1, 2, \ldots, n \tag{14}$$

Let $W_i = [w_1, w_2, \ldots, w_n]$ be the vector of local criteria weights satisfying $\sum_{i=1}^{n} W_i = 1$.

Step 4: Determining the positive ideal l (A^+) and negative ideal (A^-) solutions as (15)–(18):

In the proposed method, all criteria are considered as benefits; therefore, J' is empty, and (15) and (16) can be reduced to (17) and (18):

$$A^+ = \{v_1^+, \ldots, v_n^+\} = \left\{(max_i\ V_{ij}|j \in J), (min_i\ V_{ij}\middle|j \in J')\right\} \tag{15}$$

$$A^- = \{v_1^-, \ldots, v_n^-\} = \left\{(min_i\ V_{ij}|j \in J), (max_i\ V_{ij}\middle|j \in J')\right\} \tag{16}$$

$$A^+ = \{v_1^+, \ldots, v_n^+\} = \{(max_i\ V_{ij}|j \in J)\} \tag{17}$$

$$A^- = \{v_1^-, \ldots, v_n^-\} = \{(min_i\ V_{ij}|j \in J)\} \tag{18}$$

Step 5: Measuring the Euclidean distances between each alternative and both the positive and negative ideal, which are calculated as (19) and (20):

$$P_i^+ = \sqrt{\sum_{j=1}^{n}\left(v_{ij} - v_j^+\right)^2}\ ; i = 1, 2, \ldots, m \tag{19}$$

$$P_i^- = \sqrt{\sum_{j=1}^{n}\left(v_{ij} - v_j^-\right)^2}\ ; i = 1, 2, \ldots, m \tag{20}$$

Step 6: Computing the relative closeness to the ideal solution as (21):

$$H_i = \frac{P_i^-}{P_i^+ + P_i^-}\ ; i = 1, 2, \ldots, m; 0 \le H_1 \le 1 \tag{21}$$

Step 7: Ranking alternatives based on the H value of each parameter. $H_i = 1$ indicates the highest rank, and $H_i = 0$ indicates the lowest rank. Its calculation method is shown in Figure 3.

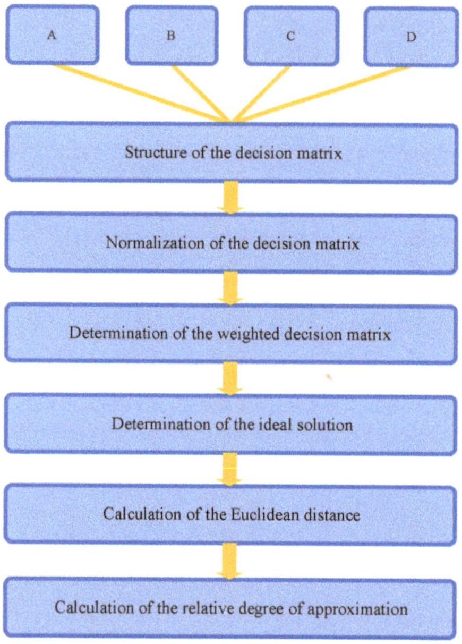

Figure 3. The TOPSIS feature ranking process integrates different FFS methods ranking.

2.8. Performance Measures

The k-fold cross-validation test, independent dataset test, subsampling test, and jackknife cross-validation test are four schemes widely used in statistical classification to check the performance of predictive models [39]. The jackknife method is widely used to estimate the generalization ability of predictive models [40,41]. However, this is time-consuming. To save computation time, ten-fold cross-validation was used in this study.

We next investigated the performance of predictive models. In k-fold cross-validation, the data are divided into k subsets, each using one of the k subsets and $k - 1$ subsets as test and training data, respectively.

2.9. Classification

In this study, we used three classification models, including the SVM, KNN, and ANN classifiers, to compare the bearing motor dataset and the CWRU dataset differences in the various fault types and normal motors and obtain accurate results through the analysis software MATLAB.

Support vector machine (SVM) [20,21]—An SVM is a supervised learning model and a machine learning model of related learning algorithms. It has relative advantages for problems such as small samples, nonlinearity, high dimensionality, and local minimum points. This is the method to use for classification or regression. Given a group of classified data, the SVM can obtain a set of models through training. Then, if there is unclassified data, the support vector machine can use the previously trained model to predict the category of this data, making it a nonprobabilistic binary linear classifier. Classification decisions are made through linear combinations of features. The characteristics of objects are usually described as eigenvalues, and in vectors, as eigenvectors. Since the support vector machine must first have classified data for training when building a model, the support vector machine is one of the methods of supervised learning.

Tuning the SVM classifier:

Using the parameter value that minimizes the cross-validation loss for the SVM and using the parameters that optimize the two-class learning, the eligible parameters are 'BoxConstraint', 'KernelFunction', 'KernelScale', 'PolynomialOrder', and 'Standardize'.

Manually adjust the parameters of the classifier according to this scheme:

Step 1: Pass the data to the SVM and set the name–value pair parameters to 'KernelScale' and 'auto'. Assume that the trained SVM model is called the SVM model. The heuristic process uses subsampling. Therefore, to reproduce the results, use rng to set the random number seed before training the classifier.

Step 2: Cross-validate a classifier by passing it to crossover. By default, the software performs 10-fold cross-validation.

Step 3: Pass the cross-validated SVM model to k-fold Loss to estimate and retain the classification error.

Step 4: Retrain the SVM classifier but adjust the 'KernelScale' and 'BoxConstraint' name–value pair arguments. As shown in Table 3.

Table 3. Support vector machine parameter setting.

Parameter	Parameter Value
BoxConstraint	1
KernelFunction	polynomial
KernelScale	auto
PolynomialOrder	2

k-Nearest Neighbor algorithm (KNN) [22]—The KNN is a nonparametric method for classification and regression prediction problems. It is one of the simplest of all machine learning algorithms. The sorting criteria are determined by a 'majority vote' of neighbors. The output of a regression model is a continuous value that is predicted to be the average of the outputs of the k-nearest neighbors. On the classification problem, the KNN adopts the majority principle and uses k-nearest neighbors to judge which group the new data belong to. The algorithm flow is very simple. The disadvantage of the KNN is that it is very sensitive to the local structure of the data, so it is extremely important to adjust the appropriate k value. First, determine the size of k. Then calculate the distance between the current new data and the adjacent data. In the third step, find out the k-nearest neighbors and see which group has the most neighbors, and then classify it into that group.

Artificial Neural Network (ANN) [26–30]—Artificial neural networks are used for supervised learning. More specifically, the ANN structure, training process, risk of overfitting, and data normalization for regression problems are analyzed. Calculations are routed through a large number of artificial neuron connections. In most cases, the artificial neural network can change its internal structure according to external information and is an adaptive system. Modern neural networks are nonlinear statistical data modeling tools, and neural networks are usually optimized by learning methods based on mathematical statistics. Artificial neural networks can have simple decision-making abilities and judgment abilities similar to human beings, and this method has more advantages than formal logical reasoning.

The different steps are described below:

Step 1: The collected input and output samples are divided into a test set and a training set. The splitting is performed randomly; usually, 80% of the samples are used for training and 20% for testing.

Step 2: The training set is subdivided into training and validation subsets. Splitting is random. Generally, 80% of the samples are used for the training subset and 20% for the validation subset.

Step 3: Set the weights and biases of the artificial neural network. In the first iteration, these values are chosen randomly. For the next iteration, a previous value of the error metric is chosen relative to the error metric obtained in the previous iteration of the training subset.

Step 4: The error metric between the ANN output and dataset output is used to evaluate training and validation subsets. Widely used metrics for a regression ANN are mean squared error, and binary cross-entropy are used for a categorical ANN.

Step 5: Compare the error metrics for the training and validation subsets to stop training when overfitting occurs. The training error metric monitors a subset to detect training improvement when the completion metric converges and stops.

Step 6: If convergence is not achieved, the error metric is used to improve the weights and biases for the next iteration.

Step 7: After training is complete, evaluate the training and test sets and compare the resulting output with the dataset output. The training set comparison is biased because the same data are already used for training. Therefore, the test set exists and provides an unbiased validity check.

Step 8: If the performance of the artificial neural network cannot meet expectations, the ANN structure, number of hidden layers, number of neurons, or training algorithm should be reset.

ANN training is not a deterministic process due to the random splitting of datasets and random initialization bias of weights. The training subset is divided into batches for training iterations. The results of each iteration are used to improve the ANN parameters. The training process is complete when all batches are complete and all samples from the training subset have been used. The training process of an artificial neural network consists of many epochs. The number of samples per batch is a parameter that can affect the training process's quality, stability, and computational cost.

2.10. Proposed Method Process

In this study, the faulty bearing detection model is based on VMD-FFT to establish the feature extraction process and the used equations. This part of feature selection is divided into four cases of individual tests, as shown in Figure 4. The specific steps are as follows:

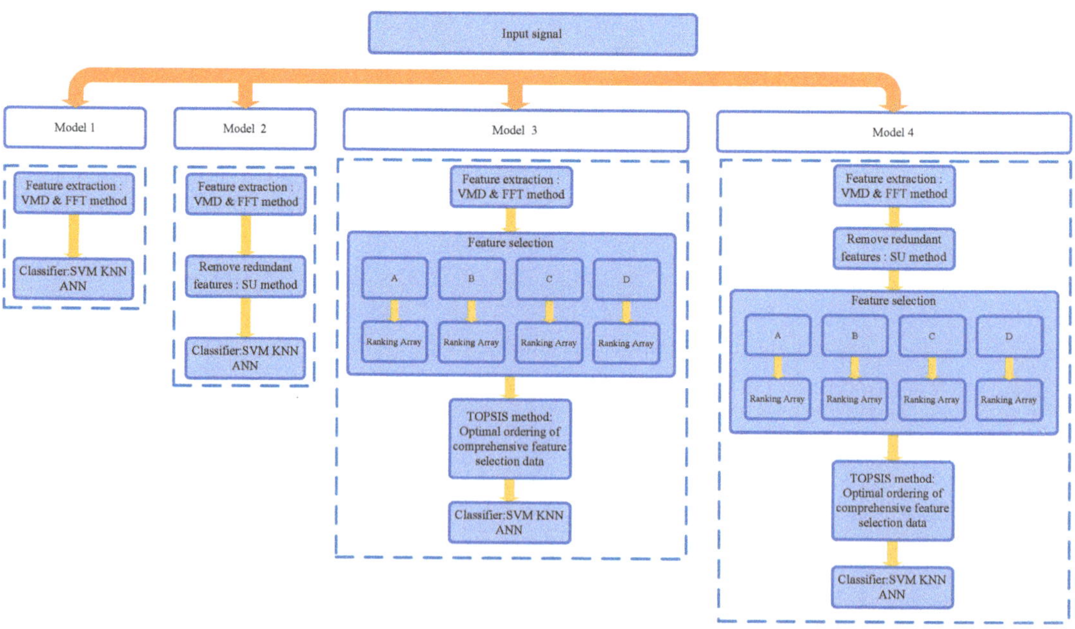

Figure 4. Propose an integrated FFS model flowchart for optimal feature selection.

Model 1: Using the VMD-FFT feature extraction process and presenting the result with a classifier.

Model 2: Using the VMD-FFT feature extraction process and SU method to remove redundant features and using the classifier to present the results.

Model 3: Using the VMD-FFT feature extraction process. In the feature selection part, the TOPSIS method (Figure 3) is used to obtain the ideal ranking, and the classifier is used to present the results.

Model 4: Using the VMD-FFT feature extraction process and using the SU method to remove redundant features. In the feature selection part, the TOPSIS method (Figure 3) is used to obtain the ideal ranking, and the classifier is used to present the results.

These four models are independent of each other. To test whether the SU method can effectively reduce redundant features and the combination of four different filtering methods selected in the TOPSIS method, the four training models of bearing faults constructed were compared. The next section introduces the bearing dataset and the CWRU dataset. We used these two datasets to test the results of the four models in the KNN, SVM, and ANN classifiers.

3. Hybrid Models

3.1. Bearing Dataset of Current Signal Measured from an Induction Motors

This section describes the specifications of the motor used in the study and measures the motor for normal and damaged bearings, broken rotor bars, and shorted stator windings. Four current signals are used for analysis. Secondly, the equipment and methods used in the experiment and the overall process of this study are introduced, and the differences between various fault types and normal motors are preliminarily compared. Finally, the accuracy results are given by MATLAB analysis software.

The equipment used in this study is a four-pole AC induction motor, as shown in Figure 5; its specifications are shown in Table 4, and the fault types are shown in Figure 6a–c. A signal acquisition device (NI PXI-1033), electricity meter, and computer were used for analysis, and the measurement data were then recorded. Raw current signals are obtained from experiments with common and three-faulted induction motors. Figure 7 shows the test bench hardware, a three-phase squirrel-cage induction motor of four types: normal, bearing failure, rotor drilled, and stator coil windings shorted. The three-phase squirrel-cage induction motor with bearing damage (aperture 1.96 mm × 0.53 mm) is shown in Figure 6a. The three-phase squirrel-cage induction motor with the rotor hole (two holes $\oint$ 8 mm and 10 mm deep) is shown in Figure 6b. A three-phase squirrel-cage induction motor with short-circuited stator coil windings (2 coils short-circuited) is shown in Figure 6c.

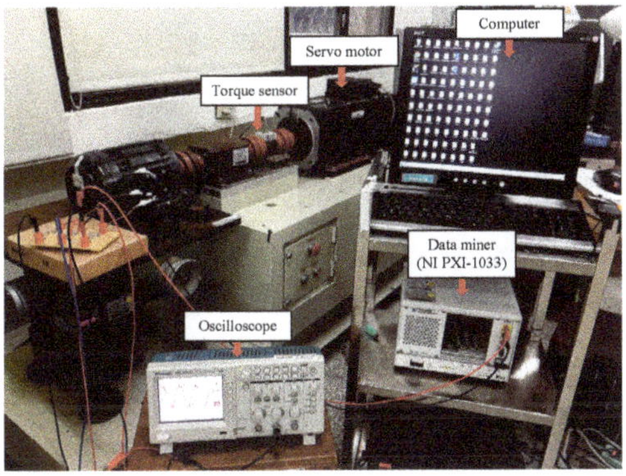

Figure 5. Torque sensor, servo motor, computer, oscilloscope, and data miner (NI PXI-1033).

Table 4. AC induction motor specifications.

Three-Phase Four-Pole Induction Motor Specifications		
Voltage	Frequency	Power Factor
220 V/380 V	60 Hz	0.8
Output	Current	Rated speed
2 Hp 1.5 kW	5.58 A/3.23 A	1764 rpm

(a)

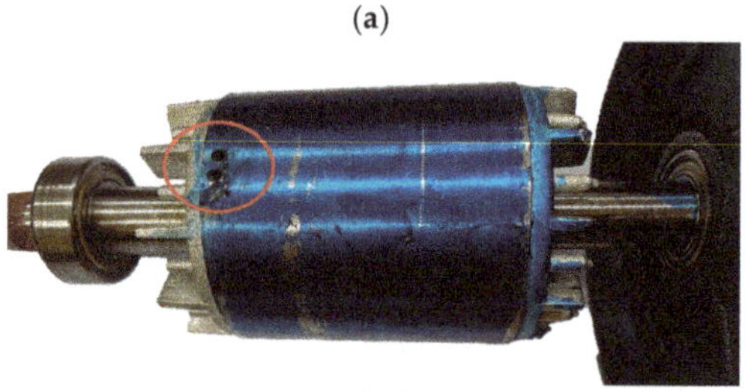

(b)

(c)

Figure 6. (**a**) Bearing damage processing (aperture 1.96 mm × 0.53 mm). (**b**) Rotor drilling failure (two holes ∮ 8 mm depth 10 mm). (**c**) Short circuit between stator layers (two coils short circuit).

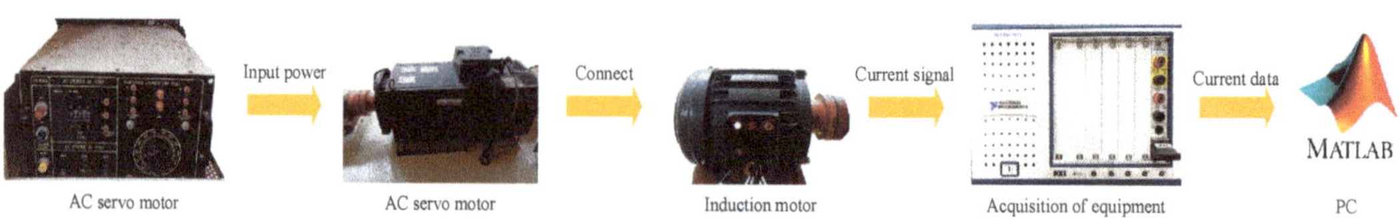

Figure 7. Signal measurement process.

3.2. Measurement Process in AC Induction Motor

First of all, this study measures the current signals of an AC induction motor in four conditions (normal, bearing, rotor, and stator) and obtains arbitrary phase data for the motor U, V, and W through the NI signal extractor. The data sampling time for each measurement is 100 s, and the collection frequency is 1000 Hz. Each signal measurement is evaluated 100 times to complete the premeasurement operation.

3.3. CWRU Benchmark Dataset

The CWRU benchmark dataset provides validation of the ball bearing test data for normal and faulty bearings [42]. The test bench hardware consists of a 2 hp induction motor, load motor, and torque encoder. The CWRU benchmark dataset is unique in that each experiment carefully records the actual test conditions of the motor as well as the bearing fault states, including four different load levels (0 hp, 1 hp, 2 hp, 3 hp), three different fault locations (inner ring, outer ring, ball), three different defect diameters (0.007″, 0.014″, 0.021″ inches), and a sampling rate of 12 kHz. The main purpose is to determine the severity and location of bearing failures. Normally, the signal is cut into 2000 data points at each level, so there are 660 samples in total except the normal signal, the signal at each level is sliced into 780 samples. The length samples for the three different defect diameters each have 2000 data points.

4. Measurement Method of the Motor Signal

In this study, the bearing dataset of the current signal measured from an induction motor and the CWRU bearing dataset are used as experimental samples for simulation. After VMF-FFT feature extraction, the comprehensive optimal SU feature removal method and TOPSIS method are used, and finally, the SVM, KNN, and ANN classifiers are used to compare the accuracy rate.

4.1. CASE STUDY 1: Bearing Motor Dataset

In order to demonstrate the performance of the proposed TOPSIS method, the bearing motor dataset was used in this case to test the results. Table 5 shows the effect of applying different feature selection techniques on various classifier architectures. On the classifier side, it was used as an evaluation measure during a 10-fold cross-validation process with 30 repetitions. For a fair performance evaluation, consider different constraints that affect classification performance, such as training dataset, classifier model, and several selected features. In this regard, we should evaluate different possible combinations of the four states applied to the three classifiers. In the case of using SVM machine learning, the average accuracy rate of the VMD-FFT signal analysis method is 87.98%, and the highest accuracy rate is 98.5%, as shown in Figure 8a. After using the VMD-FFT signal analysis method combined with the SU feature selection method, the 80 features can be reduced to 60, respectively, and the average accuracy rate is 88.09%. Compared with model 1, the average accuracy rate curve is relatively stable, as shown in Figure 8b. Using the VMD-FFT signal analysis method combined with the TOPSIS feature selection method, in Feature Number 4 and Feature Number 16, the accuracy rates are 80.50% and 93.50%. It can be seen that the six-select method is better than other selection methods, as shown in Figure 8c. It is clear that using the VMD-FFT signal analysis method combined with the TOPSIS feature selection method combined with the SU feature selection method can reduce the 80 features to 60, respectively. In Feature Number 3, Feature Number 18, and Feature Number 24, the accuracy rates are 78.70%, 98.0%, and 99.0%. Compared with the results of model 3, the curve of the six-select method in model 4 tends to stabilize faster, as shown in Figure 8d. Therefore, it can be judged that this method can delete redundant and unimportant features, obtain a better feature subset, and effectively improve accuracy.

In this case study, the proposed bearing fault diagnosis model is compared with state-of-the-art models. Since the results in Table 5 show that the six-select method achieves better results in model 3 and model 4, the six-select method is the main method in model 3 and model 4 in the three classifiers in Table 5. The accuracy of the bearing motor current signal dataset in model 4 is 78.72% for the KNN classifier, 91.82% for the SVM classifier, and 99.48% for the ANN classifier. The proposed model with the ANN classifier achieves the highest accuracy in the bearing motor current signal dataset

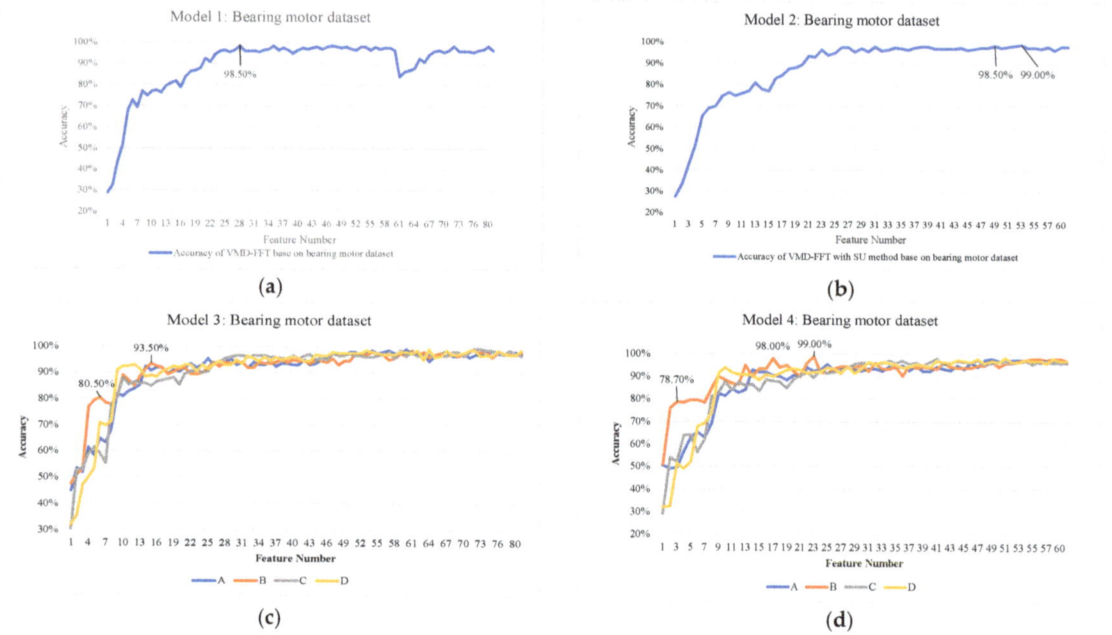

Figure 8. (**a**) Model 1: Bearing motor dataset of the VMD-FFT method in an SVM. (**b**) Model 2: Bearing motor dataset of the VMD-FFT method with redundant features removed by the SU method in an SVM. (**c**) Model 3: Bearing motor dataset of the TOPSIS method not removing features in an SVM. (**d**) Model 4: Bearing motor dataset of the TOPSIS method with redundant features removed by the SU method in an SVM.

Table 5. Result in bearing motor current signal dataset.

Bearing Motor Current Signal Dataset	KNN			SVM			ANN		
	Best Accuracy (%)	Avg (%)	Time (s)	Best Accuracy (%)	Avg (%)	Time (s)	Best Accuracy (%)	Avg (%)	Time (s)
model 1	90.50	76.75	8.47	98.50	87.98	123.95	100	99.38	1.16
model 2	90.00	77.03	6.25	98.50	88.09	124.21	100	99.41	1.04
model 3 (B)	90.50	78.63	5.77	99.00	91.68	76.83	100	99.43	1.01
model 4 (B)	91.50	78.72	4.22	99.00	91.82	69.18	100	99.48	0.93

In the case of using SVM learning, the average recognition rate of the VMD-FFT signal analysis method is 87.98%, and the highest accuracy rate is 98.5%, as shown in Figure 8a. After using the VMD-FFT signal analysis method combined with the SU feature selection method, the 80 features can be reduced to 60, respectively, and the average accuracy rate is 88.09%. Compared with model 1, the average recognition rate curve is relatively stable, as shown in Figure 8b. Using the VMD-FFT signal analysis method combined with the TOPSIS feature selection method, in Feature Number 4 and Feature Number 16, the accuracy rates are 80.50% and 93.50%. It can be seen that the six-select method is better than other selection methods, as shown in Figure 8c. Using the VMD-FFT signal analysis method combined with the TOPSIS feature selection method combined with the SU feature selection method can reduce the 80 features to 60, respectively. In Feature Number 3, Feature Number 18, and Feature Number 24, the accuracy rates are 78.70%, 98.0%, and 99.0%. Compared with the results of model 3, the curve of the six-select method in model 4 tends to stabilize faster, as shown in Figure 8d. Therefore, it can be judged that this method can delete redundant and unimportant features, obtain a better feature subset, and effectively improve accuracy.

In this case study, the proposed bearing fault diagnosis model is compared with state-of-the-art models. Since the results in Table 5 show that the six-select method achieves better results in model 3 and model 4, the six-select method is the main method in model 3 and model 4 in the three classifiers in Table 5. The accuracy of the bearing motor current signal dataset in model 4 is 78.72% for the KNN classifier, 91.82% for the SVM classifier, and 99.48% for the ANN classifier. The proposed model with the ANN classifier achieves the highest accuracy in the bearing motor current signal dataset. Therefore, the proposed bearing fault diagnosis model has better capability and can be applied to the practical task of fault diagnosis.

In this case study, the average running time of each method under different classifiers is shown in Table 5. The proposed method performs the best under each classifier. Model 4 had the shortest average running time of 4.22 s. for the KNN, 69.18 s. for the SVM, and 0.93 s. for the ANN. The SVM still has the longest average operation time and is significantly longer than the proposed method. In this case study, the proposed bearing fault diagnosis model is validated. Therefore, ANN classifiers are more suitable than those of the KNN and the SVM.

Based on the above results, in addition to showing the accuracy of each model, the performance of the three classifiers is shown, and type B of model 3 and model 4 are determined at the same time, which is an ideal solution for the feature selection method in TOPSIS.

4.2. CASE STUDY 2: CWRU Benchmark Dataset

In this case study, the proposed bearing fault diagnosis models are compared. Table 6 shows the classification of the four models of the CWRU 0 Hp benchmark dataset. The proposed model among the six-selected feature selection methods in model 4 achieves 97.52% accuracy in the KNN classifier. The accuracy of the SVM classifier is 98.60%, and the accuracy of the ANN classifier is 99.62%. In this case study, the proposed model with the ANN classifier achieves the highest accuracy, which is also higher than that of the proposed model with KNN and SVM classifiers.

Table 6. Result in CWRU bearing load 0 Hp dataset.

CWRU Bearing Load 0 Hp Dataset Data 2: 2000 × 660	KNN			SVM			ANN		
	Best Accuracy (%)	Avg (%)	Time (s)	Best Accuracy (%)	Avg (%)	Time (s)	Best Accuracy (%)	Avg (%)	Time (s)
Model 1	99.09	96.73	9.89	99.69	97.34	287.2	100	99.54	1.33
Model 2	99.09	97.03	6.71	99.84	97.35	276.3	100	99.61	1.17
Model 3	99.39	97.19	9.05	99.84	98.45	177.6	100	99.62	1.26
Model 4	99.39	97.52	8.61	99.84	98.60	176.7	100	99.62	1.21

In this case study, Table 7 shows the classification of the four models of the CWRU 1 Hp benchmark dataset. The proposed model among the six-selected feature selection methods in model 4 achieves 98.41% accuracy in the KNN classifier. The accuracy of the SVM classifier is 98.45%, and the accuracy of the ANN classifier is 99.54%. In this case study, the proposed model with the ANN classifier achieves the highest accuracy, which is also higher than the proposed model with KNN and SVM classifiers.

In this case study, Table 8 shows the classification of the four models of the CWRU 2 Hp benchmark dataset. The proposed model among the six-selected feature selection methods in model 4 achieves 98.66% accuracy in the KNN classifier. The accuracy of the SVM classifier is 98.67%, and the accuracy of the ANN classifier is 99.55%. In this case study, the proposed model with the ANN classifier achieves the highest accuracy, which is also higher than the proposed model with KNN and SVM classifiers. In this case study,

Table 9 shows the classification of the four models of the CWRU 3 Hp benchmark dataset. Among the six feature selection methods selected in model 4, the proposed model achieved 99.73% accuracy in the ANN classifier. In this case study, the proposed model with the ANN classifier achieves the highest accuracy. To confirm the credibility of the results, this study compares the results of ANN classifiers in other papers in the CWRU data. In Zhiqiang Zhang, Funa Zhou, and Sijie Li's paper [43], there are a total of six classifiers used for comparison, DNN, MDNN, MCNN, MRFNN, CMRFNN, G-CMRFNN, respectively. The method with the highest accuracy is G-CMRFNN, and the average accuracy of the classifiers is 98.20%. The average accuracy of the ANN classifier in this study is 99.62% for the CWRU 0 Hp model 4, 99.54% for the CWRU 1 Hp model 4, 99.55% for the CWRU 2 Hp model 4, and 99.73% for the CWRU 3 Hp model 4, as shown in Table 10. It can be seen from this that the model 4 method is superior in performance.

Table 7. Result in CWRU bearing load 1 Hp dataset.

CWRU Bearing Load 1 Hp Dataset Data 2: 2000 × 780	KNN			SVM			ANN		
	Best Accuracy (%)	Avg (%)	Time (s)	Best Accuracy (%)	Avg (%)	Time (s)	Best Accuracy (%)	Avg (%)	Time (s)
Model 1	98.33	95.44	12.09	99.35	97.34	287.4	99.49	98.92	1.55
Model 2	98.46	95.93	7.91	99.35	97.47	277.5	99.87	99.33	1.26
Model 3	99.61	98.22	11.60	99.84	97.38	270.3	100	99.45	1.29
Model 4	99.74	98.41	7.73	99.84	98.45	260.4	100	99.54	1.24

Table 8. Result in CWRU bearing load 2 Hp dataset.

CWRU Bearing Load 2 Hp Dataset Data 3: 2000 × 780	KNN			SVM			ANN		
	Best Accuracy (%)	Avg (%)	Time (s)	Best Accuracy (%)	Avg (%)	Time (s)	Best Accuracy (%)	Avg (%)	Time (s)
Model 1	99.23	96.31	11.58	99.74	97.21	324.3	100	99.22	1.53
Model 2	99.74	96.54	7.59	99.23	97.75	333.2	100	99.34	1.43
Model 3	99.35	98.57	11.78	99.87	98.13	176.3	100	99.50	1.35
Model 4	99.35	98.66	8.03	99.94	98.67	166.3	100	99.55	1.37

Table 9. Result in CWRU bearing load 3 Hp dataset.

CWRU Bearing load 3 Hp Dataset Data 4: 2000 × 780	KNN			SVM			ANN		
	Best Accuracy (%)	Avg (%)	Time (s)	Best Accuracy (%)	Avg (%)	Time (s)	Best Accuracy (%)	Avg (%)	Time (s)
Model 1	99.74	97.74	11.76	99.74	97.95	286.3	100	99.66	1.58
Model 2	99.74	97.38	7.53	99.87	98.07	279.2	100	99.69	1.33
Model 3	99.48	98.31	11.31	99.87	98.89	106.8	100	99.70	1.31
Model 4	99.53	98.13	7.71	99.87	98.91	100.9	100	99.73	1.27

In the paper written by Laohu Yuan, Dongshan Lian, Xue Kang, Yuanqiang Chen, and Kejia Zhai [44], there are a total of six classifiers are used for comparison, namely PNN-SFAM, BPNN, CNN-HMM, DAFD, DGNN, and CNN-SVM. The best one is the CNN-SVM model with an average accuracy of 98.75%. In addition to the accuracy results of the ANN, this study also compares the accuracy results of the SVM. The average accuracy of CWRU 0 Hp model 4 of the SVM classifier is 98.60%, and the average accuracy of CWRU 1 Hp model 4 is 98.45%. The average accuracy of the CWRU 2 Hp model 4 is 98.67%, and the average accuracy of the CWRU 3 Hp model 4 is 98.91%, as shown in Table 11. The performance of this study in SVM classification is not the best, but it is evenly matched.

Table 10. Comparison of neural network.

CWRU Dataset	Model	Average Accuracy (%)
Compare model	G-CMRFNN [43]	98.20
	CNN-SVM [44] PDC-LR-HCNN [22]	98.7593.70
Proposed model	0 Hp model 4	99.62
	1 Hp model 4	99.54
	2 Hp model 4	99.55
	3 Hp model 4	99.73

Table 11. Comparison of neural support vector machine.

CWRU Dataset	Model	Average Accuracy (%)
Compare model	CNN-SVM [44]	98.75
Proposed model	0 Hp model 4	98.60
	1 Hp model 4	98.45
	2 Hp model 4	98.67
	3 Hp model 4	98.91

The average accuracy of CWRU 3 Hp model 4 is 0.16% higher than that of the proposed CNN-SVM method. In this study, the average accuracy of the ANN classifier is 99.62%, the CWRU 0 Hp model 4, CWRU 1 Hp model 4 is 99.54%, the CWRU 2 Hp model 4 is 99.55%, CWRU 3 Hp model 4 is 99.73%, as shown in Table 10. By comparing the results with other methods, it is not difficult to see that the method in this study has achieved a high diagnostic accuracy, which further proves the effectiveness of the method.

In the paper written by Shaohui Ning and Kangning Du [22], there are a total of four classifiers to compare in this paper, namely, traditional CNN, PDC-CNN, LR-CNN, PDC-LR-CNN, and the best of the four methods is the PDC-LR-HCNN method, with an average accuracy of 93.70%. The average accuracy of the ANN classifiers in this study are as follows: the CWRU 0 Hp model 4 is 99.62%, the CWRU 1 Hp model 4 is 99.54%, the CWRU 2 Hp model 4 is 99.55%, and the CWRU 3 Hp model 4 is 99.73%, as shown in Table 10. The method research proposed in this paper can not only diagnose bearing faults quickly but also maintain the accuracy of the diagnosis, which is obviously of great significance to the actual fault diagnosis.

5. Discussion

The following two points can be summarized based on the above data results:

Improve the combination of TOPSIS selection methods: Sort by detecting the distance between the evaluation object and the optimal solution and the worst solution; if the evaluation object is the closest to the optimal solution and at the same time farthest from the most cracked, it is the best; otherwise, it is the worst. According to the assumption, the ideal solution is the optimal solution, and its various attributes have reached the best value among the alternative solutions. If the distance between the optimal solution and the most cracked solution is too large, it leads to judgment errors in the model, such as the line segment selected type A and the line segment selected type B in Figure 8d, which show that it is not choosing more reference weights to increase the accuracy rate but choosing reference weights suitable for the data that can reduce the interval between the ideal solution and the optimal solution, thereby improving the accuracy rate.

Improve the application of TOPSIS in multiobjective decision-making problems: Reduce redundant features through VMD-FFT and SU methods, as shown in Table 5. Compared with model 3, model 4 reduces 25% of the features, but in the recognition rate and running time, it is much better than model 3. Model 4 overcomes the shortcomings of poor objectivity and many assumptions and provides a more effective method for the selection of the optimal sequence

Apart from advantages, the proposed model still has flaws that need to be noted.

Model multiplicity: As mentioned in the feature selection method process, this study uses the filter method. This method does not consider which model to use in the future for learning. When selecting, it only evaluates the correlation between variables and predicted values and excludes the most irrelevant variables. Due to the relationship between variables not being considered, this study uses the TOPSIS method for aggregation. Compared to the wrapper and embedded methods, filter methods are simpler. Furthermore, when there are large datasets, testing tends to amplify into significant small differences in distributions that are not important.

Combination of filter methods in TOPSIS: This study proposes a combination of four different filter methods, as shown in Table 2. Due to the wide variety of filter methods, after excluding unsuitable types, six common filter methods were selected in this study, and only six combination methods have certain limitations on the weight of the optimal ranking, using other types of feature selection. The type of model needs further study.

6. Conclusions

Early detection of potential motor failures remains an important issue in operations and maintenance procedures. Therefore, this study proposes a motor bearing fault detection model. The symmetric uncertainty method and interpretability contained in the bearing vibration signal can effectively remove redundant features, remove irrelevant data, improve the accuracy of the learning model, reduce computational complexity, and improve the understandability of the model results. In order to overcome the shortcomings of the TOPSIS model in the multi-index decision-making process, the matrix between the original data sample and the ideal plan is used as a new decision matrix, and the ideal solution method is used to sort the plans. It overcomes the shortcomings of the traditional ideal solution, which is only based on the original data and is difficult to mine the inherent laws of the data, and provides a new idea for the decision-making problem under the condition of limited samples. At the same time, the method of combination weighting is proposed, which overcomes the shortcomings of traditional subjective and objective weighting methods. Results from measured bearing vibration data show that the proposed model 4 method outperforms traditional frequency-domain methods, feature selection methods, and other state-of-the-art filtering methods. Different FFS methods combined with different datasets in the TOPSIS method may result in different feature sets with different discriminants, so when given the wrong weights, the discrimination results may not be as expected. The results show that the proposed model 4 method helps researchers select more stable features from feature selection by integrating FFS methods. The proposed method has the advantages of stability and classification performance. However, it suffers from computational complexity issues compared to the FFS method. Still, the model 4 method has lower computational complexity compared to the filter selection method. Using the evaluation model established in this paper, through the application in the bearing fault evaluation, it shows that the result is reasonable, the calculation is simple, and it has a good application prospect.

The motor bearing fault diagnosis model proposed in this study has a high recognition rate in different datasets, but the feature selection method still needs to rely on a large amount of manual data processing in the adjustment of the TOPSIS method, which can be optimized in the future so that it can be more weighted and efficient. Future research should try to combine wrapping and embedded methods to apply the model more widely.

Author Contributions: Conceptualization, C.-Y.L., T.-A.L. and C.-Y.C.; Software, C.-Y.L., T.-A.L. and C.-Y.C.; Resources, C.-Y.L. and C.-Y.C.; Data curation, T.-A.L.; Writing—original draft, C.-Y.C. All authors have read and agreed to the published version of the manuscript.

Funding: This research received no external funding.

Data Availability Statement: Not applicable.

Conflicts of Interest: The authors declare no conflict of interest.

References

1. Hoang, D.T.; Kang, H.; Kang, J. A motor current signal-based bearing fault diagnosis using deep learning and information fusion. *IEEE Trans. Instrum. Meas.* **2020**, *69*, 3325–3333. [CrossRef]
2. Singh, S.; Kumar, N. Detection of bearing faults in mechanical systems using stator current monitoring. *IEEE Trans. Ind. Informat.* **2017**, *13*, 1341–1349. [CrossRef]
3. Chuan, L.; de Oliveira, J.V.; Cerrada, M.; Cabrera, D.; Sánchez, R.V.; Zurita, G. A systematic review of fuzzy formalisms for bearing fault diagnosis. *IEEE Trans. Fuzzy Syst.* **2019**, *27*, 1362–1382.
4. Dolenc, B.; Boškoski, P.; Juričić, D. Distributed bearing fault diagnosis based on vibration analysis. *Mech. Syst. Signal Process.* **2016**, *66–67*, 521–532. [CrossRef]
5. Attoui, I.; Fergani, N.; Boutasseta, N.; Oudjani, B.; Deliou, A. A new time-frequency method for identification and classification of ball bearing faults. *J. Sound Vib.* **2017**, *397*, 241–265. [CrossRef]
6. Zhao, H.; Yang, X.; Chen, B.; Chen, H.; Deng, W. Bearing fault diagnosis using transfer learning and optimized deep belief network. *Meas. Sci. Technol.* **2022**, *33*, 065009. [CrossRef]
7. Wu, Y.; Jiang, B.; Wang, Y. Incipient winding fault detection and diagnosis for squirrel-cage induction motors equipped on CRH trains. *ISA Trans.* **2020**, *99*, 488–495. [CrossRef] [PubMed]
8. Kaya, Y.; Kuncan, F.; Ertunç, H.M. A new automatic bearing fault size diagnosis using time-frequency images of CWT and deep transfer learning method. *Turk. J. Electr. Eng. Comput. Sci.* **2020**, *30*, 1851–1867. [CrossRef]
9. Zhang, C.H.Y.; Yuan, L.; Xiang, S. Analog circuit incipient fault diagnosis method using DBN based features extraction. *IEEE Access* **2018**, *6*, 23053–23064. [CrossRef]
10. Chen, Y.Q.; Fink, O.; Sansavini, G. Combined fault location, and classification for power transmission lines fault diagnosis with integrated feature extraction. *IEEE Trans. Ind. Electron.* **2018**, *65*, 561–569. [CrossRef]
11. Zhu, J.; Ge, Z.; Song, Z. Distributed parallel PCA for modeling and monitoring of large-scale plant-wide processes with big data. *IEEE Trans. Ind. Inf.* **2017**, *13*, 1877–1885. [CrossRef]
12. Zhao, H.; Zheng, J.; Xu, J.; Deng, W. Fault diagnosis method based on principal component analysis and broad learning system. *IEEE Access* **2019**, *7*, 99263–99272. [CrossRef]
13. Wang, Y.; Zhu, Y.; Wang, Q.; Tang, Y.; Duan, F.; Yang, Y. Complex fault source identification method for high-voltage trip-offs of wind farms based on SU-MRMR and PSO-SVM. *IEEE Access* **2020**, *8*, 130379–130391. [CrossRef]
14. Ye, X.; Hu, Y.; Shen, J.; Feng, R.; Zhai, G. An improved empirical mode decomposition based on adaptive weighted rational quartic spline for rolling bearing fault diagnosis. *IEEE Access* **2020**, *8*, 123813–123827. [CrossRef]
15. Rehman, N.U.; Aftab, H. Multivariate variational mode decomposition. *IEEE Trans. Signal Process.* **2019**, *67*, 6039–6052. [CrossRef]
16. Reddy, B.S.; Chatterji, B.N. An FFT-based technique for translation, rotation, and scale-invariant image registration. *IEEE Trans. Image Process.* **1996**, *5*, 1266–1271. [CrossRef]
17. Wang, Y.; Zheng, L.; Gao, Y.; Li, S. Vibration Signal Extraction Based on FFT and Least Square Method. *IEEE Access* **2020**, *8*, 224092–224107. [CrossRef]
18. Bayram, S.; Kaplan, K.; Kuncan, M.; Ertunç, H.M. The effect of bearings faults to coefficients obtaned by using wavelet transform. In Proceedings of the 2014 22nd Signal Processing and Communications Applications Conference (SIU), Trabzon, Turkey, 23–25 April 2014; pp. 991–994.
19. Chine, W.; Mellit, A.; Lughi, V.; Malek, A.; Sulligoi, G.; Pavan, A.M. A novel fault diagnosis technique for photovoltaic systems based on artificial neural networks. *Renew. Energy* **2016**, *90*, 501–512. [CrossRef]
20. Luo, A.; An, F.; Zhang, X.; Mattausch, H.J. A hardware-efficient recognition accelerator using Haar-like feature and SVM classifier. *IEEE Access* **2019**, *7*, 14472–14487. [CrossRef]
21. Cui, M.L.; Wang, Y.Q.; Lin, X.S.; Zhong, M.Y. Fault diagnosis of rolling bearings based on an improved stack autoencoder and support vector machine. *IEEE Sens. J.* **2021**, *21*, 4927–4937. [CrossRef]
22. Wang, Q.; Wang, S.; Wei, B.; Chen, W.; Zhang, Y. Weighted K-NN classification method of bearings fault diagnosis with multi-dimensional sensitive features. *IEEE Access* **2021**, *9*, 45428–45440. [CrossRef]
23. Hong Lan, L.T.; Tuan, T.M.; Ngan, T.T.; Son, L.H.; Giang, N.L.; Nhu Ngoc, V.T.; Hai, P.V. A New Complex Fuzzy Inference System with Fuzzy Knowledge Graph and Extensions in Decision Making. *IEEE Access* **2020**, *8*, 164899–164921. [CrossRef]
24. Roy, S.S.; Dey, S.; Chatterjee, S. Autocorrelation aided random forest classifier based on bearing fault detection framework. *IEEE Sens. J.* **2020**, *20*, 10792–10800. [CrossRef]
25. Russell, S.J.; Norvig, P. Contributing writers. In *Artificial Intelligence: A Modern Approach*, 2nd ed.; John, F.C., Jitendra, M.M., Douglas, D.E., Eds.; Prentice Hall: Englewood Cliffs, NJ, USA, 2003.
26. Zaccone, G.; Karim, R.; Menshawy, A. *Deep Learning with TensorFlow: Explore Neural Networks with Python*; Packt: Birmingham, UK, 2017.
27. Ketkar, N. *Deep Learning with Python: A Hands-On Introduction*; Apress: New York, NY, USA, 2017; pp. 195–208.

28. Kuncan, M. An intelligent approach for bearing fault diagnosis: Combination of 1D-LBP and GRA. *IEEE Access* **2020**, *8*, 137517–137529. [CrossRef]
29. Kaplan, K.; Bayram, S.; Kuncan, M.; Ertunç, H.M. Feature extraction of ball bearings in time-space and estimation of fault size with method of ANN. In Proceedings of the 16th International Conference on Mechatronics, Brno, Czech Republic, 3–5 December 2014; pp. 295–300.
30. Yang, H.; Li, X.; Zhang, W. Interpretability of deep convolutional neural networks on rolling bearing fault diagnosis. *Meas. Sci. Technol.* **2022**, *33*, 055005. [CrossRef]
31. Lai, Y.J.; Liu, T.Y.; Hwang, C.L. TOPSIS for MODM. *Eur. J. Oper. Res.* **1994**, *76*, 486–500. [CrossRef]
32. Sun, Y.; Ma, L.; Qin, N.; Zhang, M.; Lv, Q. Analog filter circuits feature selection using MRMR and SVM. In Proceedings of the 14th International Conference on Control, Automation and Systems (ICCAS 2014), Gyeonggi-do, Republic of Korea, 22–25 October 2014; pp. 1543–1547.
33. Li, X.; Zheng, Z.; Wu, L.; Li, R.; Huang, J.; Hu, X.; Guo, P. A stratified method for large-scale power system transient stability assessment based on maximum relevance minimum redundancy arithmetic. *IEEE Access* **2019**, *7*, 61414–61432. [CrossRef]
34. Feng, N.; Zhang, Y.; Zeng, Q.; Tong, M.; Joines, W.T.; Wang, G.P. Direct-splitting-based CN-FDTD for modeling 2D material nanostructure problems. *IEEE Open J. Antennas Propag.* **2020**, *1*, 309–319. [CrossRef]
35. Mohr, J.H.M. *Utility of Piotroski F-Score for Predicting Growth-Stock Returns*; MFIE Capital Working Paper: Kalken, Belgium, 2012.
36. Yu, L.; Liu, H. Feature Selection for High-Dimensional Data: A Fast Correlation-Based Filter Solution. In Proceedings of the 20th International Conference on Machine Learning (ICML-03), Washington, DC, USA, 21–24 August 2003; pp. 856–863.
37. Cekik, R.; Uysal, A.K. A novel filter feature selection method using the rough set for short text data. *Expert Syst. Appl.* **2020**, *160*, 113691. [CrossRef]
38. Saghapour, E.; Kermani, S.; Sehhati, M. A novel feature ranking method for prediction of cancer stages using proteomics data. *PLoS ONE* **2017**, *12*, e0184203. [CrossRef]
39. Ding, H.; Luo, L.; Lin, H. Prediction of Cell Wall Lytic Enzymes Using Chou's Amphiphilic Pseudo Amino Acid Composition. *Protein Pept. Lett.* **2009**, *16*, 351–355. [CrossRef]
40. Nanni, L.; Brahnam, S.; Lumini, A. Prediction of protein structure classes by incorporating different protein descriptors into general Chou's pseudo amino acid composition. *J. Theor. Biol.* **2014**, *360*, 109–116. [CrossRef] [PubMed]
41. Chou, K.C. Some Remarks on Protein Attribute Prediction and Pseudo Amino Acid Composition (50th Anniversary Year Review). *J. Theor. Biol.* **2011**, *273*, 236–247. [CrossRef] [PubMed]
42. Smith, W.A.; Randall, R.B. Rolling element bearing diagnostics using the case western reserve university data: A benchmark study. *Mech. Syst. Signal Process.* **2015**, *64–65*, 100–131. [CrossRef]
43. Zhang, Z.; Zhou, F.; Li, S. A Cross Working Condition Multiscale Recursive Feature Fusion Method for Fault Diagnosis of Rolling Bearing in Multiple Working Conditions. *IEEE Access* **2022**, *10*, 78502–78518. [CrossRef]
44. Yuan, L.; Lian, D.; Kang, X.; Chen, Y.; Zhai, K. Rolling bearing fault diagnosis based on convolutional neural network and support vector machine. *IEEE Access* **2020**, *8*, 137395–137406. [CrossRef]

mathematics

MDPI

Article

Transfer Learning-Based Intelligent Fault Detection Approach for the Industrial Robotic System

Izaz Raouf, Prashant Kumar, Hyewon Lee and Heung Soo Kim *

Department of Mechanical, Robotics and Energy Engineering, Dongguk University-Seoul, 30 Pildong-ro 1-gil, Jung-gu, Seoul 04620, Republic of Korea
* Correspondence: heungsoo@dgu.edu; Tel.: +82-2-2260-8577; Fax: +82-2-2263-9379

Abstract: With increasing customer demand, industry 4.0 gained a lot of interest, which is based on smart factories. In smart factories, robotic components are vulnerable to failure due to various industrial operations such as assembly, manufacturing, and product handling. Timely fault detection and diagnosis (FDD) is important to keep the industrial operation smooth. Previously, only the unloaded-based FDD algorithms were considered for the industrial robotic system. In the industrial environment, the robot is working under various working conditions such as speeds, loads, and motions. Hence, to reduce the domain discrepancy between the lab scale and the real working environment, we conducted experimentations under various working conditions. For that purpose, an extensive experimental setup is prepared to perform a series of various experiments mimicking the real environmental condition. In addition, in previous research work, various machine learning (ML) and deep learning (DL) approaches were proposed for robotic arm component fault detection. However, various issues are related to the DL and ML approaches. The ML models are problem-specific, and complex in computations. The DL model needs a huge amount of data. The DL model is composed of various layers that have not been thoroughly explored; as a result, the fault detection model lacks a comprehensive explanation. To overcome these issues, the transfer learning (TL) model is considered with the diverse experimental scenarios. The main contribution is to increase the generalization capabilities of the robotic PHM in the context of previously available research work. For that purpose, the VGG16 model is used because of its autonomous feature extractions for fault classification. The data are collected under a variety of different operating conditions such as loadings, speeds, and motion patterns. The 1D signal is converted to a 2D signal (scalogram) to perform the TL model. The proposed approach shows effective fault detection performance and has the capabilities of generalization under variable working conditions.

Keywords: fault detection; prognostic health management; variable working condition; bearing fault; servomotor fault

MSC: 68T01

1. Introduction

The smart factory is evolving regularly because of high flexibility, deep integration, dynamic reconfiguration, and massive volume of data. The smart factory is composed of various advancements such as artificial intelligence (AI), big data analysis, Internet of Things (IoT), industrial internet, and cloud computing [1,2]. One of the important factors of smart factories is to boost productivity. Hence, it is mandatory to keep the industrial operation smooth without the downfall of each component. Prognostic health management (PHM) can be used to keep industrial operations running smoothly and consistently. In PHM, data-based techniques are prominent because of the issues related to the physics-based modeling [3].

Machine learning (ML) and deep learning (DL) algorithms have been utilized for the PHM of different mechanical systems [2,4,5]. These techniques are composed of supervised and unsupervised approaches. In supervised approaches, the labeled data are utilized for fault classification; however, in the case of unsupervised approaches, the unlabeled data can be used for fault detection [6–8]. According to ML approaches, handcrafted features are extracted, and the feature space is then reduced by selecting the most prominent feature using feature selection methods. Afterward, the selected feature can be used for fault classification using various ML classifiers. For instance, a feature selection approach with Gaussian Ant Lion optimizer (GALO) is integrated with the K-nearest neighbor (KNN) for the fault detection and diagnosis (FDD) of rotating machines [9]. Lee et al. [10] presented an FDD technique based on the feature variable dimensional coordination to reduce the computational cost. Buchaiah et al. [11] studied the bearing FDD using an ML approach based on the Bhattacharyya distance and SVM. Guo et al. [12] presented motor current signature analysis (MCSA) for the FDD using the multi-sensor data, the improved cyclic spectral covariance matrix (ICSCM), and the MCSA combined which completely sustained the connectivity of the various sensors. The DL model has been used for the FDD because of its robustness and ease in computational complexities as compared to the hand-crafted features. Surendran et al. [13] proposed a DL model using a sailfish optimizer (SFO) to optimize the hyperparameters for accurate FDD. Ma et al. [14] proposed an ensemble DL-based FDD for the bearing system to overcome the generalization performance by integrating different DL models with multi-objective optimizations. In addition, various DL models have been proposed for the FDD of rotating machinery [15–17].

The robotic system, especially the six degree of freedom (DOF) robot, is the backbone of the smart factory; hence, its PHM is mandatory to keep the industrial operations. Over the years, various approaches have been used for robotic PHM; ferrography analysis (FA) [18], vibration analysis (VA) [19], and acoustic emission analysis (AEA) [20,21]. However, various issues are concerned related those conventional approaches, such as installation of extra sensors, real-time fault detection, bulky working environment, implementation issues, and financial expenditures, etc. To overcome these issues, the encapsulated system of the robot motor current signature analysis (MCSA) is applied for the PHM analysis [22]. For instance, a feature engineering-based ML-model is proposed for the FDD of the robotic rotate vector (RV) based on simple motion [23]. In addition, a discrete wavelet transform (DWT) is used to analyze the electrical current data and infuse feature extraction and selection for the fault classification based on ML classifier. The handcrafted features, however, are inherently problematic, and the model lacks generalization capabilities. To overcome the issue, a DL model is developed for the robotic FDD. In the proposed approach, a deep wavelet scattering (DWS) is applied for unloaded robotic strain wave gear (SWG) reducer using two different kind of motion with variable speed of operation [24]. The proposed approaches show good performance for unloaded robotic reducer. However, in the proposed algorithms only unloaded conditions are considered. In real industrial scenarios, the robot is operating at various working conditions such as speeds, loads and motions. Hence, it is needed to reduce the domain discrepancy between the lab scale and actual situations. The extensive experimental setup is required to perform a series of various experiments mimicking the real environmental condition and various loading conditions. In addition, various issues are related to the DL approaches; the DL model is made up of various layers which are not well explored, hence, the FDD model lacks comprehensive explanation. The number of parameters and hyperparameters in deeper networks is enormous, necessitating a large amount of labeled data, and computational complexities [25]. To overcome the issues related to the DL and ML, the transfer learning (TL) model can be used with less computation and generalization capabilities [26–30]. Hence, in the proposed work, the TL-based component-level FDD is considered for the actual industrial robotic system which is operating at the real working conditions, such as loading, speed and various profiles of motions.

In the current study, TL model is proposed for the robotic PHM to ensure the generalization capabilities of the model. The extensive experimental setup is prepared to perform a series of various experiments mimicking the real environmental condition, and various loading conditions are considered. The main contribution was to increase the generalization capabilities of the robotic PHM in the context of previously available research work, as given above. For that purpose, the electrical current data of the robotic system is collected under real environmental conditions such as various loadings, speeds, and motion patterns. In the proposed two different motions such as simple and welding motion are considered with variable speed of operation by considering various loading conditions. The data segmentation is performed based on a single cycle of the robotic arm. The 1D signal is converted to a 2D signal to perform the TL model. The TL model is used to overcome data-related issues and data complexities. The TL-based VGG16 model is utilized for the first time in robotic PHM under real environmental conditions. The proposed approach is used for efficient features extraction for the FDD of robotic system, that eliminates the requirement to train the DL from scratch, allowing it to converge faster. The authenticity of the model is evaluated by different FDD parameters and shows excellent results for the FDD of the industrial robotic system.

The manuscript is arranged into different sections. Section 2 is composed of the overall methodology, experimental details, data acquisition, data preprocessing, and TL model. Section 3 overviews the results and discussions. Section 4 summarizes the conclusions of the proposed research work.

2. Methodology

The proposed methodology of the research work carried out is shown in Figure 1. In this work, the FDD model for the real industrial robot (Robostar RA004) is presented. The servomotor bearing fault of axis 3 of the robotic arm is considered. The data are collected under distinct operating conditions such as speed, motion, and loading conditions. To mimic the real working conditions, only the loading-based data are collected for the effective FDD model. The data preprocessing is carried out by data segmentation and synchronization. The 1D data are converted into 2D scalogram images for the FDD model. The TL model is used to overcome data-related issues and data complexities. The VGG16-based TL model is considered for the extraction of efficient features for the FDD of the robotic system. The authenticity of the VGG16 is based on the diverse type of data with variable working conditions. For instance, overall, image-based data for various loading conditions such as 500 g, 1000 g, 1500 g, 2000 g, 2500 g, and 3000 g are considered for training the model based on the simple and welding motion, separately. Hence, for both the motions, around 80% of the data is used for the training purpose. To check the generalization capabilities of the model the highest loading conditions are used for testing and validating the model. For that purpose, 20% of the data is used for testing and validation, considering 10% for testing and 10% for validation. Hence, the health status of the bearing is predicted for the highest loading condition (3500 g) using the trained model with the lower loading condition. TL eliminates the requirement to train the DL from scratch, allowing it to converge faster. Detailed methodology is presented in the upcoming sections.

2.1. Experimental Detials

In the proposed work, the industrial robot (Robostar RA004) is under consideration. It is a 6-DOF robot, where all six axes of the robot can move independently. Each axis of the robot is powered by servomotor to operate various industrial operations and electric motor for various motion of the axes. The specification of RA004 with related information of each joint is shown in Table 1. Various parameters are mentioned such as maximum distance, payload, repetitive positioning accuracy, motion range and speed range. Two health states (healthy and faulty) are considered to carry the PHM process for the servomotor of the robotics arm. The robotic servomotor bearing PHM is considered with two health states (healthy and faulty). The inner bearing fault is induced in the inner race of the bearing at axis 3 of the robot. Figure 2 represents the flow of the experimental system used in the proposed research work.

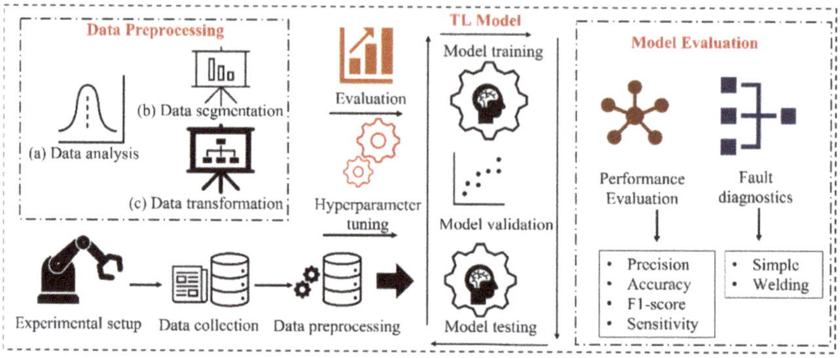

Figure 1. Proposed research methodology for the robotic FDD.

Table 1. Specifications of Robostar RA004.

Variable		Quantity (Unit)
Allowable distance		610 mm
Maximum load		4 kg
Repeated placement accuracy		±0.02 mm
Motion Range/Maximum Speed	J_1	±170°/410°/s
	J_2	−90° to +45°/410°/s
	J_3	−210° to +61°/520°/s
	J_4	±190°/560°/s
	J_5	±130°/560°/s
	J_6	±360°/900°/s

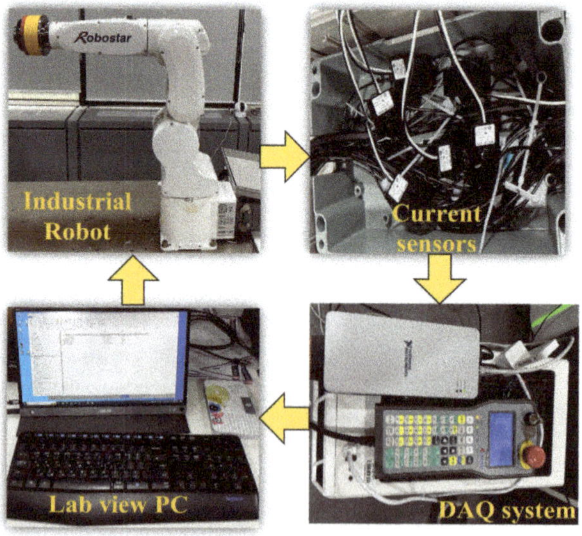

Figure 2. Demonstration of the experimental system.

2.2. Data Acquisition

The data acquisition (DAQ) system is illustrated in Figure 3. The robotic arm is powered by an electric motor and the electrical current data are collected using the current sensors (JS16FL-100). The sensors are connected to the robot power supply to observe the electrical current data. The DAQ system collects the data from the sensors and then the data are forwarded to the to the lab view personal computer (PC). The information on the collected is given in Table 2. In the experimental setup, two distinguished kinds of motion such as simple and welding motion are considered. In simple motion, the axis is simply moving forward and backward. On the other hand, all the axes are moving independently in the welding motion [22]. The electrical current data are collected for the robotic arm with 10 different speeds, such as 10% to 100% with an increment of 10%. To consider the actual environmental conditions, the data are collected under different loading conditions such as (500 g, 1000 g, 1500 g, 2000 g, 2500 g, 3000 g and 3500 g).

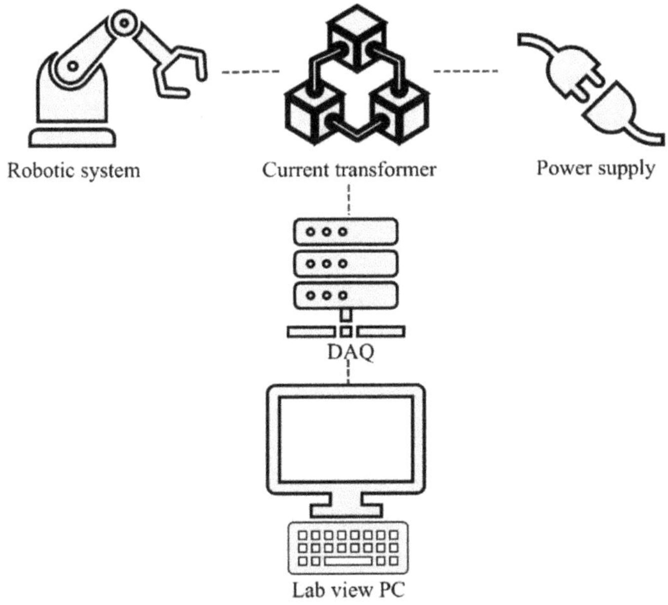

Figure 3. Demonstration of the DAQ system.

Table 2. Experimental descriptions.

Variable	Description
Data type	1st phase of electrical current
Motion	Simple and welding motion
Speed	10~100% with 10% increment
Fault type	Inner bearing fault of servomotor
Fault location	Robotic 3rd axis
Health states	Normal, faulty
Sampling frequency	5 kHz
Loading conditions	500 g, 1000 g, 1500 g, 2000 g, 2500 g, 3000 g, and 3500 g

2.3. Data Preprocessing

Data preprocessing is very crucial to clean and organize the PHM process. In the proposed work, the data preprocessing is done in two steps. Initially, all the raw data are converted to segmentation based on per cycle and then 1D signals are converted into 2D images for the TL model for the robotic PHM. The upcoming sections describe the details of the data segmentation and data conversion.

2.3.1. Data Segmentation

The collected data from the current sensors are raw and cannot be used directly for the PHM process of the robotics system. The data needs to be cleaned by removing unnecessary information. In addition, the data for the same operating conditions with different health states needs to be synchronized to reduce the probability of confusion in the fault signature because of the data pattern rather than the health states. Pre-processing of signals is required for real-time FDD. It is hard to use continuously acquired signals for PHM, hence, pre-processing is required to divide the data into a single cycle from the raw data set to analyze the failure of a single cycle. The signal segmentation is carried out by using the following steps.

I. Set a sample cycle from the overall raw signal of the collected data.
II. Perform short-time Fourier transform (STFT) on the original signal and sample data.
III. Based on the power spectral density (PSD) of the sample data from STFT, the sample data are moved by the set window.
IV. The signal is divided by finding a case where the difference between the PSD value of the sample data and the original signal is the local minimum region.
V. Finally, based on the local minimum, compute the start and end points of each cycle.

Through this operation, it is possible to divide the data into a single cycle from the repetitive raw signal, as shown in Figure 4. Hence, the segmented and synchronized data are achieved.

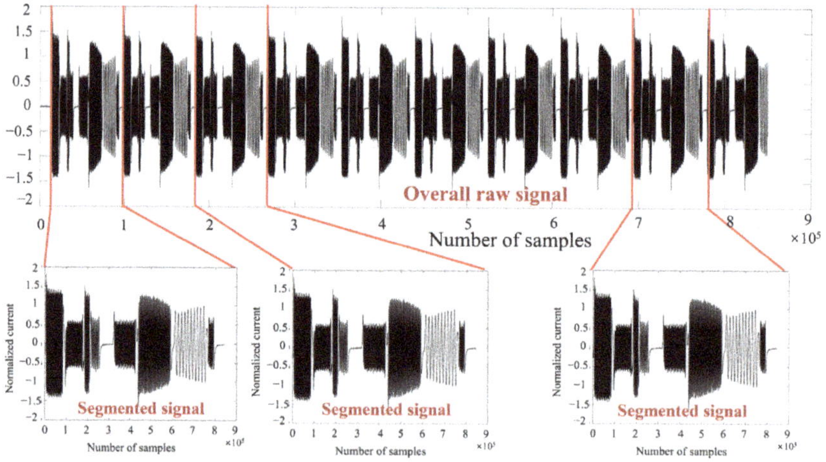

Figure 4. Data segmentation process for the raw signal.

2.3.2. Data Conversion

The input data are fed into the TL model in the form of 2D images to extract autonomous features. As a result, the time domain data must be converted into 2D images. Scalogram images are considered in the proposed method. The upcoming subsections are related to the data conversion into 2D images.

(a) Scalogram

The scalogram is a time- and frequency-dependent absolute value demonstration of a signal's continuous wavelet transform (CWT). The scalogram proves more useful than the spectrogram for evaluating real-world signals with features occurring at different scales, such as slow rate variable events interrupted by sudden transients. It can be used to improve time localization for high-frequency, short-term events as well as frequency tracking for low-frequency, longer-duration occurrences. Resampling the signal with a time-scaled and shifted wavelet yields the CWT. Wavelets oscillate and can have a wide range of values. On a prototype wavelet, scalability and transitioning operations are carried out. The CWT scaling shrinks and stretches the prototype wavelet. When the prototype wavelet is shrunk, it generates wavelets with short duration and high frequency, which are useful for detecting transient events. When the prototype wavelet is stretched, long-duration, low-frequency wavelets are produced, which can be used to isolate long-duration, low-frequency events [31]. Figure 5 shows the representation of time domain signals and their scalogram images for simple and welding motions.

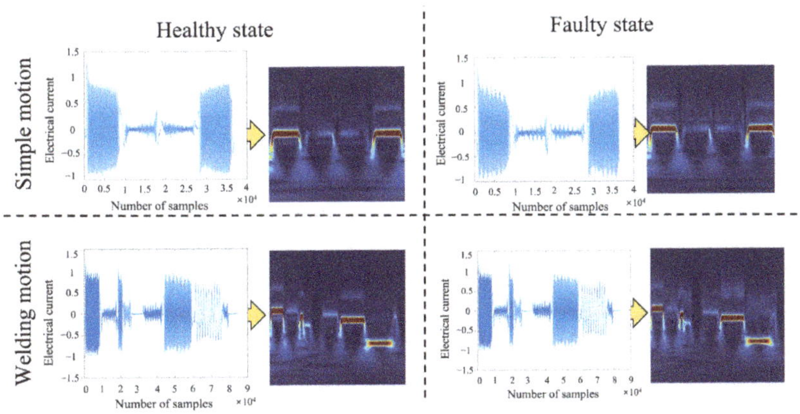

Figure 5. Scalogram representation of simple and welding motion for healthy and faulty states.

(b) Continuous wavelets transform (CWT)

The wavelet transform outperforms the conventional cosine and Fourier transforms as a time-frequency transform. The continuous wavelet transform (CWT) decomposes complex signal information and extracts interesting patterns by convolution of input sequence with mother wavelet-generated functions. Although the convolution is computed using the short-time Fourier transform, it provides different time-frequency resolutions. [32–34]. The wavelet windowing method is used for varying resolution regions. Wavelet decomposition uses a scale rather than a frequency to map a signal into a time-scale plan. This corresponds to the time-frequency plan of the short-time Fourier transform (STFT), with each scale of the time-scale plane representing a different frequency range of the time-frequency plan. The wavelet transforms a signal into sinusoids of varying frequencies, whereas the Fourier transforms a signal into transformed or sized contours from a mother wavelet.

2.4. Transfer Learning Model for Fault Detection

The general framework of TL between the target domain and source domain is shown in Figure 6. Timely fault detection of bearings in the industrial robot is crucial for minimal downtime and uninterrupted operations. The current data obtained from the servomotors were used for bearing fault detection. The current signals are the time series data. The time series data have been converted to scalogram images to better represent the data. These scalogram-based images will be used to develop the FDD model. In the real-world scenario, the availability of a huge amount of labeled data is a big challenge to train, test, and validate the DL model. The shortage of a large amount of data restricts the performance of the deep CNN model. Moreover, training the DL model from scratch is a cumbersome task. The application of transfer learning could mitigate this issue and resolve the issue of training the fault detection model from scratch. The pretrained VGG16 model (already trained on the ImageNet dataset) has been employed for knowledge transfer and fault detection. The VGG6 model has performed efficiently on the ImageNet dataset and comprises multiple convolution blocks, fully connected, and SoftMax layers as the final layer. The weights of the convolutional blocks of the VGG16 model have been transferred to the FDD model. The proposed FDD model is given in the Figure 7. These convolutional blocks (as shown in Figure 7) have been used for extracting features from the input scalogram images developed from the servomotor current signals. These extracted features have been fed to the fully connected layers and SoftMax in the final layer for the bearing fault classification. The weights of the convolutional blocks are frozen, and fully connected layers are kept trainable. The fully connected layers were optimized with the help of the adaptive gradient optimizer. The output layer must classify two states of the bearing faults of the servomotor used in the robotic arm.

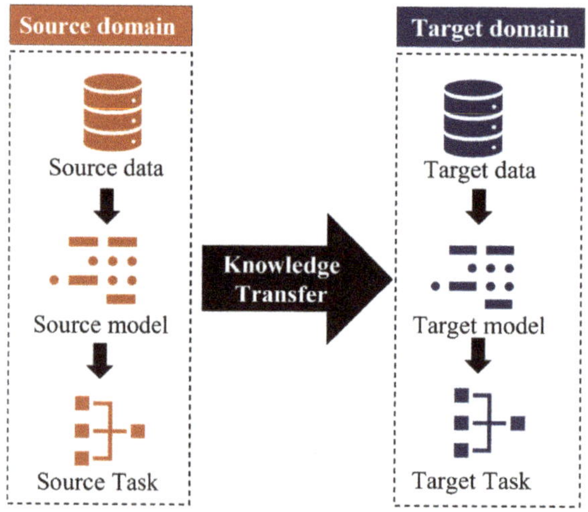

Figure 6. Framework of the TL between the source and target domain.

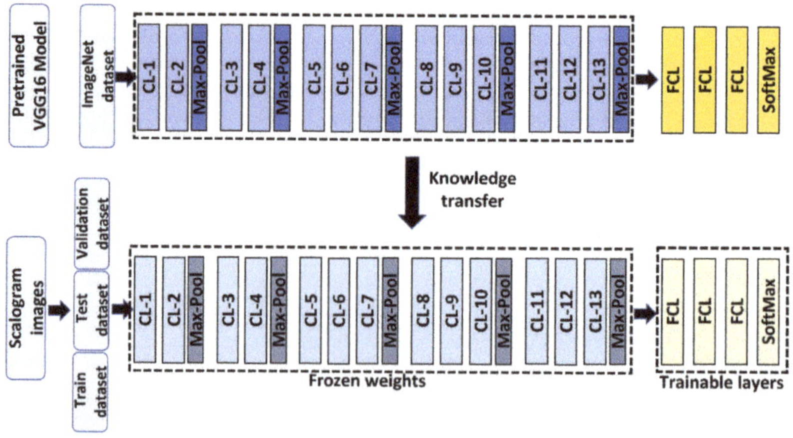

Figure 7. Block diagram of the proposed transfer learning-based fault detection model.

3. Results and Discussions

The complete analysis has been carried out on the scalogram images obtained from the current signals of the servomotor of the robotic arm. The dataset has considered various operational modes of industrial robots, including the different motion profiles, operating speeds, and multiple loading conditions. The speed variations from 10% to 100% of the rated speed have been employed during the data collection. Moreover, a variety of loading conditions, including 500 g, 1500 g, 2500 g, and 3500 g, have been considered during the current data acquisition. These 1D current data have been converted into the 2D scalogram, which has been used to develop the FDD model. The complete dataset has been divided into the training, test, and validation dataset. The two states of the servomotor, namely healthy and bearing fault, have been considered in the proposed work. Overall, image-based data for various loading conditions such as 500 g, 1000 g, 1500 g, 2000 g, 2500 g, and 3000 g are considered for training the model based on the simple and welding motion separately. Hence, for both the motions, around 80% of the data is used for the training purpose. To check the generalization capabilities of the model, the highest loading conditions are used for testing and validating the model. For that purpose, 20% of the data is used for testing and validation, considering 10% for testing and 10% for validation. Hence, the health status of the bearing is predicted for the highest loading condition (3500 g) using the trained model with the lower loading condition.

Training in deep architecture is a challenging task, as well as computationally expensive. The weights of the convolutional blocks of the VGG16 have been used for the proposed transfer learning-based fault detection model. The extracted features from the convolutional blocks have been fed to the trainable fully connected layers, with the SoftMax layer as the final layer. The model's performance was evaluated with the help of a confusion matrix and different performance metrics like accuracy, precision, sensitivity, and $F1$-score [35].

$$\text{Accuracy} = \frac{TP + TN}{TN + TP + FN + FP} \tag{1}$$

$$\text{Precision} = \frac{TP}{TP + FN} \tag{2}$$

$$\text{Sensitivity} = \frac{TP}{TP + FN} \tag{3}$$

$$F1\text{-score} = \frac{2\,TP}{2TP + FP + FN} \tag{4}$$

where TP, TN, FN and FP represent true positive, true negative, false negative and false positive, respectively.

3.1. Simple Motion

The TL model is used for the FDD of the robotic bearing using simple motion data. It is very complicated to distinguish the healthy and faulty images with the necked eyes as shown in Figure 8. Under the same operating condition of loading and speed, it is hard to see the difference between the healthy and faulty states. However, the pattern for the healthy and faulty states is changing with increasing loading. Hence, the application of the TL model is utilized to predict the health state of the data based on 3500 g from a trained model with lower loading cases.

The TL-based VGG-16 FD model consolidated after approximately 200 epochs. It is demonstrated that the model converged in 200 epochs, as illustrated the training and validation loss curves in Figure 9. For fault classification, an average accuracy of 98% is achieved. Figure 10 depicts the proposed model's confusion matrix (CM). The CM indicates that healthy and faulty states have been efficiently classified using simple motion data. The performance evaluation parameters such as precision (p), sensitivity (s), and $F1$-score are shown in Table 3. It is noted that the proposed method shows 99.9%, 98%, and 98.08% of training, testing, and validation accuracy, respectively. It is demonstrated that the presented approach of autonomous feature extraction of the TL model showed an effective FDD for the robotic servomotor using simple motion data under variable operating conditions. It is demonstrated that the health state of the higher loading conditions is predicted accurately.

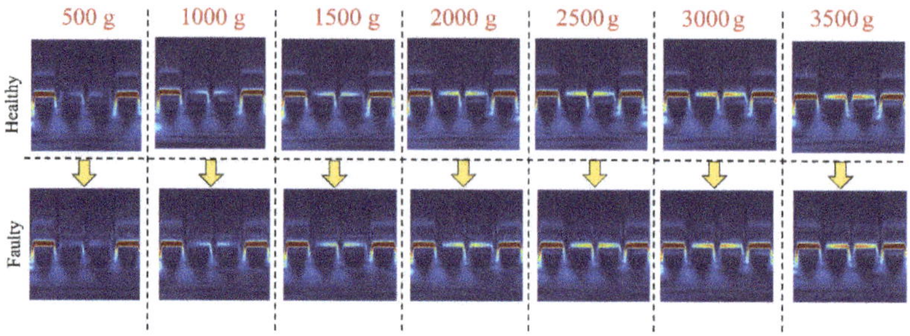

Figure 8. Scalogram representation for various loading conditions for healthy and faulty state under the same operating conditions of 10% speed.

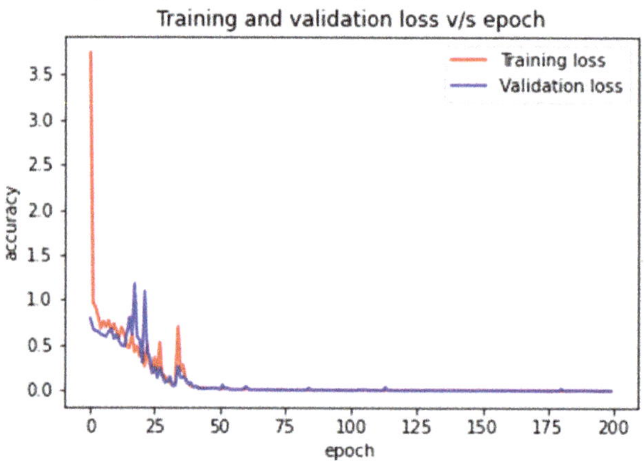

Figure 9. The proposed TL-based FDD approach's loss curve using simple motion data.

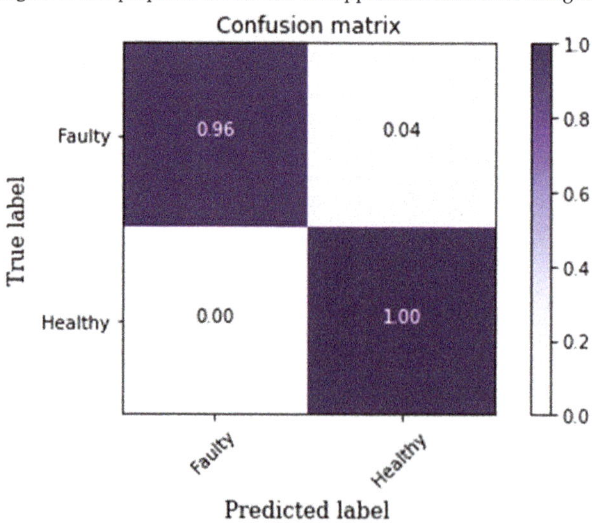

Figure 10. Simple motion-based CM for the proposed TL-based FDD approach.

Table 3. Performance metrics for the proposed TL-based model for fault detection using simple motion.

State	Precision (p)	Sensitivity (s)	$F1$-Score
Faulty	1.0	0.96	0.98
Healthy	0.96	1.0	0.98

3.2. Welding Motion

Similarly, the simple motion in the case of welding motion under the same operation condition of loading it is complicated to find the fault characteristics for healthy and faulty. However, the fault pattern of the scalogram images is changing with the increased loading on the robotic arm, as shown in Figure 11. In view of that, the electrical motor draws more electrical current with higher loading, hence the pattern changes with higher loading conditions. To provide a generalized FDD model the higher loading data (3500 g) is used for the testing and validation to predict the health state of this data set using the trained model with the lower loading conditions.

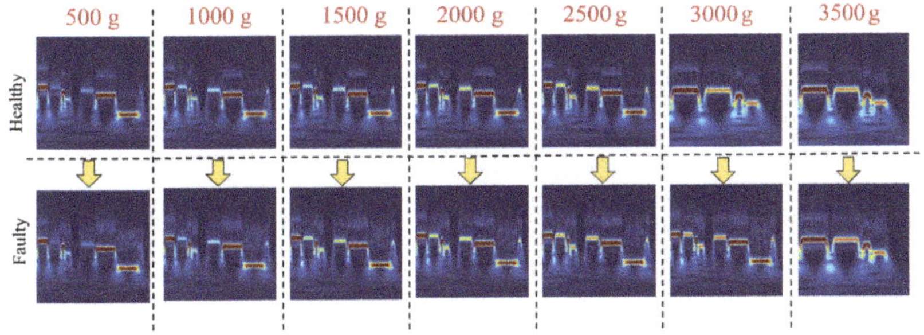

Figure 11. Scalogram representation for various loading conditions for healthy and faulty state under the same operating conditions of 10% speed.

The TL-based VGG-16 FD model converged after approximately 200 epochs. Figure 12 depicts the training and validation loss curves. For fault classification, an average accuracy of 99% is achieved. Figure 13 depicts the proposed model's confusion matrix (CM). The CM shows that conditions such as healthy, and faulty have been significantly classified using welding motion data. The values of performance evaluation parameters such as precision (p), sensitivity (s), and $F1$-score are shown in Table 4.

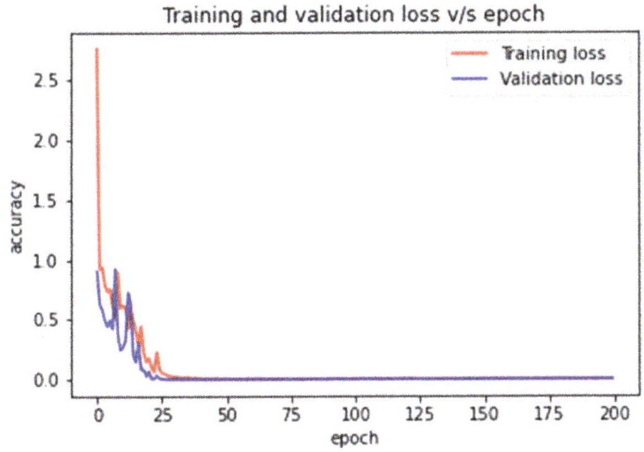

Figure 12. The proposed TL-based FDD approach's loss curve using welding motion.

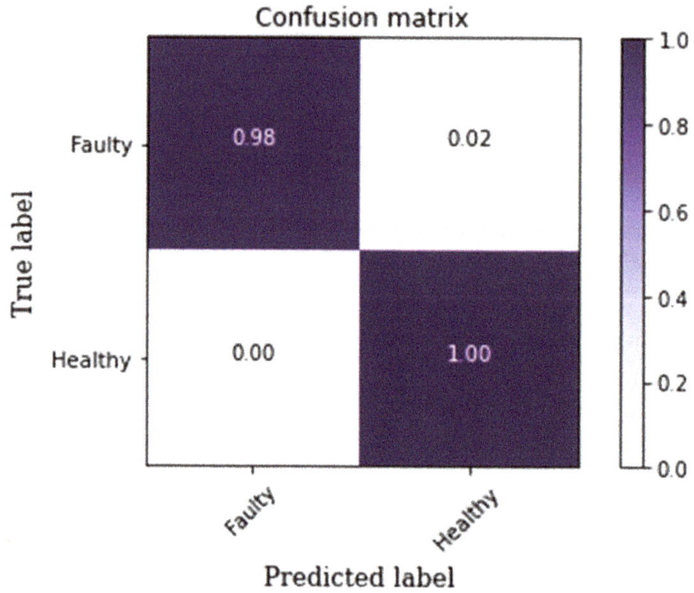

Figure 13. Welding motion-based CM for the proposed TL-based FDD approach.

Table 4. Performance metrics for the proposed TL-based FDD for welding motion.

State	Precision (p)	Sensitivity (s)	*F*1-Score
Faulty	1.0	0.98	0.99
Healthy	0.98	1.0	0.99

It is noted that the proposed method shows 99.6%, 99%, and 99.2% of training, testing, and validation accuracy, respectively. It is demonstrated that the proposed approach of autonomous feature extraction of the TL model showed an effective FDD for the robotic servomotor using simple motion data under variable operating conditions. It is demonstrated that the health state of the higher loading conditions is predicted accurately.

To sum up, in the proposed work, the issues related to the DL- and ML-based FDD are solved. In the real-world scenario, the availability of a large amount of labeled data is a big challenge to train, test, and validate the deep model. Hence, the application of TL is applied to overcome the issues related to conventional ML and DL FDD. The above results show the robustness of the proposed approach in terms of simple and welding motion data sets. In addition, the generalization capabilities of the proposed model are validated by using the highest loading conditions for testing and validation purposes. In view of that, the proposed approach can predict the health state of a new data set (unseen data). In future, more cases can be considered by evaluating a comprehensive analysis for predicting the health state of unseen data. Further, the unsupervised model can be proposed for the FDD of the robotic system.

4. Conclusions

In conclusion, the current research work proposed a robust FDD model for the robotic system under the variable working condition of speed, motion, and various loaded. To mimic real environmental conditions, the data were collected from the actual robotic system with real-world operating conditions. For that purpose, a series of different loads were integrated into the robotic manipulator. The electrical current data were collected to overcome the issues of data handling and extra sensor installation. The raw data were preprocessed using data segmentation and data synchronization. The 1D data were converted into 2D images for further processing. The application of TL was used to mitigate the issues related to the DL- and ML-based FDD. The pretrained VGG16 model (already trained on the ImageNet dataset) has been employed for knowledge transfer and fault detection. The VGG6 model performed efficiently on the ImageNet dataset and comprises multiple convolution blocks, fully connected, and SoftMax layers as the final layer. The weights of the convolutional blocks of the VGG16 model were transferred to the fault detection model. Convolutional blocks were used for extracting features from the input scalogram images developed from the servomotor current signals. These extracted features were fed to the fully connected layers and SoftMax in the final layer for the bearing fault classification. The weights of the convolutional blocks are frozen, and fully connected layers are kept trainable. The fully connected layers were optimized with the help of the adaptive gradient optimizer. The output layer classified the health states into healthy and faulty states. The proposed approach shows effective fault detection performance and has the capabilities of generalization under variable working conditions.

Author Contributions: Conceptualization, H.S.K., I.R., P.K. and H.L.; methodology, I.R. and P.K.; formal analysis I.R. and P.K.; investigation, I.R., P.K. and H.L.; resources, H.S.K.; writing—original draft preparation, I.R., P.K. and H.L.; writing—review and editing, P.K. and H.S.K.; visualization, I.R.; supervision, H.S.K.; project administration, H.S.K.; funding acquisition, H.S.K. All authors have read and agreed to the published version of the manuscript.

Funding: This work was supported by the project for Smart Manufacturing Innovation R&D funded Korea Ministry of SMEs and Startups in 2022. (Project No. RS-2022-00140460).

Institutional Review Board Statement: Not applicable.

Informed Consent Statement: Not applicable.

Data Availability Statement: Not applicable.

Conflicts of Interest: The authors declare no conflict of interest.

References

1. Wu, Y.; Dai, H.-N.; Wang, H.; Xiong, Z.; Guo, S. A Survey of Intelligent Network Slicing Management for Industrial IoT: Integrated Approaches for Smart Transportation, Smart Energy, and Smart Factory. *IEEE Commun. Surv. Tutor.* **2022**, *24*, 1175–1211. [CrossRef]
2. Raouf, I.; Khan, A.; Khalid, S.; Sohail, M.; Azad, M.M.; Kim, H.S. Sensor-Based Prognostic Health Management of Advanced Driver Assistance System for Autonomous Vehicles: A Recent Survey. *Mathematics* **2022**, *10*, 3233. [CrossRef]
3. Meng, H.; Li, Y.-F. A Review on Prognostics and Health Management (PHM) Methods of Lithium-Ion Batteries. *Renew. Sustain. Energy Rev.* **2019**, *116*, 109405. [CrossRef]
4. Kumar, P.; Hati, A.S. Deep Convolutional Neural Network Based on Adaptive Gradient Optimizer for Fault Detection in SCIM. *ISA Trans.* **2021**, *111*, 350–359. [CrossRef] [PubMed]
5. Kumar, P.; Hati, A.S. Review on Machine Learning Algorithm Based Fault Detection in Induction Motors. *Arch. Comput. Methods Eng.* **2021**, *28*, 1929–1940. [CrossRef]
6. Aggarwal, R.K.; Xuan, Q.Y.; Dunn, R.W.; Johns, A.T.; Bennett, A. A Novel Fault Classification Technique for Double-Circuit Lines Based on a Combined Unsupervised/Supervised Neural Network. *IEEE Trans. Power Deliv.* **1999**, *14*, 1250–1256. [CrossRef]
7. Vakharia, V.; Gupta, V.K.; Kankar, P.K. Ball Bearing Fault Diagnosis Using Supervised and Unsupervised Machine Learning Methods. *Int. J. Acoust. Vib.* **2015**, *20*, 244–250. [CrossRef]
8. Wang, Y.; Yang, H.; Yuan, X.; Shardt, Y.A.; Yang, C.; Gui, W. Deep Learning for Fault-Relevant Feature Extraction and Fault Classification with Stacked Supervised Auto-Encoder. *J. Process Control* **2020**, *92*, 79–89. [CrossRef]
9. Vashishtha, G.; Kumar, R. Feature Selection Based on Gaussian Ant Lion Optimizer for Fault Identification in Centrifugal Pump. In *Recent Advances in Machines and Mechanisms*; Springer: Berlin/Heidelberg, Germany, 2023; pp. 295–310.
10. Lee, Y.; Park, B.; Jo, M.; Lee, J.; Lee, C. A Quantitative Diagnostic Method of Feature Coordination for Machine Learning Model with Massive Data from Rotary Machine. *Expert Syst. Appl.* **2023**, *214*, 119117. [CrossRef]
11. Buchaiah, S.; Shakya, P. Bearing Fault Diagnosis and Prognosis Using Data Fusion Based Feature Extraction and Feature Selection. *Measurement* **2022**, *188*, 110506. [CrossRef]
12. Guo, J.; He, Q.; Zhen, D.; Gu, F.; Ball, A.D. Multi-Sensor Data Fusion for Rotating Machinery Fault Detection Using Improved Cyclic Spectral Covariance Matrix and Motor Current Signal Analysis. *Reliab. Eng. Syst. Saf.* **2023**, *230*, 108969. [CrossRef]

13. Surendran, R.; Khalaf, O.I.; Andres, C. Deep Learning Based Intelligent Industrial Fault Diagnosis Model. *CMC-Comput. Mater. Contin.* **2022**, *70*, 6323–6338. [CrossRef]
14. Ma, S.; Chu, F. Ensemble Deep Learning-Based Fault Diagnosis of Rotor Bearing Systems. *Comput. Ind.* **2019**, *105*, 143–152. [CrossRef]
15. Janssens, O.; Slavkovikj, V.; Vervisch, B.; Stockman, K.; Loccufier, M.; Verstockt, S.; Van de Walle, R.; Van Hoecke, S. Convolutional Neural Network Based Fault Detection for Rotating Machinery. *J. Sound Vib.* **2016**, *377*, 331–345. [CrossRef]
16. Zhao, X.; Jia, M. A Novel Unsupervised Deep Learning Network for Intelligent Fault Diagnosis of Rotating Machinery. *Struct. Health Monit.* **2020**, *19*, 1745–1763. [CrossRef]
17. Gong, W.; Chen, H.; Zhang, Z.; Zhang, M.; Wang, R.; Guan, C.; Wang, Q. A Novel Deep Learning Method for Intelligent Fault Diagnosis of Rotating Machinery Based on Improved CNN-SVM and Multichannel Data Fusion. *Sensors* **2019**, *19*, 1693. [CrossRef] [PubMed]
18. Peng, P.; Wang, J. Wear Particle Classification Considering Particle Overlapping. *Wear* **2019**, *422–423*, 119–127. [CrossRef]
19. Farina, M.; Osto, E.; Perizzato, A.; Piroddi, L.; Scattolini, R. Fault Detection and Isolation of Bearings in a Drive Reducer of a Hot Steel Rolling Mill. *Control Eng. Pract.* **2015**, *39*, 35–44. [CrossRef]
20. Li, C.; Sanchez, R.-V.; Zurita, G.; Cerrada, M.; Cabrera, D.; Vásquez, R.E. Gearbox Fault Diagnosis Based on Deep Random Forest Fusion of Acoustic and Vibratory Signals. *Mech. Syst. Signal Process.* **2016**, *76–77*, 283–293. [CrossRef]
21. Zhang, Y.; An, H.; Ding, X.; Liang, W.; Yuan, M.; Ji, C.; Tan, J. Industrial Robot Rotate Vector Reducer Fault Detection Based on Hidden Markov Models. In Proceedings of the 2019 IEEE International Conference on Robotics and Biomimetics (ROBIO), Dali, China, 6–8 December 2019; IEEE: Piscataway, NJ, USA, 2019; pp. 3013–3018.
22. Lee, H.; Raouf, I.; Song, J.; Kim, H.S.; Lee, S. Prognostics and Health Management of the Robotic Servo-Motor under Variable Operating Conditions. *Mathematics* **2023**, *11*, 398. [CrossRef]
23. Raouf, I.; Lee, H.; Kim, H.S. Mechanical Fault Detection Based on Machine Learning for Robotic RV Reducer Using Electrical Current Signature Analysis: A Data-Driven Approach. *J. Comput. Des. Eng.* **2022**, *9*, 417–433. [CrossRef]
24. Raouf, I.; Lee, H.; Noh, Y.R.; Youn, B.D.; Kim, H.S. Prognostic Health Management of the Robotic Strain Wave Gear Reducer Based on Variable Speed of Operation: A Data-Driven via Deep Learning Approach. *J. Comput. Des. Eng.* **2022**, *9*, 1775–1788. [CrossRef]
25. Yang, D.; Hou, N.; Lu, J.; Ji, D. Novel Leakage Detection by Ensemble 1DCNN-VAPSO-SVM in Oil and Gas Pipeline Systems. *Appl. Soft Comput.* **2022**, *115*, 108212. [CrossRef]
26. Kumar, P.; Hati, A.S.; Padmanaban, S.; Leonowicz, Z.; Chakrabarti, P. Amalgamation of Transfer Learning and Deep Convolutional Neural Network for Multiple Fault Detection in SCIM. In Proceedings of the 2020 IEEE International Conference on Environment and Electrical Engineering and 2020 IEEE Industrial and Commercial Power Systems Europe (EEEIC/I&CPS Europe), Madrid, Spain, 9–12 June 2020; IEEE: Piscataway, NJ, USA, 2020; pp. 1–6.
27. Kumar, P.; Kumar, P.; Hati, A.S.; Kim, H.S. Deep Transfer Learning Framework for Bearing Fault Detection in Motors. *Mathematics* **2022**, *10*, 4683. [CrossRef]
28. Rohan, A.; Raouf, I.; Kim, H.S. Rotate Vector (RV) Reducer Fault Detection and Diagnosis System: Towards Component Level Prognostics and Health Management (PHM). *Sensors* **2020**, *20*, 6845. [CrossRef]
29. Yan, R.; Shen, F.; Sun, C.; Chen, X. Knowledge Transfer for Rotary Machine Fault Diagnosis. *IEEE Sens. J.* **2019**, *20*, 8374–8393. [CrossRef]
30. Liu, G.; Shen, W.; Gao, L.; Kusiak, A. Knowledge Transfer in Fault Diagnosis of Rotary Machines. *IET Collab. Intell. Manuf.* **2022**, *4*, 17–34. [CrossRef]
31. Neupane, D.; Kim, Y.; Seok, J. Bearing Fault Detection Using Scalogram and Switchable Normalization-Based CNN (SN-CNN). *IEEE Access* **2021**, *9*, 88151–88166. [CrossRef]
32. Zhao, H.; Liu, J.; Chen, H.; Chen, J.; Li, Y.; Xu, J.; Deng, W. Intelligent Diagnosis Using Continuous Wavelet Transform and Gauss Convolutional Deep Belief Network. *IEEE Trans. Reliab.* **2022**. [CrossRef]
33. Wang, Y.; Yang, Z.; Shi, Z.; Ma, J.; Liu, D.; Shi, L. Periodic Error Detection and Separation of Magnetic Levitation Gyroscope Signals Based on Continuous Wavelet Transform and Singular Spectrum Analysis. *Meas. Sci. Technol.* **2022**, *33*, 065107. [CrossRef]
34. Nor, A.K.B.M.; Pedapait, S.R.; Muhammad, M. Explainable AI (XAI) for PHM of Industrial Asset: A State-of-The-Art, PRISMA-Compliant Systematic Review. *arXiv* **2021**, arXiv:2107.03869.
35. Uddin, M.G.; Nash, S.; Rahman, A.; Olbert, A.I. Performance Analysis of the Water Quality Index Model for Predicting Water State Using Machine Learning Techniques. *Process Saf. Environ. Prot.* **2023**, *169*, 808–828. [CrossRef]

mathematics

Article

Prognostics and Health Management of the Robotic Servo-Motor under Variable Operating Conditions

Hyewon Lee [1], Izaz Raouf [1], Jinwoo Song [1], Heung Soo Kim [1,*] and Soobum Lee [2]

1 Department of Mechanical, Robotics and Energy Engineering, Dongguk University Seoul, 30 Pildong-ro 1-gil, Jung-gu, Seoul 04620, Republic of Korea; leehw_410@dgu.ac.kr (H.L.); izazraouf@dongguk.edu (I.R.); jwsong0620@dgu.edu (J.S.)

2 Department of Mechanical Engineering, University of Maryland Baltimore County, Baltimore, MD 21250, USA; sblee@umbc.edu

* Correspondence: heungsoo@dgu.edu; Tel.: +82-2260-8577; Fax: +82-2-2263-9379

Abstract: A robot is essential in many industrial and manufacturing facilities due to its efficiency, accuracy, and durability. However, continuous use of the robotic system can result in various component failures. The servo motor is one of the critical components, and its bearing is one of the vulnerable parts, hence failure analysis is required. Some previous prognostics and health management (PHM) methods are very limited in considering the realistic operating conditions of industrial robots based on various operating speeds, loading conditions, and motions, because they consider constant speed data with unloading conditions. This paper implements a PHM for the servo motor of a robotic arm based on variable operating conditions. Principal component analysis-based dimensionality reduction and correlation analysis-based feature selection are compared. Two machine learning algorithms have been used to detect fault features under various operating conditions. This method is proposed as a robust fault-detection model for industrial robots under various operating conditions. Features from different domains not only improved the generalization of the model's performance but also improved the computational efficiency of massive data by reducing the total number of features. The results showed more than 90% accuracy under various operating conditions. As a result, the proposed method shows the possibility of robust failure diagnosis under various operating conditions similar to the actual industrial environment.

Keywords: artificial neural network; fault detection; feature extraction; motor current signature analysis; servo motor

MSC: 68T01

1. Introduction

With the development of the smart industry, robots, especially robotic arms, are being used in various applications, such as commercial fields and multi-robot cooperative systems. Therefore, the significance of robots is also increasing. A robot is essential in many industrial facilities due to its efficiency, accuracy, and durability [1,2].

One of the main components that comprise the robot is the servo motor, which determines the rated load and accuracy of the rotation angle of the robot. In particular, a servo motor is commonly used in industrial robots due to its high torque, small size, and precision control [3]. However, robots have many failure issues due to high torque, transformation stress, cyclic load, and impact load. After a certain period of operation, various failures such as bearing failure, broken rotor bars, and misalignment can occur. These failures cause production accidents and reduce productivity. Furthermore, if one of the robot components fails, the entire robot and production may suffer from unexpected expenses [4–6]. In this study, we deal with a fault that causes the major failure in 40% of all motor failures [7].

Prognostics and health management (PHM) can be used to detect or prevent such failures [1,8–10]. For PHM, the most representative techniques are ferrography analysis, acoustic emission analysis, vibration analysis, and motor current signature analysis (MCSA) [11]. However, in the case of vibration analysis and acoustic emission analysis, additional sensor installation is required. These additional sensors will complicate the system and incur additional costs. Besides, in the case of ferrography analysis, grease samples can be extracted directly from the reducer surface, and only internal structural defects can be diagnosed. In addition, real-time monitoring is difficult to achieve [5]. Therefore, MCSA can be used for real-time PHM without installing the extra sensors. The advantage of MCSA is that it can acquire real-time data by adding a current sensor to the electric circuit without having to attach a sensor to the device for fault diagnosis [5,12–14].

A PHM for motors based on constant speed scenarios is proposed in Reference [13]. However, in actual industrial applications, the robotic motor usually operates at variable speeds, and it is impractical to detect the constant speed of the robot's motion for fault detections. Therefore, it is very important to consider the real industrial environment of varying operational speed with acceleration and deceleration [11]. Thus, research has been developed on robot motors with acceleration and deceleration under various speeds [5]. In addition, since the robot arm can operate under various loading conditions, one study detects failure by applying various loads to the motor with constant speed [15]. On the other hand, the robot operates with various motions, i.e., simple motions and complicated motions. Research and fault detection on the various motions of the robot has been conducted [14]. However, the same is not true for robust fault diagnosis studies of the various operating conditions mentioned. Therefore, various operating conditions such as speed, motions, and loads should be considered for robust fault detection.

In this study, a PHM approach for a robotic servo motor is proposed based on feature selection and reduction methods under varying operating conditions. In addition to time domain features and frequency domain features, the time–frequency domain was decomposed using the wavelet packet decomposition (WPD) method for feature extraction. Then, dimension reduction through principal component analysis (PCA) or feature selection through correlation analysis based on the Pearson coefficient are used to reduce the number of features and develop a machine learning algorithm. After the case study, the classifier is developed through two different machine learning algorithms in order to detect robust defect features for different operating conditions [16–18]. In order to develop a robust model under various operating conditions, we propose a model using features in different domains such as time, frequency, and combined time–frequency. The proposed approach is applicable under variable working conditions of motion, speed, and loading, which mimics real environmental scenarios. The generalization of the algorithms is validated in terms of two different ML classifiers. The computational cost is reduced by using feature selection techniques.

This paper is broken up into five sections. In Section 2, the methodology, which is composed of feature extraction, feature reduction, feature selection, and classification, is discussed. In Section 3, the experimental setup is described with detailed descriptions of the data used in the experiments and an explanation of the faulty conditions. Section 4 is composed of the results and discussions of this work. Finally, in Section 5, the conclusions of the proposed method are discussed.

2. Materials and Methods

The proposed research work is shown in Figure 1. The first step is data acquisition and preprocessing. The current signal data is collected from the robot servo-motor. After a short-term Fourier transform (STFT), the continuous signal data is segmented at each cycle when the error between the sampled data and the original data is less than a criterion. After data preprocessing, features are extracted from the normalized signal. Extracting different features such as variance, standard deviation, and skewness from a signal is a common method proposed for fault detection [16,17]. However, due to the sheer volume of features, applying a classification algorithm can be time-consuming. In order to avoid such problems, feature reduction and feature selection methods are used for comparison to reduce the amount of computation. This technique is often used to avoid excessive complexity in the classification model. Among these dimension-reduction methods, PCA can be used to reduce the feature dimension and algorithm computation [18]. Also, in the feature selection method, correlation analysis is used to calculate the linear relationship between two features based on the Pearson correlation coefficient. When features with high linear correlation are determined to be equal, the number of features can be reduced by canceling them [19]. Finally, the classification performance is compared using ANN and SVM. The proposed method used a laboratory-scale experimental test bench to implement Robostar's industrial, vertically articulated 6-axis robot. To detect servo-motor faults, current data are collected for normal and fault conditions. A fault is induced in the bearing of the motor. These defects are considered at the third axis of the robot.

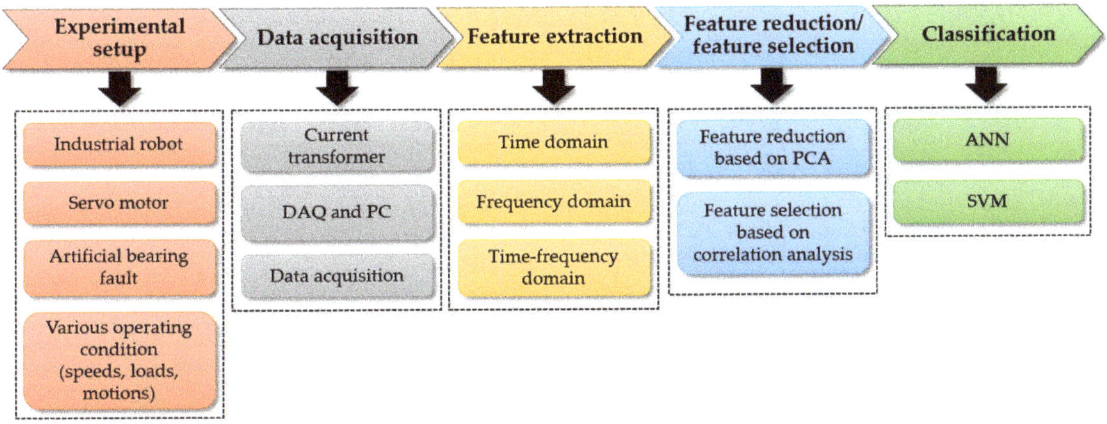

Figure 1. Flow chart of the proposed method.

2.1. Data Acquisition

The current signal is acquired from the robot servo motor through a current transformer and data acquisition module. Since the collected data is a continuous signal, the signal is divided into cycles in order to determine the fault feature in each cycle. Signal pre-processing is essential for the real-time fault detection of robot servo motors. In contrast to continuous incoming signals, preprocessing is required to separate the signal into one cycle from the original signal in order to analyze the failure of one cycle of the robot. For this purpose, the following process was carried out.

2.2. Data Pre-Processing

An arbitrary cycle was set as the model cycle in the original data. The original data and sample cycle were transformed using STFT. The original data with the length of the sample cycle were compared with the STFT value of the sample cycle, and the data were separated based on the minimum points where the error falls below the reference value. With this function, the signal can be separated into each cycle from the original signal that repeats itself. Figure 2 shows an example of signal segmentation.

2.3. Feature Extraction

A number of methods have been proposed to analyze faulty features. Among them, statistical features, sinusoidal wave shape-based features, and kinetic energy (KE)-based features were extracted in the time domain, and frequency domain features and time-frequency domain features were extracted. The feature extraction methods are described in Table 1. Where I_{mean} is the mean and I_σ is the standard deviation of the data.

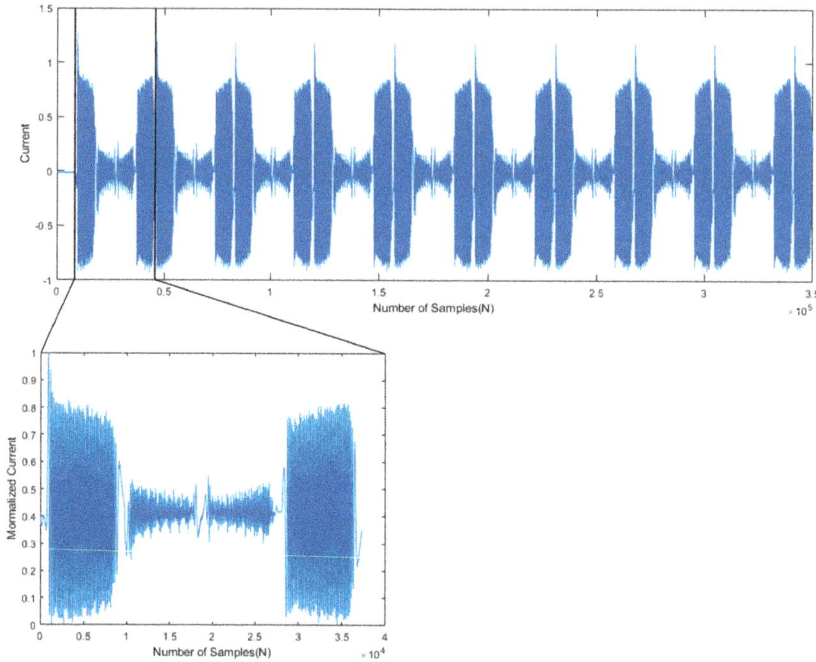

Figure 2. Signal segmentation into each cycle from the original data.

Table 1. Extracted features in different domains.

Domain	Features	Definition
Time domain	Sum [20]	$I_{sum} = \sum_{k=1}^{N}(x(k))$
	Variance [19]	$I_{var} = 1/N \sum_{k=1}^{N}(x(k) - I_{mean})$
	Standard deviation [19]	$I_{std} = \sqrt{I_{var}}$
	Root mean square [21]	$I_{RMS} = \sqrt{1/N \sum_{k=1}^{N}(x(k))^2}$
	Skewness [21]	$I_{skw} = \frac{1/N \sum_{K=1}^{N}(x(k)-I_{mean})^3}{(I_\sigma)^3}$
	Kurtosis [22]	$I_{kur} = \frac{1/N \sum_{K=1}^{N}(x(k)-I_{mean})^4}{(I_\sigma)^4}$
	Shape factor [21]	$I_{SF} = \frac{I_{RMS}}{1/N \sum_{k=1}^{N}\lvert x(k)\rvert}$
	Crest factor [21]	$I_{CF} = \frac{1/2[I_{max}-I_{min}]}{I_{RMS}}$
	Clearance factor [21]	$I_{CLF} = \frac{1/2[I_{max}-I_{min}]}{(I_{mean})^2}$
	Impulse factor [21]	$I_{IF} = \frac{1/2[I_{max}-I_{min}]}{1/N \sum_{k=1}^{N}\lvert x(k)\rvert}$
Frequency domain	Mean frequency [23]	$I_{meanf} = \sum f \times S(f) / \sum S(f)$
	Median frequency [23]	
	RMS frequency [23]	$I_{RMSf} = \sum f^2 \times S(f) / \sum S(f)$
Time-frequency domain	Energy of WPD coefficient [24]	$Ed_j^k = \sum_{i=1}^{N}(x_{k,i})^2$ $\widetilde{E}_j^k = \frac{E_j^k}{\sum E_j^k}$

In previous studies, fault diagnosis was performed by extracting features from the time and frequency domains [5,19]. However, the robot's current signal has varying speed data, and the frequency changes over time. Therefore, in this case, the feature in the time–frequency domain is also meaningful. The time–frequency domain features include continuous wavelet transforms (CWT), discrete wavelet transforms (DWT), and STFT, and WPD was used in this study. WPD is a frequency-domain signal separation method that employs frequencies. The wavelet coefficient is obtained by dividing the signal into a low-frequency region and a high-frequency region using a high-pass filter and a low-pass filter, as shown in Figure 3.

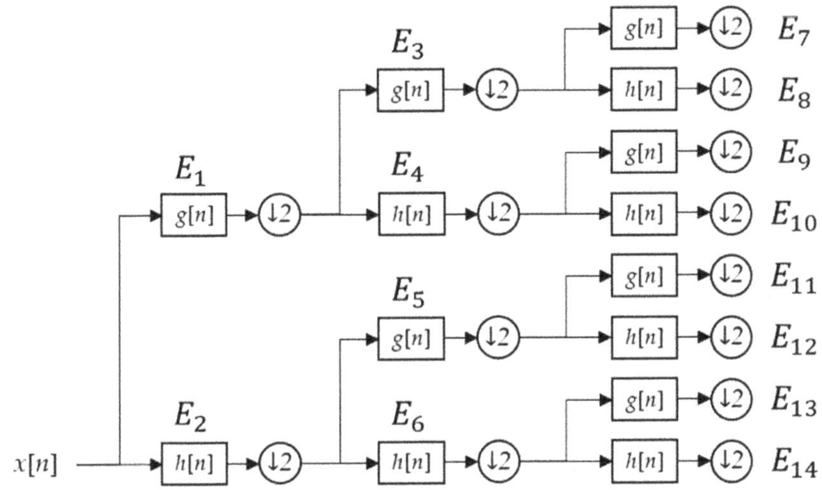

Figure 3. Description of tree decomposition of WPD.

The result can be obtained by repeating this at each level. In this study, the ratio occupying the frequency domain at each level was extracted as a feature. As shown in Table 1, after calculating the energy of the wavelet coefficient in the frequency domain of each level, the feature is extracted by calculating the ratio in the level.

2.4. Feature Reduction and Selection

In machine learning (ML), the main issue is the quality of features. Some features are relevant to the target, and some features are irrelevant. Also, some of them have similarities in certain features. A large volume of features can result in computational complexity, and moreover, poor input data will reduce the prediction accuracy. There are methods for feature selection and feature reduction to improve the quality of features and select or remove features, which can significantly affect the result. These features can be chosen, or the dimensions of redundant elements can be reduced. In this study, these two methods were compared.

2.4.1. Feature Reduction

PCA was performed as a feature reduction method that represents the variance of the original data. PCA analyzes the principal components (PCs) of features, reducing them to a lower dimension and extracting new features. The PC is calculated by the covariance of the data. After that, among the covariance eigenvectors, the component with the largest data variance is set as the first PC. Also, the component with the second largest component is set as the second PC [25]. In other words, PC_1 can explain more of the variation in the original data than PC_2. The PCs are all orthogonal to each other [26]. Through this procedure, high-dimensional data (d) can be reduced to low-dimensional data (k) where $k < d$. We compared the performance outcomes of the two methods.

2.4.2. Feature Selection

Feature selection is a method of selecting related features. For this study, Pearson correlation analysis is used to verify the linear correlation between each feature. The correlative coefficient value is between −1 and 1. The Pearson correlation method is suitable for understanding the linear relationship between two groups and is represented in Equation (1) [27].

$$P_{x,y} = \frac{\sum(x_i - \overline{x}) \sum(y_i - \overline{y})}{\sqrt{\sum(x_i - \overline{x})^2 \cdot \sum(y_i - \overline{y})^2}} \quad (1)$$

where x and y are the values of the feature and $\overline{x}$ and $\overline{y}$ represent the mean of x and y. The correlation coefficient $P_{x,y}$ ranges from −1 to 1. A value closer to 1 indicates a positive linear relationship, 0 indicates less correlation, and −1 indicates a negative correlation. Since two features with high correlation are judged to be almost identical, only one of the two features with high correlation is selected to reduce features for further analysis [28]. Correlation analysis determines the correlation by calculating the covariance of two different variables. If the correlation coefficient $P_{x,y}$ is larger than an arbitrary r value, then the correlation is estimated to be high. Only one of the two variables was selected to reduce the number of features. Correlation analysis was performed as a feature selection method [24].

2.5. Classification

2.5.1. Artificial Neural Network (ANN)

ANN is developed as part of artificial intelligence (AI), which involves a process similar to how the human brain works [29]. ANN is a computational model consisting of artificial neurons connected with weights, which are the coefficients that make up the neural structure. ANN have a lot of use in pattern recognition, in particular when the system has noise and variation [29]. For classification, the ANN model is composed of 4 different types of layers for binary classification: the input layer, the hidden layer, the sigmoid layer, and the output layer [30]. Figure 4 shows the structure of the ANN model used in this study.

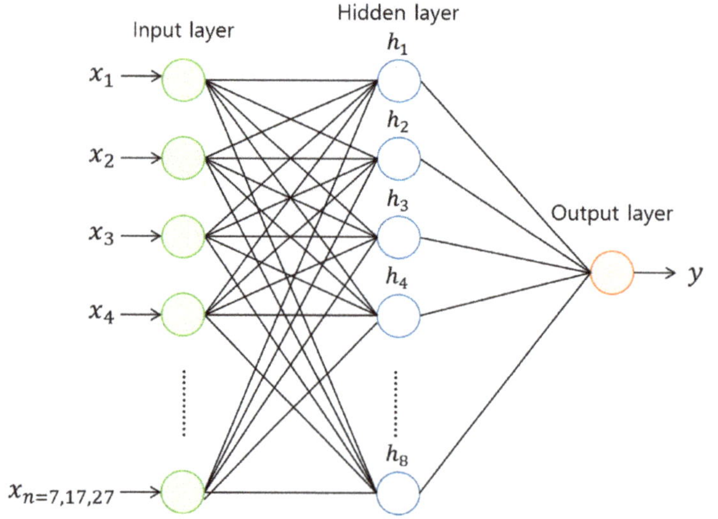

Figure 4. Structure of the ANN process.

The input data is transformed into higher features through nonlinear transformation in the hidden layer as:

$$h_1 = \sigma(W_1 x + b_1) \tag{2}$$

$$h_l = \sigma(W_l h_{l-1} + b_l),\ l = \{2, \cdots, d\} \tag{3}$$

where x is the input data and h_l are hidden features; W_l and b_l are the weight matrices and the vectors of bias, respectively, and d is the number of hidden layers. σ is the activation function and is responsible for making the above transformation nonlinear. In this study, the rectified linear unit(ReLU) is used. The formula is in Equation (4) [30]:

$$\sigma = \max(0, x) \tag{4}$$

The sigmoid layer is used to calculate the output value from the last hidden layer using the following sigmoid function (5) [31]:

$$\mathrm{S}(y) = \frac{1}{1 + e^{-y}}, \tag{5}$$

where $\mathrm{S}(y)$ is output value and has a range from 0 to 1, and y is the value of the last hidden layer. The sigmoid function is normally used for binary classification [31].

2.5.2. Support Vector Machine (SVM)

We used SVM to classify faults based on features in the time, frequency, and time–frequency domains. SVM is one of the most commonly used classifier-based PHM techniques [32]. This technique is a non-stochastic linear classification model that classifies classes of data in a given population into a supervised learning classification model. The input data is non-linearly mapped to the feature space, and the features in the feature space are characterized by the hyperplane with the maximum-margin [33]. The margin is defined as the vertical distance between support vectors, as shown in Figure 5. In this case, the support vector is the only limiting factor that determines the boundary. Also, although SVM is a linear classifier, there are cases where functions cannot be classified linearly in general. For this purpose, kernel functions such as linear kernels, polynomial kernels, and radial basis functions map to a high-dimensional feature space where linear separation is possible. These functions are widely used for their infinite smoothness, ease of calibration, and adequate robustness [34]. The following equations show different Kernel functions, such as Equation (6), which represents the linear Kernel function; Equation (7), which is a polynomial function; and Equation (8), which represents a radial basis function [32]:

$$K(x, x_j) = x \cdot x^T \tag{6}$$

$$K(x, x_j) = \left(1 + x \cdot x_i^T\right)^d \tag{7}$$

$$\left(\vec{x_i}, \vec{x_j}\right) = \exp\left(-\gamma \|\vec{x_i} \cdot \vec{x_j}\|^2\right) \tag{8}$$

where x is the input data and d is the degree of the kernel function. γ is the kernel function parameter and is greater than 0. Among the linear and polynomial kernel functions, the one most suitable for this data was selected as the radial basis function.

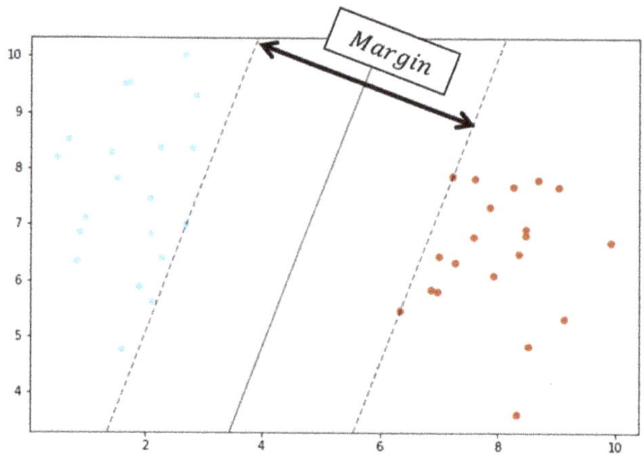

Figure 5. Basic example of an SVM process to set hyperplane with the maximum margin.

3. Experimental Setup

The Robostar robot is used in this study to detect a bearing fault in a servo motor. The focus of this study is the robot model R004, which has a payload capacity of 4 kg and is a 6-axis articulated robot with a faulty third-axis servo motor, as shown in Figure 6. There are two different states: normal and faulty. The servo motor considered in this work is shown in Figure 7a, and Figure 7b shows the bearing which is used in the servo motor of the robotic arm. In this study the inner race bearing fault is considered, which is artificially induced by grinding. Figure 8 shows the details of the data acquisition system which is composed of 6-axis, vertically articulated robot, current transformer, DAQ modules, and PC.

As the MCSA method is used, the current data of the third axis motor is collected from the robot through the current transformer JS16FL-100 sensors. A description of data acquisition is shown in Figure 9. The current transformer sensor is mounted and observes the current signal through the robot's wire. The DAQ module collects the signal from the current transformer sensors. The signal sent by the current transformer sensor is received by the DAQ module. After that, the collected signals are stored in the PC. The current signal was extracted for the first phase of the three-phase current signal, and the data were acquired at a sampling rate of 5000 Hz. After data acquisition, all of the data were divided for each cycle.

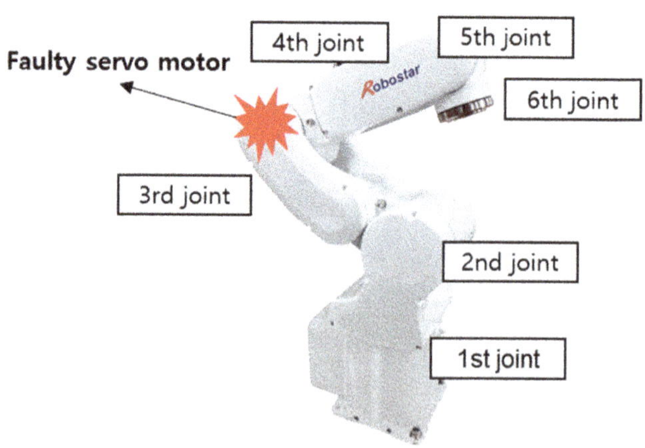

Figure 6. Description of the robot servo motor fault location in the robot.

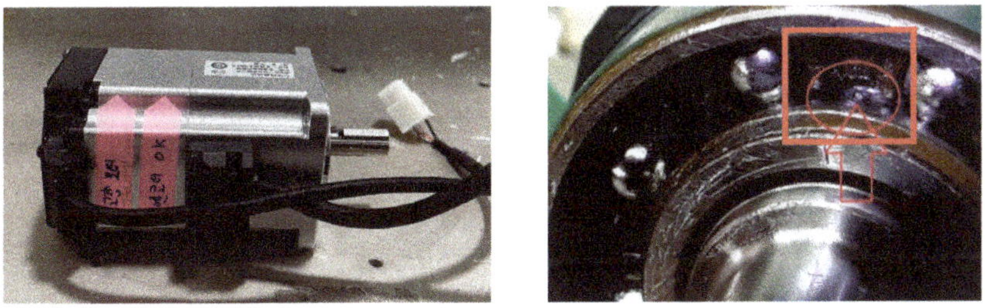

(**a**) (**b**)

Figure 7. (**a**) Used servo motor in the robot arm; (**b**) faulty servo motor with an inner race bearing fault.

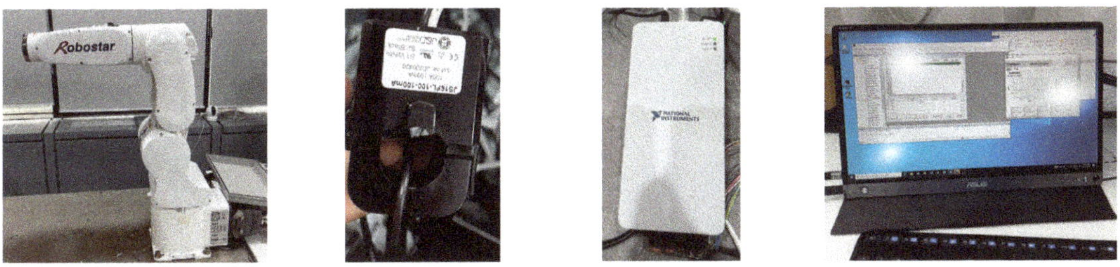

(**a**) (**b**) (**c**) (**d**)

Figure 8. Description of the data acquisition system (**a**) 6-axis, vertically articulated robot; (**b**) current transformer; (**c**) DAQ module; (**d**) PC.

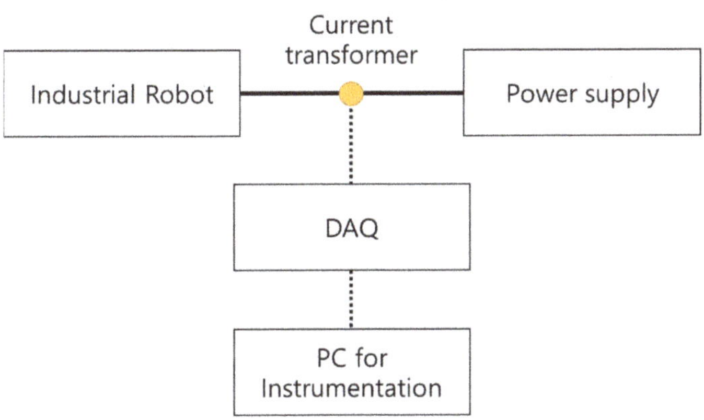

Figure 9. Flow diagram of the DAQ system of the experiment.

Data were acquired at 8 different loading conditions of 0 g, 500 g, 1000 g, 1500 g, 2000 g, 2500 g, 3000 g, and 3500 g and 10 different speeds ranging from 10% to 100% in 10% increment. Also, data were extracted from two different types of motions: simple motion and complex motion. For the simple motion, only the third axis with a fault moves at −50 +50 +50 −50 while the other axes are fixed; 8 to 10 cycles each were collected from 10 different rates. A total of 2748 datasets were collected. There are 658 normal datasets and 629 fault datasets for simple motion, and 737 normal datasets and 724 fault datasets for complex motion. "Complex motion" describes a welding motion in which all the axes of robot move together or independently. In order to confirm that the PHM model is robust under various operating conditions, various data were collected. A brief description is given in Table 2.

Table 2. Detailed information about the collected data.

Parameters	Description
Component	Robostar Robot R004
Data types	Normal, Faulty
Current phases	First phase
Sampling frequency	5000 Hz
Motion	Simple and complex motion
Speed	10 different speeds
Loading	8 different loading
Number of cycles	8–10 cycles per each speed of each state
Fault	3-axis servo motor fault (Bearing fault)
Total Number of cycles	2748

4. Results and Discussion

This section analyzes the results of the feature reduction and feature selection methods and the classification model based on feature extraction to detect the fault features of the robot. Figure 10 represents the trend of each feature for electric current data in the time domain, frequency domain, and time–frequency domain. It shows different trends for different speeds and different loading conditions. These six features are best represented by the classification of faulty and normal data. Also, some features show a distinguishable difference between normal and faulty data. Normal and faulty data are very clear on the larger scale of the graph. Most features are load- and speed-dependent. Among them, it was confirmed that the higher the load and speed of the WPD features and mean frequency feature, the better the fault features were observed at higher frequencies. The combination of these various features allows machine learning algorithm for learning process.

All raw data are normalized between 0 and 1 based on the maximum and minimum value of each cycle before feature extraction [35]. Since the data are biased with respect to equipment condition, this has been used to reduce the contribution of feature values caused by biased data when the data are free of outliers [30]. As shown in Figure 11, a total of six case studies are compared. A total of 27 features are extracted for Case I, Case II, Case III, Case IV, Case V, and Case VI.

After feature extraction, all features are used for Case I without any technique. After feature extraction, ANN, a deep learning algorithm, is trained with all of the extracted features. The ANN algorithm consists of two dense layers, where the first layer is composed of eight nodes and the second layer is consists of a single node. For Case II, after feature extraction, SVM, which is a machine learning algorithm, is trained with all of the extracted features. For Cases III and IV, after feature extraction, PCA is conducted in order to reduce the dimensionality of the features, as high dimensionality may overfit and confuse the machine learning algorithm. When the PCs are calculated, a total of 27 new PCs are computed depending on how they explain the variance of the original feature. The first 7 PCs, which explain 95% of the original variance, are generated by PCA. A total of 7 PCs become new features, and the original 27 features are reduced to 7. After feature reduction, new features are trained and tested using two machine learning techniques. For Case III, ANN is trained, and for Case IV, SVM is used. For Cases V and VI, features are selected using the feature selection method after feature extraction. Figure 12 is a heat map based on the Pearson correlation coefficient matrix of all of the data. The higher the correlation between each feature, the deeper the red color, and the more deeply the variables are related. By selecting only one of the features with a correlation coefficient of 0.9 or more, the number of features was reduced to 17, as shown in Figure 13. All of the features and

17 selected features are shown in Table 3. After feature selection, ANN is trained for Case V, and SVM is used for Case VI.

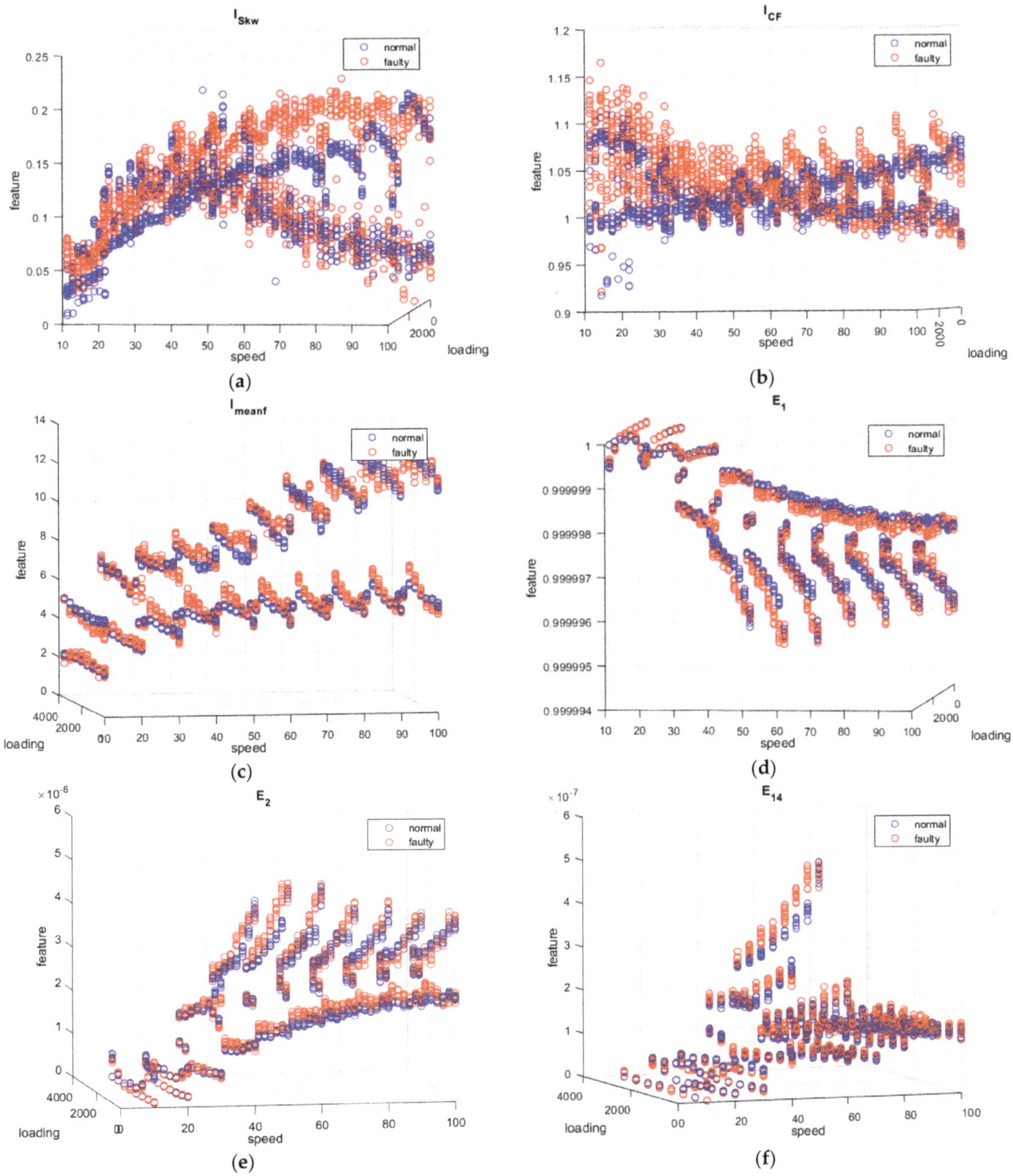

Figure 10. Representative extracted features: (**a**) skewness, (**b**) crest factor, (**c**) mean frequency, (**d**) first energy of WPD, (**e**) second energy of WPD, and (**f**) fourteenth energy of WPD.

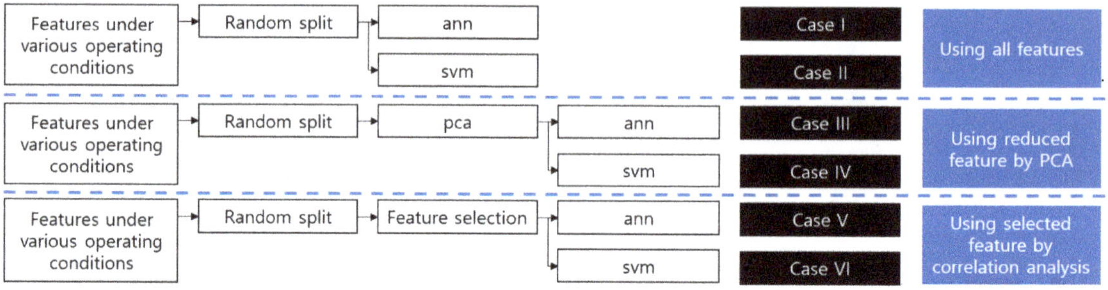

Figure 11. Description of the case study.

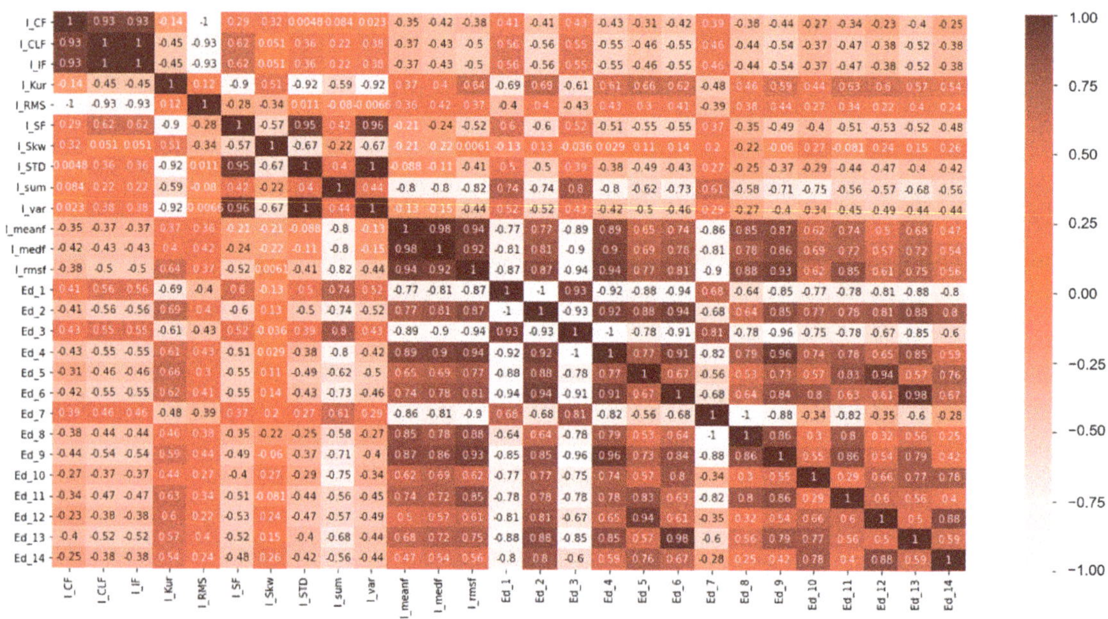

Figure 12. The correlation coefficients between all 27 features.

Figure 14 shows overall results of the proposed work related to fault classification. To elaborate further, Case I and Case II are based on the ANN and SVM classifiers, respectively, where all 27 features are used with random split for fault classification. Herein, 10-fold cross validation is used to overcome the overfitting issue. It is observed that the ANN-based fault classification shows a 92.15% training and 88.97% testing accuracy. On the other hand, the SVM-based classifier yields 91.5% and 92.97% of training and testing accuracy, respectively. The two proposed approaches show good classification performance, however, the number of features is higher, and it is computationally complicated to extract too many features. Besides, the ML classifier usually shows good performance with a large amount of data, and overfitting can be caused. In order to overcome these issues, the feature space is reduced using PCA and correlation analysis. In light of this, Case III and Case IV are based on the reduced feature space using PCA, and seven features are used. In Case III, the ANN classifier is used, achieving an 83.57% training and 81.45% testing accuracy. The SVM classifier is used in Case IV with a 90.01% and 90.67% training and testing accuracy, respectively. It is observed that the proposed feature selection method based on PCA shows good performance for fault classification. However, it is impossible to identify the exact type of feature in the process of feature reduction using PCA. For that reason, the feature space is reduced using the correlation analysis, as presented in Case V and Case VI, where 17 features are selected out of the original 27. In Case V, the ANN classifier is applied with an 87.05% training and 84.36% testing accuracy. On the other hand, the SVM classifier (Case VI) shows an effective performance with a 90% training accuracy and 91.76% testing accuracy. Overall, Case VI shows good performance in terms of the number of features and the classification performance. In conclusion, no significant difference was observed in the classification accuracy; however, the proposed approach overcomes the issues related to overfitting and computational complexities.

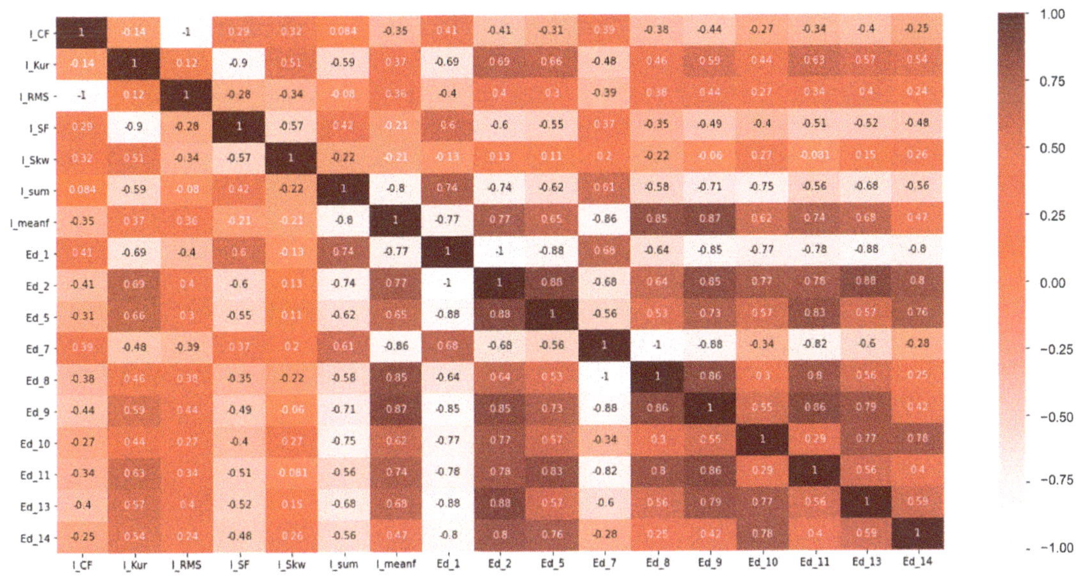

Figure 13. Features selected by removing one of the features whose correlation coefficient exceeds the r value.

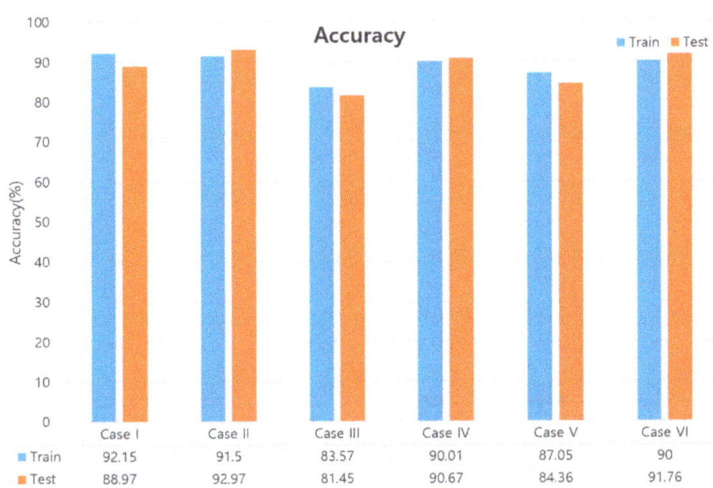

Figure 14. Accuracy evaluation of training and testing for all presented cases.

Table 3. All extracted features and features.

No	Parameters	Description/Values
1	I_{CF}	I_{CF}
2	I_{CLF}	I_{Kur}
3	I_{IF}	I_{RMS}
4	I_{Kur}	I_{SF}
5	I_{RMS}	I_{skw}
6	I_{SF}	I_{sum}
7	I_{skw}	I_{meanf}
8	I_{STD}	E_1
9	I_{sum}	E_2
10	I_{var}	E_5
11	I_{meanf}	E_7
12	I_{medf}	E_8
13	I_{rmsf}	E_9
14	E_1	E_{10}
15	E_2	E_{11}
16	E_3	E_{13}
17	E_4	E_{14}
18	E_5	
19	E_6	
20	E_7	
21	E_8	
22	E_9	
23	E_{10}	
24	E_{11}	
25	E_{12}	
26	E_{13}	
27	E_{14}	

Table 4 summarizes the precision, sensitivity, and F-1 score for all six cases. Precision represents the proportion of actual normal data to the predicted normal data. The formula is as follow [36]:

$$\text{Precision} = \frac{True\ Positive}{True\ Positive + False\ Positive} \tag{9}$$

Table 4. Precision, sensitivity, F-1 score, and accuracy evaluation for the various presented cases.

	Case I	Case II	Case III	Case IV	Case V	Case VI
Precision	94.01	94.26	85.79	93.77	88.03	94.01
Sensitivity	84.34	91.53	79.81	87.85	88.25	89.55
F-1 score	89.92	92.87	82.69	90.71	88.14	91.73
Accuracy	88.97	92.97	81.45	90.67	84.36	91.76

Sensitivity (called recall) represents the ratio of predicted normal data to actual normal data. The formula is as follows [36]:

$$\text{Sensitivity} = \frac{True\ Positive}{True\ Positive + False\ Negative} \tag{10}$$

F score is the weight harmonic average of precision and sensitivity, and the case where the weight is 1 is called the F-1 score. The formula is as follows [36]:

$$\text{F} - 1\ \text{score} = 2\frac{\text{Precision}\ \times\ \text{Sensitivity}}{\text{Precision}\ + \text{Sensitivity}} \tag{11}$$

These are the performance evaluation parameters that are generally used to evaluate the performance of the classifiers. In general, compared to other performance evaluation indicators, it shows good performance in precision at 94.01 (Case I), 94.26 (Case II), 85.79 (Case III), 93.77 (Case IV), 88.03 (Case V), 94.01 (Case VI) and weak sensitivity at 84.34 (Case I), 91.53 (Case II), 79.81 (Case III), 87.85 (Case IV), 88.25 (Case V), and 89.55 (Case VI). This indicates that the models have high reliability in predicting normal data, but low reliability in predicting actual normal data. In addition, the F-1 score is almost similar to the accuracy, indicating that there is no imbalance problem in the data and that the amount of normal data and failure data is balanced.

To sum up, the proposed study is a robust approach for the fault detection of the robotic serve-motor. Our team proposed MCSA for fault detection in the robotic system for the first time. Using this method, the issues related to data handling and the installation of extra sensors are resolved. In order to reduce the discrepancy of a lab-scale model with real-world applications and increase the robustness of the model, various experiments are performed under variable working conditions, such as motion, speed, and loading. In this study, a feature engineering framework is proposed for fault classification based on ML applications. In the proposed work, various issues are resolved regarding overfitting and computational complexities. In future consideration, deep learning and transfer learning approaches can be used to improve the generalization capabilities of the fault detection model. With this research, we developed a fault detection model that generally works under different operating conditions than previous works. However, even though the proposed model does a good job of classifying the robot's different modes of operation, data preprocessing needs to be made easier for real-time fault detection.

5. Conclusions

This study presented a method for developing a robust fault detection model for the servo motor of a robotic arm under various operating conditions. A method was proposed to improve classification performance under various operating conditions of robot arm speed, load, and motions. Performance was evaluated by comparing feature reduction methods or feature selection methods following feature extraction. The normal and abnormal data of a 6-axis industrial vertical robot's third-axis servo motor were collected. MCSA was used to detect the faulty features of the inner race-bearing fault of the servo motor.

The proposed model extracts a total of 27 features in the time domain, frequency domain, and time–frequency domain, and the generalization ability of the model is improved by extending the range of feature extraction. When a fault occurred, the fault features were detected in various features of each cycle, and it was confirmed that the features were distinguished, especially in the high-frequency region. Cases in which features were reduced by PCA analysis were divided into those where the number of features was selected by correlation analysis. The two machine learning algorithms were trained for each case. Through case studies, cases with the highest accuracy were selected based on their computational efficiency.

As a result of comparing the accuracy of the learned model with the data from each test, it was confirmed that the original data with all features showed the highest accuracy—92.97%—in Case I. However, in Case VI, it was confirmed that a good classification model of 91.76% accuracy could be obtained as a result of a feature selection method that is computationally economical with little sacrifice of accuracy. Therefore, the present study shows that failures can be detected with an accuracy of more than 90% for various operating conditions such as the speed, load, and motions of the robot.

Conclusively, the main contributions are:

1. This method works for various operating speeds, loads, and motions of the robot with acceleration and deceleration.
2. Using time-domain, frequency-domain, and time–frequency-domain features, the range of feature extraction is extended, and the generalization ability of models is improved.
3. The computational speed and the amount of feature computation can be reduced by using feature reduction and feature selection methods.
4. A classification accuracy of over 90% can be achieved under various robot operating conditions.

The robustness of the proposed method under various operating conditions was evaluated using datasets with various speeds, loads, and motions. The classification accuracy of the proposed approach is above 90%.

Author Contributions: Conceptualization, H.S.K., S.L., I.R. and H.L.; methodology, H.L. and J.S.; formal analysis H.L., I.R. and J.S.; investigation, H.L.; resources, H.S.K.; writing—original draft preparation, H.L., J.S., S.L., I.R. and H.S.K.; writing—review and editing, H.S.K., J.S., I.R. and S.L.; visualization, H.L.; supervision, H.S.K. and S.L.; project administration, H.S.K.; funding acquisition, H.S.K. All authors have read and agreed to the published version of the manuscript.

Funding: This research was supported by the MOTIE (Ministry of Trade, Industry, and Energy) in Korea under the Fostering Global Talents for Innovative Growth Program (P0017307) supervised by the Korea Institute for Advancement of Technology (KIAT).

Data Availability Statement: No applicable.

Conflicts of Interest: The authors declare no conflict of interest.

References

1. Qiao, G.; Weiss, B.A. Advancing Measurement Science to Assess Monitoring, Diagnostics, and Prognostics for Manufacturing Robotics. *IJPHM* **2016**, *7*, 3. [CrossRef]
2. Huang, Y.; Zhang, Y.; Xiao, H. Multi-Robot System Task Allocation Mechanism for Smart Factory. In Proceedings of the 2019 IEEE 8th Joint International Information Technology and Artificial Intelligence Conference (ITAIC), Chongqing, China, 24–26 May 2019; IEEE: Piscataway, NJ, USA, 2019; pp. 587–591.
3. Sun, H.; Zhang, J. Health Monitoring of Strain Wave Gear on Industrial Robots. In Proceedings of the 2019 IEEE 8th Data Driven Control and Learning Systems Conference (DDCLS), Dali, China, 24–27 May 2019; IEEE: Piscataway, NJ, USA, 2019; pp. 1166–1170.
4. Qian, H.-M.; Li, Y.-F.; Huang, H.-Z. Time-Variant Reliability Analysis for Industrial Robot RV Reducer under Multiple Failure Modes Using Kriging Model. *Reliab. Eng. Syst. Saf.* **2020**, *199*, 106936. [CrossRef]
5. Raouf, I.; Lee, H.; Kim, H.S. Mechanical Fault Detection Based on Machine Learning for Robotic RV Reducer Using Electrical Current Signature Analysis: A Data-Driven Approach. *J. Comput. Des. Eng.* **2022**, *9*, 417–433. [CrossRef]
6. Zheng, J.; Yang, W. Failure Analysis of a Flexspline of Harmonic Gear Drive in STC Industrial Robot: Microstructure and Stress Distribution. *IOP Conf. Ser. Mater. Sci. Eng.* **2018**, *452*, 042148. [CrossRef]
7. Kim, Y.; Bae, H.; Kim, S.; Vachtsevanos, G. Fault Diagnosis of AC Servo Motor with Current Signals Based on Wavelet Decomposition and Template Matching Methods. *IFAC Proc. Vol.* **2008**, *41*, 7239–7244. [CrossRef]
8. Zhang, J.; Jiang, Y.; Li, X.; Huo, M.; Luo, H.; Yin, S. An Adaptive Remaining Useful Life Prediction Approach for Single Battery with Unlabeled Small Sample Data and Parameter Uncertainty. *Reliab. Eng. Syst. Saf.* **2022**, *222*, 108357. [CrossRef]
9. Zhang, J.; Jiang, Y.; Li, X.; Luo, H.; Yin, S.; Kaynak, O. Remaining Useful Life Prediction of Lithium-Ion Battery with Adaptive Noise Estimation and Capacity Regeneration Detection. *IEEE/ASME Trans. Mechatron.* **2022**, *72*, 1–12. [CrossRef]
10. Zhang, J.; Li, X.; Tian, J.; Jiang, Y.; Luo, H.; Yin, S. A Variational Local Weighted Deep Sub-Domain Adaptation Network for Remaining Useful Life Prediction Facing Cross-Domain Condition. *Reliab. Eng. Syst. Saf.* **2023**, *231*, 108986. [CrossRef]

11. Peng, P.; Wang, J. NOSCNN: A Robust Method for Fault Diagnosis of RV Reducer. *Measurement* **2019**, *138*, 652–658. [CrossRef]
12. Jung, J.-H.; Lee, J.-J.; Kwon, B.-H. Online Diagnosis of Induction Motors Using MCSA. *IEEE Trans. Ind. Electron.* **2006**, *53*, 1842–1852. [CrossRef]
13. Raghunath, A.S.; Sreekumar, K.T.; Kumar, C.S.; Ramachandran, K.I. Improving Speed Independent Performance of Fault Diagnosis Systems through Feature Mapping and Normalization. In Proceedings of the 2016 15th IEEE International Conference on Machine Learning and Applications (ICMLA), Anaheim, CA, USA, 18–20 December 2016; pp. 764–767.
14. Raouf, I.; Lee, H.; Noh, Y.R.; Youn, B.D.; Kim, H.S. Prognostic Health Management of the Robotic Strain Wave Gear Reducer Based on Variable Speed of Operation: A Data-Driven via Deep Learning Approach. *J. Comput. Des. Eng.* **2022**, *9*, 1775–1788. [CrossRef]
15. Qiao, M.; Yan, S.; Tang, X.; Xu, C. Deep Convolutional and LSTM Recurrent Neural Networks for Rolling Bearing Fault Diagnosis Under Strong Noises and Variable Loads. *IEEE Access* **2020**, *8*, 66257–66269. [CrossRef]
16. Abid, A.; Khan, M.T.; Iqbal, J. A Review on Fault Detection and Diagnosis Techniques: Basics and Beyond. *Artif. Intell. Rev.* **2021**, *54*, 3639–3664. [CrossRef]
17. Singh, A.; Thakur, N.; Sharma, A. A Review of Supervised Machine Learning Algorithms. In Proceedings of the 2016 3rd International Conference on Computing for Sustainable Global Development (INDIACom), New Delhi, India, 16–18 March 2016; pp. 1310–1315.
18. Errichello, R. How to Analyze Gear Failures. *Pract. Fail. Anal.* **2002**, *2*, 8–16. [CrossRef]
19. Devendiran, S.; Manivannan, K.; Kamani, S.C.; Refai, R. An Early Bearing Fault Diagnosis Using Effective Feature Selection Methods and Data Mining Techniques. *Int. J. Eng. Technol.* **2015**, *7*, 16.
20. Attaran, B.; Ghanbarzadeh, A. Bearing Fault Detection Based on Maximum Likelihood Estimation and Optimized ANN Using the Bees Algorithm. *JACM* **2015**, *1*, 35–43. [CrossRef]
21. Kharche, P.P.; Kshirsagar, D.S.V. Review of Fault Detection in Rolling Element Bearing. *Int. J. Innov. Res. Adv. Eng.* **2014**, *1*, 169–174.
22. Park, J.; Hamadache, M.; Ha, J.M.; Kim, Y.; Na, K.; Youn, B.D. A Positive Energy Residual (PER) Based Planetary Gear Fault Detection Method under Variable Speed Conditions. *Mech. Syst. Signal Process.* **2019**, *117*, 347–360. [CrossRef]
23. Hamadache, M.; Jung, J.H.; Park, J.; Youn, B.D. A Comprehensive Review of Artificial Intelligence-Based Approaches for Rolling Element Bearing PHM: Shallow and Deep Learning. *JMST Adv.* **2019**, *1*, 125–151. [CrossRef]
24. Kimotho, J.K.; Sextro, W. An Approach for Feature Extraction and Selection from Non-Trending Data for Machinery Prognosis. *PHM Soc. Eur. Conf.* **2014**, *2*, 1. [CrossRef]
25. Ringnér, M. What Is Principal Component Analysis? *Nat Biotechnol* **2008**, *26*, 303–304. [CrossRef] [PubMed]
26. Granato, D.; Santos, J.S.; Escher, G.B.; Ferreira, B.L.; Maggio, R.M. Use of Principal Component Analysis (PCA) and Hierarchical Cluster Analysis (HCA) for Multivariate Association between Bioactive Compounds and Functional Properties in Foods: A Critical Perspective. *Trends Food Sci. Technol.* **2018**, *72*, 83–90. [CrossRef]
27. Zhou, H.; Deng, Z.; Xia, Y.; Fu, M. A New Sampling Method in Particle Filter Based on Pearson Correlation Coefficient. *Neurocomputing* **2016**, *216*, 208–215. [CrossRef]
28. Huang, J.; Huang, N.; Zhang, L.; Xu, H. A Method for Feature Selection Based on the Correlation Analysis. In Proceedings of the 2012 International Conference on Measurement, Information and Control, Harbin, China, 18–20 May 2012; Volume 1, pp. 529–532.
29. Agatonovic-Kustrin, S.; Beresford, R. Basic Concepts of Artificial Neural Network (ANN) Modeling and Its Application in Pharmaceutical Research. *J. Pharm. Biomed. Anal.* **2000**, *22*, 717–727. [CrossRef]
30. Heo, S.; Lee, J.H. Fault Detection and Classification Using Artificial Neural Networks. *IFAC Pap.* **2018**, *51*, 470–475. [CrossRef]
31. Sharma, S.; Sharma, S.; Athaiya, A. Activation functions in neural networks. *IJEAST* **2020**, *4*, 310–316. [CrossRef]
32. Patle, A.; Chouhan, D.S. SVM Kernel Functions for Classification. In Proceedings of the 2013 International Conference on Advances in Technology and Engineering (ICATE), Mumbai, India, 23–25 January 2013; pp. 1–9.
33. Liu, Q.; Chen, C.; Zhang, Y.; Hu, Z. Feature Selection for Support Vector Machines with RBF Kernel. *Artif. Intell. Rev.* **2011**, *36*, 99–115. [CrossRef]
34. Michel, P.; Kaliouby, R.E. Real Time Facial Expression Recognition in Video Using Support Vector Machines. In Proceedings of the 5th International Conference on Multimodal Interfaces, Vancouver, BC, Canada, 5–7 November 2003; pp. 258–264.
35. Singh, D.; Singh, B. Investigating the Impact of Data Normalization on Classification Performance. *Appl. Soft Comput.* **2020**, *97*, 105524. [CrossRef]
36. Luque, A.; Carrasco, A.; Martín, A.; de las Heras, A. The Impact of Class Imbalance in Classification Performance Metrics Based on the Binary Confusion Matrix. *Pattern Recognit.* **2019**, *91*, 216–231. [CrossRef]

mathematics

MDPI

Article

Deep Transfer Learning Framework for Bearing Fault Detection in Motors

Prashant Kumar [1], Prince Kumar [2], Ananda Shankar Hati [2] and Heung Soo Kim [1,*]

1 Department of Mechanical, Robotics, and Energy Engineering, Dongguk University-Seoul, 30 Pil-dong 1 gil, Jung-gu, Seoul 04620, Republic of Korea
2 Department of Electrical Engineering, Indian Institute of Technology (Indian School of Mines), Dhanbad 826004, Jharkhand, India
* Correspondence: heungsoo@dgu.edu; Tel.: +82-2-2260-8577; Fax: +82-2-2263-9379

Abstract: The domain of fault detection has seen tremendous growth in recent years. Because of the growing demand for uninterrupted operations in different sectors, prognostics and health management (PHM) is a key enabling technology to achieve this target. Bearings are an essential component of a motor. The PHM of bearing is crucial for uninterrupted operation. Conventional artificial intelligence techniques require feature extraction and selection for fault detection. This process often restricts the performance of such approaches. Deep learning enables autonomous feature extraction and selection. Given the advantages of deep learning, this article presents a transfer learning–based method for bearing fault detection. The pretrained ResNetV2 model is used as a base model to develop an effective fault detection strategy for bearing faults. The different bearing faults, including the outer race fault, inner race fault, and ball defect, are included in developing an effective fault detection model. The necessity for manual feature extraction and selection has been reduced by the proposed method. Additionally, a straightforward 1D to 2D data conversion has been suggested, altogether eliminating the requirement for manual feature extraction and selection. Different performance metrics are estimated to confirm the efficacy of the proposed strategy, and the results show that the proposed technique effectively detected bearing faults.

Keywords: deep learning; transfer learning; prognostics and health management; bearing fault; electrical motor

MSC: 68T07

1. Introduction

Electrical motors are the prime movers of modern industries. However, unwanted faults in the motors can lead to the complete shutdown of the industry. Bearings are the critical components of electrical motors (EMs). The bearing separates the stationary part from the moving part. Generally, it is on both ends, i.e., on both the drive and nondrive sides of the motor. Bearing fault (BF) is the most common fault in electrical motors. It is responsible for more than half of all motor defects. Bearing fault includes the inner race fault (IRF), outer race fault (ORF), and bearing ball defect (BBD) [1,2]. The PHM of the bearing is crucial for the uninterrupted operation of the motor. Timely fault diagnosis of the BFs in the EMs could help avoid the complete shutdown of the production or manufacturing facility in the industry. The BFs can be caused by harsh operating conditions, overloading, overspeeding, manufacturing defects, overheating, dielectric stress, and aging. Symptoms of the faults can be unbalanced voltages and line currents, excessive vibration, unwarranted heating, enhanced losses, efficiency decline, reduction in the median torque, and higher torque pulsation. To keep the EMs in the industries operating without interruption, timely fault detection (FD) is crucial.

The conventional bearing FD approach includes current and vibration monitoring techniques. Motor current signature analysis is the favored method for fault diagnosis in EMs. In addition, vibration-based FD approaches are famous for bearing FD. Both these methods require a lot of human expertise and past knowledge about EMs. Researchers have recently used artificial intelligence (AI) for FD in EMs. In recent years, the use of AI in the bearing FD has improved fault detection accuracy while making the fault detection approaches more reliable [3]. Conventional machine-learning (ML) algorithms, such as support vector machine (SVM), decision tree (DT), random forest (RF), and k-nearest neighbor (kNN), have been extensively used to develop a bearing FD approach in electrical motors and rotating machines [4,5]. These FD approaches rely on efficient input data, i.e., input features. Feature extraction and selection (FES) are essential for fault detection using these conventional ML approaches. Either the frequency domain signals or the time-domain signals can yield the features. Statistical features, such as standard deviation, mean, and variance, among many more, can be used. Feature selection is a big challenge for these conventional ML approaches, and the overall performance of these approaches is dependent on these features. Manual feature extraction and selection require prior knowledge and human expertise. In addition, optimization algorithms are used to optimize the models [6]. Konar et al. [7] proposed the bearing FD using the continuous wavelet transformation (CWT) and SVM model. The CWT has been used to analyze the vibration of the frame of the induction motor (IM) during the starting operation. Li et al. [8] developed an FD strategy for the bearing with the help of the SVM model and ant colony optimization. Gryllias et al. [9] suggested an FD methodology for bearing operating in the industrial environment using the SVM model. An FD strategy for the bearing fault was developed in [10], using permutation entropy, ensemble empirical decomposition, and SVM. Amarnath et al. [11] used the sound signals for the bearing FD by using the DT-based FD model. The DT algorithm–based model for bearing FD was fed data from statistical features acquired from acoustic signals. Sugumaran et al. [12] developed a bearing FD strategy by using the DT algorithm to select features with the help of vibration signals and feeding to the proximal SVM model. Tian et al. [13] propounded a bearing FD strategy using spectral kurtosis and cross-correlation for the FES from the vibration signals. These features were applied to develop the health index with the help of principal component analysis and kNN. Pandya et al. [14] developed a rolling element-bearing FD strategy using empirical mode decomposition and kNN. The features were extracted with the help of the Hilbert–Huang transformation from the acoustic signals. Sharma et al. [15] developed a bearing FD approach using vibration-based time-domain features and feeding to the weighted kNN classifier. The conventional ML-based bearing FD strategy requires efficient features as inputs. Feature extraction, as well as feature selection, is a tedious and often challenging task. The manual FES also requires prior knowledge and human expertise. It is difficult to develop the generic features that can be given to the traditional ML-centered FD approaches. This often restricts the performance of these ML-based FD approaches.

Given the problem associated with the abovementioned approaches, researchers have started to use deep learning (DL) algorithms in the domain of PHM. In recent years, DL algorithms have drawn a lot of attention for FD in EMs. The DL algorithms, such as convolutional neural network (CNN), autoencoder (AE), deep Boltzmann machine (DBM), deep belief network (DBN), and recurrent neural network (RNN), have been considered useful in the FD domain [15–18]. These algorithms are popular in the domain of image classification, biomedical, and many more [18,19]. The DL-based FD approaches overcome one of the major lacunae of the conventional ML-based FD approaches, i.e., FES. The DL algorithms, such as CNN, facilitate autonomous FES. The CNN is extensively used in the image classification problem. The inherent advantages of CNN have attracted researchers to apply it in the PHM domain. Several research papers have efficiently used the CNN-based model for the bearing FD in electrical motors, as well as other rotating machines. Janssens et al. [20] proposed the bearing FD in rotating machinery using the CNN-based model. The vibration signals collected under various states of the bearing were used for the analysis and development of the CNN-based model. Magar et al. [21] proposed an FD approach employing the CNN-based FD model. The model was tested on the Case Western Reserve University Bearing dataset [22]. Mukesh et al. [23] developed a bearing defect identification and classification methodology using the CNN-based FD model. The three-bearing condition, i.e., normal condition, ORF, and IRF, were considered and were efficiently detected. Zhao et al. [24] propounded a deep CNN model for planet-bearing FD. The DL-based model was composed of multiple CNN layers and achieved reasonable accuracy. The Hilbert transformation was applied to the input signal to develop input for the deep CNN model. Wang et al. [25] proposed a bearing FD approach with the help of a multiscale neural network comprising one- and two-dimensional convolution channels. The three states of the bearing, namely healthy, ORF, and IRF, were included for the analysis. Islam et al. [26] developed a bearing FD scheme with the help of an adaptive deep CNN model that utilized the 2D input information from the acoustic signals. Wang et al. established an FD model for the rolling element bearings in combination with hidden Markov models (HMM) and CNN. CNN layers were employed for the FES from the vibration data, and HMM was used as a tool for fault classification. Zhang et al. [27] have proposed a bearing FD using transfer learning (TL) in variable operating conditions. Zhu et al. [28] have developed a TL-based method for bearing FD under changing working conditions. A locomotive bearing FD approach has been proposed using TL from laboratory to practical usage bearings [29]. Shao et al. [30] have proposed a machine FD using wavelet-based images and transfer learning. Zheng et al. [31] have proposed a bearing FD using the TL-based framework using a sufficient dataset of bearings from different sources. Hasan and Kim [32] have developed a bearing FD approach using the vibration data conversion by Stockwell transformation and transfer learning. Lu et al. [33] have proposed an intelligent bearing FD using CNN and TL. Wen et al. [34] have used the VGG19 model with TL for the bearing FD.

The deep model offers advantages, such as better domain adaptabilities, and generalization capabilities [35]. Most of the previously used models have been shallow in nature. The previous works have used relatively shallow models, and the potential of the deep models with over 50 layers has not previously been investigated. In addition, most of the papers have used dedicated signal-processing tools for converting 1D data to the 2D data before the analysis [30]. Moreover, the challenges of training such deep models can be effectively addressed by transfer learning (TL) [36]. Only a limited number of papers are available that have used both transfer learning and deeper network for the bearing FD. The present work aims to use deep models with the application of the TL for the bearing FD. The developed work uses the state-of-the-art ResNet50V2 (RNV2) [37] model for FES from the input signals, and final classification is conducted with the fully connected layers and the SoftMax function. The key contributions of the present work may be summarized as follows:

1. A deep model with transfer learning is proposed, which can perform efficient feature extraction and fault detection.
2. Without using any particular signal-processing transformation, such as a wavelet or short-time Fourier transformation, the input signals are transformed to 2D images.
3. Transfer learning inhibits the need to train the deep model from scratch, which helps the model converge more quickly.
4. To the best of the author's knowledge, this is the first work that has used the ResNet50V2 model for the bearing FD.

The rest of this article is structured as follows: Section 2 describes transfer learning and the ResNet50V2 model in detail. Section 3 presents the proposed methodology. Section 4 provides the results and assessment. Finally, Section 5 concludes the work.

2. Detailed Description of Transfer Learning and ResNet50V2

2.1. Transfer Learning (TL)

TL is a popular method in image classification problems, text classification, building utilization, and spam filtering. This consists of learning features on one task and applying them to them on the other task. To avoid having to train the new model from the start, TL entails using the features from the previously trained model. The pretrained framework is generally trained on a large dataset comprising a lot of data. The application of TL facilitates the new model with lower training time and lower generalization error. Figure 1 shows the fundamental layout of the standard TL process. The transfer from the source model can be weights, which could be used for the weight initialization of the target model. These pretrained models are generally trained on large datasets, such as ImageNet. The transfer learning process involves steps such as selecting the pretrained model, creating the base model, weight transfer, training the new layers on the target dataset, and improving the model via fine-tuning. Figure 2 shows a flowchart of the TL process.

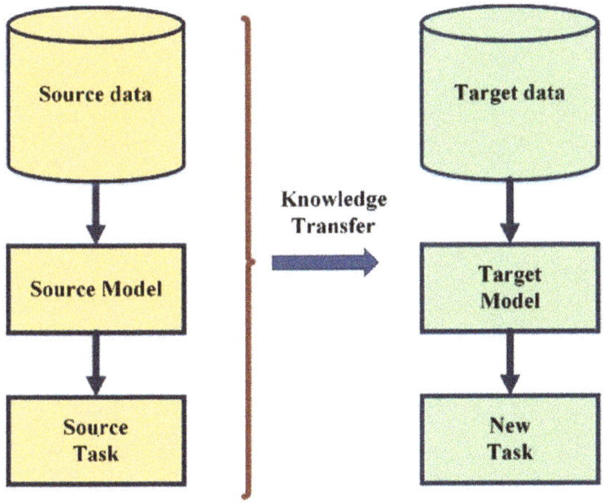

Figure 1. Basic layout of the standard transfer learning process.

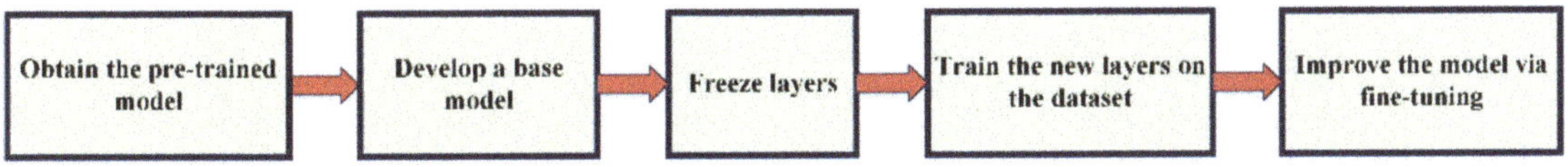

Figure 2. Flowchart of the transfer learning process.

2.2. ResNet50V2 (RNV2)

ResNet50V2 [37] is a modified version of the ResNet50, and it performs better than the ResNet50 and ResNet101 on the ImageNet dataset. ResNet stands for the residual neural network. An RNN is a form of deep neural network (DNN) and draws inspiration from the cerebral cortex's pyramidal cells. ResNet implements this functionality by employing shortcuts to go over particular layers or skip connections. The ResNet models are typically run with double- or triple-layer skips that have batch normalization and nonlinearities (ReLU) in between. The skip weights can also be learned using an additional weight matrix; these models are referred to as highway nets. DenseNets are models that include numerous parallel skips. ResNet allows the deep network training of more than 150 layers. Before the ResNet, the training of DNNs was a challenging task owing to the problem of vanishing gradients. The core of the ResNet is the residual blocks. Assume that the input is x, the learning-derived underlying mapping is $f(x)$, and $f(x)$ is the input to the activation function. The portions in the dotted line boxes in Figure 3a, must learn the mapping $f(x)$, whereas in Figure 3b, they must learn the mapping $f(x) - x$. The term "residual block" was acquired in this manner. Given that the necessary underlying mapping is the identity function $f(x) = x$, the residual mapping is significantly easier to train because it simply has to set the weights and biases of the top weight layer (such as the fully connected layer and convolutional layer) to zero. The solid line in Figure 3b that connects the layer input x to the addition operator is referred to as a residual connection (or shortcut connection). The residual blocks provide faster input propagation across layers via the residual connections. In RNV2, a modification was made for the ResNet50 model in the propagation formulations of the links between the blocks. The core idea of the RNV2 is the application of the identity shortcut connection that skips one or more layers.

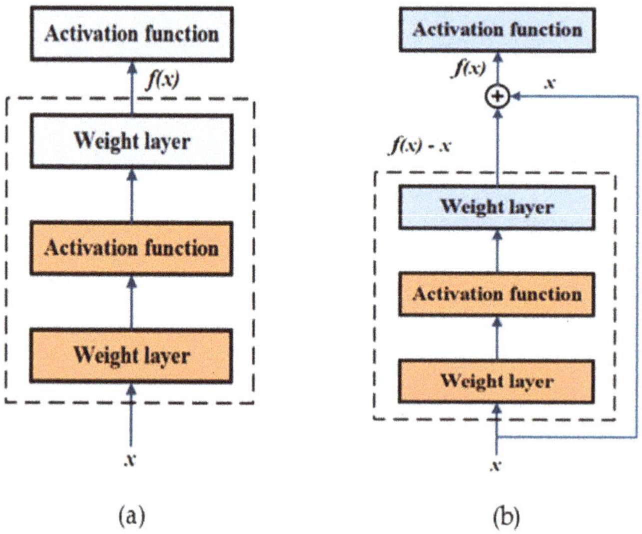

Figure 3. (**a**) Normal block and (**b**) residual block.

3. The Proposed Methodology

The bearing fault detection model is crucial for the uninterrupted operation of the motors. The core idea of the proposed method is to apply transfer learning to minimize the computational burden of the deep fault detection model. The proposed method combines transfer learning with deep learning to develop an efficient fault detection approach for the bearings. A simple 1D to 2D conversion technique has been proposed. In addition, the details of the fault detection model have been described in this section.

3.1. Data Preprocessing

Timely bearing fault detection is crucial to avoid unwanted downtime in industries. Generally, the data obtained from the sensors are time series data. The model training is dependent on the data condition. If the data include noises and irrelevant information, then they make model training a challenging task. Data preparation involves steps such as data integration, data cleaning, data segmentation, dimensionality reduction, and transformation. These steps can help in cleaning the raw data. Because data-driven approaches struggle to handle raw signals, the traditional ML-based FD approach necessitates extensive preprocessing before analysis. Data conditioning involves the optimal FES from the raw signals and is based on human expertise and prior knowledge. FD is strongly reliant on FES, and as incorrect FES can lead to fault misclassification. Because of FD's dependence on the FES, it is both a difficult and crucial task. Xu et al. [38] have proposed wavelet transformation–based images for the motor imagery (MI) EEG signals. Saucedo-Dorantes et al. [39] have extracted the deep features for the FD in the bearings. A stacked autoencoder has been used for extracting the fault features. Azamfar [40] et al. have developed the gearbox FD approach with the help of the 2D CNN and current signature analysis. Authors have used the fused data from the multiple sensors before applying it to the CNN model. Dedicated signal-processing tools such as wavelet transformation (WT) or short-time Fourier transformation (STFT) offer advantages such as localization in the time and frequency domain, efficient data representation, time-frequency information, and more. However, applying a dedicated signal-processing tool is also challenging. WT has disadvantages too, such as computationally intensive, shift sensitivity, and poor directionality. The fact that STFT has a fixed window is a serious flaw. It often restricts the efficient representation of the data. Moreover, applying any dedicated signal-processing tools requires expertise and extensive knowledge of the data. Many other authors have also used 1D data to 2D conversion for the fault diagnosis [41,42]. The proposed TL-based FD model takes the image as input. A simple yet effective technique has been utilized to transform the 1D vibration data into 2D images. To build the 2D images, the acquired 1D data is divided to obtain signal samples for the various physical conditions of the bearing. The color images are in RGB format (i.e., a matrix), which means that each image has height, width, and three channels: red (R), green (G), and blue (B). The RGB pictures, or color images, are made up of many pixels. The pixel is a composition of a triplet of R, G, and B elements. R, G, and B elements have a range (0–255). The fact that color images have numerous pixels means they have several triplets of R, G, and B. $Pixel(p,q,c)$ represents the RGB matrix, where $p = 1,\ldots,d$, $q = 1,\ldots,d$, and the third dimension c includes the red ($c = 1$), green ($c = 2$), and blue ($c = 3$) channels. With the aid of Equation (1), segments (S) are created from the time-domain signal samples (S) to create a root matrix (RM). The sample's maximum and lowest values, given by Equation (2), are used to normalize the root matrix. Finally, Equation (3) is computed to estimate $Pixel(p,q,c)$ from the normalized root matrix. The red, green, and blue components of $Pixel(p,q,c)$ are identical to one another, and the range of their pixel values is (0–255). Python was used to implement this technique. Figure 4 illustrates the proposed method.

$$RM(p,q) = S((p-1) \times D + q) \tag{1}$$

$$NRM(P,Q) = \frac{RM(P,Q) - min_{p,q}(RM(P,Q))}{max_{p,q}(RM(P,Q)) - min_{p,q}(RM(P,Q))} \tag{2}$$

$$Pixel(p,q,c) = NRM(p,q),\ c = 1,2,3 \tag{3}$$

where k represent the number of samples and S represents the strength values of the given samples.

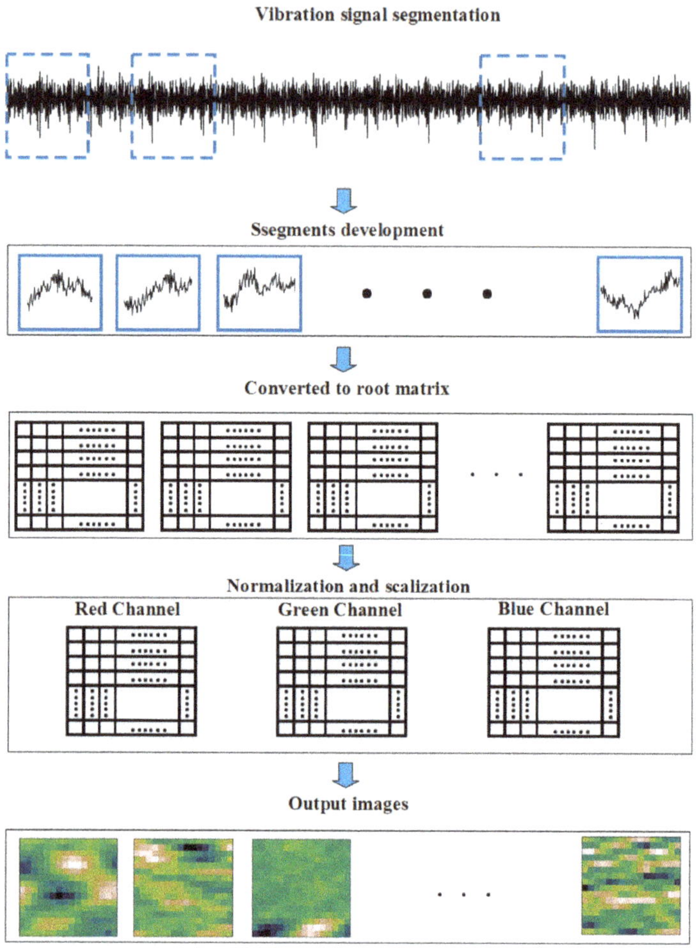

Figure 4. 1D signal to image conversion.

3.2. Fault Detection Model

In the FD field, it is challenging to generate a considerable number of labeled fault data. The availability of large, labeled fault data is a challenging issue, and these data are quite low, compared with the ImageNet dataset. The performance of deep CNN architecture for FD is constrained by the lack of large quantities of labeled fault data, which makes training difficult. Transfer learning can mitigate these issues and helps in the overall improvement of the fault detection models. The pretrained RNV2 model is used for knowledge transfer and fault diagnosis. RNV2 shows an example of excellent image segregation performance. Its layers can perform FES from the input. Figure 4 shows the composition of the purported RNV2-based FD model. The fault detection dataset's class labels were fitted by using the ResNet layers of RNV2. There are two types of blocks present in the structure, namely ResNet-Block-1 and ResNet-Block-2. Both blocks comprise the convolutional layers, batch normalization, ReLu activation, and shortcut connections. The difference between the two blocks lies in the shortcut connection. ResNet-Block-1 has an identity function in the shortcut connection, whereas ResNet-Block-2 has convolutional layers and batch normalization in the shortcut connection. The depth of the network and efficient feature extraction layers of the RNV2-based FD model would help improve the performance and achieve high accuracy in FD. The proposed model extracts feature from images generated from a 1D signal using RNV2. The mined bottleneck features were used as an input to the classifier, including one FCL and SoftMax activation function with four output nodes. Weights were randomly initialized for fully connected layers (FCLs). The hyperparameters tuning was conducted for the fully connected layers. ResNet blocks utilize the same weight of the pretrained RNV2 model (i.e., weights are locked and represented by a lock symbol), and the remaining block is fine-tuned (represented by an unlocking symbol), as shown in Figure 5. The training of FCLs is conducted with the help of the Adam optimizer's having a preliminary learning rate of 0.001.

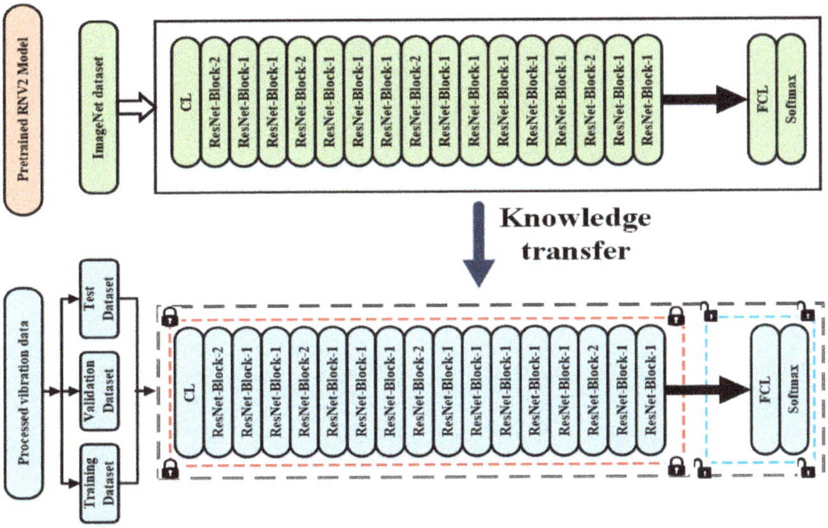

Figure 5. Block diagram of the proposed FD methodology.

A complete analysis has been conducted on the vibration data of the CWRU-bearing dataset [22]. Figure 6 shows a view of the test setup. It comprises a motor, a torque transduce/encoder (center), a dynamometer (right), and control circuits (not shown). The bearing faults were induced with the help of electro-discharge machining. The bearings faults were emulated with the help of electro-discharge technology, having fault diameters of (0.007, 0.014, and 0.021) inches. The input vibration data was acquired for different loading conditions, such as (0, 1, 2, and 3) hp, including the various fault conditions, such as IRF, ORF, BBD, and healthy bearings. The vibration signal was collected at the sampling frequency of 12 kHz. The vibration data were acquired employing sensors fitted on the drive side of the motor. These data were processed using the method described in Section 3. The 1D signals have been converted to the images for the FD using the IRNV2 model and are shown in Table 1. The randomness of the data points distribution helps to avoid the bias problem and facilitates an equal chance of selection. The four states of the bearing are under consideration, namely healthy, IRF, ORF, and BBD. Overall, 24,000 images were generated for the proposed TL-based FD approach. Of the 24,000 images, 70% (16,800) of data were employed for the training, 15% (3600) for validation, and 15% (3600) for the model testing. Each state of the bearing contains 4200 images for training, 900 images for validation, and 900 images for testing.

Figure 6. Test setup for the analysis comprising 2 hp motor.

Table 1. Samples of images created for various states of the bearing.

Bearing State	Image
BBD	
IRF	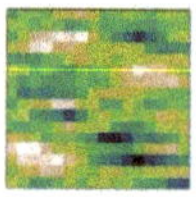
ORF	
Healthy	

4. Results and Discussion

Deep architecture training from scratch without the TL is a challenging task. The ResNet blocks of the RNV2 were utilized as feature extractors. These features were given to the FCLs, with the SoftMax layer as the last layer. The pretrained RNV2 framework was utilized as the base model, their weights were frozen, and new top layers were added and trained. These top layers were trained with random weight initialization on extracted features from the ResNet blocks. The fact that the base model was run only once on the training data, rather than once for each training period, was a substantial advantage of the proposed method. Thus, it is much faster and cheaper. The model was trained multiple times and fine-tuned for efficient performance. The model's performance was evaluated by estimating the confusion matrix (CM) and different performance metrics such as the accuracy (acc), precision (p), sensitivity (s), and $F1$-score. The CM is a tabular arrangement that visualizes and encapsulates the performance of a classification model. The values of these performance metrics, such as p, s, and $F1$-score, can be calculated as:

$$acc = \frac{tp + tn}{tp + tn + fp + fn} \tag{4}$$

$$p = \frac{tp}{tp + fp} \tag{5}$$

$$s = \frac{tp}{tp + fn} \tag{6}$$

$$F1 = \frac{2 \times p \times s}{p + s} \quad (7)$$

where tp denotes actual positive trials, tn denotes actual negative trials, fp denotes incorrect positive trials, and fn denotes incorrect negative trials.

The TL-based FD model converged at around 50 epochs. The training and validation accuracy curve is given in Figure 7. The training and validation loss curve is given in Figure 8. Figures 7 and 8 show that the model converged in 50 epochs. The model achieved an average accuracy of more than 99% for fault classification. Figure 9 shows the CM for the proposed model. It is apparent from the CM (Figure 9) that all the states of the bearing, such as healthy, IRF, ORF, and BBD, have been efficiently classified. The average accuracy is 99.50% for the developed framework. Table 2 presents the values of the performance metrics, such as accuracy (acc), precision (p), sensitivity (s), and $F1$-score.

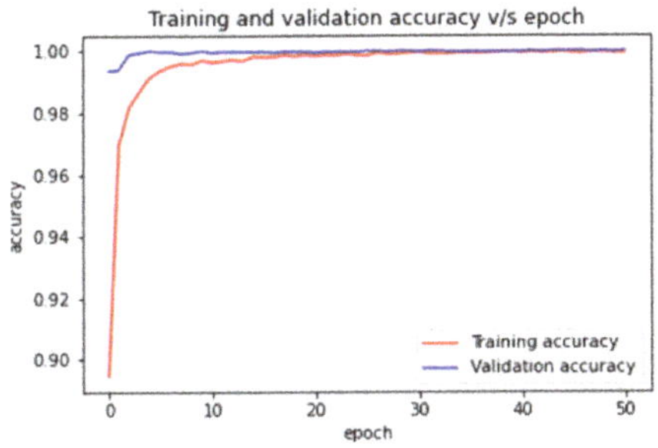

Figure 7. Accuracy vs. epoch curve for the proposed TL-based bearing FD approach.

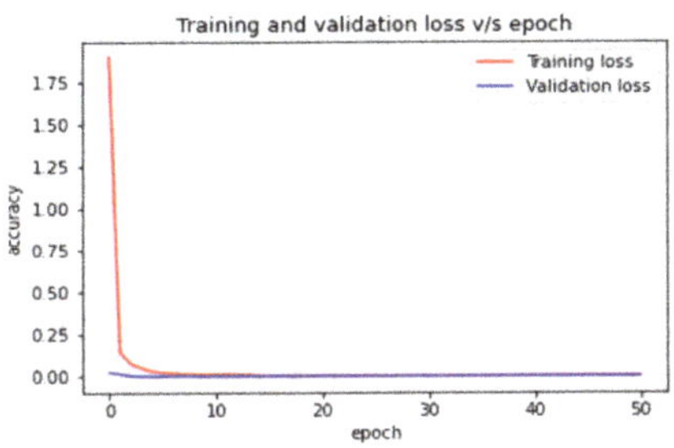

Figure 8. Loss curve for the proposed TL-based bearing FD approach.

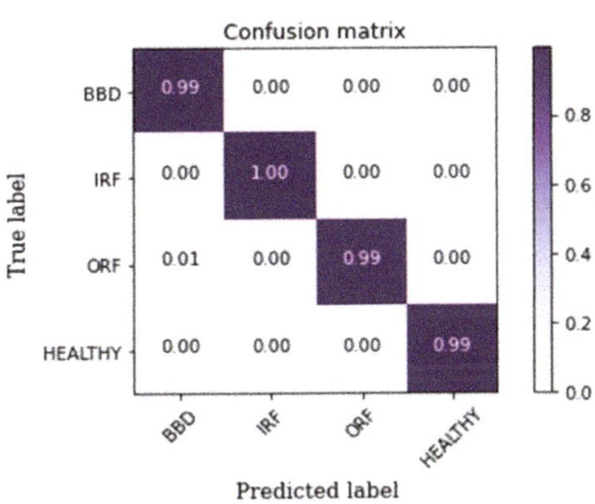

Figure 9. Confusion matrix for the proposed TL-based FD model.

Table 2. Performance metrics of the proposed model.

State	Precision (p)	Sensitivity (s)	$F1$-Score
BBD	1.0	0.99	0.99
IRF	1.0	1.0	1.0
ORF	0.99	1.0	0.99
HEALTHY	1.0	1.0	1

It is evident from Table 2 that the values of various performance metrics are more than 99%, which demonstrates that all the states of the bearing are efficiently classified. The CM (Figure 9) shows that states such as healthy, IRF, ORF, and BBD are classified reasonably, with more than 99% accuracy.

In addition, a comparative study was conducted on the proposed and existing DL-based FD methods. Multiple DL-based FD methods were assessed to inspect the functioning of the proposed IRNV2-based FD model. The proposed model was compared with two DL-based FD methods employing the sparse filters [43] and DBN [44]. Lei et al. [43] employed sparse filters for FES from the vibration data and SoftMax to classify faults. Gan and Wang [44] developed an FD network by using DBNs for FD in the mechanical system. In addition, comparisons were made with many CNN-based FD models, such as the hierarchical CNN (HCNN) model [45], adaptive deep CNN (ADCNN) model [46], multiple sensors-based CNN (MCNN) model [47], 1D CNN model [48], CNN model using vibration images (CNNVM) [49], stacked autoencoder and DBN model (SAE–DBN) [50], and CNN long short-term memory (CNN–LSTM) model [51]. Lu et al. [45] developed a bearing FD approach using a DL method by employing CNN. Guo et al. [46] used hierarchical adaptive deep CNN for the bearing FD. Xia et al. [47] incorporated sensor fusion and CNN for efficient fault detection in rotating machines. Eren [48] proposed a 1D CNN model for the bearing FD. Hoang and Kang [49] developed a CNN-based FD methodology for the bearing FD utilizing vibration images. Chen and Li [50] developed a SAE–DBN model for the bearing FD using the multisensory feature fusion. Wang et al. [51] developed a motor fault diagnosis model using the multilevel information fusion and combination of CNN and LSTM. Table 3 lists the accuracy of the various models. Table 3 shows that the developed model surpasses FD techniques utilizing sparse filters, DBNs, and other CNN models. The proposed fault detection approach surpasses the different CNN models and has a superior accuracy of 99.50%. In addition, the developed FD approach was compared with an FD method by using a DBN and outperformed it. The developed method shows superior accuracy to that of other DL-based FD procedures, as reflected in Table 3, owing to its higher depth, autonomous FES properties, and fault categorization capabilities. Moreover, the profundity of the model facilitates better domain adaptabilities and generalization capabilities.

Deep architectures (proposed model) learn distributed and sparse representations. These features are efficient in comparison to features learned by shallow ML frameworks. It is expedient to utilize a deep framework in comparison with a shallow ML framework for better data representation. The depth of the networks enables more-effective FES. The deep framework makes domain adaptivity simple. The benefits of the purported approach over the standard ML-based fault detection techniques include automatic FES and good domain adaptation. The proposed method outperforms existing methods and offers accurate fault analysis with minimal human interaction. Additionally, it shows that fine-tuning and modeling with TL together produce superior accuracy in a small number of training epochs to a model created from scratch. When training a CNN model with more depth from scratch, it takes a long time to process. The current study efficiently applies TL to overcome the deep CNN's shortcomings. Despite being a deep network, the proposed technique reduces the computational cost.

Table 3. Comparison of the proposed model with various DL-based FD approaches.

Model	Accuracy (%)
Sparse filter [43]	96.40
DBN [44]	99.03
HCNN [45]	92.60
ADCNN [46]	98.1
MCNN [47]	99.41
1DCNN [48]	97.10
CNNVM [49]	97.74
SAE–DBN [50]	96.40
CNN–LSTM [51]	98.10
Proposed Model	99.50

5. Conclusions

This article proposes a TL-based fault detection approach for the bearing fault. A thorough analysis was conducted of the bearing dataset from the CWRU-bearing data center. The proposed model effectively performed the bearing fault detection with reasonable accuracy. The depth of the model aids in efficient domain learning capabilities. In addition, the proposed model mitigated the need for manual FES, which is a cumbersome task. Despite the high depth of the model, owing to transfer learning, the model was not required to be trained from scratch. This helped in saving time, and it worked with low computational power. The average accuracy of the model was more than 99%, and the values of the other performance metrics were also on the higher side. These results justify the performance of the proposed IRNV2-based bearing FD model. Thereby, it can be established that the developed model enables an intelligent and computationally viable solution for bearing fault detection.

Author Contributions: Conceptualization, P.K. (Prashant Kumar), A.S.H., P.K. (Prince Kumar) and H.S.K.; methodology, P.K. (Prashant Kumar); software, P.K. (Prashant Kumar) and P.K. (Prince Kumar); validation, P.K. (Prashant Kumar), A.S.H. and H.S.K.; formal analysis, P.K. (Prashant Kumar); investigation, P.K. (Prashant Kumar); resources, H.S.K.; data curation, P.K. (Prashant Kumar) and A.S.H.; writing—original draft preparation, P.K. (Prashant Kumar) and P.K. (Prince Kumar); writing—review and editing, P.K. (Prashant Kumar), A.S.H., P.K. (Prince Kumar) and H.S.K.; supervision, A.S.H. and H.S.K.; funding acquisition, H.S.K. All authors have read and agreed to the published version of the manuscript.

Funding: This work was supported by a project for Smart Manufacturing Innovation R&D funded Korea Ministry of SMEs and Startups in 2022 (Project No. RS-2022-00140460) and supported by BK21FOUR.

Institutional Review Board Statement: Not applicable.

Informed Consent Statement: Not applicable.

Data Availability Statement: Not applicable.

Conflicts of Interest: The authors declare no conflict of interest. The funders had no role in the design of the study, in the collection, analyses, or interpretation of data; in the writing of the manuscript; or in the decision to publish the results.

References

1. Tavner, P.J. Review of Condition Monitoring of Rotating Electrical Machines. *IET Electr. Power Appl.* **2008**, *2*, 215–247. [CrossRef]
2. Kumar, P.; Hati, A.S. Review on Machine Learning Algorithm Based Fault Detection in Induction Motors. *Arch. Comput. Methods Eng.* **2021**, *28*, 1929–1940. [CrossRef]
3. Zhao, L.; Zhu, Y.; Zhao, T. Deep Learning-Based Remaining Useful Life Prediction Method with Transformer Module and Random Forest. *Mathematics* **2022**, *10*, 2921. [CrossRef]
4. Raouf, I.; Lee, H.; Kim, H.S. Mechanical Fault Detection Based on Machine Learning for Robotic RV Reducer Using Electrical Current Signature Analysis: A Data-Driven Approach. *J. Comput. Des. Eng.* **2022**, *9*, 417–433. [CrossRef]
5. Raouf, I.; Lee, H.; Noh, Y.R.; Youn, B.D.; Kim, H.S. Prognostic Health Management of the Robotic Strain Wave Gear Reducer Based on Variable Speed of Operation: A Data-Driven via Deep Learning Approach. *J. Comput. Des. Eng.* **2022**, *9*, 1775–1788. [CrossRef]
6. Deng, W.; Zhang, L.; Zhou, X.; Zhou, Y.; Sun, Y.; Zhu, W.; Chen, H.; Deng, W.; Chen, H.; Zhao, H. Multi-Strategy Particle Swarm and Ant Colony Hybrid Optimization for Airport Taxiway Planning Problem. *Inf. Sci.* **2022**, *612*, 576–593. [CrossRef]
7. Konar, P.; Chattopadhyay, P. Bearing Fault Detection of Induction Motor Using Wavelet and Support Vector Machines (SVMs). *Appl. Soft Comput.* **2011**, *11*, 4203–4211. [CrossRef]
8. Li, X.; Zheng, A.; Zhang, X.; Li, C.; Zhang, L. Rolling Element Bearing Fault Detection Using Support Vector Machine with Improved Ant Colony Optimization. *Measurement* **2013**, *46*, 2726–2734. [CrossRef]
9. Gryllias, K.C.; Antoniadis, I.A. A Support Vector Machine Approach Based on Physical Model Training for Rolling Element Bearing Fault Detection in Industrial Environments. *Eng. Appl. Artif. Intell.* **2012**, *25*, 326–344. [CrossRef]
10. Zhang, X.; Liang, Y.; Zhou, J.; Zang, Y. A Novel Bearing Fault Diagnosis Model Integrated Permutation Entropy, Ensemble Empirical Mode Decomposition and Optimized SVM. *Measurement* **2015**, *69*, 164–179. [CrossRef]
11. Amarnath, M.; Sugumaran, V.; Kumar, H. Exploiting Sound Signals for Fault Diagnosis of Bearings Using Decision Tree. *Measurement* **2013**, *46*, 1250–1256. [CrossRef]
12. Sugumaran, V.; Muralidharan, V.; Ramachandran, K.I. Feature Selection Using Decision Tree and Classification through Proximal Support Vector Machine for Fault Diagnostics of Roller Bearing. *Mech. Syst. Signal Process.* **2007**, *21*, 930–942. [CrossRef]
13. Tian, J.; Morillo, C.; Azarian, M.H.; Pecht, M. Motor Bearing Fault Detection Using Spectral Kurtosis-Based Feature Extraction Coupled with K-Nearest Neighbor Distance Analysis. *IEEE Trans. Ind. Electron.* **2015**, *63*, 1793–1803. [CrossRef]
14. Pandya, D.H.; Upadhyay, S.H.; Harsha, S.P. Fault Diagnosis of Rolling Element Bearing with Intrinsic Mode Function of Acoustic Emission Data Using APF-KNN. *Expert Syst. Appl.* **2013**, *40*, 4137–4145. [CrossRef]
15. Sharma, A.; Jigyasu, R.; Mathew, L.; Chatterji, S. Bearing Fault Diagnosis Using Weighted K-Nearest Neighbor. In Proceedings of the 2018 2nd International Conference on Trends in Electronics and Informatics (ICOEI), Tirunelveli, India, 11–12 May 2018; pp. 1132–1137.
16. Zhang, B.; Zhou, C.; Li, W.; Ji, S.; Li, H.; Tong, Z.; Ng, S.-K. Intelligent Bearing Fault Diagnosis Based on Open Set Convolutional Neural Network. *Mathematics* **2022**, *10*, 3953. [CrossRef]
17. Kumar, P.; Shankar Hati, A. Convolutional Neural Network with Batch Normalisation for Fault Detection in Squirrel Cage Induction Motor. *IET Electr. Power Appl.* **2021**, *15*, 39–50. [CrossRef]
18. Yu, Y.; Hao, Z.; Li, G.; Liu, Y.; Yang, R.; Liu, H.; Yu, Y.; Hao, Z.; Li, G.; Liu, Y.; et al. Optimal Search Mapping among Sensors in Heterogeneous Smart Homes. *MBE* **2023**, *20*, 1960–1980. [CrossRef]
19. Ren, Z.; Han, X.; Yu, X.; Skjetne, R.; Leira, B.J.; Sævik, S.; Zhu, M. Data-Driven Simultaneous Identification of the 6DOF Dynamic Model and Wave Load for a Ship in Waves. *Mech. Syst. Signal Process.* **2023**, *184*, 109422. [CrossRef]
20. Janssens, O.; Slavkovikj, V.; Vervisch, B.; Stockman, K.; Loccufier, M.; Verstockt, S.; Van de Walle, R.; Van Hoecke, S. Convolutional Neural Network Based Fault Detection for Rotating Machinery. *J. Sound Vib.* **2016**, *377*, 331–345. [CrossRef]
21. Magar, R.; Ghule, L.; Li, J.; Zhao, Y.; Farimani, A.B. FaultNet: A Deep Convolutional Neural Network for Bearing Fault Classification. *IEEE Access* **2021**, *9*, 25189–25199. [CrossRef]
22. Loparo, K.A. Case Western Reserve University Bearing Data Center. Bearings Vibration Data Sets, Case Western Reserve University. 2012, pp. 22–28. Available online: https://engineering.case.edu/bearingdatacenter (accessed on 5 October 2022).
23. Bhadane, M.; Ramachandran, K.I. Bearing Fault Identification and Classification with Convolutional Neural Network. In Proceedings of the 2017 International Conference on Circuit, Power and Computing Technologies (ICCPCT), Kollam, India, 20–21 April 2017; pp. 1–5.
24. Zhao, D.; Wang, T.; Chu, F. Deep Convolutional Neural Network Based Planet Bearing Fault Classification. *Comput. Ind.* **2019**, *107*, 59–66. [CrossRef]
25. Wang, D.; Guo, Q.; Song, Y.; Gao, S.; Li, Y. Application of Multiscale Learning Neural Network Based on CNN in Bearing Fault Diagnosis. *J. Signal Process. Syst.* **2019**, *91*, 1205–1217. [CrossRef]
26. Islam, M.M.M.; Kim, J.-M. Automated Bearing Fault Diagnosis Scheme Using 2D Representation of Wavelet Packet Transform and Deep Convolutional Neural Network. *Comput. Ind.* **2019**, *106*, 142–153. [CrossRef]
27. Zhang, R.; Tao, H.; Wu, L.; Guan, Y. Transfer Learning with Neural Networks for Bearing Fault Diagnosis in Changing Working Conditions. *IEEE Access* **2017**, *5*, 14347–14357. [CrossRef]
28. Zhu, J.; Chen, N.; Shen, C. A New Deep Transfer Learning Method for Bearing Fault Diagnosis Under Different Working Conditions. *IEEE Sens. J.* **2020**, *20*, 8394–8402. [CrossRef]

29. Yang, B.; Lei, Y.; Jia, F.; Xing, S. An Intelligent Fault Diagnosis Approach Based on Transfer Learning from Laboratory Bearings to Locomotive Bearings. *Mech. Syst. Signal Process.* **2019**, *122*, 692–706. [CrossRef]
30. Shao, S.; McAleer, S.; Yan, R.; Baldi, P. Highly Accurate Machine Fault Diagnosis Using Deep Transfer Learning. *IEEE Trans. Ind. Inform.* **2018**, *15*, 2446–2455. [CrossRef]
31. Zheng, Z.; Fu, J.; Lu, C.; Zhu, Y. Research on Rolling Bearing Fault Diagnosis of Small Dataset Based on a New Optimal Transfer Learning Network. *Measurement* **2021**, *177*, 109285. [CrossRef]
32. Hasan, M.J.; Kim, J.-M. Bearing Fault Diagnosis under Variable Rotational Speeds Using Stockwell Transform-Based Vibration Imaging and Transfer Learning. *Appl. Sci.* **2018**, *8*, 2357. [CrossRef]
33. Lu, T.; Yu, F.; Han, B.; Wang, J. A Generic Intelligent Bearing Fault Diagnosis System Using Convolutional Neural Networks With Transfer Learning. *IEEE Access* **2020**, *8*, 164807–164814. [CrossRef]
34. Wen, L.; Li, X.; Li, X.; Gao, L. A New Transfer Learning Based on VGG-19 Network for Fault Diagnosis. In Proceedings of the 2019 IEEE 23rd International Conference on Computer Supported Cooperative Work in Design (CSCWD), Porto, Portugal, 6–8 May 2019; pp. 205–209.
35. Goodfellow, I.; Bengio, Y.; Courville, A. *Deep Learning*; MIT Press: Cambridge, MA, USA, 2016.
36. Weiss, K.; Khoshgoftaar, T.M.; Wang, D. A Survey of Transfer Learning. *J. Big Data* **2016**, *3*, 9. [CrossRef]
37. He, K.; Zhang, X.; Ren, S.; Sun, J. Identity Mappings in Deep Residual Networks. In *Proceedings of the Computer Vision—ECCV 2016*; Leibe, B., Matas, J., Sebe, N., Welling, M., Eds.; Springer International Publishing: Cham, Switzerland, 2016; pp. 630–645.
38. Xu, B.; Zhang, L.; Song, A.; Wu, C.; Li, W.; Zhang, D.; Xu, G.; Li, H.; Zeng, H. Wavelet Transform Time-Frequency Image and Convolutional Network-Based Motor Imagery EEG Classification. *IEEE Access* **2019**, *7*, 6084–6093. [CrossRef]
39. Saucedo-Dorantes, J.J.; Arellano-Espitia, F.; Delgado-Prieto, M.; Osornio-Rios, R.A. Diagnosis Methodology Based on Deep Feature Learning for Fault Identification in Metallic, Hybrid and Ceramic Bearings. *Sensors* **2021**, *21*, 5832. [CrossRef] [PubMed]
40. Azamfar, M.; Singh, J.; Bravo-Imaz, I.; Lee, J. Multisensor Data Fusion for Gearbox Fault Diagnosis Using 2-D Convolutional Neural Network and Motor Current Signature Analysis. *Mech. Syst. Signal Process.* **2020**, *144*, 106861. [CrossRef]
41. Wen, L.; Li, X.; Gao, L. A Transfer Convolutional Neural Network for Fault Diagnosis Based on ResNet-50. *Neural Comput. Appl.* **2020**, *32*, 6111–6124. [CrossRef]
42. Xie, T.; Huang, X.; Choi, S.-K. Intelligent Mechanical Fault Diagnosis Using Multisensor Fusion and Convolution Neural Network. *IEEE Trans. Ind. Inform.* **2022**, *18*, 3213–3223. [CrossRef]
43. Lei, Y.; Jia, F.; Lin, J.; Xing, S.; Ding, S.X. An Intelligent Fault Diagnosis Method Using Unsupervised Feature Learning towards Mechanical Big Data. *IEEE Trans. Ind. Electron.* **2016**, *63*, 3137–3147. [CrossRef]
44. Gan, M.; Wang, C. Construction of Hierarchical Diagnosis Network Based on Deep Learning and Its Application in the Fault Pattern Recognition of Rolling Element Bearings. *Mech. Syst. Signal Process.* **2016**, *72*, 92–104. [CrossRef]
45. Lu, C.; Wang, Z.; Zhou, B. Intelligent Fault Diagnosis of Rolling Bearing Using Hierarchical Convolutional Network Based Health State Classification. *Adv. Eng. Inform.* **2017**, *32*, 139–151. [CrossRef]
46. Guo, X.; Chen, L.; Shen, C. Hierarchical Adaptive Deep Convolution Neural Network and Its Application to Bearing Fault Diagnosis. *Measurement* **2016**, *93*, 490–502. [CrossRef]
47. Xia, M.; Li, T.; Xu, L.; Liu, L.; De Silva, C.W. Fault Diagnosis for Rotating Machinery Using Multiple Sensors and Convolutional Neural Networks. *IEEE/ASME Trans. Mechatron.* **2017**, *23*, 101–110. [CrossRef]
48. Eren, L. Bearing Fault Detection by One-Dimensional Convolutional Neural Networks. *Math. Probl. Eng.* **2017**, *2017*, 8617315. [CrossRef]
49. Hoang, D.-T.; Kang, H.-J. Rolling Element Bearing Fault Diagnosis Using Convolutional Neural Network and Vibration Image. *Cogn. Syst. Res.* **2019**, *53*, 42–50. [CrossRef]
50. Chen, Z.; Li, W. Multisensor Feature Fusion for Bearing Fault Diagnosis Using Sparse Autoencoder and Deep Belief Network. *IEEE Trans. Instrum. Meas.* **2017**, *66*, 1693–1702. [CrossRef]
51. Wang, J.; Fu, P.; Zhang, L.; Gao, R.X.; Zhao, R. Multilevel Information Fusion for Induction Motor Fault Diagnosis. *IEEE/ASME Trans. Mechatron.* **2019**, *24*, 2139–2150. [CrossRef]

mathematics

MDPI

Review

Prognostics and Health Management of Rotating Machinery of Industrial Robot with Deep Learning Applications—A Review

Prashant Kumar, Salman Khalid and Heung Soo Kim *

Department of Mechanical, Robotics and Energy Engineering, Dongguk University-Seoul, Seoul 04620, Republic of Korea; prashantkumar@dgu.ac.kr (P.K.); salmankhalid@dgu.ac.kr (S.K.)
* Correspondence: heungsoo@dgu.edu; Tel.: +82-2-2260-8577; Fax: +82-2-2263-9379

Abstract: The availability of computational power in the domain of Prognostics and Health Management (PHM) with deep learning (DL) applications has attracted researchers worldwide. Industrial robots are the prime mover of modern industry. Industrial robots comprise multiple forms of rotating machinery, like servo motors and numerous gears. Thus, the PHM of the rotating components of industrial robots is crucial to minimize the downtime in the industries. In recent times, deep learning has proved its mettle in different areas, like bio-medical, image recognition, speech recognition, and many more. PHM with DL applications is a rapidly growing field. It has helped achieve a better understanding of the different condition monitoring signals, like vibration, current, temperature, acoustic emission, partial discharge, and pressure. Most current review articles are component- (or system-) specific and have not been updated to reflect the new deep learning approaches. Also, a unified review paper for PHM strategies for industrial robots and their rotating machinery with DL applications has not previously been presented. This paper presents a review of the PHM strategies with various DL algorithms for industrial robots and rotating machinery, along with brief theoretical aspects of the algorithms. This paper presents a trend of the up-to-date advancements in PHM approaches using DL algorithms. Also, the restrictions and challenges associated with the available PHM approaches are discussed, paving the way for future studies.

Keywords: prognostics and health management (PHM); deep learning (DL); industrial robots; rotating machinery

MSC: 68T01

1. Introduction

Industrial robots (IRs) have drawn a lot of attention over the past two decades due to the availability of cutting-edge technologies and the need for high production. Industrial robots have found applications in almost every sector, like manufacturing, underwater exploration, hazardous material disposal, steel exploration, and entertainment [1–5]. IRs include multiple forms of rotating machinery, like servo motors and gears, which are also prone to failures [6]. In general, IRs are robust machines; however, faults are inevitable. The rotating machines are vital components of the IRs and act as a driving force [7]. IRs have seen a surge in their applications in recent years [1,8–14]. This has aided human efforts to reduce the operational costs. The World Robotics 2021 industrial reports show that more than three million IRs are operating globally, almost 10% more than the previous year. In 2020, despite the global epidemic, new robot sales climbed by 0.5%, with 384,000 units shipped worldwide [15]. With a compound annual growth rate (CAGR) of 11.7% between 2021 and 2030, the size of the worldwide IRs market is predicted to increase from USD 37,876.0 million in 2020 to USD 116,848.7 million by 2030 [15]. In 2021, the size of the global IRs market was estimated at USD 15.60 billion [16]. The market for IRs was estimated to be worth USD 26.52 billion in 2022 and is anticipated to grow at a CAGR of 10.5% between

2023 and 2030 [17]. The global trend of publications containing the keywords "industrial robot fault" in the title that were published per year, as determined by the Web of Science and PubMed, is given in Figure 1.

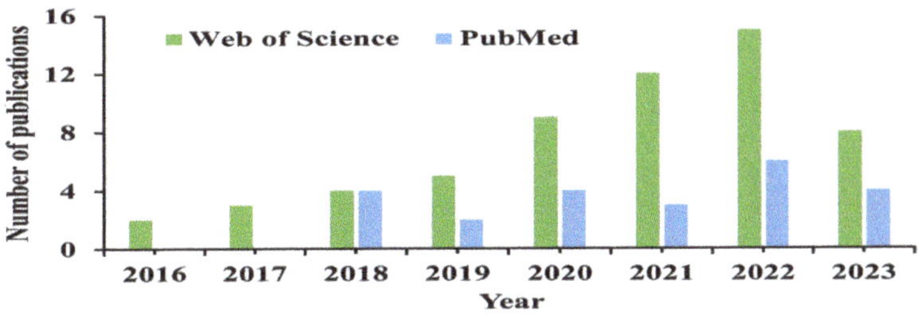

Figure 1. Global trend of the publications containing the Keyword "industrial robot fault" in the title that were published per year, as determined by the Web of Science and PubMed.

The market trend shows that IRs will be a driving force in industry. The robot system applications in those industries help to improve productivity, efficiency, and quality. The technological improvement in sensors, motors, and drives has improved the performance and efficiency of IRs. Due to advancements in robot system position and trajectory precision, arc welding has gained popularity over spot welding in various applications.

The technologies involved in robots have become complex and require a lot of feedback from the environment for efficient operation and precise control. The reliability of robots and their associated components is critical for minimum downtime and maximum production [18]. Robotic system health monitoring, diagnostics, prognostics, and maintenance have received a lot of attention as a result of the high-reliability requirements. The PHM of advanced robotics setup in industries are crucial for the smooth functioning of production and serviceable units. An efficient PHM approach for industrial robots and their rotating machines is the need of the hour [19]. A holistic framework for PHM [20–24] is shown in Figure 2. It comprises the data collection, data conditioning, fault detection (FDT), fault diagnosis (FDG), fault prognosis (FP), and decision support in a chronological manner [25–28]. The domains of fault detection, diagnosis, and prognosis have been extensively studied. The focus of this paper will be restricted to these topics.

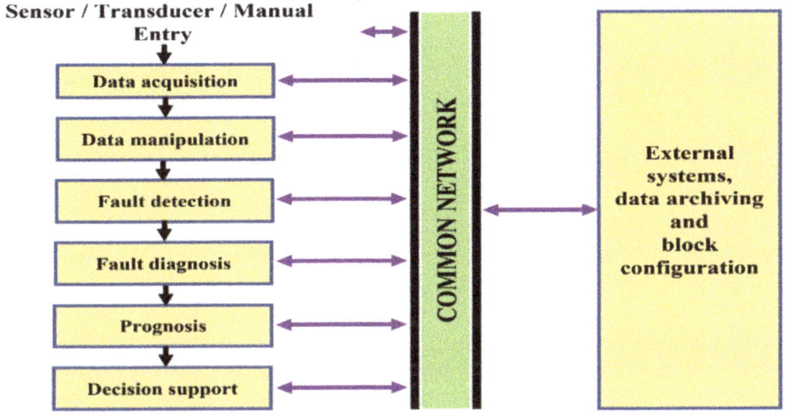

Figure 2. Holistic framework of PHM.

PHM is a modern engineering strategy that amalgamates advanced sensing methodologies, failure physics, statistical analysis, artificial intelligence (AI), and reliability analysis to enable the real-time health monitoring and prognostics of a system's future state based on the existing data [27]. PHM refers to a collection of strategies and processes for monitoring, diagnosing, prognosticating, and maintaining a machine or process [29]. Manufacturing systems use PHM technologies to reduce unplanned downtime and expenses. PHM aids engineers in transforming data into interpretable information and assessing health, improving the system's understanding. It makes it possible to create strategies for the system's efficient and planned operation. Initially, aerospace industries used PHM strategies, but they have also found applications in several fields, like manufacturing, automobile, and railways [9–13]. The ability to estimate a system's remaining useful life (RUL) through PHM while it is in use makes condition-based maintenance (CBM) possible. It helps develop a maintenance strategy in which only damaged parts are repaired or replaced [30–34]. CBM is a systematic approach that combines hardware and software to continuously assess the equipment performance and deterioration without interfering with the system's normal operations [35,36]. CBM uses the actual condition of the equipment as opposed to system/component breakdowns or planned maintenance. Prognostics is a vital element for CBM as it enables timely maintenance decisions [37–39]. The concept of preventive maintenance leads to a rise in expenses for many industrial companies, as many components are replaced before the end of their lifecycle. Therefore, maintenance should be carried out as needed to ensure a high level of safety and dependability. This is the core concept of CBM, and PHM is the key technology for realizing it.

At present, diagnostics is conducted with the help of instruments, like sensors, meters, controllers, and computational devices [40]. These devices are used to obtain signals from the machine or process for diagnostic purposes. The root causes of failure can be identified using sophisticated diagnostic approaches [41,42]. The diagnostic task is a reactive maintenance process that is performed when a fault actually occurs. The standalone application of diagnostic approaches does not have a significant effect on reducing the occurrence of downtime and the related expenses. To improve the management of the maintenance scheduling and production optimization, maintenance should be conducted in a proactive manner [43]. This can be accomplished by switching maintenance strategies from typical break-and-repair (diagnostics) to predict-and-avoid (prognostics). The aim of PHM is to establish and deliver an integrated strategy for viewing the machine's health to users. PHM involves both prognostics and diagnostics [44]. By identifying and establishing the causal connection between cause and effect, diagnostics is the method of discovering defects and identifying the primary causes of failure. The practice of evaluating and predicting health, which includes anticipating an impending failure and the remaining usable life, is known as prognostics [17–19]. Implementing timely and suitable maintenance actions and making precise logistics decisions based on the diagnostic and prognostic outputs, available resources, and operational demand are all parts of health management.

With the advancement in sensor technology and computational power, artificial intelligence (AI) has attracted researchers to improving the existing PHM approaches, as well as developing new methodologies. Different AI algorithms, like support vector machine (SVM), random forest (RF), k-nearest neighbor (kNN), decision trees (DT), artificial neural network (ANN), and many more, have been used for fault diagnosis (FD) and fault prognosis (FP) [44]. FD and FP methodologies using these AI algorithms require suitable features as input, which requires prior knowledge and expertise of the fault. This creates a hindrance in developing PHM solutions with generalization capabilities. The availability of cloud computing, huge data storage capabilities, sensors, communication technologies, and a complex engineered setup have led to huge data generation and collection [20–22,45–50]. Important details regarding the condition of the system are provided by this data. The development of multidimensional and heterogeneous data streams has a tremendous impact on the operation of traditional AI methods, like SVM, kNN, RF, and DT [51–53]. More refined analytical tools and improved approaches are required to efficiently and inherently harvest the features concealed in actual-time measured systems.

Over the last decade, deep learning (DL) has attracted researchers from different domains like biomedical, image recognition, natural language processing, and voice recognition systems worldwide, owing to its excellent properties [23–28]. A deep learning algorithm has immense potential. Deep networks are used to spontaneously manage extremely non-linear and sophisticated feature extraction from unprocessed information, eliminating the necessity for manual feature development [54–60]. DL can spontaneously discover hierarchical features from enormous and multidimensional industrial data, making it a viable tool for the PHM solution [61–64]. Lee et al. [65] have proposed a fault detection approach for the robotic servo-motor under varying working conditions. Rauf et al. [66] have proposed a transfer learning-based DL approach for fault detection in the industrial robotic system. Zhou et al. [67] have proposed a harmonic reducer fault diagnosis using the deep learning-based model. Adam et al. [68] developed a multiple fault diagnosis approach with the help of a convolutional neural network-based algorithm. Yin et al. [69] have developed a dual-driven transfer network for fault diagnosis in industrial robots. Figure 3 shows the various ways in which PHM strategies can be developed. The task of feature extraction and selection is primarily emphasized in traditional data-driven techniques. It is heavily reliant on signal processing techniques and human knowledge. These approaches require numerous adjustments when working with big volumes of data and do not operate in real time. DL models are capable of automatically discovering and removing pertinent features from unprocessed data. By doing so, manual feature engineering—which can be time-consuming and prone to mistakes in fault detection tasks—is no longer necessary. DL models have the capacity to immediately learn intricate patterns and representations from the data, improving defect detection. DL models can effectively handle complicated datasets. They have the capacity to learn from a variety of data sources and identify subtle patterns that conventional approaches can find challenging. DL models can handle complex fault patterns and nonlinear interactions. The nonlinear behaviors of many industrial systems can be difficult to model using conventional techniques. End-to-end learning, where the model learns directly from the input data to the output predictions, is made possible by DL models. As a result, manual intervention at crucial points in the pipeline for fault detection is no longer required. In a nutshell, DL provides an end-to-end framework and facilitates a unified PHM system.

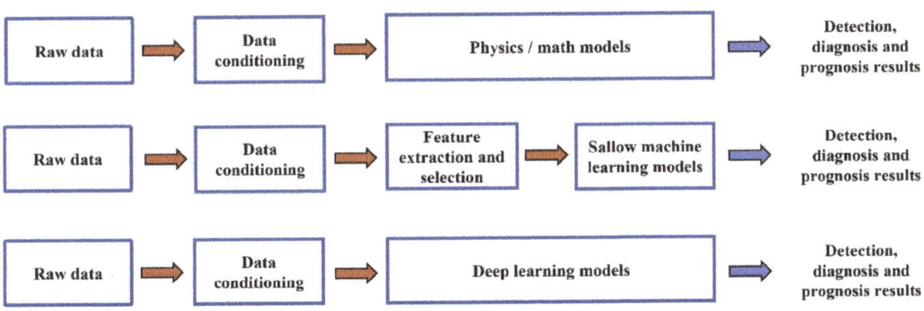

Figure 3. Various PHM methods with Physics/math models, ML-based model, and DL-based models.

Most current review articles are component- (or system-)specific, and do not reflect the advancement in DL-based strategies. This is a burgeoning field, and several studies are being conducted to develop more refined approaches and improved strategies. Many advanced methods are emerging each month, and there is a need to review the latest trends and PHM strategies. Few papers have reviewed the DL-based PHM strategies for rotating components of the IRs. This paper examines the PHM strategies based on the DL-based approaches for industrial robots and their rotating machinery. Section 2 discusses faults and failures in industrial robots and their rotating components. Section 3 illustrates the PHM methodologies, together with the conventional PHM cycle, and details the PHM performance metrics and DL-based PHM. Section 4 presents a brief description of the various DL algorithms. Section 5 presents a detailed study of the existing DL framework-based PHM for the rotating machinery of the IRs. Section 6 briefly discusses the PHM strategies with DL applications and future possibilities. Finally, Section 7 concludes the work.

2. Industrial Robot Configuration and Faults

Industrial robots are complex and require continuous monitoring for optimum performance and minimum downtime. A robot is described by the International Standards Organisation (ISO 8373) as a machine that has automatic control, reprogramming, and manipulation capabilities [70]. This machine is flexible and has numerous configurable axes. It is made to be used in a variety of industrial applications and can be either stationary or mobile. An IR is a general-purpose programmable machine that possesses the characteristics of the human arm. It can be programmed by its computer to move its arm through sequences of motion to perform some useful tasks. It can perform a similar motion over and over until it is reprogrammed to perform other functions. Many industrial operations involve robots working together with other equipment. The main features of the robot include:

- A robot can produce a job with consistent quality at a steady state with practically zero rework and wastage.
- Robots can work continuously throughout the work cycle with proper maintenance solutions.
- Robots' upkeeping cost is increasing at a lower price in comparison to the labor maintenance cost every year.
- The capital cost for the robot is paid once only.
- Robots can take up repeated tasks and challenging jobs even in an unsafe and unhealthy environment.
- Robots can work precisely at higher speeds and can exert larger force than in humanly possible.

IR comprises different components, like robotic arms, body, arm, actuators, rotate vector reducers, sensors, end-effectors, switches, gears, and linkages. There can be numerous faults in a robotics system due to its complex nature. Figure 4 shows a block diagram of the robot system. Three essential parts make up a robotic system: the power sources, the computer used to manage the robot, and the robot's mechanical framework. All necessary pneumatic, hydraulic, and electro-mechanical components are included in the robot's mechanical design. This includes electrical actuators, which are motors used for rotational operations, as well as non-electric actuators that utilize hydraulic or pneumatic systems, or both. These components collectively enable the robot to carry out its intended functions. The robot has many internal sensors, which are mainly used for measuring the rotary positions of the motor shafts, gears to reduce the speed between the motors and the joints, switches, and relays for creating selected operations. These motions will have to be performed when certain conditions are met. The robot has an end effector, such as a tool or a gripper. The entire mechanical structure is interfaced with the robot control computer. The robotic system's computer comes equipped with a variety of software applications required for the structure of the robot to function. These software packages incorporate coordinated transformation software, which makes it easier for the robot's movements to be seamlessly coordinated. To control the actuators' speed and location, control software is also present. Additionally, the computer has interfaces for teaching and learning particular tasks, enabling users to guide the robot successfully. Additionally, it includes safety precautions to guard against any potential harm to the robot structure, thus creating a safe working environment. Figure 5 shows a pictorial view of the IR, while Figure 6 depicts the faults in the reducers of the IR. Figure 5 demonstrates the six degrees of freedom (DOF) IR. The six DOF means that the 6-axis of the IR can move independently. There are several types of IRs, which include the non-servo robot, servo robot, programable robot, and computer programmable robot. A non-servo robot is typically used for moving objects, like picking up an object and transporting it to another place. The manipulators and effectors—robotic appendages that serve as the robot's arms and hands and provide it enhanced flexibility and greater movement—enable the servo robots to perform a range of tasks. A programmable IR can execute the repeating task a certain number of times based on fed programs. A servo robot that can be programmed by a computer and controlled remotely is known as a computer-programmable robot. Also, IRs have many structural configurations that suit several applications in the industry.

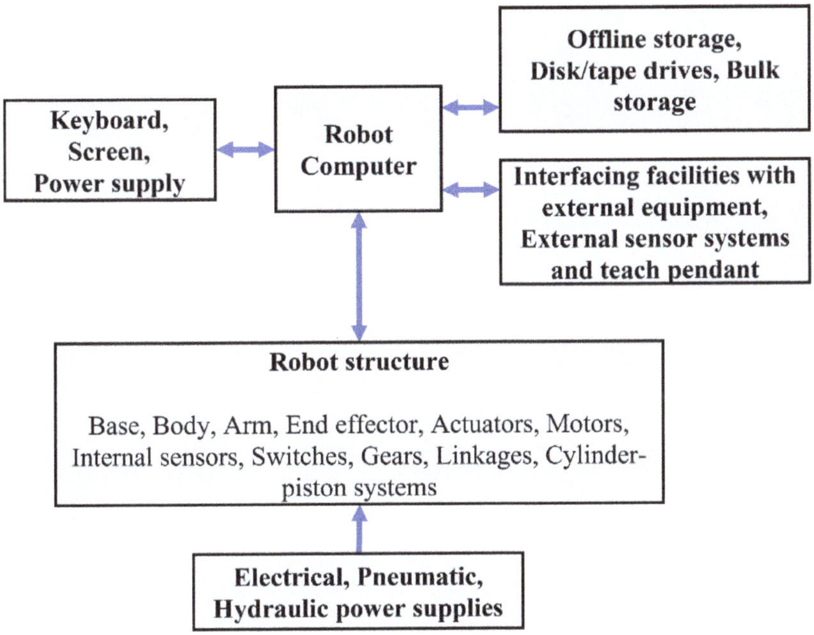

Figure 4. Block diagram of IR system.

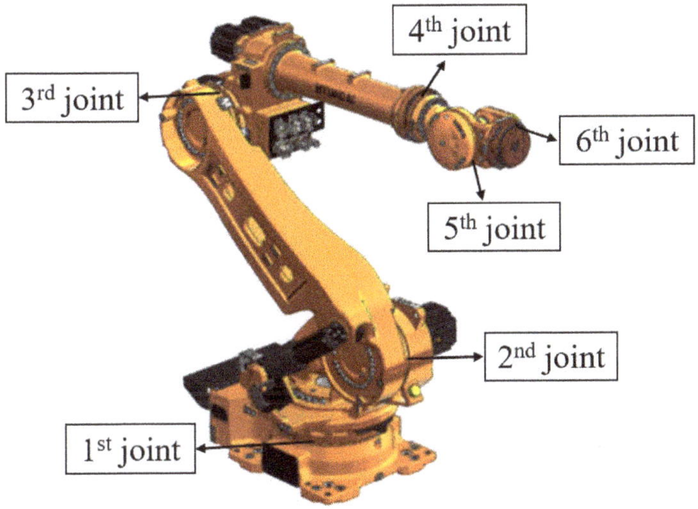

Figure 5. Industrial robot with 6 degrees-of-freedom [48].

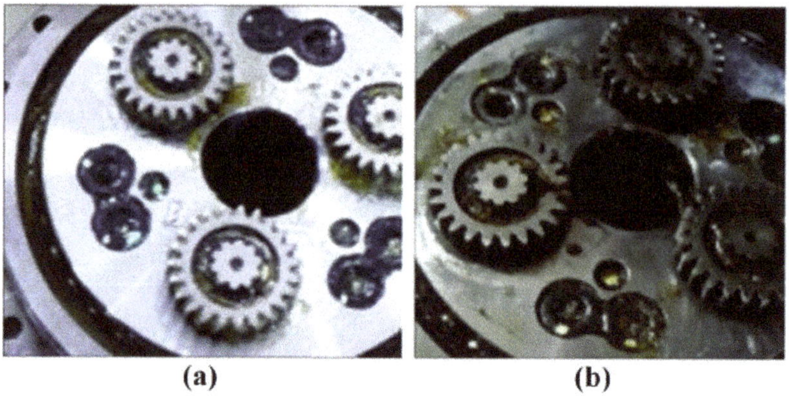

Figure 6. Faults in the industrial robots (a) Faulty reducer, and (b) Faulty Aged reducer [48].

It is vital to detect faults in a timely manner, and research on the PHM of the robotic system could be vital for efficient FDT. Faults, soft failures, and hard failures are the three types of faults that can be found. A fault is a systemic issue, such as a defect, an inaccurate signal value, or a poor decision. A fault may cause the degradation of the system's performance and can lead to failure [71]. Faults in the system can cause the system to wear out faster. The system may nevertheless be able to achieve the desired productivity and output product quality. A soft failure is characterized by deterioration, 'wear and tear', and exterior variations, which result in system damage. A soft failure occurs when a system continues to function, but its performance begins to deteriorate. In the case of a soft failure, the system's productivity decreases, and it is unable to meet the required objective. With time, its productivity decreases and its performance worsens, and ultimately decreases to a point below the required standards. A hard failure can be referred to as a breakdown of the component/equipment of the system, which leads to a pause in the functioning of the system [71]. Under such conditions, the manufacturing process is compromised, and cannot meet the required demand. The whole process completely shuts down. The system's PHM should be capable of detecting both soft and hard failures. PHM should be designed in such a way that it can detect failures early enough to prevent significant breakdowns. The majority of PHM solutions are centered on component monitoring and failure. There is a necessity for system-level monitoring, which will be applied to track the source of the failure to the point of genesis, or wherever it may have originated, by monitoring the health of the components, as well as the system.

The rotating components of the IR are crucial as well as being vulnerable to the faults. The rotating components, such as the motors, gears, and reducers, are also vulnerable to faults. The PHM of these rotating components could significantly reduce downtime and help in scheduling maintenance. The faults in the rotating components include faults in the gearboxes, centrifugal pumps, motors, alternators, and many more. The faults in the rotating machinery can include bearing defects, rotor defects, eccentricity, gear wear, cavitation, and misalignment [72–74]. Bearing defects can be segregated into outer race defects, inner race defects, ball defects, and train defects. Eccentricity can be divided into static, dynamic, and mixed eccentricity. Rotor defects are the major issue in the induction motors, alternators, and generators. High starting torque and frequency switching are the major causes of rotor damage in the motors [75]. The symptoms of the faults can include high vibration, increased current demand, torque pulsation, and excessive heating [75]. Timely maintenance of the rotating machinery is essential to avoid a complete shutdown. The PHM of rotating machines is critical in achieving the aim of uninterrupted operations in industries.

3. PHM Methodologies

PHM has previously existed in the medical and aerospace fields. PHM involves three subfields; namely, fault detection, fault diagnosis, and fault prognosis [76]. FDT aims to detect instances when the machine starts to behave differently from its normal behavior. It can be treated as a dual categorization job, i.e., to categorize whether the machine is running well or unwell [77]. Fault diagnosis involves fault identification, fault localization, and recognition of the severity. The next phase, diagnostics, should be able to pinpoint what went wrong and should build on the understanding that something went wrong. The analysis and prediction of the fault diagnosis should be more thorough than that of FDT. In the fault prognosis, the RUL is estimated. Prognostic models and physics-based models are typically utilized. The RUL is estimated with the help of the degradation trajectory [78]. From a practical perspective, the correct RUL estimation is crucial, as an incorrect estimation will lead to over-maintenance or complete shutdown. An accurate RUL assessment will help in adequate maintenance scheduling. The PHM solution combines these three groups to provide an optimized solution to the machine's maintenance. FDT application through applying DL can be categorized into two groups: supervised and unsupervised [79,80]. Supervised learning involves the availability of labelled data in the training and test dataset. Any DL approach can be chosen depending on the nature and availability of the data. Fault diagnosis can be viewed from the perspective of AI as a multi-class classification problem. It entails categorizing the detected fault according to a particular set of fault type, location, and severity. As the target value is in the actual world, FP in AI applications may be viewed as a regression problem [81]. The prediction seeks to create a learning function that could translate the state of the machine to its RUL [82–85].

The variety of the sensors data are used for the PHM of IRs. These sensors data help in assessing the health of the IRs. Accelerometers, encoders, temperature sensors, current and voltage sensors, vision systems, and force/torque sensors are a few of the frequently utilized sensors. The vibration sensor data have been significantly used for the PHM of IRs. The joints and actuators of the robot are measured in terms of their position, velocity, and direction using encoders. The system can find differences between the actual position and the expected position, which may point to faults with the robot's mobility or control system. Robotic joints, motors, electronics, and other parts are all monitored for their temperature using temperature sensors. Overheating or other potential defects can be indicated by sudden temperature fluctuations or by exceeding the predetermined thresholds. The electrical parameters of the robot's motors and actuators are monitored using current and voltage sensors. Variations in the current or voltage levels may be a sign of electrical problems, such as overloading, short circuits, or other issues. The forces and torques applied by the robot during its interactions with the environment are measured by force and torque sensors. These sensors can identify anomalies, such as sudden contact forces or high torques, which could be signs of an impending collision or malfunction. Robotic vision systems are used to keep an eye on its surroundings. These systems include cameras and image processing software. The system can discover possible issues through their ability to spot visual irregularities such as erroneous part arrangement, missing objects, or variations from the typical visual patterns.

For a long time, vibration-based analysis has been widely utilized for prognostics due to its superior capabilities, and many applications still employ this traditional method [37–40]. The vibration data have been widely used for developing a PHM strategy in rotating machines. It is one of the PHM topics that has been the subject of the most research. Other techniques, like acoustic emission, temperature analysis, and ultrasonic, are also widely used. Processing is conducted on the sensor data and is amalgamated using the sensor fusion techniques, owing to their innate advantages [86–90]. Model-based, data-driven, and hybrid prognostic techniques are the three types of prognostic technologies currently available [91].

A model is created and simulated for the healthy and fault states in a typical model-based process. The assessment of the developed model under the system's many functional modes is used to approximate the system's remaining useful life (RUL). This is created by combining the time-averaged model probability and the weighted predictions from each mode. The reliability of many models is under scrutiny, and if it is unavailable, data-driven techniques are utilized to estimate the RUL. This is generally accomplished by visualizing the developing fault's trajectory and the time it takes to obtain to the preset threshold value. The two famous fault prediction tools are the Kalman filter and the Alpha–Beta–Gamma tracking filter, which are often used in aerospace PHM and many other fields [43–47,92]. In hybrid approaches, both model-based techniques and data-driven methods are amalgamated and used for fault prognosis and diagnosis [93–97]. The traditional method of PHM is based on analytical models that draw on physical principles and subject-matter expertise. Systems with well-understood physics and well-defined failure mechanisms may respond well to this strategy. Analytical models for complex systems can be difficult and time-consuming to create, and they may not be correct in the presence of unexpected or unpredictable behavior. Machine learning algorithms that learn to recognize patterns in the data provide the foundation of the DL approach to PHM. This method can be used to analyze complicated systems with a wide range of failure modes as it is not constrained by the requirement to comprehend the underlying physics of the system. Deep learning algorithms are more resistant to unforeseen or unpredictable behavior because they may learn to adapt to changes in the system.

An efficient PHM strategy should detect incipient faults, diagnose faults, and estimate the RUL of the component or sub-elements. Both products and processes can benefit from PHM. The focus of product PHM is on a physical object. Monitoring a robot arm is an example of product PHM. In comparison to process PHM, product PHM is more readily available in the automobile, aerospace, and power generation industries [49–56].

3.1. Conventional PHM Cycle

Prognostics and Health Management comprise multiple tasks to lower the overall lifecycle cost of the component/system. The PHM strategies involve multiple steps (as shown in Figure 7), like data collection, feature development, dimensionality reduction, model development, decision making, and remaining useful life calculation. The data acquisition step involves collecting the data, like the vibration and current temperature, from multiple sensors, including the accelerometers, acoustic emission sensors, thermometers, and hall sensors. These data contain information regarding the health of the machine. The feature extraction step involves the application of signal processing tools, like fast Fourier transform (FFT), Short-time Fourier transform (STFT), Wavelet packet transform (WPT), and Hilbert Huang transformation (HHT). The statistical features based on time-domain signals are kurtosis, root mean square (RMS), skewness, etc., and are used to develop PHM strategies [98–108]. Also, some of the frequency-domain signatures, like spectral, envelope, and wavelet packets, are widely employed for PHM strategies [20,57–60]. The feature selection step involves removing redundant and irrelevant features and is accomplished by selecting the essential features using filters, wrappers, or embedded methods. Also, dimensionality-reduction tools, like principal component analysis (PCA), linear discriminant analysis (LDA), and kernel PCA, are used for feature dimensionality reduction, as well as for retaining rich information about the health of the intact machines [109,110].

The traditional method for anomaly detection includes SVM, Hidden Markov models, the Bayesian network, and ensemble methods. These methods have been applied efficiently for the health assessment of different machines [111,112]. PHM involves three tasks: diagnostics, prognostics, and decision support. Diagnostics is the crucial task following FDT to understand the system's health by analyzing the severity level of faults. The conventional machine learning approaches involve the SVM, kNN, DT, and RF trained on a labeled dataset for fault identification and classification [111,113,114]. Prognostics refer to the detection of incipient faults and related RUL for the predictive maintenance of the system. The data-driven approaches, like ANN, HMM, the Kalman filter, and the extended Kalman filter, have been utilized for the prognosis [43,67–69]. The PHM strategy's health management system is referred to as decision support, which utilizes the outcome of the diagnostics and prognostics for making timely, suitable, and logical judgments to schedule the maintenance or replacement of components [115–121]. To determine the best maintenance task and time to apply it, mathematical programming, Markov decision processes, and Reinforcement learning (RL) methods are prominently used [71–73].

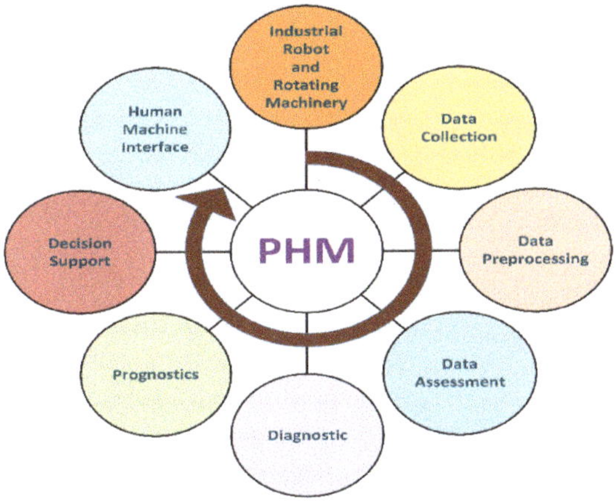

Figure 7. Framework for the conventional PHM.

3.2. PHM Performance Metrics

The performance analysis of the PHM approach determines the system's reliability. The complexity of the PHM system requires the appropriate performance metrics, which are listed in Table 1. These metrics are employed to assess the RUL prediction for prognostics. The performance metrics offer a thorough examination of how well the PHM techniques function with DL applications.

Table 1. Performance metrics for PHM evaluation.

Diagnostics	Prognostics
Accuracy [122]	Mean absolute error [123]
Error rate [122]	Root mean square error [124]
Precision [125]	Mean absolute percentage error [124]
Sensitivity [126] (p. 202)	Prediction horizon [127]
F1-score [126]	Convergence [127]
Correlation coefficient [128]	Relative accuracy [127]
Area under curve [129]	Confidence interval [130]
Detection error trade off [129]	Exponential transformed accuracy [131]

3.3. DL-Based PHM

The application of DL in PHM has gained momentum in the last few years. With the inherent capabilities of DL-based models, the disadvantages of conventional ML-based models have been seized. The DL algorithms like CNN, RNN, AE, etc., offer automatic feature development, which significantly improves the model's performance. The DL-based model has been efficiently used for FDT, FDG, and FP. All of the major PHM fields have a universal framework as a result of DL. This can be illustrated by the simple diagram shown in Figure 8. The application of DL provides an end-to-end learning framework for PHM. The type of data available and the application domain influence the choice of the DL model. When there is a scarcity of labeled data, which often happens in practical problems, FDT requires unsupervised learning. A multi-class classification challenge could be said to exist in the fault diagnosis scenario. The objective of the DL created for fault diagnosis is to map the detected fault to a certain combination of fault type, location, and severity. A typical DL model will involve the SoftMax layer to the final layer for achieving the fault diagnosis task. A common choice for the loss function is categorical cross-entropy. The model is trained based on this loss function. Also, after training a DL model, the t-SNE method can be used for feature visualization. The prognosis task can be considered as the regression task. The RUL prediction might be reduced to a normalized range by the final layer of the DL model, which could be a single neuron with a linear activation function or sigmoid function. The accurate estimation of the RUL is a grueling task as an overestimation could lead to unnecessary maintenance and an underestimation could lead to a complete shutdown of the machine. One of the most important tasks in the prognosis is penalizing the delayed RUL estimations (i.e., the predicted RUL is higher than the actual RUL). The input data for the PHM solution for robots and their rotating machinery can include vibration data, current data, imagery data, temperature data, etc.

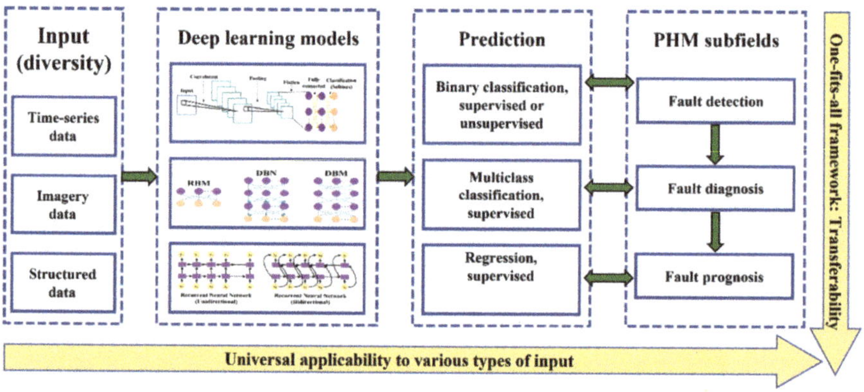

Figure 8. DL-based framework for the PHM including its subfield like fault detection, fault diagnosis, and fault prognosis for various types of input.

Deep learning framework-based PHM systems often incorporate different deep learning architectures, including deep Boltzmann machines, autoencoders (AEs), convolutional neural networks (CNNs), and recurrent neural networks (RNNs). An in-depth explanation of how these designs are applied in PHM systems is provided below:

- Restricted Boltzmann Machines (RBMs): RBMs have a wide range of applications; their direct use in PHM systems built on deep learning frameworks has been relatively less common. RBMs, however, can contribute to PHM in many ways. In PHM, RBMs can be utilized to find anomalies. An RBM can learn the underlying distribution of the normal behavior by being trained on data from typical operational scenarios [132]. The RBM may assess the reconstruction error or energy of fresh data instances during the inference stage. Higher reconstruction errors or energies signify abnormalities or flaws because they deviate from the expected behavior. In PHM systems, RBMs can be used as a step in the pre-processing pipeline. RBMs are capable of extracting features from high-dimensional sensor input or learning a compressed representation. The hidden units of an RBM can be trained on the input data to identify significant latent characteristics or patterns that can be used as inputs to later models, such as fault classifiers or prognostics models [133].
- Autoencoders (AEs): Autoencoders are able to pick up on a system or component equipment's typical working behavior and recognize abnormalities or departures from it. Autoencoders identify probable errors or anomalies by highlighting variations between the original and reconstructed input data [134]. In PHM, AEs can serve as feature extractors. The encoder portion of an autoencoder can capture meaningful representations of the sensor data by being trained on a sizable dataset. These rep-

resentations can then be utilized as inputs for later supervised models, such as fault classifiers or prognostics models [135]. High-dimensional sensor data can have its dimensions reduced by AEs, allowing for more effective processing and storage. AEs preserve important information while simplifying later modelling efforts by lowering the dimensions of the input they compress into a lower-dimensional latent space [136].

- Convolutional Neural Networks (CNNs): The capacity of CNNs to efficiently extract spatial patterns and features from the sensor data, such as images or time-series data, makes them a common tool in PHM. CNNs can be used for fault detection or classification tasks in applications where images or visual data are accessible (such as thermal imaging or photos from visual inspection) [137]. CNNs develop hierarchical representations of the images they process, identifying pertinent details and patterns linked to errors or anomalies [138]. It can be used to analyze spectrogram data, which displays the frequency content of time-series sensor measurements in signal-based PHM. In order to perform tasks like fault detection, classification, or regression, CNNs may extract spatial patterns from spectrograms [139].
- Recurrent Neural Networks (RNNs): RNNs are made to identify sequential patterns and temporal dependencies in time-series data. Sequential sensor measurements are frequently used in PHM applications, making RNNs an excellent choice for this type of data analysis [140]. RNNs can simulate temporal dependencies in time-series sensor data, especially those with Long Short-Term Memory (LSTM) or Gated Recurrent Unit (GRU) variations. Using RNNs, it is possible to detect faults and perform diagnostics and prognostics on sequential data by capturing patterns, long-term dependencies, and dynamics [141]. In PHM, time-series forecasting tasks can be performed using RNNs. RNNs can forecast future sensor readings, remaining usable life (RUL), or failure probabilities by learning from the existing sensor data, which enables proactive maintenance planning [142].

4. Overview of Deep Learning Models

Deep learning has gained popularity owing to the availability of high computational resources. The idea of DL dates back to the 1940s [143], but appears to be a new concept, as it was relatively unknown for several years before gaining traction, and it was known by a variety of names prior to being termed "deep learning". DL developed in three stages: cybernetics in the 1940s–1960s, connectionism in the 1980s–1990s, and the present revival under the name DL, which began in 2006 [143]. Deep networks are based on the human brain's hierarchical architecture and attempt to learn simple patterns; they transform them into more abstract representations [144–146]. The generic structure of a feed-forward deep neural network (DNN) contains an input layer, numerous hidden layers, and an output layer. When multi-layer perceptron (MLP) obtains the input data, the output is generated along with the successive layers of the model in a straightforward manner. The non-linear activation functions of each hidden/middle layer neuron are given the biased weight sum of the preceding layer outputs to generate the neuron's output. The DL model's hierarchical design allows for efficient feature learning, which aids in comprehending the underlying correlations and patterns in enormous amounts of data [147,148]. The following section briefly describes the available DL algorithms that are applied in the PHM strategies.

4.1. Restricted Boltzmann Machine

The Restricted Boltzmann machine (RBM) is a generative stochastic neural network framework. It can discover a probability distribution within a collection of inputs. The RBMs are undirected bipartite graphical models with n_x visible and n_h hidden units that allow no intralayer connections and are widely employed as generative models (GMs). Due to their stochastic processing units, RBMs can learn the original data's recreated form. They are generally used as a pre-processor for various frameworks to complete the job in supervised classification, but can also be utilized as a standalone classifier. Goodfellow et al. [143] provides a step-by-step strategy for training RBMs. In the coming sections, we briefly discuss two generative deep neural network (DNN) models based on the RBM; namely, the deep belief network (DBN), and deep Boltzmann machines (DBMs). Figure 9 shows the structures of the RBM, DBN, and DBM.

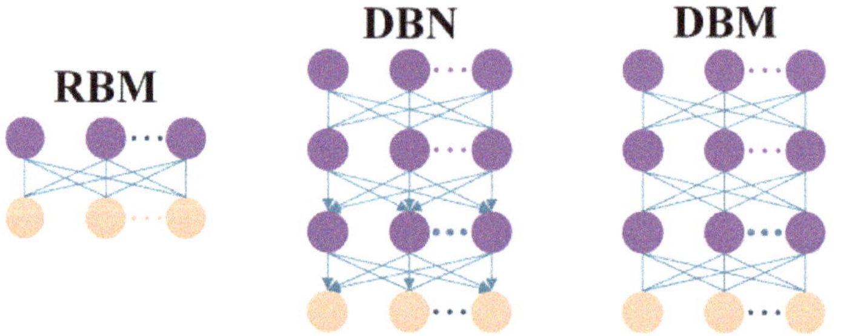

Figure 9. Structure of the RBM, DBN, and DBM (shaded boxes in lavender color represent hidden units).

4.1.1. Deep Belief Network

The DBN is a deep probabilistic GM constructed by stacking several RBMs, and consists of several layers of stochastic, latent variables [149]. Hidden units or feature detectors are terms used to describe latent variables that have binary values. The two layers at the top are linked by undirected and symmetric connections, which form an associative memory. The upper layer sends directed links down to the lower layers. The states of the units produce the data vector in the lowest tier. Links in the lower layers are top-down directed, whereas the top layers are undirected. An effective layer-by-layer process is utilized to learn the generative weights. These weights specify the relationship between the variables in different layers. After learning, a single bottom–up run is performed. It begins with the help of a detected data vector in the end layer. To determine the values of the latent variables in each layer, the weights generation process is reversed. The nets of DBN perform one layer of learning at a time when inferring the data. This is conducted by employing the latent variable values of one layer as the training data for the coming layer. It can also be amalgamated with other learning methods. It can help in fine-tuning all the weights that will boost the multiplicative or discriminatory operation of the complete framework.

4.1.2. Deep Boltzmann Machine

The Deep Boltzmann machine is a deep GM with layers that are organized hierarchically. The DBM is formed by stacking layers of the RBM, such that odd-numbered layer units and even-numbered layer units are independent. DBM is a totally undirected model, unlike the deep belief network. The latent variable in a DBM contains numerous layers, whereas RBMs only have one. Within each layer of a DBM, the variables are mutually independent and conditioned on the variables of the neighboring levels. The DBM's energy function incorporates a weight matrices-based connection between hidden units (latent variables). A DBM can also be arranged in a bipartite graph. In contrast to a DBN, which may be taught layer-by-layer, a DBM is trained as a joint model. As a result, DBM training is more computationally expensive than DBN training.

4.2. Auto-Encoder

An auto-encoder (AE) is an efficient neural network model that employs an unsupervised learning method for learning efficient data coding in an unsupervised way. It is made up of two parts: an encoder and a decoder. The encoder is utilized to encode the input, and in some cases, to compress the data. Each layer of the encoder has a decreasing number of hidden units. It allows only the most significant and representative attributes to be mined from the data. The decoding part of the framework is the second component. Each layer of the decoder has an increasing number of hidden units, and the decoder tries reconstructing the original input using the encoded data. Consider the encoder, which uses a non-linear mapping to turn the input i into a hidden representation e, and given by [143,150]:

$$e = \phi(W * i + b) \tag{1}$$

where, ϕ denotes a non-linear activation function (AF). SoftMax, relu, tanh, sigmoid, and other activation functions are often employed. In the same way, the decoder maps the hidden representation as follows [143]:

$$d = \phi(W' * i + b') \tag{2}$$

In addition to traditional auto-encoders and sparse auto-encoders, there are a few altered variations available, such as denoising AE, contractive AE, and variational AE. Vincent et al. have suggested that a denoising AE can be used as training criteria to learn and extract the essential features, which can yield an efficient high-level feature from the input [151]. An explicit regularizer is introduced to the objective function of a contractive AE, forcing the model to grasp an encoding that is resilient to minor input value fluctuations. The variational auto-encoder is a type of generative model that is classified as an auto-encoder because of its architectural similarity to the basic auto-encoders [152]. The deep auto-encoders offer many advantages, like [143]:

- Deep AE facilitates the reduction in the computational power required for the representation of some functions.
- Deep AE facilitates the reduction in the computational training data required for learning some functions.

AEs are trainable in an unsupervised way. The stacked denoising AE (SDA) can offer an efficient pre-training solution. The model is trained by instantiating the weights of a DNN. When the SDA has been trained layer-by-layer, the auto-encoders' parameters can be used to initialize all of the DNN's layers. Then, on the labelled training data, supervised fine-tuning is used to reduce the prediction error. To map the output of the final layers to the targets, a SoftMax layer is typically placed on top of the AE-based structure; Figure 10 illustrates this step. The pretraining method using SDA improves the convergence speed of the DNN models compared to the random weight initialization. Training of the DNN includes issues like vanishing/exploding gradient problems. This is due to the commonly used nonlinear activation functions (tanh or sigmoid). As a result, auto-encoder-provided unsupervised training is valuable and effective.

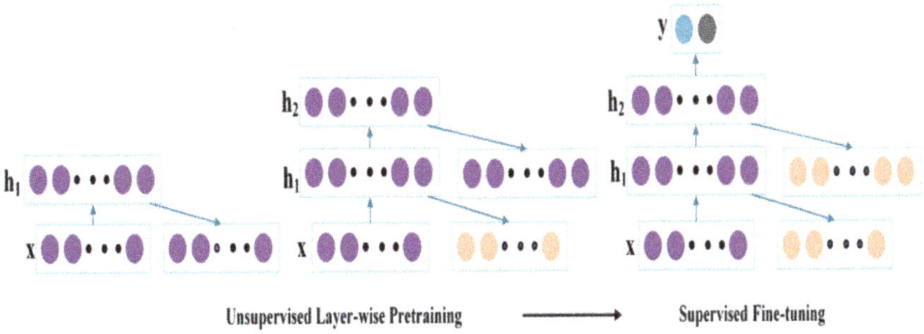

Figure 10. Framework for unsupervised pre-training and supervised fine-tuning of stacked denoising auto-encoder based DNN model.

4.3. Convolutional Neural Network

The visual cortex of the human brain is the inspiration for the convolutional neural network (CNN), which was first proposed by LeCun [153] for image processing. The CNN has found its application in multiple domains, including image segregation, speech recognition, object recognition, and many more. The CNNs are analogous to traditional ANNs as they also consist of neurons that self-optimize through learning. Like ANN, CNN is also composed of multiple layers, including an input layer, hidden layer, and output layer. In the CNN, the layers performing convolution operations are the hidden layers. The CNN is mainly composed of the convolutional layers (CLs), pooling layers (PLs), and fully-connected layers (FCLs) [126]. Figure 11 gives a simple architecture of CNN. The details of these layers are given below:

- CL: This is the core component of a CNN. The majority of the computation occurs in this block only. The input to this layer is the tensor with shape (number of images) × (image height) × (image width) × (input channels). The name convolution comes from the mathematical operation, termed 'convolution', in this layer. Convolution is a linear operation in a CNN that performs a weight multiplication with the input. The CNNs have traditionally been designed for 2-D inputs, with multiplication occurring between a 2-D array of input data and a 2-D array of weights, also known as a kernel or filter. The size of the kernel is a fraction of the input data. Between the filter-sized input matrix and the filter, the dot product is utilized, which is then summed to provide a single value. The tiny-sized filter allows the input array to multiply the same filter (set of weights) several times at various points on the input. The filter is convoluted all over the input data's portion/segment/patch. This is conducted left-to-right and top-to-bottom. The multiplication of the filter and input yields a single value. The input filtering is characterized as a 2-D array of output values obtained by repeatedly applying the filter to the input array. Consequently, a 2-D array obtained through this operation is referred to as a "feature map". The values in the feature map are passed through a non-linearity, such as a Rectified Linear Unit (ReLu), once it has been developed [143]. It can be explained mathematically in the following way:

$$G[m,n] = (f * h)[m,n] = \sum_{j}\sum_{k} h[j,k]\cdot f[m-j,n-k] \tag{3}$$

  where f denotes the input array, h denotes the kernel, j and k denote the input matrix size, and m and n represent the row and column indices of the resultant matrix.
- PL: The PL performs the down-sampling operation, typically applied after a convolution layer. This helps in achieving spatial invariance. It prevents overfitting by aggressively lowering the spatial dimension of the network's representation to decrease the quantum of the parameters and calculations. As it computes a constant input function, it introduces no parameters. In general, max and average pooling are often used in the analysis. Each pooling operation in the max pooling scheme selects the current view's maximum value. Similarly, each pooling action in average pooling averages the current view's value.
- FCL: Similar to conventional neural networks, the FCL neurons are fully connected to the preceding layer. Consequently, a matrix multiplication followed by a bias offset can be utilized to calculate their activations.

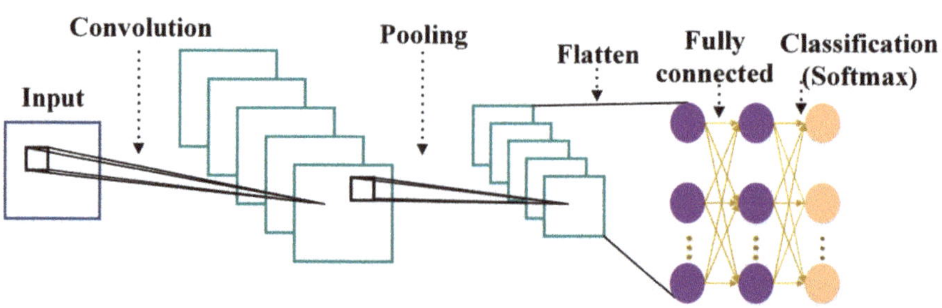

Figure 11. Framework of CNN model.

4.4. Recurrent Neural Network

A recurrent neural network (RNN) is an AI algorithm that performs efficiently on the time series or sequential data. A RNN is well-suited for a variety of problems, like language transformation, natural language processing, voice recognition, and picture captioning. It has found applications in famous applications, like Siri and Google translator. The RNNs, like feedforward and CNNs, learn from training input. They are distinguished by their "memory", which enables them to alter the present action and output by employing information from previous inputs. The RNN differs from other DL algorithms in that its output is reliant on the preceding elements of the input sequence. RNNs use the backpropagation through time (BPTT) technique, which is fundamentally different from traditional backpropagation because it is tailored to sequence data in order to determine the gradients. Traditional backpropagation employs the same concepts as BPTT, wherein the model self-trains by computing the errors from its output to its input layer. These computations allow for the precise modification and adjustment of the model's parameters. BPTT varies from conventional techniques in that errors are accumulated at each time step, whereas feedforward networks do not need to accumulate total errors [143]. This is because feedforward networks do not share parameters between layers. Figure 12 shows the basic structure of a RNN.

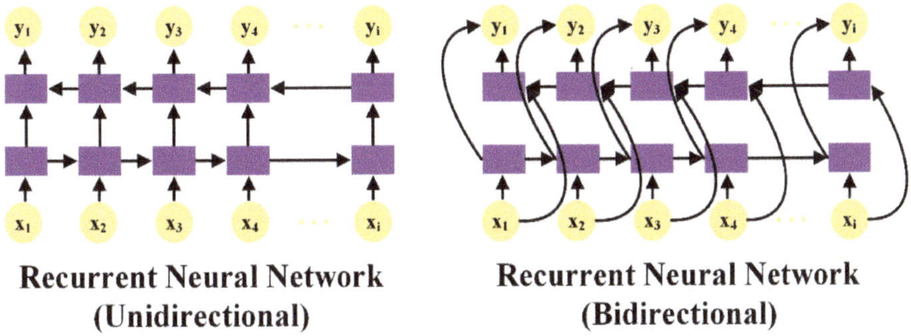

Figure 12. Framework of RNN model.

5. Deep Learning for the PHM of Rotating Machinery of Industrial Robots

This section discusses the existing deep learning framework-based PHM of the rotating machinery of IRs. The existing deep learning frameworks for PHM are discussed in the following sections.

5.1. Deep Belief Network for PHM

The DBN is among the most popular algorithms in the domain of PHM. It is among the first models employed for the PHM strategy. Dash et al. [154] (p. 20) developed a DBN-based probabilistic generative model to detect robotic manipulator failure. Failures have been identified at every position and instance of robotic manipulators using the DBN-based model. Elsewhere, Chen and Li proposed a DBN-based model that utilizes the features extracted with the help of auto-encoders from the vibration data for bearing FDT [155]. Ren et al. propounded a FDT methodology using DBN models [156]. The DBN model was trained on historical datasets and applied to real-time measurement data to generate outputs. These outputs and measurements were used to extract residuals, and based on the adaptive threshold for the residuals, faults were detected in the complex system. Xing et al. proposed an invariant DBN model for gear-FDG with the help of raw vibration data [157]. The propounded fault diagnosis model learned the distributed-invariant features directly, utilizing the raw vibration data, and performed the FDG. Jiao and Zheng proposed a combination of the DBN-based model and wavelet transformation of the vibration signals for the fault diagnosis of industrial robots [158]. The vibration signal was denoised, decomposed, and reconstructed using the wavelet transformation. The normalized eigenvector was developed and used to input the DBN-based model. Elsewhere, Ji et al. proposed a methodology for the FDG of the reducers of industrial robots with the help of the deep-level probability-directed graph DBN model [159]. Shao et al. proposed a FDG technique using a DBN-based model for the motors used in the manufacturing process [160]. The DBN model comprises the stacked RBMs (as shown in Figure 13) and is trained with the help of a layer-by-layer pre-training method. This model assesses the motor's health by automatically learning aspects from the sensor data. Most of these methods still require hand-crafted features and efficient signal processing techniques. These dependencies restrict the model's performance. The training of DBN-based models is cumbersome, and tracking the loss function is challenging. It also limits the provision of end-to-end learning solutions for fault diagnosis and prognosis.

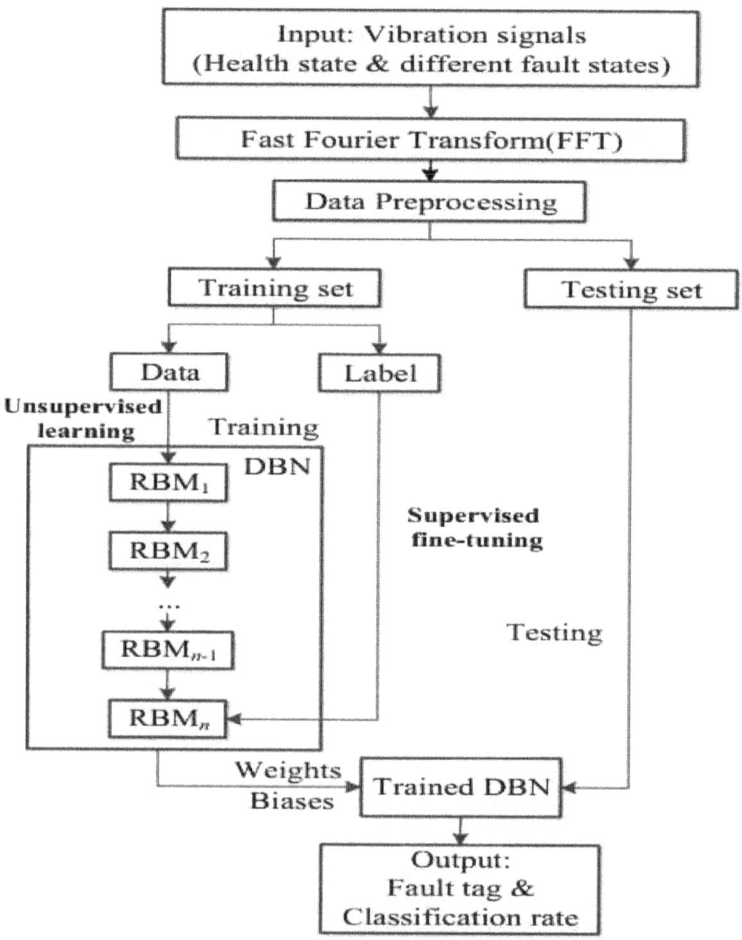

Figure 13. DBN-based framework for fault diagnosis of the induction motor used in manufacturing process [160].

5.2. Deep Boltzmann Machine for PHM

The Deep Boltzmann machines are powerful DL models that conduct the interpretation and training process in cooperation with the bottom–up and top–down directions.

This helps improve the representation of the input features. Despite being a powerful deep learning model, limited works are related to the DBM-based PHM strategies. Elsewhere, Hu et al. proposed a FDG approach for industrial fault diagnosis that included the DBM and multi-grained scanning forest ensemble [161]. Deng et al. proposed a bearing FDG employing the DBM-based FDG paradigm [162]. The time and frequency domain features were retrieved and fed into the DBM-based model as input. Li et al. used the Gaussian–Bernoulli DBM for high-level feature development using the vibration data in three modalities [163]. Figure 14 illustrates the design of the purported framework, and three distinct modalities were fed to the Gaussian–Bernoulli DBM for gearbox FDG. A SVM classifier was utilized to fuse the representative features and perform the fault classification. This approach has been verified on both spur and helical gearboxes. Wang et al. purported the Gaussian–Bernoulli DBM for compressor health management in smart manufacturing [164]. The DBM Gaussian neurons were used to pre-process the vibration signals for health management, and the created model was able to infer the complicated features from the input sequence. Hyperparameter optimization was carried out using the Particle Swarm Optimizer algorithm. Also, a tailored Liu–Storey conjugate gradient algorithm was used to improve the convergence rate. The application of DBM-based models requires intensive computation, and conducting a weight update is challenging. However, DBM-based models also have advantages, like efficient learning of complex representations and good uncertainty propagation. Mitrevski and Ploger [165] have proposed robot fault detection and diagnosis using the DBM-based model.

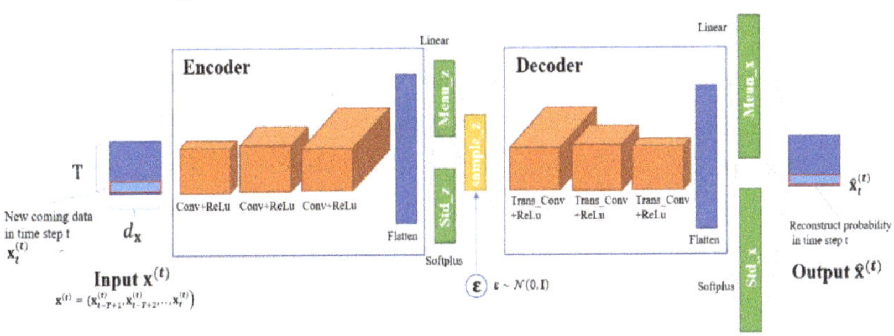

Figure 14. Gaussian–Bernoulli DBM framework for fault diagnosis [166].

5.3. *Auto-Encoder for PHM*

Auto-encoders are very popular in the PHM field, and have been extensively used by researchers for FDG and FP. Hong et al. presented a FDG approach for multi-joint industrial robots using a deep sparse auto-encoder model using an attitude dataset [167]. A test rig was used to help create the dataset, and analysis was performed on the results. Reference [166] proposed a fault diagnosis approach for the industrial robot using the sliding-window convolutional variational auto-encoder-based model and multivariate time series data. Figure 15 shows the framework of this approach, where the input data is $x^{(t)}$ with a time-step of t, and the model output is the reconstruction probabilities of each point in the sliding window. Xiao et al. propounded a denoising AE-based model using acoustic signals for fault diagnosis [168]. Elsewhere, Yun et al. proposed a fault diagnosis approach for the robot arm using the stacked auto-encoder (SAE)-based FDT framework [169]. Two stethoscopes were used for sound data acquisition, and feature extraction was performed using the STFT spectrogram. The auto-encoder model was trained and tested using these features. Sun et al. developed a FDT approach for induction motors using a sparse AE for the feature learning from the vibration signals [170]. Partial corruption was added using the denoising coding and fed into the SAE-based model for feature learning. These features have been fed to the neural network classifier for fault identification and classification. In another work, Li et al. proposed an intelligent FDG using a fully connected AE for bearing FDG [171]. The proposed model imposed a lifespan sparseness on the encoded features, and the soft polling method was applied to boost the accuracy and stability. Also, a dataset was developed by adding Gaussian noise, and the performance was evaluated to validate the performance in a noisy environment. Sohaib et al. developed an approach for the FDG approach for rotary machine bearings with the SAE model [172]. The complex envelope spectrum aided in making the frequency component more distinct in the signal and facilitated efficient feature extraction from the given input signals. Also, automatic feature extraction helped in tackling the problems associated with manual feature extraction and selection. AE-based approaches require a dedicated classifier for fault diagnosis. These approaches require a high computational cost, and selecting the specific features for the fault diagnosis is challenging. However, AE-based techniques also offer advantages, like flexible architecture, dimensionality reduction, and no requirement for labeled data.

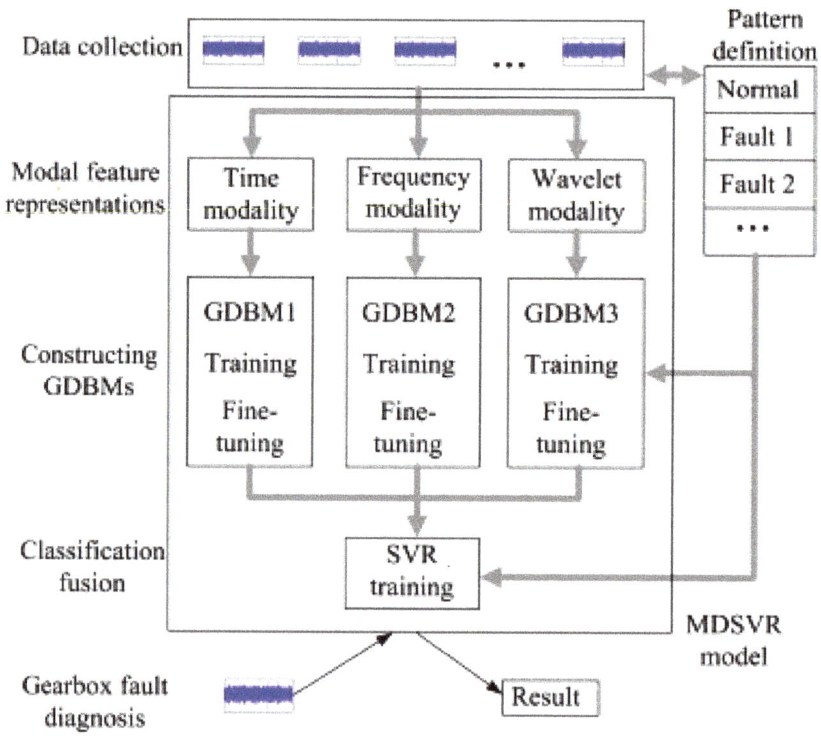

Figure 15. Convolutional variational auto-encoder framework for fault diagnosis in industrial robots [163].

5.4. Convolutional Neural Network for PHM

The CNN is efficiently used in PHM due to its excellent automatic feature learning capabilities and segregation capabilities. Chen et al. developed a CNN-based FDG model for the heavy-duty industrial robot system [173]. A FDT model was designed with a series combination of spectrum calculation fault diagnosis networks. Elsewhere, Kim et al. suggested a FDG methodology for industrial robot servo systems utilizing multiple sensor signals as an input to the one-dimensional CNN model [174]. Figure 16 shows the framework, and it is comprised of one plain convolutional block, three stacked residual blocks with a skip connection, a global average pooling (GAP) layer, and two fully connected layers. Also, the model was validated on the Case Western Reserve University (CWRU) data and the IMS bearing database of the University of Cincinnati. Yang et al. developed a FDT technique for the rotating vector reducer for industrial robots using a CNN-based model [175]. Meanwhile, Ma et al. [176] suggested a FDT methodology for the industrial robot by employing the one-dimensional CNN and data improvisation through random sampling and mix-up data augmentation. The dataset includes the torque, speed, position, and current data of the robot. Li et al. proposed a multi-axis IR FDG approach using the multi-label one-dimensional CNN [177]. Elsewhere, Liu at al. proposed a dilated CNN model for the cross-axial industrial robotics FDG [178]. The sliding window and key feature extraction method pre-processed the input data. These data are fed to the dilated CNN model for feature mining, and the self-attention network is used for its feature attention capability. Lu et al. propounded a dual-module attentive CNN for industrial robot fault diagnosis [179]. Two parallel CNN models with different attentions were capitalized for feature learning, and the features were fused for efficient fault diagnosis. In another work, Janssens et al. proposed a CNN-based technique for different types of bearing faults and rotor imbalances [180]. The CNN-based FDT approach helped eradicate the need for manually engineered features like the ball pass frequencies of the raceway, kurtosis, RMS, and variance. It demonstrated that a CNN-based feature learning system outperforms classic feature-engineered techniques. Plakias et al. developed an attentive dense CNN fault diagnosis technique for bearings [181]. The attentive deep CNN model considers the temporal coherence of the data, which helps to improve the feature learning. Cheng et al. developed a FDT technique for rotating machinery using the CNN model and continuous wavelet transformation [182]. The proposed model used a local binary convolutional layer for faster training and to avoid overfitting issue. The model was tested on the bearing faults and gearbox compound FDG. Guo et al. developed a CNN-based FDT approach for rotating machinery employing the continuous wavelet transformation of vibration signals [183]. Also, the model was tested on different pieces of rotor equipment for validation of the proposed methodology. Liang et al. purported an intelligent FDT approach for rotating machinery using the combination of the wavelet transformation, generative adversarial nets, and CNN [184]. The wavelet transformation was used to obtain the time–frequency image characteristics from the one-dimensional raw signals. Generative adversarial nets were employed to develop the training images, and the CNN model was used for FDT. Li et al. propounded a FDG approach for rotating machinery with the amalgamation of the DBN and one-dimensional CNN [185]. The DBN was created by combining the three RBMs for high-dimensional data feature abstraction and dimensionality reduction. For FDG, these low-dimensional features are loaded into a one-dimensional CNN model. To evaluate the effectiveness of the model, the proposed approach was applied to two experimental datasets. These CNN-based methods facilitate efficient feature extraction and safeguard spatial information. Also, the performance of these models relies on parameter initialization and lacks global feature extraction capabilities.

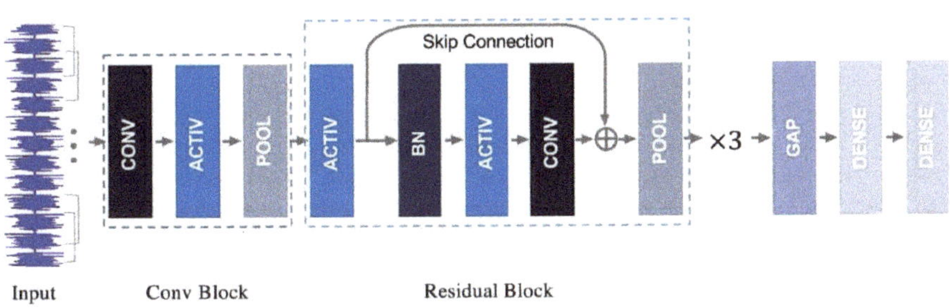

Figure 16. Residual CNN framework for fault diagnosis in industrial robots [174].

5.5. Recurrent Neural Network for PHM

The RNN provides the inherent advantage of retaining the temporal information of the time–series data. This property of the RNN is advantageous for PHM as it retains the information throughout the training. The RNN can recall temporal dependencies and understand the failure's dynamic comportment. Vanilla RNNs (basic RNNs), on the other hand, are unable to learn long-term temporal dependencies due to the vanishing/exploding gradient problem. Gradient clipping is a technique that uses a threshold value to restrict the magnitude of a gradient. Various gating strategies have been proposed to deal with the vanishing gradient. Long Short-Term Memory (LSTM) and Gated Recurrent Unit (GRU) are the two most well-known RNN versions for dealing with these problems. For example, An et al. developed a bearing FDT method with the help of an RNN-based FDT model [186]. Figure 17 shows a framework of the propounded model and training strategy. The input network extends the dimensions of the input, LSTM cells have been used for the recurrent framework, and hidden inputs are used as an input to the two-layer network. Also, the physical interpretation of the network learning was given with the help of the maximum mean discrepancy and t-SNE [187]. Zhang et al. developed an RNN-based FDT model for rotating machinery [188]. GRU is used to extract temporal information from the time–series data and to learn the relevant attributes from the produced images. Finally, MLP is used to implement FDT. Liu et al. propounded a FDT method for the rolling element bearing using the recurrent neural network [189]. The reconstruction error between the output data and the following period data was utilized to detect and categorize different fault kinds after the vibration signals were employed as an input to the GRU-based denoising AE-based model. Elsewhere, Jaing et al. developed a bearing FDT method using the deep RNN model [190]. The frequency signals are used to construct the input data without the manual feature development, and the adopted DL strategy was applied for the training process. Qiao et al. suggested a FDT model through the combination of the CNN and LSTM for bearing fault diagnosis [191]. The spatial sequence characteristics were extracted from the input signal by the model's convolution and LSTM layers, and the final classification was performed by the dense layers. Also, the model was substantiated on the public domain data sets of the CWRU. Meanwhile, Oh et al. proposed a bearing fault diagnosis of the rotating machinery using the combination of a denoising AE and a multi-scale convolution RNN [192]. The denoising AE is used to pre-process the data, and the multi-scale convolution RNN is applied to categorize the bearing defects. Li et al. [193] proposed a mobile robot bearing FD using the DWT and LSTM models. The vibration signals were decomposed into six frequency bands for the bearing FD task. Zhi et al. [194] developed a FD model for harmonic reducers, which is a key component of IRs. A combination of the CNN and LSTM has been employed for the FD using the wavelet regional correlation threshold denoising algorithm. Wang et al. [195] proposed a FD method for the motor drive system of IRs, where the CNN has been used for the feature extraction and LSTM for the prediction of the system's health. RNN-based approaches are among the most efficient methods for RUL estimation. The RNN is well suited to time–series data and sequential data. The conventional RNN structure often suffers from the vanishing gradient problem. However, a modified version of the RNN, like LSTM, helps solve the vanishing gradient problem. The training time of these models requires a long duration, and the structures are often complex. Generally, these models do not support parallel computing. Overall, a few DL-based PHM strategies have been encapsulated in Table 2.

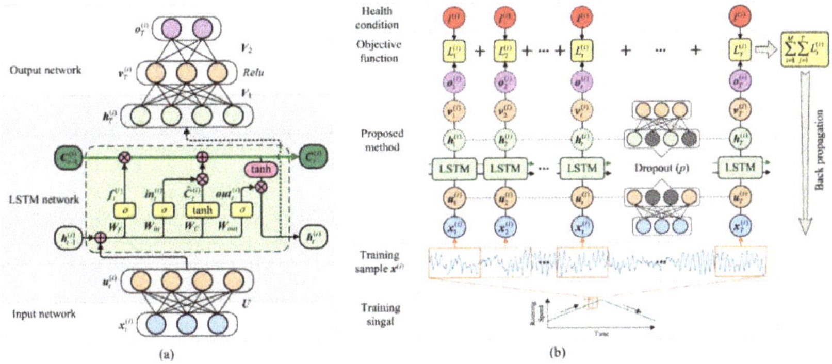

Figure 17. Illustration of (**a**) RNN framework for fault diagnosis in bearings, and (**b**) training methodology [186].

Table 2. PHM Methods with DL-based strategies.

PHM Methods Based on Deep Learning Methods					
	Reference	**Dataset**	**Datatype**	**Model**	**Accuracy**
Fault diagnosis	Sohaib et al. [196]	CWRU bearing data	Vibration	SAE-DNN	99.5%
	Xu et al. [197]	CWRU and Xi'an Jiaotong University (XJTU-SY) bearing data	Vibration	Wavelet Transform-CNN	99.4%
	Hoang and Kang et al. [198]	KAT bearing dataset by Paderborn University, Germany	Current	CNN	99.47%
	Li et al. [199]	CWRU	Vibration	CNN-LSTM	99.74%
		Gear Box	Vibration	DBM	99.94%
	Chen et al. [200]	Gear Box	Vibration	SAE	99.55%
		Gear Box	Vibration	DBN	98.73%
	Chen et al. [201]	CWRU	Vibration	Cyclic Spectral Coherence-CNN	98.93%
	Verstraete et al. [202]	CWRU	Vibration	2D-CNN	99.9%
	Liu et al. [203]	Test setup with motor and faulty bearings	Vibration	STFT-SAE	97.84%
	Shi et al. [204]	UNSW planetary test rig	Vibration	Bidirectional-convolutional LSTM	95.83%
	Ravikumar et al. [205]	Test setup with IC engine gearbox	Vibration	Stacked LSTM	94.33%
	Chen et al. [173]	IR system	Current	Improved CNN	99.59%
	Long et al. [206]	IR system	Attitude data	SAE-SVM	96.74%
Fault prognosis	Kamat et al. [207]	PRONOSTIA bearings dataset	Vibration	AE-LSTM	90%
	Wang et al. [208]	PRONOSTIA bearings dataset	Vibration	Spatiotemporal-3DCNN	98.25%
	Ding et al. [209]	NASA IMS dataset	Vibration	Deep CNN	0.0052 (RMSE)
	Li et al. [210]	Test setup with milling machine	Current	LSTM	0.0950 (RMSE)
	Qin et al. [211]	Test setup with gear	Vibration	Macroscopic-microscopic attention LSTM	0.142 (NRMSE)

6. Discussion, Challenges and Future Aspects of PHM

Prognostics and Health Management using DL has proved to be a fast-growing field, with a lot of studies being conducted on it worldwide. It has brought significant improvement and has proven to be a key technology to improve system reliability. A good PHM strategy provides strong economic benefits, minimum downtime, and maximum productivity. The main objective that the PHM system must accomplish, depending on the applications, poses challenges for their requirements. The most obvious ones are accuracy and precision. It needs to be quantified with the set of performance indicators and evaluated against their decision-making. In certain instances, incredibly superior accuracy and precision are essential to making a confident decision. Such a decision may include stopping a system in case of a warning of FDT, replacement of the component upon FDG, and delaying or predicting planned maintenance based on the RUL estimations. High levels of precision and accuracy might not be necessary in some circumstances, and they might conflict with other goals. In some circumstances, the decision-making in the crucial applications of the IR systems depends on the transparency, explicability, and interpretability of the PHM models. PHM solutions offer a practical and intelligent approach to condition-based maintenance and preventive maintenance, but they also have some security flaws. The PHM's technological foundation is made up of numerous devices and different communication protocols. There is always an issue of data integrity, data privacy, and substantiation. These issues are required to be properly addressed to ensure the robustness and efficiency of the PHM solution. Inaccurate PHM models, data availability issues, limited knowledge of the machine's current state, randomness in the machine's future usage profile, and unreliable sensor data values are some issues that arise when using PHM in real-world applications. Also, it is crucial to understand the feasibility of the different sensor signals and signal analysis used for the PHM of IRs. This has been included in Table 3 to demonstrate the signals used, along with the signal processing tools and their pertinency.

Moreover, the characteristics of the rotating machinery in IRs and traditional rotating machinery can differ in a number of ways. Some of the differences are given below:

- Dimension and scale: Compared to conventional rotating machinery, IRs often possess smaller, more compact rotating machinery. Traditional rotating machinery can be substantially larger in size and have higher power ratings, such as large-scale industrial machinery or power generation turbines. Industrial robots, on the other hand, need smaller motors and systems to carry out their specialized tasks quickly and accurately.
- Operating Speed and Precision: Due to the high-speed, precise tasks that IRs are built for, their rotating machinery must operate with outstanding speed and control precision. These robots frequently carry out actions that require the quick acceleration and deceleration of the rotating components.
- Duty Cycle and Constant Operation: IRs frequently work in cycles or sequences, carrying out particular tasks intermittently with brief spikes in activity. Their rotating equipment must be able to resist repeated start-stop cycles and adjust to different load scenarios. Turbines used in power generation or other types of conventional rotating machinery frequently run continuously for long periods of time without undergoing repeated start-stop cycles.
- Maintenance and Serviceability: The frequent and demanding actions of industrial robots necessitate frequent maintenance and service. These robots' rotating machinery needs to be built with access points for inspections, lubrication, and component replacement in mind. Depending on their individual applications, traditional rotating machinery may have distinct maintenance needs that necessitate more involved maintenance processes and extended downtime intervals.

Table 3. Signals and signals processing applicable to the PHM of IRs with their applicability.

Article	Signal	Signal Processing	Feasibility
[212]	Encoder	Singular spectrum analysis (SSA) Hilbert transform (HT) Empirical mode decomposition HT (EMDHT)	Easy availability of signal Simple to apply
[213]	Vibration	Wavelet transform (WT)	Signal easily accessible with sensors Highly feasible
[214]	Vibration	WT	Signal easily accessible with sensors Easy to apply
[215]	Acoustic Emission (AE)	WT	Easily accessible Signal interpretation is cumbersome High background noise Generalization is difficult
[216]	Current	WT	Non-intrusive approach Highly feasible Multi-resolution analysis
[217]	Vibration	Discrete WT	Multi-resolution analysis Localization of Fault Signatures Noise Suppression
[218]	Vibration	Continuous WT	Time-Frequency Localization Continuous Frequency Coverage Adaptability to Signal Variability Improved Accuracy in Transient Detection
[48]	Current	Statistical analysis	Simple applicability Efficient feature development Feature selection needs expertise
[56]	Current	Discrete WT	Non-invasive approach Early fault detection Real-time monitoring
[219]	Vibration	Discrete WT	Multi-resolution analysis Localization of Fault Signatures Efficient feature extraction
[69]	Vibration	Short-time Fourier Transform (STFT) Wavelet decomposition	Time-Frequency localization Simplicity and Computational Efficiency
[220]	Current	STFT Wavelet packet decomposition (WPD)	Non-invasive approach Early fault detection Wide applicability Cost effective
[221]	Vibration	Discrete WT	Multi-resolution analysis Localization of Fault Signatures Interpretability
[222]	Vibration	STFT	Efficient Frequency Resolution Interpretability Fast computation
[169]	Vibration	STFT	Efficient Frequency Resolution Noise suppression Easy to implement

Deep learning has brought significant improvements to the PHM approaches by learning complex representations of the data. The capability of DL frameworks to automatically extract and learn features provides an edge over the conventional machine learning models.

Despite multiple advantages, DL-based PHM still has a long way to go. The DL algorithms, like RBM, DBN, DBM, AE, CNN, and RNN, have brought significant improvements to the PHM strategies. Table 4 compares the different DL algorithms. The algorithms are chosen based on the type and availability of the data. Only a small amount of research work is available for the PHM strategies with DL applications for industrial robots. However, many PHM strategies with DL applications for rotating machinery are available. In recent years, researchers worldwide have used DL algorithms for FDT, FDG, and FP. The DL algorithms have challenges associated with them too. Many improvements are needed for industrial acceptance of the PHM strategies with DL algorithms, and questions need to be answered. Here are some of the important aspects of the DL-based PHM strategies:

- Data insufficiency: In the real-time environment, the unavailability of a large amount of data is the major hurdle that restricts the application of PHM strategies with DL algorithms. It is well-known that DL algorithms require a substantial volume of data, and that the availability of large volumes of data is not feasible. Some of the established DL frameworks, like VGG16, VGG19, ResNe-50, and InceptionResNet-v2, have used millions of images for training [223–225]. However, in a real-time context, such a massive amount of data is not feasible. Researchers have used techniques like data augmentation to increase the training samples in the training datasets by developing synthetic data. Basic data augmentation methods like window cropping, wrapping, and flipping can be applied to time-series data to create a variety of data structures [226]. Generic algorithms are also frequently used to create new data that is similar to the original data. In some cases, new GMs are used to construct the linked time-series data, keeping the temporal dependency of the original data. Researchers have also looked into the concept of transfer learning to address the data insufficiency problem for FDG and FP [227,228]. Many new innovations are coming, and they will aid in improving the PHM strategies with DL applications.
- Data quality: The performance of any artificial intelligence-based model relies heavily on the data quality. The success and efficiency of DL-based PHM strategies depend heavily on data quality. The availability of cloud computing, the industrial internet of things, and intelligent sensors have aided in collecting an enormous amount of data. However, the growing volume of data brings included noises and disturbances. Also, the ambient and operating conditions affect the quality of the data. In industrial data, there are the problems of data duplicity, unlabeled data, imbalanced data, and many more. These concerns have not been addressed thoroughly in most of the available research works. Also, the majority of solutions focus on a minimally imbalanced scenario, ignoring the problems associated with the substantially under-represented instances, which are common in real-world industrial workplaces. Furthermore, real-world data is generally unstructured, multi-modal, and diverse, making the model far more challenging. More attention is required in the future for developing a generic deep model that can work on diverse data without sacrificing the training efficiency.
- Data pre-processing: This is among the most crucial components of an AI-based model's effective performance. It is crucial for both machine learning and DL models. The model's success is mainly reliant on the condition of the input data. Pre-processing includes data normalization, the removal of data duplicity, and standardization. It also includes tackling incomplete data problems, outliers and missing values, and labeling data. In certain cases, signal processing tools, like FFT, STFT, wavelet transformation, and Hilbert–Huang transformation, are also used to process the input signals. In the future, research will be required to build a standardized approach for pre-processing data prior to their input to the AI-based model.
- Model selection and explainability: The appropriate DL framework selection is one of the vital steps for the development of an efficient PHM strategy. There are many DL algorithms, and choosing the appropriate model based on the available data is critical. Most of the available PHM strategies have been based on the models that require handcrafted features. These models are prone to errors and lack generalization

capabilities. The application of DL algorithms has helped to resolve the problems associated with the handcrafted features. However, setting up the hyper-parameters of the DL-based model is itself a big challenge. There are only a few papers that deal with setting up the DL models and their hyper-parameters' optimization. There is a need to develop a strategy that would allow the autonomous optimization of models and their hyper-parameters as per the given input data. This can be investigated in the future. Despite the good performance of DL models for PHM strategies, the acceptance of such an approach has a lot of roadblocks. The DL models are like black box models and lack interpretability. The decision-making part of PHM is heavily dependent on the DL models. However, only a few papers have dealt with the interpretability and explainability of DL models for PHM [126]. There is a need to develop a PHM strategy with DL applications, but with transparency, interpretability, and explainability.

Table 4. Pros and cons of DL-based PHM.

Algorithms	Pros	Cons
DBN [78–80]	Global feature extraction possible	Training is cumbersome
	Supports dimensionality reduction	Tracking loss function is difficult
	Can work on less data	Parameters optimization is difficult
DBM [161,163]	Can learn internal representation	Weight update is difficult
	Robust to ambiguous inputs	Slow training
CNN [36,96,98,115]	Excellent feature extraction properties	Cannot obtain global features
	Supports multiple dimension data	Cannot interpret time dimension information
Auto-encoder [166,168]	Unsupervised learning	Requirement of dedicated classifier for fault diagnosis
	No label data requirement	High data requirement
	Supports dimensionality reduction	Difficult to determine the importance of data
	Supports flexible framework	Selecting specific features not possible
	Availability of multiple forms	No interpretability
RNN [109,111–113]	Performs well on sequence problem	Slow training speed
	Capitalizes the time dimension of input data	No parallel computing
	Supports unlimited input length data	Problem of vanishing gradient

The application of PHM to IRs offers several challenges. It can be more difficult compared to applying it to the other rotating machines or components. Some of the challenges pertaining to the PHM of IRs are listed below:

- Industrial Robots' Complexity: IRs are sophisticated systems with numerous vulnerable parts. This makes it challenging to gather and examine the data that might be used to anticipate problems.
- Dynamic Operating Conditions: IRs are frequently utilized in a range of settings with various operating circumstances. Because of this, creating PHM models that can correctly forecast failures under all operating circumstances can be challenging.
- Lack of Sufficient Training Data: For the development of reliable FDT and prediction models, it can be difficult to obtain enough labelled training data. In IR systems, labelled data collection can be time-consuming and expensive for different fault scenarios. Furthermore, gathering data for uncommon or catastrophic failure situations might be very difficult.

- Adaptability and Generalization: Systems for IRs might differ greatly in terms of their models, configurations, and working environments. PHM systems must be flexible and able to be generalized to various robot kinds and settings. To achieve dependable and scalable PHM, it is challenging to create models and algorithms that can adjust to differences in robot systems, including changes in the load, operational conditions, or task requirements.

Deep learning algorithms in PHM systems built on the DL framework have a number of possibilities for development. The following are some ideas for potential enhancements:

- Model Architectures: The performance can be enhanced by investigating and creating new model architectures designed specifically for PHM workloads. This entails creating deep neural networks with specialized layers, such as recurrent or attention processes that can efficiently capture temporal dependencies and persistent patterns in the sensor input. In order to capture complicated interactions in multi-modal or graph-structured data, architectural innovations like transformer models or graph neural networks can also be researched.
- Uncertainty Quantification: DL models often lack the ability to provide reliable uncertainty estimates, which is crucial for decision-making in PHM systems. Model uncertainty can be better understood and characterized by including uncertainty quantification approaches, like Bayesian deep learning or Monte Carlo dropout. As a result, it will be easier to spot circumstances when the model's predictions may not be as accurate and make the appropriate decisions.
- Robustness to Adversarial Attacks: Small changes in the input data can cause inaccurate predictions or misclassification in deep learning models, making them vulnerable to adversarial attacks. To increase the resilience of deep learning models in PHM systems, adversarial robustness strategies might be investigated, such as adversarial training or input regularization. With the help of these methods, models should be more resistant to adversarial examples and perform consistently, even when there are subtle attacks or data abnormalities present.

PHM is a promising technology that has the potential to increase the dependability and uptime of industrial robots despite these difficulties. The technology is anticipated to become more accessible and less expensive as it advances. As a result, PHM will be a more appealing option for more producers. IR prognostics and health management is a developing field with a number of promising future developments. Future PHM capabilities for industrial robots include the following:

- Real-time Monitoring and Adaptive Control: Future PHM systems for IRs will place a strong emphasis on real-time monitoring and adaptive control techniques. Continuous assessment of the robot's health is made possible via real-time monitoring, allowing for the quick identification and remediation of any potential problems. In response to recognized flaws or degradation, adaptive control approaches can modify the robot's operational settings or control algorithms, improving the performance and lowering the likelihood of failure.
- Human–Robot Collaboration and Safety: Collaboration between people and robots in shared workspaces will rise in the future of industrial robotics, as will safety concerns. The safety and wellbeing of human operators will be greatly enhanced by PHM systems. PHM systems can initiate safety routines, such as reducing the robot speed, changing the motion trajectories, or shutting down the robot in critical conditions, by monitoring the robot's health and identifying probable defects. For the creation of secure and effective human–robot collaborative environments, this PHM feature will be crucial.
- Predictive Maintenance and Spare Parts Management: Predictive maintenance and improved spare parts management are the future directions for PHM systems for IRs. These systems can calculate the remaining useful life of crucial components and schedule maintenance procedures appropriately by utilizing predictive models and

real-time monitoring. This method ensures that IR systems operate well by minimizing unplanned downtime, lowering the maintenance costs, and optimizing the spare parts inventory.

- Cloud Computing and Remote Monitoring: The use of cloud computing and remote monitoring tools will make it possible to centrally monitor and analyze a number of IRs spread out across several places. Distributed robot data can be gathered and analyzed via cloud-based PHM platforms, enabling benchmarking, trend-tracking, and comparison analysis. Experts can remotely monitor and help with IR system troubleshooting thanks to remote access and diagnostics, which promote proactive maintenance and support.
- Big Data Analytics and Deep Learning: IR sensor data is becoming more widely available, creating new opportunities for using big data analytics and DL methods. Large amounts of sensor data can be analyzed to find patterns and anomalies that improve issue identification and diagnosis. On the basis of the previous data, DL algorithms can be trained to create predictive models that can foretell errors or performance declines in the future. PHM systems for IRs may be more accurate and reliable when using this data-driven approach.

7. Conclusions

This paper has presented a review of the PHM strategies with different deep learning algorithms. The application of different DL algorithms, like RBM, DBN, DBM, AE, CNN, and RNN, in PHM for the rotating machines of industrial robots has been discussed, along with the brief theoretical aspects of the algorithms. DL algorithms have significantly improved the performance of the PHM strategies. However, the industrial application of such approaches requires further improvement in terms of the high data requirements, required computational power, and model optimization. The optimization of deep models is a difficult task and involves significant improvements to be made. With the availability of an enormous volume of data with intelligent sensors, cloud computing, and IIoT, PHM with DL algorithms for industrial robots and its rotating machinery is undergoing a huge boost. PHM for industrial robots has a very bright future. The following possibilities could arise as technology advances:

- More Accurate and Reliable Predictions: DL algorithms will grow more potent and sophisticated, enabling us to make forecasts regarding the health of industrial robots that are more dependable and accurate. Less unplanned outages and downtime will result from this, which will increase productivity and save organizations money.
- Improved Decision-making: PHM systems will provide industries with better data concerning the condition of their robots, enabling them to choose more wisely between maintenance and repairs; operations will become more effective and efficient as a result.
- Earlier Detection of Failures: Early failure detection using PHM systems will provide companies more time to take corrective action. Catastrophic failures, which can be expensive and harmful, will be less likely as a result.

Moreover, there is also a need to develop an effective, transparent, interpretable, and explainable PHM approach with DL applications for the rotating machinery of industrial robots.

Author Contributions: Conceptualization, P.K., S.K. and H.S.K.; methodology, P.K.; software, P.K. and S.K.; validation, P.K., S.K. and H.S.K.; formal analysis, P.K.; investigation, P.K.; resources, H.S.K.; data curation, P.K. and S.K.; writing—original draft preparation, P.K. and S.K.; writing—review and editing, P.K., S.K. and H.S.K.; supervision, H.S.K.; funding acquisition, H.S.K. All authors have read and agreed to the published version of the manuscript.

Funding: This work was supported by a project for Smart Manufacturing Innovation R&D funded the Korea Ministry of SMEs and Startups in 2022 (Project No. RS-2022-00140460).

Institutional Review Board Statement: Not applicable.

Informed Consent Statement: Not applicable.

Data Availability Statement: Not applicable.

Conflicts of Interest: The authors declare no conflict of interest. The funders had no role in the design of the study; in the collection, analyses, or interpretation of the data; in the writing of the manuscript; or in the decision to publish the results.

References

1. Afsari, K.; Gupta, S.; Afkhamiaghda, M.; Lu, Z. Applications of collaborative industrial robots in building construction. In Proceedings of the 54th ASC Annual International Conference Proceedings, Minneapolis, MN, USA, 18–21 April 2018; pp. 472–479.
2. Evjemo, L.D.; Gjerstad, T.; Grøtli, E.I.; Sziebig, G. Trends in smart manufacturing: Role of humans and industrial robots in smart factories. *Curr. Robot. Rep.* **2020**, *1*, 35–41. [CrossRef]
3. Rao, J. *History of Rotating Machinery Dynamics*; Springer Science & Business Media: Berlin/Heidelberg, Germany, 2011; Volume 20.
4. Ruishu, Z.; Chang, Z.; Weigang, Z. The status and development of industrial robots. In Proceedings of the IOP Conference Series: Materials Science and Engineering, Kuala Lumpur, Malaysia, 13–14 August 2018; IOP Publishing: Bristol, UK, 2018; Volume 423, p. 012051.
5. Singh, B.; Sellappan, N.; Kumaradhas, P. Evolution of industrial robots and their applications. *Int. J. Emerg. Technol. Adv. Eng.* **2013**, *3*, 763–768.
6. *Industrial Robotics*; Industrial Press: South Norwalk, CT, USA, 2008; Available online: https://books.industrialpress.com/9780831133580/industrial-robotics (accessed on 29 November 2022).
7. Engelberger, J.F. *Robotics in Practice: Management and Applications of Industrial Robots*; Springer Science & Business Media: Berlin/Heidelberg, Germany, 2012; ISBN 978-1-4684-7120-5.
8. Nof, S.Y. *Handbook of Industrial Robotics*; John Wiley & Sons: Hoboken, NJ, USA, 1999; ISBN 978-0-471-17783-8.
9. Chatterjee, P.; Manikrao Athawale, V.; Chakraborty, S. Selection of industrial robots using compromise ranking and outranking methods. *Robot. Comput.-Integr. Manuf.* **2010**, *26*, 483–489. [CrossRef]
10. Choi, S.; Zhang, G.; Fuhlbrigge, T.; Watson, T.; Tallian, R. Applications and requirements of industrial robots in meat processing. In Proceedings of the 2013 IEEE International Conference on Automation Science and Engineering (CASE), Madison, WI, USA, 17–20 August 2013; pp. 1107–1112.
11. Karabegović, I. The Role of Industrial Robots in the Development of Automotive Industry in China. *Int. J. Eng. Work.* **2016**, *3*, 92–97.
12. Bader, F.; Rahimifard, S. A methodology for the selection of industrial robots in food handling. *Innov. Food Sci. Emerg. Technol.* **2020**, *64*, 102379. [CrossRef]
13. Olsson, T.; Haage, M.; Kihlman, H.; Johansson, R.; Nilsson, K.; Robertsson, A.; Björkman, M.; Isaksson, R.; Ossbahr, G.; Brogårdh, T. Cost-efficient drilling using industrial robots with high-bandwidth force feedback. *Robot. Comput.-Integr. Manuf.* **2010**, *26*, 24–38. [CrossRef]
14. Zhang, G.Q.; Li, X.; Boca, R.; Newkirk, J.; Zhang, B.; Fuhlbrigge, T.A.; Feng, H.K.; Hunt, N.J. Use of Industrial Robots in Additive Manufacturing—A Survey and Feasibility Study. In Proceedings of the ISR/Robotik 2014, 41st International Symposium on Robotics, Munich, Germany, 2–3 June 2014; pp. 1–6.
15. International Federation of Robotics. *Executive Summary World Robotics 2020 Industrial Robots.* 2020.
16. Industrial Robots Market Size, Share & Growth Report. 2029. Available online: https://www.fortunebusinessinsights.com/industry-reports/industrial-robots-market-100360 (accessed on 22 May 2023).
17. Global Industrial Robotics Market Size & Share Report. 2030. Available online: https://www.grandviewresearch.com/industry-analysis/industrial-robotics-market (accessed on 22 May 2023).
18. Jaber, A.A. *Design of an Intelligent Embedded System for Condition Monitoring of an Industrial Robot*; Springer: Berlin/Heidelberg, Germany, 2016.
19. Scott, M.J.; Verhagen, W.J.C.; Bieber, M.T.; Marzocca, P. A Systematic Literature Review of Predictive Maintenance for Defence Fixed-Wing Aircraft Sustainment and Operations. *Sensors* **2022**, *22*, 7070. [CrossRef]
20. Arnaiz, A.; Iung, B.; Adgar, A.; Naks, T.; Tohver, A.; Tommingas, T.; Levrat, E. Information and Communication Technologies Within E-maintenance. In *E-Maintenance*; Holmberg, K., Adgar, A., Arnaiz, A., Jantunen, E., Mascolo, J., Mekid, S., Eds.; Springer: London, UK, 2010; pp. 39–60; ISBN 978-1-84996-205-6.
21. Sheppard, J.W.; Kaufman, M.A.; Wilmer, T.J. IEEE Standards for Prognostics and Health Management. *IEEE Aerosp. Electron. Syst. Mag.* **2009**, *24*, 34–41. [CrossRef]
22. *Condition Monitoring and Diagnostics of Machines. Data Processing, Communication and Presentation: General Guidelines*; BSI British Standards: London, UK, 2003.
23. *Condition Monitoring and Diagnostics of Machines. Data Processing, Communication and Presentation: Data Processing*; BSI British Standards: London, UK, 2015.

24. *Condition Monitoring and Diagnostics of Machines. Data Processing, Communication and Presentation: Communication*; BSI British Standards: London, UK, 2007.
25. Medjaher, K.; Zerhouni, N.; Gouriveau, R. *From Prognostics and Health Systems Management to Predictive Maintenance 1: Monitoring and Prognostics*; John Wiley & Sons: Hoboken, NJ, USA, 2016; ISBN 978-1-119-37102-1.
26. Pecht, M.G.; Kang, M. *Prognostics and Health Management of Electronics: Fundamentals, Machine Learning, and the Internet of Things*; John Wiley & Sons: Hoboken, NJ, USA, 2018; ISBN 978-1-119-51535-7.
27. Kim, N.-H.; An, D.; Choi, J.-H. *Prognostics and Health Management of Engineering Systems*; Springer International Publishing: Cham, Switzerland, 2017.
28. Goodman, D.; Hofmeister, J.P.; Szidarovszky, F. *Prognostics and Health Management: A Practical Approach to Improving System Reliability Using Condition-Based Data*; John Wiley & Sons: Hoboken, NJ, USA, 2019; ISBN 978-1-119-35670-7.
29. Raouf, I.; Khan, A.; Khalid, S.; Sohail, M.; Azad, M.M.; Kim, H.S. Sensor-Based Prognostic Health Management of Advanced Driver Assistance System for Autonomous Vehicles: A Recent Survey. *Mathematics* **2022**, *10*, 3233. [CrossRef]
30. Baptista, M.; de Medeiros, I.P.; Malere, J.P.; Nascimento, C., Jr.; Prendinger, H.; Henriques, E.M. Comparative case study of life usage and data-driven prognostics techniques using aircraft fault messages. *Comput. Ind.* **2017**, *86*, 1–14. [CrossRef]
31. Kwon, D.; Hodkiewicz, M.R.; Fan, J.; Shibutani, T.; Pecht, M.G. IoT-based prognostics and systems health management for industrial applications. *IEEE Access* **2016**, *4*, 3659–3670. [CrossRef]
32. Liu, Z.; Jia, Z.; Vong, C.-M.; Han, J.; Yan, C.; Pecht, M. A patent analysis of prognostics and health management (PHM) innovations for electrical systems. *IEEE Access* **2018**, *6*, 18088–18107. [CrossRef]
33. Theissler, A.; Pérez-Velázquez, J.; Kettelgerdes, M.; Elger, G. Predictive maintenance enabled by machine learning: Use cases and challenges in the automotive industry. *Reliab. Eng. Syst. Saf.* **2021**, *215*, 107864. [CrossRef]
34. Wong, S.Y.; Chuah, J.H.; Yap, H.J. Technical data-driven tool condition monitoring challenges for CNC milling: A review. *Int. J. Adv. Manuf. Technol.* **2020**, *107*, 4837–4857. [CrossRef]
35. Liu, C.; Cichon, A.; Królczyk, G.; Li, Z. Technology development and commercial applications of industrial fault diagnosis system: A review. *Int. J.Adv. Manuf. Technol.* **2022**, *118*, 3497–3529. [CrossRef]
36. Ranasinghe, K.; Sabatini, R.; Gardi, A.; Bijjahalli, S.; Kapoor, R.; Fahey, T.; Thangavel, K. Advances in Integrated System Health Management for mission-essential and safety-critical aerospace applications. *Prog. Aerosp. Sci.* **2022**, *128*, 100758. [CrossRef]
37. Djurdjanovic, D.; Lee, J.; Ni, J. Watchdog Agent—An infotronics-based prognostics approach for product performance degradation assessment and prediction. *Adv. Eng. Inform.* **2003**, *17*, 109–125. [CrossRef]
38. Nuñez, D.L.; Borsato, M. OntoProg: An ontology-based model for implementing Prognostics Health Management in mechanical machines. *Adv. Eng. Inform.* **2018**, *38*, 746–759. [CrossRef]
39. Gao, R.; Wang, L.; Teti, R.; Dornfeld, D.; Kumara, S.; Mori, M.; Helu, M. Cloud-enabled prognosis for manufacturing. *CIRP Ann.* **2015**, *64*, 749–772. [CrossRef]
40. Pech, M.; Vrchota, J.; Bednář, J. Predictive maintenance and intelligent sensors in smart factory. *Sensors* **2021**, *21*, 1470. [CrossRef] [PubMed]
41. Khalid, S.; Hwang, H.; Kim, H.S. Real-world data-driven machine-learning-based optimal sensor selection approach for equipment fault detection in a thermal power plant. *Mathematics* **2021**, *9*, 2814. [CrossRef]
42. Khalid, S.; Song, J.; Raouf, I.; Kim, H.S. Advances in Fault Detection and Diagnosis for Thermal Power Plants: A Review of Intelligent Techniques. *Mathematics* **2023**, *11*, 1767. [CrossRef]
43. Moore, R. *Making Common Sense Common Practice*; Butterworth–Heinemann: Oxford, UK, 2004.
44. Lin, Y.; Li, X.; Hu, Y. Deep diagnostics and prognostics: An integrated hierarchical learning framework in PHM applications. *Appl. Soft Comput.* **2018**, *72*, 555–564. [CrossRef]
45. Booyse, W.; Wilke, D.N.; Heyns, S. Deep digital twins for detection, diagnostics and prognostics. *Mech. Syst. Signal Process.* **2020**, *140*, 106612. [CrossRef]
46. Qiao, G.; Weiss, B.A. Advancing measurement science to assess monitoring, diagnostics, and prognostics for manufacturing robotics. *Int. J. Progn. Health Manag.* **2016**, *7*, 013. [CrossRef]
47. Xu, J.; Wang, Y.; Xu, L. PHM-oriented integrated fusion prognostics for aircraft engines based on sensor data. *IEEE Sens. J.* **2013**, *14*, 1124–1132. [CrossRef]
48. Raouf, I.; Lee, H.; Kim, H.S. Mechanical fault detection based on machine learning for robotic RV reducer using electrical current signature analysis: A data-driven approach. *J. Comput. Des. Eng.* **2022**, *9*, 417–433. [CrossRef]
49. Siddiqa, A.; Karim, A.; Gani, A. Big data storage technologies: A survey. *Front. Inf. Technol. Electron. Eng.* **2017**, *18*, 1040–1070. [CrossRef]
50. Yang, C.; Huang, Q.; Li, Z.; Liu, K.; Hu, F. Big Data and cloud computing: Innovation opportunities and challenges. *Int. J. Digit. Earth* **2017**, *10*, 13–53. [CrossRef]
51. Nath, A.G.; Udmale, S.S.; Singh, S.K. Role of artificial intelligence in rotor fault diagnosis: A comprehensive review. *Artif Intell Rev* **2021**, *54*, 2609–2668. [CrossRef]
52. Arinez, J.F.; Chang, Q.; Gao, R.X.; Xu, C.; Zhang, J. Artificial Intelligence in Advanced Manufacturing: Current Status and Future Outlook. *J. Manuf. Sci. Eng.* **2020**, *142*, 110804. [CrossRef]
53. Dalzochio, J.; Kunst, R.; Pignaton, E.; Binotto, A.; Sanyal, S.; Favilla, J.; Barbosa, J. Machine learning and reasoning for predictive maintenance in Industry 4.0: Current status and challenges. *Comput. Ind.* **2020**, *123*, 103298. [CrossRef]

54. Alam, M.; Samad, M.D.; Vidyaratne, L.; Glandon, A.; Iftekharuddin, K.M. Survey on deep neural networks in speech and vision systems. *Neurocomputing* **2020**, *417*, 302–321. [CrossRef]
55. Lundervold, A.S.; Lundervold, A. An overview of deep learning in medical imaging focusing on MRI. *Z. Für Med. Phys.* **2019**, *29*, 102–127. [CrossRef]
56. Rohan, A.; Raouf, I.; Kim, H.S. Rotate vector (Rv) reducer fault detection and diagnosis system: Towards component level prognostics and health management (phm). *Sensors* **2020**, *20*, 6845. [CrossRef]
57. Shamshirband, S.; Fathi, M.; Dehzangi, A.; Chronopoulos, A.T.; Alinejad-Rokny, H. A review on deep learning approaches in healthcare systems: Taxonomies, challenges, and open issues. *J. Biomed. Inform.* **2021**, *113*, 103627. [CrossRef]
58. Tobore, I.; Li, J.; Yuhang, L.; Al-Handarish, Y.; Kandwal, A.; Nie, Z.; Wang, L. Deep learning intervention for health care challenges: Some biomedical domain considerations. *JMIR Mhealth Uhealth* **2019**, *7*, e11966. [CrossRef]
59. Yamashita, R.; Nishio, M.; Do, R.K.G.; Togashi, K. Convolutional neural networks: An overview and application in radiology. *Insights Imaging* **2018**, *9*, 611–629. [CrossRef]
60. Kanjo, E.; Younis, E.M.; Ang, C.S. Deep learning analysis of mobile physiological, environmental and location sensor data for emotion detection. *Inf. Fusion* **2019**, *49*, 46–56. [CrossRef]
61. Li, X.; Zhang, W.; Ding, Q. Deep learning-based remaining useful life estimation of bearings using multi-scale feature extraction. *Reliab. Eng. Syst. Saf.* **2019**, *182*, 208–218. [CrossRef]
62. Wang, J.; Ma, Y.; Zhang, L.; Gao, R.X.; Wu, D. Deep learning for smart manufacturing: Methods and applications. *J. Manuf. Syst.* **2018**, *48*, 144–156. [CrossRef]
63. Duan, L.; Xie, M.; Wang, J.; Bai, T. Deep learning enabled intelligent fault diagnosis: Overview and applications. *J. Intell. Fuzzy Syst.* **2018**, *35*, 5771–5784. [CrossRef]
64. Li, G.; Deng, C.; Wu, J.; Chen, Z.; Xu, X. Rolling Bearing Fault Diagnosis Based on Wavelet Packet Transform and Convolutional Neural Network. *Appl. Sci.* **2020**, *10*, 770. [CrossRef]
65. Lee, H.; Raouf, I.; Song, J.; Kim, H.S.; Lee, S. Prognostics and Health Management of the Robotic Servo-Motor under Variable Operating Conditions. *Mathematics* **2023**, *11*, 398. [CrossRef]
66. Raouf, I.; Kumar, P.; Lee, H.; Kim, H.S. Transfer Learning-Based Intelligent Fault Detection Approach for the Industrial Robotic System. *Mathematics* **2023**, *11*, 945. [CrossRef]
67. Zhou, X.; Zhou, H.; He, Y.; Huang, S.; Zhu, Z.; Chen, J. Harmonic reducer in-situ fault diagnosis for industrial robots based on deep learning. *Sci. China Technol. Sci.* **2022**, *65*, 2116–2126. [CrossRef]
68. Adam, H.E.A.; Kimotho, J.K.; Njiri, J.G. Multiple faults diagnosis for an industrial robot fuse quality test bench using deep-learning. *Results Eng.* **2023**, *17*, 101007. [CrossRef]
69. Yin, T.; Lu, N.; Guo, G.; Lei, Y.; Wang, S.; Guan, X. Knowledge and data dual-driven transfer network for industrial robot fault diagnosis. *Mech. Syst. Signal Process.* **2023**, *182*, 109597. [CrossRef]
70. Nagarajan, R. *Introduction to Industrial Robotics*; Pearson Education India: Delhi, India, 2016.
71. Parhami, B. Defect, fault, error, . . . , or failure? *IEEE Trans. Reliab.* **1997**, *46*, 450–451. [CrossRef]
72. Lee, J.; Wu, F.; Zhao, W.; Ghaffari, M.; Liao, L.; Siegel, D. Prognostics and health management design for rotary machinery systems—Reviews, methodology and applications. *Mech. Syst. Signal Process.* **2014**, *42*, 314–334. [CrossRef]
73. Heng, A.; Zhang, S.; Tan, A.C.; Mathew, J. Rotating machinery prognostics: State of the art, challenges and opportunities. *Mech. Syst. Signal Process.* **2009**, *23*, 724–739. [CrossRef]
74. Kumar, P.; Hati, A.S. Review on machine learning algorithm based fault detection in induction motors. *Arch. Comput. Methods Eng.* **2021**, *28*, 1929–1940. [CrossRef]
75. Tavner, P.J. Review of condition monitoring of rotating electrical machines. *IET Electr. Power Appl.* **2008**, *2*, 215–247. [CrossRef]
76. Zhang, L.; Lin, J.; Liu, B.; Zhang, Z.; Yan, X.; Wei, M. A Review on Deep Learning Applications in Prognostics and Health Management. *IEEE Access* **2019**, *7*, 162415–162438. [CrossRef]
77. Gálvez, A.; Diez-Olivan, A.; Seneviratne, D.; Galar, D. Fault Detection and RUL Estimation for Railway HVAC Systems Using a Hybrid Model-Based Approach. *Sustainability* **2021**, *13*, 6828. [CrossRef]
78. Yan, B.; Ma, X.; Huang, G.; Zhao, Y. Two-stage physics-based Wiener process models for online RUL prediction in field vibration data. *Mech. Syst. Signal Process.* **2021**, *152*, 107378. [CrossRef]
79. Liu, H.; Zhou, J.; Xu, Y.; Zheng, Y.; Peng, X.; Jiang, W. Unsupervised fault diagnosis of rolling bearings using a deep neural network based on generative adversarial networks. *Neurocomputing* **2018**, *315*, 412–424. [CrossRef]
80. Cheng, C.; Zhou, B.; Ma, G.; Wu, D.; Yuan, Y. Wasserstein distance based deep adversarial transfer learning for intelligent fault diagnosis with unlabeled or insufficient labeled data. *Neurocomputing* **2020**, *409*, 35–45. [CrossRef]
81. Lu, W.; Liang, B.; Cheng, Y.; Meng, D.; Yang, J.; Zhang, T. Deep Model Based Domain Adaptation for Fault Diagnosis. *IEEE Trans. Ind. Electron.* **2017**, *64*, 2296–2305. [CrossRef]
82. Calabrese, F.; Regattieri, A.; Bortolini, M.; Gamberi, M.; Pilati, F. Predictive Maintenance: A Novel Framework for a Data-Driven, Semi-Supervised, and Partially Online Prognostic Health Management Application in Industries. *Appl. Sci.* **2021**, *11*, 3380. [CrossRef]
83. Rezamand, M.; Kordestani, M.; Carriveau, R.; Ting, D.S.-K.; Orchard, M.E.; Saif, M. Critical Wind Turbine Components Prognostics: A Comprehensive Review. *IEEE Trans. Instrum. Meas.* **2020**, *69*, 9306–9328. [CrossRef]

84. Jin, X.; Sun, Y.; Que, Z.; Wang, Y.; Chow, T.W.S. Anomaly Detection and Fault Prognosis for Bearings. *IEEE Trans. Instrum. Meas.* **2016**, *65*, 2046–2054. [CrossRef]
85. Sikorska, J.Z.; Hodkiewicz, M.; Ma, L. Prognostic modelling options for remaining useful life estimation by industry. *Mech. Syst. Signal Process.* **2011**, *25*, 1803–1836. [CrossRef]
86. Byington, C.; Watson, M.; Sheldon, J.; Swerdon, G. Shaft coupling model-based prognostics enhanced by vibration diagnostics. *Insight-Non-Destr. Test. Cond. Monit.* **2009**, *51*, 420–425. [CrossRef]
87. Fisher, C.; Baines, N. Multi-sensor condition monitoring systems for gas turbines. *J. Cond. Monit.* **1988**, *1*, 57–68.
88. Kemerait, R. New cepstral approach for prognostic maintenance of cyclic machinery. In Proceedings of the IEEE SOUTHEASTCON, Tampa, FL, USA, 5–8 April 1987; Volume 1987, pp. 256–262.
89. Muir, D.; Taylor, B. Oil debris monitoring for aeroderivative gas turbine. *ASME Power Div. (Publ.) PWR* **1997**, *32*, 547–553.
90. Crow, E.C.; Reichard, K.; Rogan, C.; Callen, J.; Seifert, E. Integrated multi-sensor package (IMSP) for unmanned vehicle operations. In Proceedings of the Unmanned/Unattended Sensors and Sensor Networks IV, International Society for Optics and Photonics. Florence, Italy, 18–20 September 2007; Volume 6736, p. 673604.
91. Liao, L.; Köttig, F. A hybrid framework combining data-driven and model-based methods for system remaining useful life prediction. *Appl. Soft Comput.* **2016**, *44*, 191–199. [CrossRef]
92. Lee, M.-S.; Shifat, T.A.; Hur, J.W. Kalman Filter Assisted Deep Feature Learning for RUL Prediction of Hydraulic Gear Pump. *IEEE Sens. J.* **2022**, *22*, 11088–11097. [CrossRef]
93. Liu, Z.-X.; Wang, Z.-Y.; Wang, Y.; Ji, Z.-C. Optimal Zonotopic Kalman Filter-based State Estimation and Fault-diagnosis Algorithm for Linear Discrete-time System with Time Delay. *Int. J. Control Autom. Syst.* **2022**, *20*, 1757–1771. [CrossRef]
94. Maynard, K.P. Interstitial processing: The application of noise processing to gear fault detection. In Proceedings of the international conference on Condition monitoring, University of Wales, Swansea, UK, 12–16 April 1999; Volume 12, pp. 77–86.
95. Patton, R.J. Fault detection and diagnosis in aerospace systems using analytical redundancy. In Proceedings of the IEE Colloquium on Condition Monitoring and Fault Tolerance, London, UK, 6 November 1990; IET: London, UK, 1990.
96. Tudoroiu, N.; Khorasani, K. Satellite fault diagnosis using a bank of interacting Kalman filters. *IEEE Trans. Aerosp. Electron. Syst.* **2007**, *43*, 1334–1350. [CrossRef]
97. Hansen, R.J.; Hall, D.L.; Kurtz, S.K. A new approach to the challenge of machinery prognostics. In Proceedings of the Turbo Expo: Power for Land, Sea, and Air, The Hague, The Netherlands, 13–16 June 1994; American Society of Mechanical Engineers: New York, NY, USA, 1994; Volume 78873, p. V005T15A001.
98. Denkena, B.; Litwinski, K.; Brouwer, D.; Boujnah, H. Design and analysis of a prototypical sensory Z-slide for machine tools. *Prod. Eng.* **2013**, *7*, 9–14. [CrossRef]
99. Holland, S.W.; Barajas, L.G.; Salman, M.; Zhang, Y. PHM for automotive manufacturing & vehicle applications. In Proceedings of the Prognostics & Health Management Conference, Portland, OR, USA, 10–14 October 2010.
100. Hu, S.J.; Koren, Y. Stream-of-variation theory for automotive body assembly. *CIRP Ann.* **1997**, *46*, 1–6. [CrossRef]
101. Sahir Arıkan, M.; Balkan, T. Process modeling, simulation, and paint thickness measurement for robotic spray painting. *J. Robot. Syst.* **2000**, *17*, 479–494. [CrossRef]
102. Shen, T.; Wan, F.; Cui, W.; Song, B. Application of prognostic and health management technology on aircraft fuel system. In Proceedings of the 2010 Prognostics and System Health Management Conference, Macau, China, 12–14 January 2010; IEEE: New York, NY, USA, 2010; pp. 1–7.
103. Siegel, D.; Zhao, W.; Lapira, E.; AbuAli, M.; Lee, J. A comparative study on vibration-based condition monitoring algorithms for wind turbine drive trains. *Wind Energy* **2014**, *17*, 695–714. [CrossRef]
104. Siegel, D.; Lee, J.; Dempsey, P. Investigation and Evaluation of Condition Indicators, Variable Selection, and Health Indication Methods and Algorithms For Rotorcraft Gear Components. In Proceedings of the MFPT 2014 Conference, Virginia Beach, VA, USA, 10–12 June 2014.
105. Bin, G.; Gao, J.; Li, X.; Dhillon, B. Early fault diagnosis of rotating machinery based on wavelet packets—Empirical mode decomposition feature extraction and neural network. *Mech. Syst. Signal Process.* **2012**, *27*, 696–711. [CrossRef]
106. Li, W.; Zhu, Z.; Jiang, F.; Zhou, G.; Chen, G. Fault diagnosis of rotating machinery with a novel statistical feature extraction and evaluation method. *Mech. Syst. Signal Process.* **2015**, *50*, 414–426. [CrossRef]
107. Zhu, H.; He, Z.; Wei, J.; Wang, J.; Zhou, H. Bearing fault feature extraction and fault diagnosis method based on feature fusion. *Sensors* **2021**, *21*, 2524. [CrossRef]
108. Widodo, A.; Yang, B.-S. Application of nonlinear feature extraction and support vector machines for fault diagnosis of induction motors. *Expert Syst. Appl.* **2007**, *33*, 241–250. [CrossRef]
109. Cheng, G.; Chen, X.; Li, H.; Li, P.; Liu, H. Study on planetary gear fault diagnosis based on entropy feature fusion of ensemble empirical mode decomposition. *Measurement* **2016**, *91*, 140–154. [CrossRef]
110. Zimroz, R.; Bartkowiak, A. Two simple multivariate procedures for monitoring planetary gearboxes in non-stationary operating conditions. *Mech. Syst. Signal Process.* **2013**, *38*, 237–247. [CrossRef]
111. Kumar, P.; Hati, A.S. Support Vector Classifier-Based Broken Rotor Bar Detection in Squirrel Cage Induction Motor. In *Machines, Mechanism and Robotics*; Springer: Berlin/Heidelberg, Germany, 2022; pp. 429–438.
112. Moghaddass, R.; Sheng, S. An anomaly detection framework for dynamic systems using a Bayesian hierarchical framework. *Appl. Energy* **2019**, *240*, 561–582. [CrossRef]

113. Cabrera, D.; Sancho, F.; Sánchez, R.-V.; Zurita, G.; Cerrada, M.; Li, C.; Vásquez, R.E. Fault diagnosis of spur gearbox based on random forest and wavelet packet decomposition. *Front. Mech. Eng.* **2015**, *10*, 277–286. [CrossRef]
114. Tian, J.; Morillo, C.; Azarian, M.H.; Pecht, M. Motor bearing fault detection using spectral kurtosis-based feature extraction coupled with K-nearest neighbor distance analysis. *IEEE Trans. Ind. Electron.* **2015**, *63*, 1793–1803. [CrossRef]
115. Chen, J.; Ma, C.; Song, D.; Xu, B. Failure prognosis of multiple uncertainty system based on Kalman filter and its application to aircraft fuel system. *Adv. Mech. Eng.* **2016**, *8*, 1–13. [CrossRef]
116. Singleton, R.K.; Strangas, E.G.; Aviyente, S. Extended Kalman filtering for remaining-useful-life estimation of bearings. *IEEE Trans. Ind. Electron.* **2014**, *62*, 1781–1790. [CrossRef]
117. Soualhi, A.; Clerc, G.; Razik, H.; Guillet, F. Hidden Markov models for the prediction of impending faults. *IEEE Trans. Ind. Electron.* **2016**, *63*, 3271–3281. [CrossRef]
118. Niu, G. *Data-Driven Technology for Engineering Systems Health Management*; Springer: Berlin/Heidelberg, Germany, 2017.
119. Aissani, N.; Beldjilali, B.; Trentesaux, D. Dynamic scheduling of maintenance tasks in the petroleum industry: A reinforcement approach. *Eng. Appl. Artif. Intell.* **2009**, *22*, 1089–1103. [CrossRef]
120. Chan, G.; Asgarpoor, S. Optimum maintenance policy with Markov processes. *Electr. Power Syst. Res.* **2006**, *76*, 452–456. [CrossRef]
121. Wu, S.; Gebraeel, N.; Lawley, M.A.; Yih, Y. A neural network integrated decision support system for condition-based optimal predictive maintenance policy. *IEEE Trans. Syst. Man Cybern.-Part A Syst. Hum.* **2007**, *37*, 226–236. [CrossRef]
122. Ali, J.B.; Fnaiech, N.; Saidi, L.; Chebel-Morello, B.; Fnaiech, F. Application of empirical mode decomposition and artificial neural network for automatic bearing fault diagnosis based on vibration signals. *Appl. Acoust.* **2015**, *89*, 16–27.
123. Zhu, J.; Chen, N.; Peng, W. Estimation of bearing remaining useful life based on multiscale convolutional neural network. *IEEE Trans. Ind. Electron.* **2018**, *66*, 3208–3216. [CrossRef]
124. Deutsch, J.; He, D. Using deep learning-based approach to predict remaining useful life of rotating components. *IEEE Trans. Syst. Man Cybern. Syst.* **2017**, *48*, 11–20. [CrossRef]
125. Shao, H.; Jiang, H.; Lin, Y.; Li, X. A novel method for intelligent fault diagnosis of rolling bearings using ensemble deep auto-encoders. *Mech. Syst. Signal Process.* **2018**, *102*, 278–297. [CrossRef]
126. Kumar, P.; Hati, A.S. Deep convolutional neural network based on adaptive gradient optimizer for fault detection in SCIM. *ISA Trans.* **2021**, *111*, 350–359. [CrossRef]
127. Saxena, A.; Celaya, J.; Saha, B.; Saha, S.; Goebel, K. Metrics for offline evaluation of prognostic performance. *Int. J. Progn. Health Manag.* **2010**, *1*, 4–23. [CrossRef]
128. Lou, X.; Loparo, K.A. Bearing fault diagnosis based on wavelet transform and fuzzy inference. *Mech. Syst. Signal Process.* **2004**, *18*, 1077–1095. [CrossRef]
129. Batista, L.; Badri, B.; Sabourin, R.; Thomas, M. A classifier fusion system for bearing fault diagnosis. *Expert Syst. Appl.* **2013**, *40*, 6788–6797. [CrossRef]
130. Chen, N.; Tsui, K.L. Condition monitoring and remaining useful life prediction using degradation signals: Revisited. *IIE Trans.* **2013**, *45*, 939–952. [CrossRef]
131. Nectoux, P.; Gouriveau, R.; Medjaher, K.; Ramasso, E.; Chebel-Morello, B.; Zerhouni, N.; Varnier, C. PRONOSTIA: An experimental platform for bearings accelerated degradation tests. In Proceedings of the IEEE International Conference on Prognostics and Health Management, PHM'12, Paris, France, 31 May–2 June 2012; IEEE Catalog Number: CPF12PHM-CDR. 2012; pp. 1–8.
132. Erfani, S.M.; Rajasegarar, S.; Karunasekera, S.; Leckie, C. High-dimensional and large-scale anomaly detection using a linear one-class SVM with deep learning. *Pattern Recognit.* **2016**, *58*, 121–134. [CrossRef]
133. Chen, S.; Yu, J.; Wang, S. One-dimensional convolutional auto-encoder-based feature learning for fault diagnosis of multivariate processes. *J. Process Control* **2020**, *87*, 54–67. [CrossRef]
134. Givnan, S.; Chalmers, C.; Fergus, P.; Ortega-Martorell, S.; Whalley, T. Anomaly Detection Using Autoencoder Reconstruction upon Industrial Motors. *Sensors* **2022**, *22*, 3166. [CrossRef]
135. Yang, Z.; Xu, B.; Luo, W.; Chen, F. Autoencoder-based representation learning and its application in intelligent fault diagnosis: A review. *Measurement* **2022**, *189*, 110460. [CrossRef]
136. Peyron, M.; Fillion, A.; Gürol, S.; Marchais, V.; Gratton, S.; Boudier, P.; Goret, G. Latent space data assimilation by using deep learning. *Q. J. R. Meteorol. Soc.* **2021**, *147*, 3759–3777. [CrossRef]
137. d'Acremont, A.; Fablet, R.; Baussard, A.; Quin, G. CNN-Based Target Recognition and Identification for Infrared Imaging in Defense Systems. *Sensors* **2019**, *19*, 2040. [CrossRef]
138. Shi, Y.; Yang, J.; Qi, Z. Unsupervised anomaly segmentation via deep feature reconstruction. *Neurocomputing* **2021**, *424*, 9–22. [CrossRef]
139. Karabacak, Y.E.; Gürsel Özmen, N. Common spatial pattern-based feature extraction and worm gear fault detection through vibration and acoustic measurements. *Measurement* **2022**, *187*, 110366. [CrossRef]
140. Wen, Y.; Fashiar Rahman, M.; Xu, H.; Tseng, T.-L.B. Recent advances and trends of predictive maintenance from data-driven machine prognostics perspective. *Measurement* **2022**, *187*, 110276. [CrossRef]
141. Zhang, J.; Zeng, Y.; Starly, B. Recurrent neural networks with long term temporal dependencies in machine tool wear diagnosis and prognosis. *SN Appl. Sci.* **2021**, *3*, 442. [CrossRef]

142. Chen, C.; Zhu, Z.H.; Shi, J.; Lu, N.; Jiang, B. Dynamic Predictive Maintenance Scheduling Using Deep Learning Ensemble for System Health Prognostics. *IEEE Sens. J.* **2021**, *21*, 26878–26891. [CrossRef]
143. Goodfellow, I.; Bengio, Y.; Courville, A. *Deep Learning*; MIT Press: Cambridge, MA, USA, 2016.
144. Dargan, S.; Kumar, M.; Ayyagari, M.R.; Kumar, G. A Survey of Deep Learning and Its Applications: A New Paradigm to Machine Learning. *Arch. Comput. Methods Eng* **2020**, *27*, 1071–1092. [CrossRef]
145. Arel, I.; Rose, D.C.; Karnowski, T.P. Deep Machine Learning—A New Frontier in Artificial Intelligence Research [Research Frontier]. *IEEE Comput. Intell. Mag.* **2010**, *5*, 13–18. [CrossRef]
146. Aggarwal, C.C. *Neural Networks and Deep Learning: A Textbook*; Springer: Berlin/Heidelberg, Germany, 2018; ISBN 978-3-319-94463-0.
147. Alzubaidi, L.; Zhang, J.; Humaidi, A.J.; Al-Dujaili, A.; Duan, Y.; Al-Shamma, O.; Santamaría, J.; Fadhel, M.A.; Al-Amidie, M.; Farhan, L. Review of deep learning: Concepts, CNN architectures, challenges, applications, future directions. *J. Big Data* **2021**, *8*, 53. [CrossRef] [PubMed]
148. Shrestha, A.; Mahmood, A. Review of Deep Learning Algorithms and Architectures. *IEEE Access* **2019**, *7*, 53040–53065. [CrossRef]
149. Hinton, G.E. Deep belief networks. *Scholarpedia* **2009**, *4*, 5947. [CrossRef]
150. Ng, A. Sparse autoencoder. *CS294A Lect. Notes* **2011**, *72*, 1–19.
151. Vincent, P.; Larochelle, H.; Lajoie, I.; Bengio, Y.; Manzagol, P.-A.; Bottou, L. Stacked denoising autoencoders: Learning useful representations in a deep network with a local denoising criterion. *J. Mach. Learn. Res.* **2010**, *11*, 3371–3408.
152. An, J.; Cho, S. Variational autoencoder based anomaly detection using reconstruction probability. *Spec. Lect. IE* **2015**, *2*, 1–18.
153. Le Cun, Y.; Boser, B.; Denker, J.S.; Henderson, D.; Howard, R.E.; Hubbard, W.; Jackel, L.D. Handwritten digit recognition with a back-propagation network. In Proceedings of the 2nd International Conference on Neural Information Processing Systems, Denver, CO, USA, 27–30 November 1989; pp. 396–404.
154. Dash, P.B.; Naik, B.; Nayak, J.; Vimal, S. Deep belief network-based probabilistic generative model for detection of robotic manipulator failure execution. *Soft Comput.* **2021**, *27*, 363–375. [CrossRef]
155. Chen, Z.; Li, W. Multisensor feature fusion for bearing fault diagnosis using sparse autoencoder and deep belief network. *IEEE Trans. Instrum. Meas.* **2017**, *66*, 1693–1702. [CrossRef]
156. Ren, H.; Chai, Y.; Qu, J.; Ye, X.; Tang, Q. A novel adaptive fault detection methodology for complex system using deep belief networks and multiple models: A case study on cryogenic propellant loading system. *Neurocomputing* **2018**, *275*, 2111–2125. [CrossRef]
157. Xing, S.; Lei, Y.; Wang, S.; Jia, F. Distribution-invariant deep belief network for intelligent fault diagnosis of machines under new working conditions. *IEEE Trans. Ind. Electron.* **2020**, *68*, 2617–2625. [CrossRef]
158. Jiao, J.; Zheng, X. Fault Diagnosis Method for Industrial Robots Based on DBN Joint Information Fusion Technology. *Comput. Intell. Neurosci.* **2022**, *2022*, 4340817. [CrossRef] [PubMed]
159. Ji, C.; Wang, K.; Yuan, D. Health assessment method of industrial robot reducer based on deep belief network. In Proceedings of the 2021 IEEE 11th Annual International Conference on CYBER Technology in Automation, Control, and Intelligent Systems (CYBER), Jiaxing, China, 27–31 July 2021; IEEE: New York, NY, USA, 2021; pp. 442–446.
160. Shao, S.-Y.; Sun, W.-J.; Yan, R.-Q.; Wang, P.; Gao, R.X. A deep learning approach for fault diagnosis of induction motors in manufacturing. *Chin. J. Mech. Eng.* **2017**, *30*, 1347–1356. [CrossRef]
161. Hu, G.; Li, H.; Xia, Y.; Luo, L. A deep Boltzmann machine and multi-grained scanning forest ensemble collaborative method and its application to industrial fault diagnosis. *Comput. Ind.* **2018**, *100*, 287–296. [CrossRef]
162. Deng, S.; Cheng, Z.; Li, C.; Yao, X.; Chen, Z.; Sanchez, R.-V. Rolling bearing fault diagnosis based on Deep Boltzmann machines. In Proceedings of the 2016 Prognostics and System Health Management Conference (PHM-Chengdu), Chengdu, China, 19–21 October 2016; IEEE: New York, NY, USA, 2016; pp. 1–6.
163. Li, C.; Sanchez, R.-V.; Zurita, G.; Cerrada, M.; Cabrera, D.; Vásquez, R.E. Multimodal deep support vector classification with homologous features and its application to gearbox fault diagnosis. *Neurocomputing* **2015**, *168*, 119–127. [CrossRef]
164. Wang, J.; Wang, K.; Wang, Y.; Huang, Z.; Xue, R. Deep Boltzmann machine based condition prediction for smart manufacturing. *J. Ambient Intell. Humaniz. Comput.* **2019**, *10*, 851–861. [CrossRef]
165. Mitrevski, A.; Plöger, P.G. Data-Driven Robot Fault Detection and Diagnosis Using Generative Models: A Modified SFDD Algorithm. In Proceedings of the 30th International Workshop on Principles of Diagnosis DX'19, Kla-genfurt, Austria, 11–13 November 2019.
166. Chen, T.; Liu, X.; Xia, B.; Wang, W.; Lai, Y. Unsupervised anomaly detection of industrial robots using sliding-window convolutional variational autoencoder. *IEEE Access* **2020**, *8*, 47072–47081. [CrossRef]
167. Hong, Y.; Sun, Z.; Zou, X.; Long, J. Multi-joint Industrial Robot Fault Identification using Deep Sparse Auto-Encoder Network with Attitude Data. In Proceedings of the 2020 Prognostics and Health Management Conference (PHM-Besançon), Besancon, France, 4–7 May 2020; IEEE: New York, NY, USA, 2020; pp. 176–179.
168. Xiao, D.; Qin, C.; Yu, H.; Huang, Y.; Liu, C.; Zhang, J. Unsupervised machine fault diagnosis for noisy domain adaptation using marginal denoising autoencoder based on acoustic signals. *Measurement* **2021**, *176*, 109186. [CrossRef]
169. Yun, H.; Kim, H.; Jeong, Y.H.; Jun, M.B. Autoencoder-based anomaly detection of industrial robot arm using stethoscope based internal sound sensor. *J. Intell. Manuf.* **2021**, *34*, 1427–1444. [CrossRef]

170. Sun, W.; Shao, S.; Zhao, R.; Yan, R.; Zhang, X.; Chen, X. A sparse auto-encoder-based deep neural network approach for induction motor faults classification. *Measurement* **2016**, *89*, 171–178. [CrossRef]
171. Li, C.; Zhang, W.; Peng, G.; Liu, S. Bearing fault diagnosis using fully-connected winner-take-all autoencoder. *IEEE Access* **2017**, *6*, 6103–6115. [CrossRef]
172. Sohaib, M.; Kim, J.-M. Reliable fault diagnosis of rotary machine bearings using a stacked sparse autoencoder-based deep neural network. *Shock Vib.* **2018**, *2018*, 2919637. [CrossRef]
173. Chen, L.; Cao, J.; Wu, K.; Zhang, Z. Application of Generalized Frequency Response Functions and Improved Convolutional Neural Network to Fault Diagnosis of Heavy-duty Industrial Robot. *Robot. Comput.-Integr. Manuf.* **2022**, *73*, 102228. [CrossRef]
174. Oh, Y.; Kim, Y.; Na, K.; Youn, B.D. A deep transferable motion-adaptive fault detection method for industrial robots using a residual–convolutional neural network. *ISA Trans.* **2021**, *128*, 521–534. [CrossRef]
175. Yang, S.; Luo, X.; Li, C. Fault Diagnosis of Rotation Vector Reducer for Industrial Robot Based on a Convolutional Neural Network. *Stroj. Vestn. /J. Mech. Eng.* **2021**, *67*, 489–500. [CrossRef]
176. Ma, Z.; Xiao, H.; Pan, Y.; Jiang, W.; Xiong, M.; He, Z. Multi-axis Industrial Robot Fault Diagnosis Model Based on Improved One-Dimensional Convolutional Neural Network. In Proceedings of the International Conference on Data Mining and Big Data, Guangzhou, China, 20–22 October 2021; pp. 397–410.
177. Li, P.; Xiao, H.; Jiang, W.; Ning, D. Compound Fault Diagnosis of Industrial Robot Based on Improved Multi-label One-Dimensional Convolutional Neural Network. In Proceedings of the International Conference on Data Mining and Big Data, Guangzhou, China, 20–22 October 2021; Springer: Berlin/Heidelberg, Germany, 2021; pp. 205–216.
178. Liu, Y.; Chen, C.; Wang, T.; Cheng, L. An attention enhanced dilated CNN approach for cross-axis industrial robotics fault diagnosis. *Auton. Intell. Syst.* **2022**, *2*, 11. [CrossRef]
179. Lu, K.; Chen, C.; Wang, T.; Cheng, L.; Qin, J. Fault diagnosis of industrial robot based on dual-module attention convolutional neural network. *Auton. Intell. Syst.* **2022**, *2*, 12. [CrossRef]
180. Janssens, O.; Slavkovikj, V.; Vervisch, B.; Stockman, K.; Loccufier, M.; Verstockt, S.; Van de Walle, R.; Van Hoecke, S. Convolutional neural network based fault detection for rotating machinery. *J. Sound Vib.* **2016**, *377*, 331–345. [CrossRef]
181. Plakias, S.; Boutalis, Y.S. Fault detection and identification of rolling element bearings with Attentive Dense CNN. *Neurocomputing* **2020**, *405*, 208–217. [CrossRef]
182. Cheng, Y.; Lin, M.; Wu, J.; Zhu, H.; Shao, X. Intelligent fault diagnosis of rotating machinery based on continuous wavelet transform-local binary convolutional neural network. *Knowl.-Based Syst.* **2021**, *216*, 106796. [CrossRef]
183. Guo, S.; Yang, T.; Gao, W.; Zhang, C. A novel fault diagnosis method for rotating machinery based on a convolutional neural network. *Sensors* **2018**, *18*, 1429. [CrossRef] [PubMed]
184. Liang, P.; Deng, C.; Wu, J.; Yang, Z. Intelligent fault diagnosis of rotating machinery via wavelet transform, generative adversarial nets and convolutional neural network. *Measurement* **2020**, *159*, 107768. [CrossRef]
185. Li, Y.; Zou, L.; Jiang, L.; Zhou, X. Fault diagnosis of rotating machinery based on combination of deep belief network and one-dimensional convolutional neural network. *IEEE Access* **2019**, *7*, 165710–165723. [CrossRef]
186. An, Z.; Li, S.; Wang, J.; Jiang, X. A novel bearing intelligent fault diagnosis framework under time-varying working conditions using recurrent neural network. *ISA Trans.* **2020**, *100*, 155–170. [CrossRef]
187. Van der Maaten, L.; Hinton, G. Visualizing data using t-SNE. *J. Mach. Learn. Res.* **2008**, *9*, 2579–2605.
188. Zhang, Y.; Zhou, T.; Huang, X.; Cao, L.; Zhou, Q. Fault diagnosis of rotating machinery based on recurrent neural networks. *Measurement* **2021**, *171*, 108774. [CrossRef]
189. Liu, H.; Zhou, J.; Zheng, Y.; Jiang, W.; Zhang, Y. Fault diagnosis of rolling bearings with recurrent neural network-based autoencoders. *ISA Trans.* **2018**, *77*, 167–178. [CrossRef]
190. Jiang, H.; Li, X.; Shao, H.; Zhao, K. Intelligent fault diagnosis of rolling bearings using an improved deep recurrent neural network. *Meas. Sci. Technol.* **2018**, *29*, 065107. [CrossRef]
191. Qiao, M.; Yan, S.; Tang, X.; Xu, C. Deep convolutional and LSTM recurrent neural networks for rolling bearing fault diagnosis under strong noises and variable loads. *IEEE Access* **2020**, *8*, 66257–66269. [CrossRef]
192. Oh, S.; Han, S.; Jeong, J. Multi-scale convolutional recurrent neural network for bearing fault detection in noisy manufacturing environments. *Appl. Sci.* **2021**, *11*, 3963. [CrossRef]
193. Li, S.; Zhao, Y.; Ding, M. Mobile robot motor bearing fault detection and classification on discrete wavelet transform and lstm network. *J. Mech. Med. Biol.* **2018**, *18*, 1840034. [CrossRef]
194. Zhi, Z.; Liu, L.; Liu, D.; Hu, C. Fault Detection of the Harmonic Reducer Based on CNN-LSTM With a Novel Denoising Algorithm. *IEEE Sens. J.* **2022**, *22*, 2572–2581. [CrossRef]
195. Wang, T.; Zhang, L.; Wang, X. Fault detection for motor drive control system of industrial robots using CNN-LSTM-based observers. *CES Trans. Electr. Mach. Syst.* **2023**, 1–9. [CrossRef]
196. Sohaib, M.; Kim, C.-H.; Kim, J.-M. A Hybrid Feature Model and Deep-Learning-Based Bearing Fault Diagnosis. *Sensors* **2017**, *17*, 2876. [CrossRef]
197. Xu, Y.; Li, Z.; Wang, S.; Li, W.; Sarkodie-Gyan, T.; Feng, S. A hybrid deep-learning model for fault diagnosis of rolling bearings. *Measurement* **2021**, *169*, 108502. [CrossRef]
198. Hoang, D.T.; Kang, H.J. A Motor Current Signal-Based Bearing Fault Diagnosis Using Deep Learning and Information Fusion. *IEEE Trans. Instrum. Meas.* **2020**, *69*, 3325–3333. [CrossRef]

199. Li, X.; Zhang, W.; Ding, Q. Understanding and improving deep learning-based rolling bearing fault diagnosis with attention mechanism. *Signal Process.* **2019**, *161*, 136–154. [CrossRef]
200. Chen, Z.; Chen, X.; Li, C.; Sanchez, R.-V.; Qin, H. Vibration-based gearbox fault diagnosis using deep neural networks. *J. Vibroengineering* **2017**, *19*, 2475–2496. [CrossRef]
201. Chen, Z.; Mauricio, A.; Li, W.; Gryllias, K. A deep learning method for bearing fault diagnosis based on Cyclic Spectral Coherence and Convolutional Neural Networks. *Mech. Syst. Signal Process.* **2020**, *140*, 106683. [CrossRef]
202. Verstraete, D.; Ferrada, A.; Droguett, E.L.; Meruane, V.; Modarres, M. Deep Learning Enabled Fault Diagnosis Using Time-Frequency Image Analysis of Rolling Element Bearings. *Shock Vib.* **2017**, *2017*, e5067651. [CrossRef]
203. Liu, H.; Li, L.; Ma, J. Rolling Bearing Fault Diagnosis Based on STFT-Deep Learning and Sound Signals. *Shock Vib.* **2016**, *2016*, e6127479. [CrossRef]
204. Shi, J.; Peng, D.; Peng, Z.; Zhang, Z.; Goebel, K.; Wu, D. Planetary gearbox fault diagnosis using bidirectional-convolutional LSTM networks. *Mech. Syst. Signal Process.* **2022**, *162*, 107996. [CrossRef]
205. Ravikumar, K.N.; Yadav, A.; Kumar, H.; Gangadharan, K.V.; Narasimhadhan, A.V. Gearbox fault diagnosis based on Multi-Scale deep residual learning and stacked LSTM model. *Measurement* **2021**, *186*, 110099. [CrossRef]
206. Long, J.; Mou, J.; Zhang, L.; Zhang, S.; Li, C. Attitude data-based deep hybrid learning architecture for intelligent fault diagnosis of multi-joint industrial robots. *J. Manuf. Syst.* **2021**, *61*, 736–745. [CrossRef]
207. Kamat, P.V.; Sugandhi, R.; Kumar, S. Deep learning-based anomaly-onset aware remaining useful life estimation of bearings. *PeerJ Comput. Sci.* **2021**, *7*, e795. [CrossRef]
208. Wang, X.; Wang, T.; Ming, A.; Han, Q.; Chu, F.; Zhang, W.; Li, A. Deep Spatiotemporal Convolutional-Neural-Network-Based Remaining Useful Life Estimation of Bearings. *Chin. J. Mech. Eng.* **2021**, *34*, 62. [CrossRef]
209. Ding, H.; Yang, L.; Cheng, Z.; Yang, Z. A remaining useful life prediction method for bearing based on deep neural networks. *Measurement* **2021**, *172*, 108878. [CrossRef]
210. Li, H.; Wang, W.; Li, Z.; Dong, L.; Li, Q. A novel approach for predicting tool remaining useful life using limited data. *Mech. Syst. Signal Process.* **2020**, *143*, 106832. [CrossRef]
211. Qin, Y.; Xiang, S.; Chai, Y.; Chen, H. Macroscopic–Microscopic Attention in LSTM Networks Based on Fusion Features for Gear Remaining Life Prediction. *IEEE Trans. Ind. Electron.* **2020**, *67*, 10865–10875. [CrossRef]
212. Algburi, R.N.A.; Gao, H. Health Assessment and Fault Detection System for an Industrial Robot Using the Rotary Encoder Signal. *Energies* **2019**, *12*, 2816. [CrossRef]
213. Jaber, A.; Bicker, R. Industrial Robot Fault Detection Based on Wavelet Transform and LabVIEW. In Proceedings of the 2014 First International Conference on Systems Informatics, Modelling and Simulation, Sheffield, UK, 29 April–1 May 2014.
214. Jaber, A.A.; Bicker, R. The optimum selection of wavelet transform parameters for the purpose of fault detection in an industrial robot. In Proceedings of the 2014 IEEE International Conference on Control System, Computing and Engineering (ICCSCE 2014), Penang, Malaysia, 28–30 November 2014; pp. 304–309.
215. Zhang, Y.; An, H.; Ding, X.; Liang, W.; Yuan, M.; Ji, C.; Tan, J. Industrial Robot Rotate Vector Reducer Fault Detection Based on Hidden Markov Models. In Proceedings of the 2019 IEEE International Conference on Robotics and Biomimetics (ROBIO), Dali, China, 6–8 December 2019; pp. 3013–3018.
216. Bonci, A.; Longhi, S.; Nabissi, G.; Verdini, F. Predictive Maintenance System using motor current signal analysis for Industrial Robot. In Proceedings of the 2019 24th IEEE International Conference on Emerging Technologies and Factory Automation (ETFA), Zaragoza, Spain, 10–13 September 2019; pp. 1453–1456.
217. Jaber, A.A.; Bicker, R. Fault diagnosis of industrial robot gears based on discrete wavelet transform and artificial neural network. *Insight-Non-Destr. Test. Cond. Monit.* **2016**, *58*, 179–186. [CrossRef]
218. Chen, Z.; Wu, K.; Wu, J.; Deng, C.; Wang, Y. Residual shrinkage transformer relation network for intelligent fault detection of industrial robot with zero-fault samples. *Knowl.-Based Syst.* **2023**, *268*, 110452. [CrossRef]
219. Jaber, A.A.; Bicker, R. Industrial Robot Backlash Fault Diagnosis Based on Discrete Wavelet Transform and Artificial Neural Network. *Am. J. Mech. Eng.* **2016**, *4*, 21–31. [CrossRef]
220. Yang, Q.; Li, X.; Wang, Y.; Ainapure, A.; Lee, J. Fault Diagnosis of Ball Screw in Industrial Robots Using Non-Stationary Motor Current Signals. *Procedia Manuf.* **2020**, *48*, 1102–1108. [CrossRef]
221. Jaber, A.A.; Bicker, R. Development of a Condition Monitoring Algorithm for Industrial Robots based on Artificial Intelligence and Signal Processing Techniques. *Int. J. Electr. Comput. Eng. (IJECE)* **2018**, *8*, 996–1009. [CrossRef]
222. Nentwich, C.; Reinhart, G. A Method for Health Indicator Evaluation for Condition Monitoring of Industrial Robot Gears. *Robotics* **2021**, *10*, 80. [CrossRef]
223. He, K.; Zhang, X.; Ren, S.; Sun, J. Deep residual learning for image recognition. In Proceedings of the IEEE Conference on Computer Vision and Pattern Recognition, Las Vegas, NV, USA, 27–30 June 2016; pp. 770–778.
224. Simonyan, K.; Zisserman, A. Very deep convolutional networks for large-scale image recognition. *arXiv* **2014**, arXiv:1409.1556.
225. Szegedy, C.; Ioffe, S.; Vanhoucke, V.; Alemi, A.A. Inception-v4, inception-resnet and the impact of residual connections on learning. In Proceedings of the Thirty-First AAAI Conference on Artificial Intelligence, San Francisco, CA, USA, 4–9 February 2017.
226. Li, X.; Zhang, W.; Ding, Q.; Sun, J.-Q. Intelligent rotating machinery fault diagnosis based on deep learning using data augmentation. *J. Intell. Manuf.* **2020**, *31*, 433–452. [CrossRef]

227. Kumar, P.; Hati, A.S. Transfer learning-based deep CNN model for multiple faults detection in SCIM. *Neural Comput. Appl.* **2021**, *33*, 15851–15862. [CrossRef]
228. Shao, S.; McAleer, S.; Yan, R.; Baldi, P. Highly accurate machine fault diagnosis using deep transfer learning. *IEEE Trans. Ind. Inform.* **2018**, *15*, 2446–2455. [CrossRef]

mathematics

MDPI

Review

Advances in Fault Detection and Diagnosis for Thermal Power Plants: A Review of Intelligent Techniques

Salman Khalid, Jinwoo Song, Izaz Raouf and Heung Soo Kim *

Department of Mechanical, Robotics, and Energy Engineering, Dongguk University-Seoul, 30 Pildong-ro 1-gil, Jung-gu, Seoul 04620, Republic of Korea
* Correspondence: heungsoo@dgu.edu; Tel.: +82-2-2260-8577; Fax: +82-2-2263-9379

Abstract: Thermal power plants (TPPs) are critical to supplying energy to society, and ensuring their safe and efficient operation is a top priority. To minimize maintenance shutdowns and costs, modern TPPs have adopted advanced fault detection and diagnosis (FDD) techniques. These FDD approaches can be divided into three main categories: model-based, data-driven-based, and statistical-based methods. Despite the practical limitations of model-based methods, a multitude of data-driven and statistical techniques have been developed to monitor key equipment in TPPs. The main contribution of this paper is a systematic review of advanced FDD methods that addresses a literature gap by providing a comprehensive comparison and analysis of these techniques. The review discusses the most relevant FDD strategies, including model-based, data-driven, and statistical-based approaches, and their applications in enhancing the efficiency and reliability of TPPs. Our review highlights the novel and innovative aspects of these techniques and emphasizes their significance in sustainable energy development and the long-term viability of thermal power generation. This review further explores the recent advancements in intelligent FDD techniques for boilers and turbines in TPPs. It also discusses real-world applications, and analyzes the limitations and challenges of current approaches. The paper highlights the need for further research and development in this field, and outlines potential future directions to improve the safety, efficiency, and reliability of intelligent TPPs. Overall, this review provides valuable insights into the current state-of-the-art in FDD techniques for TPPs, and serves as a guide for future research and development.

Keywords: thermal power plant; fault detection and diagnosis (FDD); boiler tube leakage; turbine; data-driven method; model-based method; and signal-based methods

MSC: 68T01

1. Introduction

TPPs continue to play a crucial role in the generation of electricity globally, with 83% of the world's electricity production being generated from fossil fuels, 12.6% from renewable sources, and 6.3% from nuclear energy, as per the British Petroleum Statistical Review of World Energy 2021 [1]. Despite the increasing popularity of renewable energy, thermal power generation remains essential in supporting the variable output of renewables, and maintaining energy security. As the demand for electricity continues to grow, TPP equipment is becoming larger and more complex, which in the event of a fault can pose challenges. Quickly diagnosing and repairing faults can be difficult, due to a lack of information and manpower, leading to prolonged downtime and increased production losses [2]. A previous literature survey shows that identifying faults in boilers and turbines is a time-consuming process that often requires expert experience and technical support from the original manufacturer [3]. To address these challenges, the use of FDD techniques in TPPs has been proposed as a solution. The implementation of these techniques has the potential to improve the safety, efficiency, and reliability of TPP operations, ultimately reducing downtime and production losses. FDD techniques help to quickly and accurately detect and diagnose faults, reducing the time needed to repair equipment, and minimizing the impact on production [4]. In addition to the boiler and turbine sections, other sections in thermal power plants can experience faults. For instance, scaling and fouling can occur in the cooling system of thermal power plants, leading to reduced heat transfer efficiency and negatively impacting overall plant performance [5–7]. The generator and electrical equipment may also be prone to faults, such as insulation breakdown, voltage instability, and rotor winding issues [8]. Additionally, the fuel system may also have potential faults, including fuel quality issues such as high moisture content or impurities that can cause combustion problems and damage to the combustion chamber or exhaust system [9]. The emission control system may also experience faults, such as a malfunctioning scrubber or catalytic converter, leading to violations of environmental regulations and affecting the overall efficiency of the power plant [10]. Although the majority of the literature on fault detection and diagnosis in thermal power plants focuses on the boiler and turbine sections, it is crucial to consider potential faults in other areas. Addressing these faults can improve efficiency and reliability, reduce maintenance costs, and ensure compliance with environmental regulations.

FDD is an important process that is used to identify and isolate faults in a system. This process starts with the detection of faults, followed by isolation to determine the location of the fault, and then identification, which involves calculation of the fault's time-variant characteristics. The FDD methods can be divided into three categories: model-based methods [11,12], data-driven methods [13], and statistical methods [14]. Model-based methods are efficient solutions for simple fault detection problems. However, they can be challenging to apply to complex industrial processes. In such cases, data-driven approaches and statistical methods have become popular. These methods involve the use of machine learning algorithms [15], ANN [16], and multivariate statistical techniques, such as PCA [17]. The concept of e-maintenance [18,19], also known as condition-based maintenance, has recently been introduced. This system uses advanced FDD methods to identify faults in TPPs. These methods use real-time data from advanced data acquisition systems to detect and diagnose faults. TPPs are equipped with various acoustic emissions [20,21] and process monitoring sensors [22], which generate a large amount of data. These data can be used for performance monitoring and intelligent FDD by learning from the stored historical data. Boiler tube leakage and turbine failures are the major equipment faults in TPPs [23,24]. According to a survey conducted from 2013 to 2017 [22,25], boiler tube leaks were the most common cause of failure in TPPs, constituting 54% of the total power plant outages. Among these leaks, water wall tube leakage was the dominant type, followed by the second superheater, first reheater, and first superheater, as shown in Figure 1. The cost of repairing these leaks can range from USD 2 to 10 million per leak [26]. Therefore, the implementation of intelligent FDD methods is essential for TPPs to ensure safe and reliable equipment operation and to reduce maintenance costs.

In recent years, AI and machine learning have gained prominence as effective tools for fault detection and diagnosis (FDD) in thermal power plants. They offer a significant advantage in handling and processing large amounts of data from various sources, such as sensors and control systems [27,28]. By analyzing and interpreting these data in real-time, AI algorithms can identify potential faults, providing valuable insights into the performance of the power plant. Machine learning algorithms can continuously learn and adapt to new data, improving their accuracy and effectiveness over time. These algorithms can be applied to various FDD techniques, including model-based, data-driven, and statistical-based approaches. For example, in model-based approaches, AI algorithms can develop more accurate and robust models of the thermal power plant to detect and diagnose faults [29]. Similarly, in data-driven approaches, AI algorithms can analyze historical data to identify patterns and anomalies that may indicate potential faults in the power plant [30]. However, challenges exist in implementing AI and machine learning for FDD in thermal power plants. There is a need for large amounts of high-quality data to train the algorithms effectively, and advanced computing capabilities to handle the computational complexity of these algorithms. Despite these challenges, several successful applications of AI and machine learning have been reported, such as Cui et al. [31] who developed a machine learning system for early fault diagnosis and warning of temperature deviation in power plant boiler reheater. The system can predict and issue alarms when the deviation exceeds a certain threshold, thus improving the efficiency and safety of power plants. The study findings showed that the model can identify the influencing factors of temperature deviation and provide reference guidance for the operation of power plant boilers. Dhini et al. [32] developed a fault diagnosis system for steam turbines in thermal power plants using extreme learning machine-radial basis function networks (ELM-RBF). Tested with real fault data, the system demonstrated high accuracy and fast computation, with ELM-RBF being faster than backpropagation neural networks (BPNN) without significant loss of accuracy. The proposed system can prevent unplanned breakdowns and accurately classify potential faults, improving the efficiency and safety of thermal power plants. Therefore, the use of AI and machine learning for FDD in thermal power plants holds great promise for improving the efficiency and reliability of these systems. In addition to AI-based approaches, recently, new technologies such as IoT, IoE, and smart grids are gaining increasing attention in sustainable energy development. They have the potential to significantly improve energy efficiency, reduce carbon emissions, and enable efficient integration of renewable energy sources into the grid [33–35].

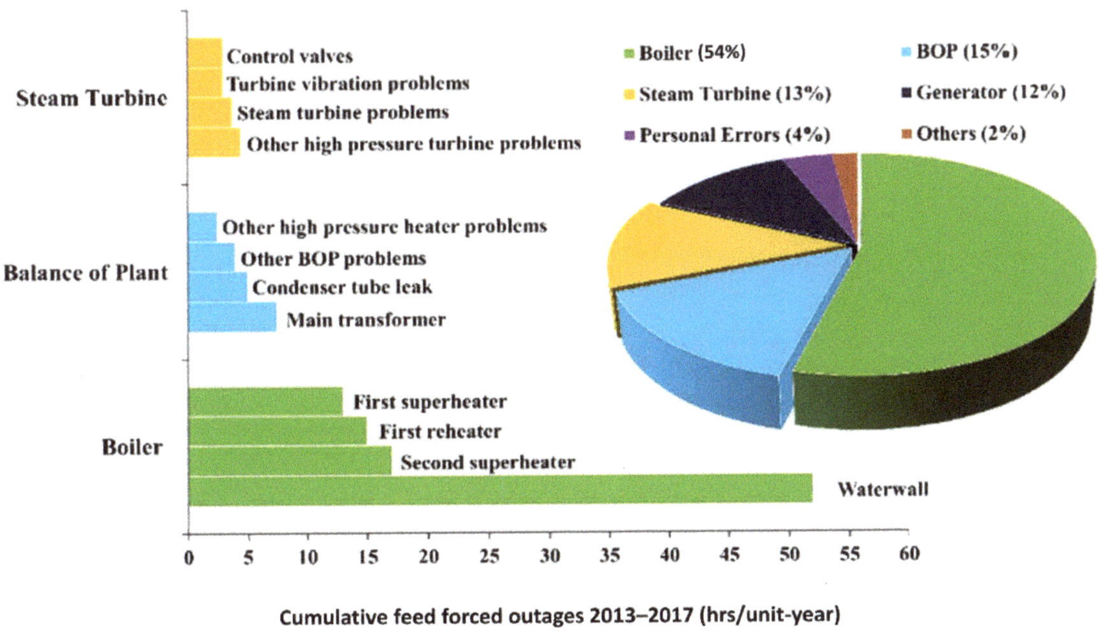

Figure 1. Graph Depicting the Severity of Power Plant Faults and their Resulting Percentage of Outages [22].

This survey provides a comprehensive overview of the current advancements in FDD techniques and their practical applications in modern TPPs. The aim of this review is to bring the challenges faced by TPPs to the attention of the FDD research community, and to summarize the different FDD approaches and their applications in identifying faults in key power plant equipment, such as boilers and turbines. The FDD methods are categorized into three types: model-based methods, data-driven methods, and statistical methods. The survey focuses on the real-world applications of these methods in detecting faults in power plant equipment, and provides a detailed explanation of the principles behind these approaches, practical examples of their use, and a discussion of future trends and areas for further development. Based on our review of the literature, there is a clear gap in the research on the use of intelligent techniques for fault detection and diagnosis in thermal power plants (TPPs). While there has been significant research on fault detection and diagnosis in TPPs, particularly on model-based and data-driven approaches, there is a lack of comprehensive analysis and comparison of these techniques. Our paper addresses this gap by providing a systematic review of the most relevant FDD strategies, including model-based, data-driven, and statistical-based approaches, as well as their classifications and applications in improving the efficiency and reliability of TPPs. By highlighting the novel and innovative aspects of these techniques, our review emphasizes their importance in the sustainable development of the energy sector and their potential to ensure the long-term viability of thermal power generation. Overall, our paper provides valuable insights into the state-of-the-art in FDD for TPPs and identifies opportunities for further research and development in this field.

2. TPP Equipment and Common Faults: An Overview

This section presents an overview of the major equipment, critical faults, and their causes in the TPP.

2.1. Major Equipment in TPPs

The TPPs are facilities that produce electricity by harnessing heat from sources such as coal, natural gas, oil, and nuclear reactions. These plants include several critical pieces of equipment that are crucial to the energy generation process, for which equipment includes boilers, steam turbines, generators, and condensers [36]:

1. Boiler

The boiler is one of the most important pieces of equipment in a TPP, and is responsible for heating the water that will be turned into steam and used to drive the turbine. Boilers are typically fueled by coal, natural gas, or oil, and can reach temperatures of over 1000 degrees Celsius. The heat generated in the boiler is used to convert water into steam, which is then transported to the turbine through a series of pipes [37].

2. Steam Turbine

The steam turbine is the next key piece of equipment in a thermal power plant, and uses the steam generated by the boiler to produce mechanical energy, which is then used to drive the generator. Turbines come in a variety of sizes and shapes, but the basic principle behind them all is the same. They work by using steam to spin a rotor, which is connected to a shaft that drives the generator. The faster the steam flows, the more energy the turbine can produce [38].

3. Generator

The generator is the next piece of equipment in the TPP process. It takes the mechanical energy generated by the turbine, and converts it into electrical energy that can be used to power homes and businesses. Generators use magnetic fields to produce electrical currents, which are then fed into the electrical grid to be distributed to users. Generators can range in size from small units that are used to power individual homes, to large units that can generate hundreds of megawatts of electricity [39].

4. Condenser

The condenser is a critical component in the operation of a TPP. It is used to cool the steam produced by the turbine, condensing it back into the water, so that it can be reused in the boiler. The steam is typically condensed by running it through a series of tubes, which are surrounded by cool water that is pumped in from a nearby source, such as a river or lake [40].

These major pieces of equipment in a TPP play a crucial role in the energy generation process. From the boiler that heats the water to the turbine that produces mechanical energy, to the generator that converts that energy into electricity, each of these pieces of equipment must work together seamlessly to produce the energy that powers homes and businesses. Additionally, condensers play an important role in maintaining the efficiency of the energy generation process, helping to prevent damage to the equipment, and keeping the plant running smoothly. Figure 2 shows a schematic diagram of a coal-fired thermal power plant, which is a type of power plant that generates electricity by burning coal to produce steam that drives a turbine connected to a generator. The process begins with the coal being transported to the plant and fed into a boiler, where it is burned at high temperatures to produce steam. The steam then flows through a series of pipes and turbines, where it expands and turns the blades, generating mechanical energy that is then converted into electrical energy by the generator. After the steam passes through the turbines, it is cooled and condensed back into water and returned to the boiler to repeat the cycle. The diagram also includes other essential components of the power plant, such as the cooling tower and transformer [22].

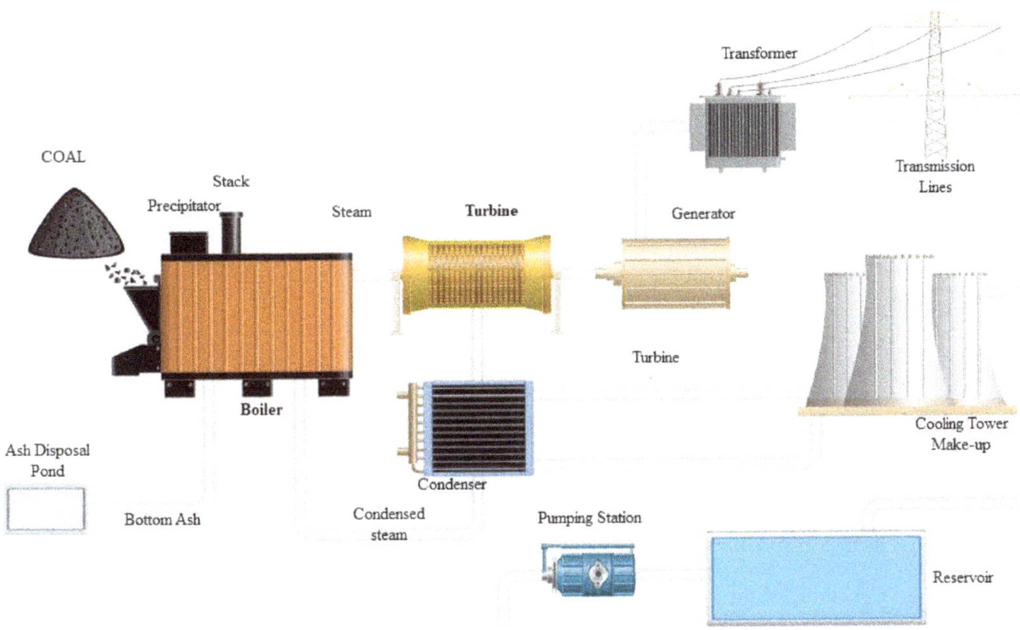

Figure 2. Schematic of the coal-fired TPP representing major equipment [22].

2.2. Common Faults in TPPs

This section summarizes in detail the two major equipment faults (boiler tube leakage and steam turbine failure) in the TPP.

2.2.1. Steam Turbine Faults

The steam turbine is a critical component in the energy generation process, converting the energy from steam into mechanical energy that can be used to generate electricity. The turbine converts high thermal energy from high-pressure vapor at high temperatures into rotational energy through a series of moving blades. This process involves multiple stages of energy conversion as the vapor passes through static blades. The rotation of the turbine rotor, connected to the generator's axle, ultimately produces electrical energy [41]. Steam turbine fault detection is an important aspect of maintaining the efficient operation of a

TPP. Any faults in the steam turbine can result in reduced efficiency, increased downtime, and potentially catastrophic failure. Several common faults can occur in steam turbines, which include blade failure, bearing failure, and rotor imbalance [42]. These faults can cause vibrations and other symptoms that can be detected and monitored using a range of diagnostic tools and techniques. Figure 3 offers an overview of the different faults that may occur in steam turbines, which are further explored in the following sections.

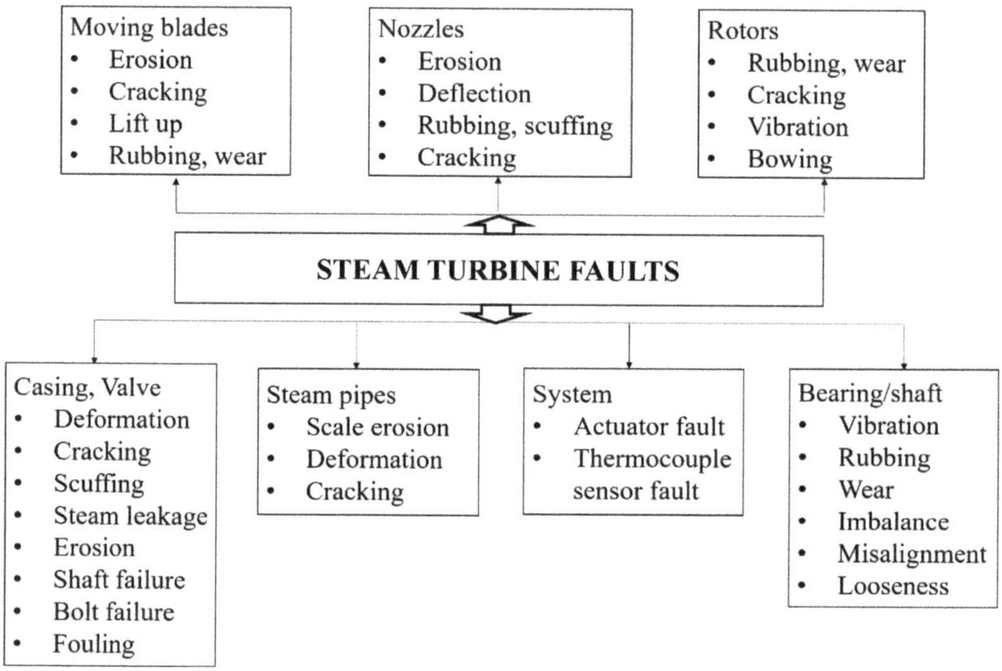

Figure 3. Steam turbine fault types and the causes of failures.

1. Unbalancing and misalignment

Unbalance is a frequent cause of vibration in steam turbines, but can be resolved by proper balancing of the components. Vibrations in overhung and flexible rotors are mainly radial, i.e., horizontal, vertical, or axial. The magnitude of unbalance is proportional to the amplitude of vibrations. Misalignment, such as the bearing not being aligned with the shaft, between bearings, or with the clamping halves, can result in excessive stress on the bearing, leading to damage due to fatigue. A bent shaft can also cause misalignment. Radial and axial vibrations are important in determining misalignment, with axial vibration being the key factor. The three types of misalignment are angular, parallel, and their combination [43].

2. Mechanical looseness

Mechanical looseness can compromise the operation of a steam turbine, affecting its power production. Regular monitoring can be costly in terms of reducing maintenance downtime, but if a fault is diagnosed, it offers sufficient notice to prepare for necessary corrective actions [44].

3. Actuator Fault

A faulty actuator can impact the turbine controller's output, causing a slower response to the required flow rates. A broken spindle can lead to leakage in the overflow valve, reducing turbine performance [45].

4. Thermocouple sensors fault

A malfunction in the thermocouple sensor in the steam path of the turbine can result in gradually increasing or decreasing readings over time [46].

5. Fouling fault

Accumulated deposits in the steam route can cause deviations in the steam velocity, resulting in pressure drops, reduced turbine capacity and efficiency, and extra rotor thrust. Uneven fouling can lead to unbalanced rotors and vibration issues. The deposits can cause nozzles and blades to deviate from their original configuration, and increase the resistance to the flow of steam [47].

Traditionally, to maintain the efficient operation of a TPP, various methods of fault detection have been utilized for steam turbines, including the following:

1. Vibration analysis: This involves measuring the vibration levels of the steam turbine components, and analyzing the data to detect any deviations from the normal operating conditions. Vibration analysis can help identify faults, such as unbalance, misalignment, or mechanical looseness [48].
2. Thermography: This involves using thermal cameras to measure the temperature of the steam turbine components and detect any anomalies. Thermography can help to identify faults, such as a broken spindle or fouling [49].
3. Acoustic monitoring: This involves listening for changes in the sound produced by the steam turbine, and analyzing the data to detect any deviations from the normal operating conditions. Acoustic monitoring can help to identify faults, such as mechanical looseness or bearing damage [50].
4. Oil analysis: This involves testing the lubricating oil for contaminants or other signs of wear and tear, and analyzing the data to detect any anomalies. Oil analysis can help identify faults, such as actuator malfunction or a thermocouple sensor fault [51].

2.2.2. Boiler Tube Leakage

Boiler tube leakage in a TPP can be a serious issue, as it can lead to reduced efficiency, increased downtime, and even catastrophic failure. Boiler tubes, which are used to carry hot gases from the combustion process to the steam turbine, are subjected to high temperatures and pressures. Over time, these tubes can become damaged, leading to leakage, and ultimately reducing the efficiency of the power plant. There are several reasons why boiler tubes may leak. One common cause is corrosion [52,53], which can occur as a result of exposure to high temperatures and corrosive chemicals, such as those found in the combustion gases. Other factors that can lead to boiler tube leakage include mechanical stress, thermal stress, and improper maintenance [54]. The consequences of boiler tube leakage can be significant. Leaks can reduce the efficiency of a power plant, as they allow hot gases to escape, instead of being directed to the steam turbine. This can lead to increased fuel consumption and decreased output, ultimately affecting the bottom line of the power plant. Additionally, leaks can cause damage to other components in the system, such as the steam turbine, increasing the likelihood of unscheduled downtime and repair costs.

The most dominant occurrence of boiler tube leakage lies in the water wall tube section [55]. Waterwall tubes are a critical component in a TPP, as they are responsible for containing and directing the flow of hot water and steam. However, water wall tubes are also subjected to high temperatures and pressures, and over time they can become damaged and leak. Waterwall tube leakage can have serious consequences, including reduced efficiency, increased downtime, and even catastrophic failure. There are several causes of waterwall tube leakage in a TPP. Another common cause of waterwall tube leakage is thermal stress, which occurs when the tubes are subjected to repeated fluctuations in temperature. This can cause the tubes to expand and contract, leading to cracking and eventual failure. In addition to these causes, there are other factors that can contribute to waterwall tube leakage; these include mechanical fatigue [56], erosion [57], and inadequate design. For example, if the waterwall tubes are not properly supported, they may be subjected to excessive stress and vibrations, leading to cracking and failure.

Yang et al.'s study on coal quality discovered that the high ash content in the coal used in TPPs leads to corrosion in the water wall tubes. They proposed that proper coal blending could help to minimize this corrosion [58]. Additionally, Xue et al. analyzed the boiler water, and found that the presence of NaOH causes corrosion-induced perforations and leakage in the water wall tubes. To prevent these leakages, it is important for power plant inspectors to regularly monitor the water quality and perform necessary tests to ensure the tubes do not leak [59]. Similarly, superheater and reheater tubes in a steam power plant are constantly exposed to high temperatures and pressures, making them susceptible to damage and leakage over time. Purbolaksono et al. found localized short-term overheating to be the main cause of failure in primary superheater tubes [60]. Khalil et al. looked into the reasons behind failures in both cold and hot reheater tubes, and concluded that poor maintenance practices and improper feed water chemistry were the main contributing factors [61]. These findings highlight the importance of proper maintenance and monitoring to ensure the longevity and reliable operation of superheater and reheater tubes in a power plant.

Boiler tube leakage in power plants can have serious consequences. Leaks reduce the efficiency of the plant, as hot water and steam escape, instead of being directed to the steam turbine. This results in higher fuel consumption, reduced output, and negative impact on the plant's financial performance. Furthermore, leaks can cause damage to other system components, such as the steam turbine, leading to unplanned downtime and costly repairs. To minimize the risk of tube leakage, it is crucial to conduct regular inspections and maintenance of the waterwall tubes [62]. This includes checking for signs of corrosion or damage, replacing damaged tubes, and cleaning to remove corrosive build-up. Proper operation within design parameters is also important to avoid overloading the system, and reduce the risk of leakage.

To detect and prevent boiler tube leaks, several traditional fault detection techniques that are commonly used in TPPs are

1. Ultrasonic Testing: High-frequency sound waves are used to detect faults in the tubes. The location and size of the leak can be determined by transmitting sound waves through the tube wall [63].
2. Eddy Current Testing: Magnetic fields are used to detect faults in the tubes. The location and size of the leak can be determined by inducing an eddy current in the tube wall [64].
3. Leak Detection Dye: A water-soluble dye is injected into the steam system, and the location of the dye observed as it leaks out of the tubes. This can provide visual indication of the location and size of the leak [65].
4. Pressure Testing: The pressure drop in the steam system is measured over time. A sudden drop in pressure can indicate a leak in the tubes.
5. Thermographic Imaging: Infrared cameras are used to detect changes in temperature in the tubes. The location and size of the leak can be determined by detecting changes in temperature [66].

3. FDD Approaches in Intelligent TPPs

The FDD is a crucial process in identifying faults within a system. It involves detecting faults, determining their location, and characterizing them based on size and other attributes [67]. The two main categories of FDD methods are model-based and model-free, with the latter further divided into data-driven and statistical methods, as shown in Figure 4. Model-based FDD [68] involves using a mathematical model to predict normal system behavior, and comparing it to actual observations to detect and diagnose faults. However, its implementation can be limited by the requirement of an accurate model, which can be difficult to obtain [69]. In contrast, data-driven FDD [70] methods identify correlations between system measurements to detect and diagnose faults. These relationships are established by training an empirical model using normal, fault-free data, and evaluating the estimation residuals of new measurements to identify faults. On the other hand, statistical-based methods compare features extracted from a signal to the desired normal baseline values to make FDD decisions [71]. Both data-driven and statistical-based methods have been widely adopted across various industries for FDD purposes.

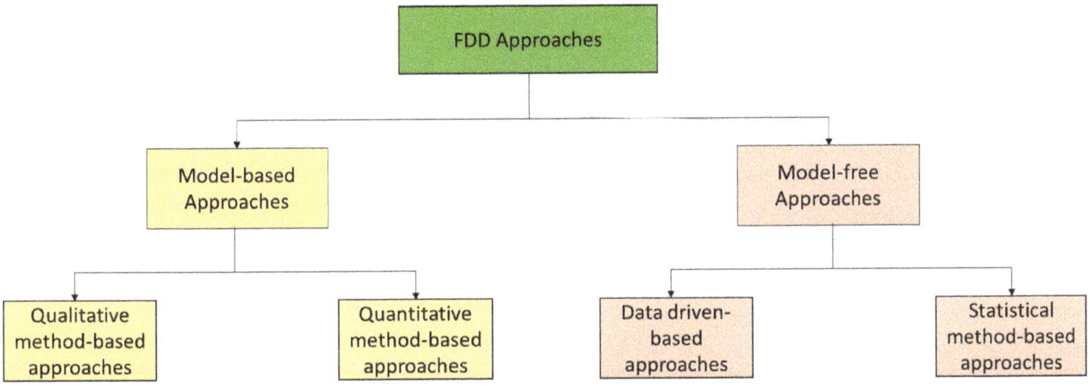

Figure 4. Diagram of Various Fault Detection Techniques in Power Plant Systems.

3.1. FDD Approaches for Steam Turbine

In this section, we delve into the application of FDD approaches, including both model-based methods and model-free methods, in the context of steam turbine TPPs.

3.1.1. Model-Based Fault Detection

Model-based fault detection is a widely used approach to detect and diagnose faults in steam turbines in TPPs [72]. This approach involves the use of mathematical models to simulate the behavior of the steam turbine system, and to identify any deviations from normal operating conditions that may indicate the presence of a fault. The first step in model-based fault detection is to develop a mathematical model of the steam turbine system that accurately represents its behavior under normal operating conditions. This model can be based on physical laws, empirical data, or a combination of both. The model should include all of the important components and interactions of the steam turbine system, such as the steam flow rate, temperature, pressure, and power output. Once the model has been developed, it can be used to monitor the behavior of the steam turbine system in real-time. The model can be compared to the actual operating data from the steam turbine system, and any deviations from the model predictions can be used to identify potential faults. For example, if the model predicts a certain steam flow rate, and the actual steam flow rate is significantly different, this may indicate the presence of a fault, such as a leak in the steam flow system.

Similarly, if the model predicts a certain power output, and the actual power output is significantly lower, this may indicate the presence of a fault, such as an inefficient turbine blade [73]. Model-based fault detection offers several advantages over other fault detection approaches. For example, it provides a more comprehensive and accurate view of the steam turbine system, it can be more sensitive to subtle changes in the system behavior, and it can be used to diagnose the root cause of faults, which can be useful for maintenance and repair purposes. In summary, model-based fault detection is a valuable tool for detecting and diagnosing faults in steam turbines in TPPs. By using mathematical models to simulate the behavior of the steam turbine system, it provides a more comprehensive and accurate view of the system, which can be used to identify and diagnose faults, and to improve the efficiency and reliability of the steam turbine system. Figure 5 illustrates the model-based fault detection approaches for thermal power plants. It depicts the types of models, including non-linear, linearized, LPV, and Fuzzy T-S models, and their corresponding approaches such as set membership, fault estimation, neural network, and fuzzy inference. The figure also shows how residual generation and evaluation are used to detect and diagnose faults in the power plant, thereby improving its efficiency and reliability. The residual evaluation is carried out using threshold check and feature extraction, along with Bayesian approaches, which ensures the accurate detection and diagnosis of faults. In summary, the techniques presented in Figure 5 are critical in enabling prompt corrective action and ensuring the long-term viability of thermal power generation.

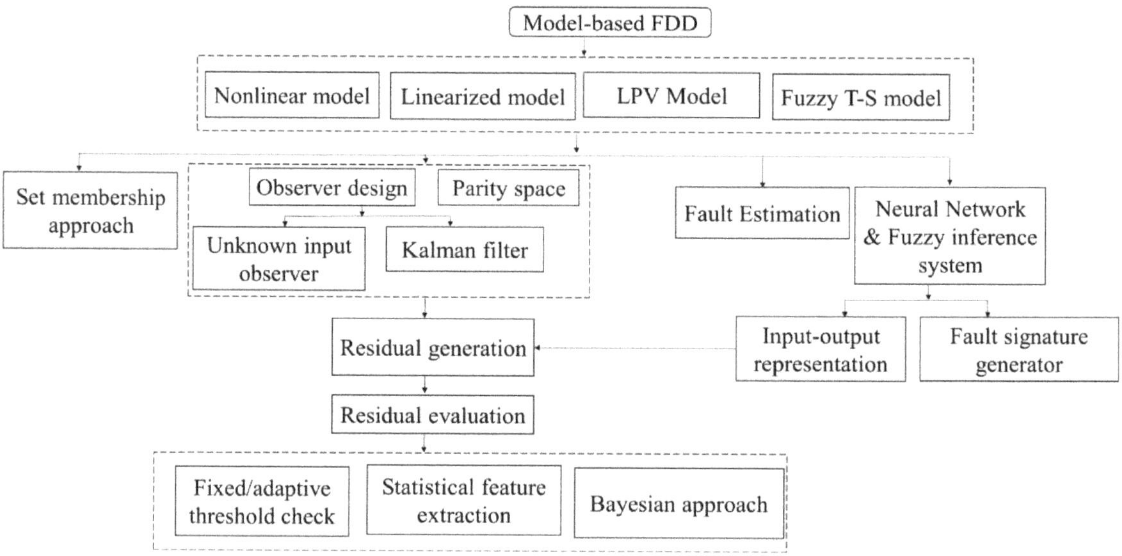

Figure 5. Illustration of Model-Based Fault Detection TPP Systems.

The application of FDD approaches in steam turbine TPPs has received significant attention in recent years. Researchers have proposed a variety of model-based approaches to improve the accuracy of FDD in steam turbines. Table 1 shows the different types of model-based approaches and the corresponding faults that they can detect and diagnose. For example, Salashoor et al. combined a support vector machine (SVM) classifier and an adaptive neuro-fuzzy inference system (ANFIS) classifier to improve the FDD assignments [74]. Another study proposed an FDD system based on the ANFIS technique for four different faults in steam turbines [75]. The proposed system was tested for its effectiveness in diagnosing 12 major faults under various noise and data manipulation conditions. Li et al. presented a Moving Exponential Double-Sided Sensitivity filter (MEDSS filter) based on the Kalman filter, which enhanced the FDD of the regular sinusoidal synthesis (SS) method [76]. The effectiveness of the model was validated through simulations and real-world case studies. Sha et al. proposed an improved Locality-Preserving Projection (ILPP) scheme using the Riemannian metric for the diagnosis of fouling faults in steam turbines [77]. The results of this method showed significant improvement, compared to other existing approaches. Huang et al. proposed a Riemannian algorithm for the fault detection of valve stiction in steam turbines [78]. The effectiveness of the proposed method was compared to traditional FDD methods through experiments and simulations. Figure 6 depicts the proposed FDD approach.

Martnez et al. [45] proposed a fault tolerant control (FTC) for the turbine in a TPP, which was evaluated in a practical case study and dynamic simulator with various scenarios, such as initial stage pressure, superheated pressurized steam, and drum pressure. The proposed approach was shown to be applicable to a broad range of situations with strong nonlinear dynamics [50]. The FTC scheme was also integrated with a data-driven approach, using ANFIS and SVM classifiers for FDD. The FTC scheme demonstrated effective fault accommodation and improved steam turbine availability [79]. Zhang et al. presented a graph model approach to categorize healthy and faulty conditions in the dead zone of the control valve, with high diagnostic accuracy that can be applied in the real industrial environment [80]. Another study used a Modified Locality-Preserving Projection (MLPP) based on the Riemannian approach to overcome limitations in intrinsic feature space for effective fault diagnosis. A framework for process monitoring was established, and kernel density estimation was used to approximate confidence bounds. The proposed approach was tested under various noisy scenarios, with results showing its accuracy [81].

Table 1. Comparison of Model-Based Approaches for Turbine Fault Detection in Power Plant Systems.

Fault Detection Approach	Fault/Consequence	Outcome
Integrated SVM with ANFIS [74]	List of different faults, such as, fouling, TS, boiler pressure.	The proposed FDD system is primarily appealing due to the potential advantages of lowering maintenance costs, increased productivity, and enhanced steam turbine accessibility.
ANFIS technique [75]	Various faults: Boiler pressure, fouling, TS, etc.	The proposed FDD model showed the generalization capabilities for variable operating conditions, such as alteration in the fault behavior over time.
MEDSS model using Kalman filter [76]	Rotor-to-stator rubbing fault.	The MEDSS filter has demonstrated promise in detecting distinctive uncontrollable fault attributes in rotating machines, particularly in low SNR scenarios.
Kalman filter [82]	Turbine blade fault due to fatigue.	By assessing deterioration severity and replacement scheduling, overall performance and reliability prediction can be used to enhance accessibility and implement maintenance until failure happens.
ILPP scheme using Riemannian metric [77]	Fouling fault.	The performance of the proposed approached is effective, as compared to the other conventional techniques.
Riemannian algorithm [78]	Valve stiction fault of the steam turbine.	Applicability of the approach in both single control loop and cascaded control loop.
FTC approach [45]	Actuator fault.	Applicable to use in broader range of situations with strong nonlinear dynamics.
FTC approach based on ANFIS [79]	Various faults: actuator fault, TS fault, fouling, etc.	Applicability of the proposed FTC approach under various types of steam turbine fault circumstances.
Graph model approach [80]	Control valve fault	Effectively applicable in the real industrial environment, enhancing economic advantages and execution safety.
MLPP based on Riemannian [81]	Blades fouled fault	Applicable under variable operating conditions (validated using various noisy conditions).
Unsupervised fuzzy C-means (FCM) algorithm [83]	Misaligned and amplified data	Generalization and capable of working on unseen data.

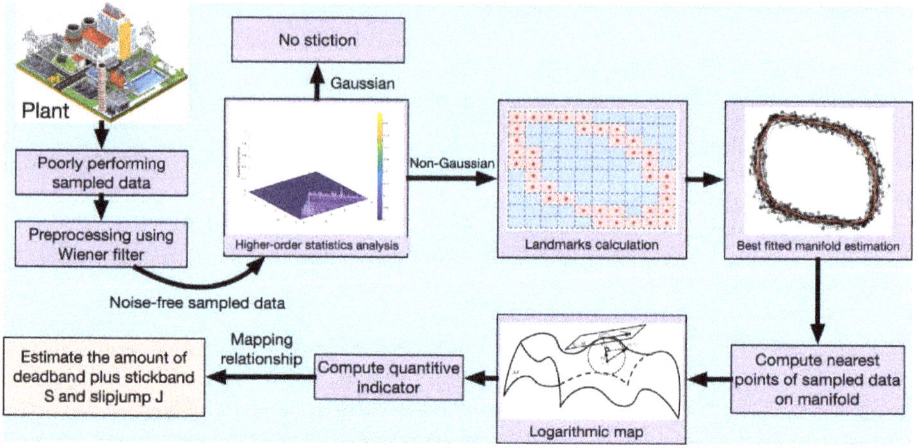

Figure 6. Diagram of the Proposed Riemannian-based Fault Detection Method for Power Plant Systems [78].

3.1.2. Data-Driven Based Fault Detection

The field of FDD in steam turbines of TPPs has recently seen a shift toward data-driven approaches. These approaches, known as "knowledge-based FDD", utilize artificial intelligence and machine learning algorithms to analyze large amounts of data and detect potential faults in real-time. Unlike model-based and signal-based FDD, data-driven approaches do not rely on prior information, and, instead, learn from historical data. Advances in artificial intelligence and machine learning have made data-driven approaches a popular research topic in recent years [84]. The use of these techniques results in improved efficiency, reduced downtime, and increased plant reliability. The data-driven methods make use of a range of techniques, such as signal processing, machine learning, and data analytics, to identify deviations from normal behavior that may indicate a fault. One popular approach is to use machine learning algorithms, such as ANNs and SVMs, to build a model of the normal behavior of the steam turbine. The model is then used to compare actual data with expected data, and determine if deviations are significant enough to indicate a fault. In summary, the use of data-driven techniques in steam turbine FDD has the potential to greatly improve the reliability and efficiency of TPPs by enabling the early detection and correction of faults. The continued development and implementation of these techniques will play a crucial role in the future of the thermal power industry.

There have been several advancements in data-driven techniques for FDD in the steam turbines of TPPs. In recent years, data-driven approaches have gained popularity due to the advancements in AI and machine learning. These techniques make use of data analysis, signal processing, and machine learning algorithms to identify faults in real-time. By analyzing large amounts of data generated by the plant, data-driven methods can detect faults early, which can reduce downtime, improve efficiency, and increase plant reliability.

Studies have shown the effectiveness of using data-driven techniques, such as deep learning, machine learning, supervised and unsupervised learning, and hybrid approaches for FDD. For example, Salahshoor et al. [75] used adaptive neuro-fuzzy inference classifiers to identify 12 major faults in a steam turbine. Another study proposed a neural network-based approach for fault detection in a steam turbine, which involved data collection in both laboratory and real-world conditions [42]. Figure 7 highlights the application of deep learning for FDD in steam turbines. The data used in this study were collected in both laboratory and real-world environments, and underwent a preprocessing stage, which included segmentation. The model was then trained, followed by the fault diagnosis process. This approach is an example of the use of data-driven methods in the field of FDD in steam turbines [85].

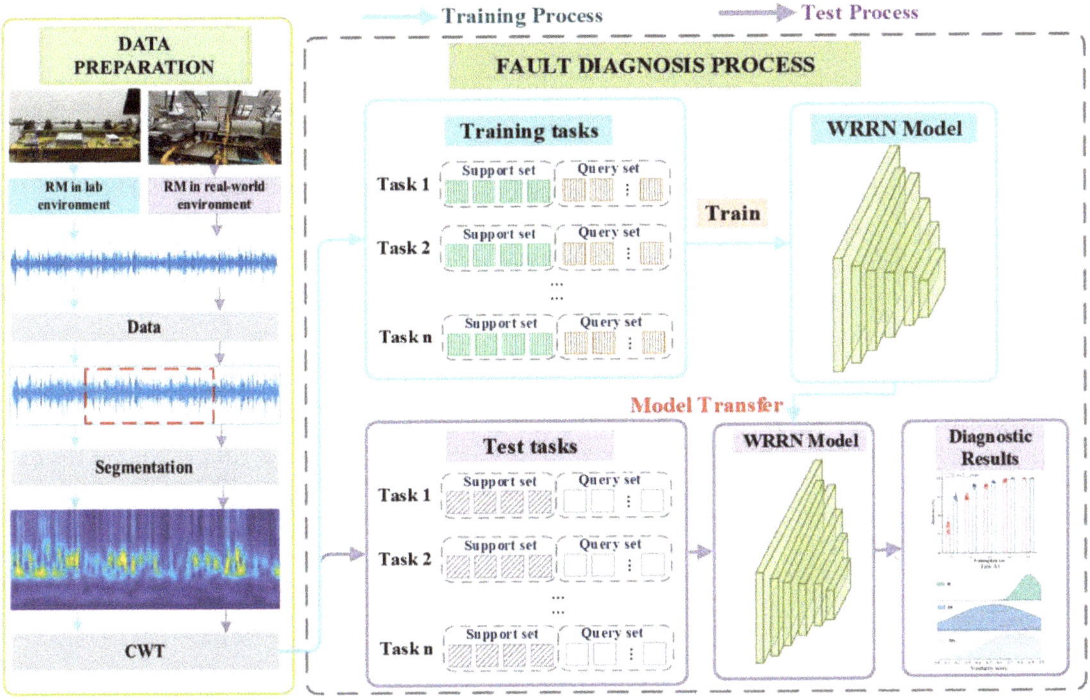

Figure 7. Illustration of Data-Driven Deep Learning Based FDD Approach for Power Plant Systems [85].

Table 2 highlights the various knowledge-based data-driven approaches for steam turbine FDD. Dhini et al. [42] compared the performance of a neural network (NN) classifier across three different scenarios, with the last two scenarios (with and without PCA) outperforming the first scenario, which only used selected process parameters. Chen et al. [86] evaluated the fault detection performance of a support vector machine (SVM)-based framework, and compared it to linear discriminant analysis (LDA) and backpropagation neural network (BPN). The study found that the SVM performed better than the other two methods. In another study [32], a novel extreme learning machine-radial basis function network (ELMRBF) was proposed for steam turbine FDD, and its efficiency was compared to backpropagation neural networks (BPNN). Ashraf et al. [87] proposed ANN and SVM models based on relative vibration modeling for steam turbine shaft bearing FDD, and found that the ANN model performed better than the SVM model. Que et al. [88] presented a semi-supervised framework based on GAN and particle filter (PF) for FDD and remaining useful life (RUL) prediction of steam turbine, and verified its efficiency through real-world examples. Fang et al. [89] proposed a data-driven approach based on ANNs for the vibration FDD of the steam turbine, and found that the features extracted using ANN outperformed those extracted using empirical mode decomposition (EMD). Wang et al. [90] used a residual network to diagnose misalignment and imbalance faults in the steam turbine, which eliminated the limitations of conventional signal processing techniques, and improved precision and reliability. Helin et al. [91] proposed a compressive approach for steam turbine FDD, consisting of unsupervised PCA and an NN-based autoencoder.

Table 2. Comparison of Data-Driven Based FDD Approaches for Steam TPP Systems.

Approach	Fault	Outcomes
Neural network with PCA [42]	Various faults, such as misalignment, robot bowing, blade erosion.	Good classification performance under real industrial applications.
SVM based fault classification [86]	Various faults such as flow, erosion of blade, failure of bearing, etc.	The presented work is capable of real application.
Extreme learning machine-radial basis function networks (ELMRBF) approach [32]	Various faults in the turbine, such as case cracking, blade cracking, rotor bowing, misalignment.	This study identifies characteristics that have a significant impact on the given specification.
ANN and SVM based FDD [87]	Bearing fault of the steam turbine	Vibration reduction of the bearing of the steam turbine's high-speed shaft can inhibit downtimes and costly maintenance, contributing to the machinery's safe and constant execution.
Semi-supervised model based on GAN and PF [88]	Anomaly detection: generator power is used as a health indicator (HI)	Applicable in the real application, and can be used to determine the HI and RUL.
Feature extraction based on ANN [89]	Imbalance and rubbing	The extracted feature outperforms the conventional feature based on EMD.
Residual network [90]	Misalignment and imbalance	This solves the limitations of traditional techniques, and reduces the computational cost.
Various approaches, such as unsupervised, PCA, and NN based autoencoder [91]	Anomaly detection of steam turbine	Long-term data are utilized; hence, the problem evaluation on big data (two years) is considered, which effectively detects anomalies in the steam turbine.
ANN approach [92]	Steam turbine bearing fault	Computationally less expensive model, as compared to previous models.
Deep learning based wide residual relation network (WRRN) [85]	Imbalance, misalignment	It is demonstrated that the WRRN can reliably detect rotating machine fault types using small, or even single, samples.

3.1.3. Statistical Method-Based Fault Detection

An effective and efficient way to detect and diagnose faults in steam turbines is through the implementation of statistical methods. This approach involves the collection of data from various sources within the turbine, such as vibration sensors, temperature sensors, and pressure gauges. The data are then processed using statistical techniques, such as regression analysis, principal component analysis, and clustering algorithms, to identify patterns and anomalies in the system [93,94]. For example, a sudden increase in vibration readings from a certain part of the turbine may indicate a problem with a bearing, or a misaligned rotor. Similarly, elevated temperature readings may indicate a problem with the cooling system, while changes in pressure readings can indicate a leak in a pipe. By detecting these faults early on, plant operators can take prompt corrective action to avoid costly downtime and repairs. Additionally, statistical-based fault detection and diagnosis can help to identify the root cause of a problem, allowing for targeted repairs and improved maintenance strategies.

Table 3 shows statistical-based approaches that have recently been used for the FDD of the steam turbine. Zhao et al. [95] proposed CWT for different fault evaluation of the steam turbine. The power distribution of the signal in the time and frequency domain can be easily depicted using a time–frequency contour map. In summary, it provides an effective method for identifying steam turbine faults involving a breakdown change. Ajami et al. [96] presented statistical approach based on independent component analysis (ICA) for a real turbine (model V94.2). As a preliminary step in ICA, the input data undergo whitening and centering. This process involves transforming the original signals into variables with a mean value of zero, and then linearly transforming these centered signals so that they are uncorrelated, and have unity variance. Figure 8 illustrates the mixing and separation process of the ICA algorithm.

Mubaraali et al. [97] proposed a statistical approach for the turbine FDD by using the CWT to remove noise from the signal. The features are extracted using statistic filter (SF) and Hilbert transform (HT) integrated with moving-peak-hold method (M-PH). Zhang et al. presented a kernel generalized discriminant analysis (KGDA), where the data are transformed from the original set to high-dimensional feature space. The statistic length among normal and test data are then calculated to determine the presence or absence of a malfunction. If a fault happens, a comparable analysis is used to identify the type of fault. The results show that the proposed technique can prevent systematic errors and fault misdiagnosis caused by changes in the operating environment and model insecurity. Lin et al. [98] proposed grey clustering analysis (GCA) using (FFT) analysis. In summary, the highest and lowest values of the power spectrum imply a vibration fault at a specific frequency, and frequency trends are used to diagnose mechanical vibration faults.

Table 3. Comparison of Statistical-based Fault Detection Techniques for steam turbine Power Plant Systems.

FDD Approach	Fault/Signal Type	Advantages
CWT approach [95]	Vibration signal with various kinds of faults, such as rubbing, oil whip, looseness, loss of component, unbalance.	The proposed model is effective, and can potentially be used in real-world application.
CWT based SF and HT combined with M-PH [97]	Vibration data, bearing fault.	The proposed method outperforms other approaches in terms of fault signal extraction and fault diagnosis of low-speed bearings.
Kernel generalized discriminant analysis (KGDA) [99]	Vibration data/various kind of fault; unbalance, misalignment, oil whip, radial rubbing.	This approach captures the nonlinear correlation, and proficiently synthesizes changing information in multiple process factors.
ICA based statistical approach [96]	Different thermal parameters related to the flow.	The model can compensate for environmental and model uncertainty.
GCA analysis based on FFT [98]	Vibration signal.	Ease of implementation, practical application with high accuracy.
Wavelet spectrum based FDD of turbine generator [100]	Thermal signal measurement.	The early fault can be detected using the energy profile based on wavelet spectrum.

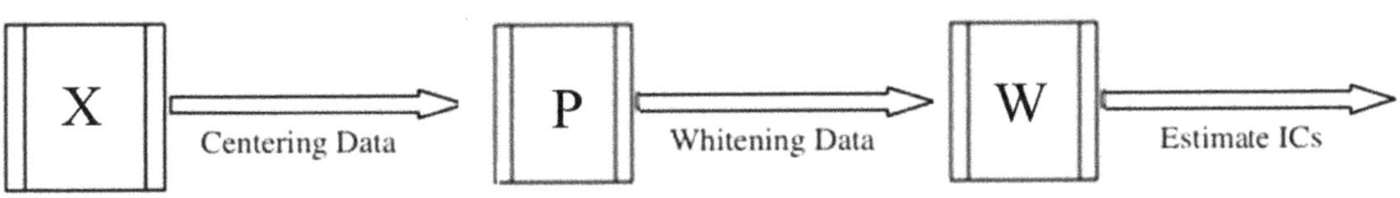

Figure 8. Illustration of the Mixing and Separation Process using ICA Algorithm [96].

3.2. Application of FDD Approaches in Boiler Tube Leakage Detection

In this section, we examine the use of FDD techniques, including both model-based and model-free approaches, in the context of the boiler in a TPP.

3.2.1. Model-Based Methods

In the area of boiler tube leak detection, various mathematical models have been widely used [69]. This conventional approach takes into account both the steady and dynamic aspects of process variables, making it a suitable solution for various fault diagnosis applications. However, in some cases, this method may not provide precise results, as it can be difficult to establish a valid mathematical model of the process for specific industrial scenarios. Panday et al. [101] designed a straightforward monitoring tool to detect leaks in the boiler section of a 300 MW power plant. They compared the amount of feedwater needed to produce steam under normal and faulty conditions, and established the ratio of feedwater flow rate to steam flow rate as the key parameter for anomaly detection, since the available data did not include other indicators used in previous studies, such as water level, blowdown, or make-up water. To minimize false alarms, they set a threshold for the difference in slope between the normal and leaky data sets. They also applied an EMA filter to reduce noise in the raw signals. The results showed that a decrease in economizer outlet temperature represents a leak, as shown in Figure 9. This tool was created as a simple and effective solution for real-time leak detection when other critical measurements are not available.

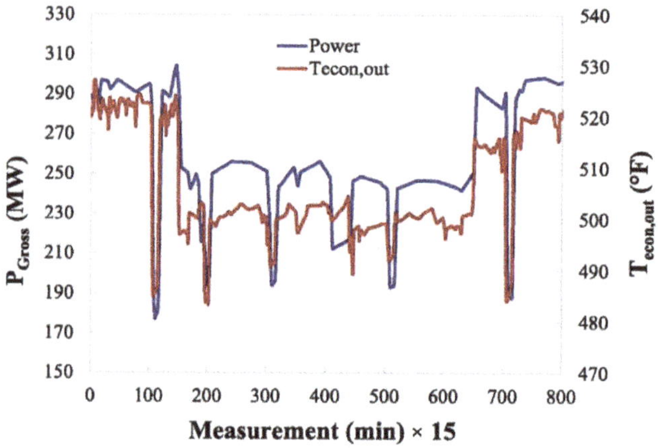

Figure 9. Consequence of a Leak: A Graph Showing the Decrease in Economizer Outlet Temperature [101].

Sun et al. [102] proposed a model-based algorithm that incorporates a time-varying forgetting factor to identify leaks in boiler steam–water systems [94]. They used system identification methods to analyze the steam drum, taking into account the material balance relationship and measuring feedwater flow rate, steam flow rate, pressure change rate, and drum level. Chen et al. [69] developed a steam boiler leak detection system that uses a model-based least squares algorithm. The model includes heat and mass balance equations, and was tested in real-world conditions at Syncrude Canada, demonstrating its ability to provide early leak warnings. Li et al. [103] put forward the use of the group method of data handling (GMDH) technique to detect water leakage from interior tubing into steam space in high-pressure feedwater heaters. However, they pointed out that the GMDH model's complexity increases with the number of layers, making the evaluation of all possible nodes computationally intensive, which could be challenging for practical applications. Lang et al. [26] developed a leak detection system for generator tubes and heat exchangers that utilized an input/loss model based on heat and mass balance governing equations to calculate fuel flow, heating values, and fuel chemistry. The model was implemented at the Boardman coal plant, and was shown to effectively predict tube leaks. David et al. [104] introduced a simple model-based algorithm that was developed by creating a mathematical model of various boiler sub-systems, such as the furnace, boiler tubes, drums, and heat exchangers. The model's outputs were obtained by using real-time plant measurement data during the boiler operation. The fault detection in the model utilized a Kalman filter algorithm, which estimated all process variables at the input and output side of the boiler.

The residuals, generated by measuring the difference between the estimated and measured values, were used to determine if there was a fault in the boiler. If the residual value exceeded the threshold, it indicated a fault in the boiler. Table 4 compares the model-based fault detection techniques for boiler water wall tube leakage detection.

Table 4. Comparison of Model-based Fault Detection Techniques for Boiler water wall tube leakage detection.

FDD Approach	Fault	Advantages
Exponential Moving average filter and Kalman Filter [101]	Economizer tube leakage detection.	The proposed technique was simple, and can be extended to other sections of the boiler.
Least square algorithm [69,102,103]	Complete boiler.	Provided a simple and effective solution based on heat and mass balance relationships.
GMDH Model [103]	High-pressure feed water heater.	Simple and effective methods based on heat mass balance relationships.
Input/loss method [26]	Generator tubes and heat ex-changers.	Ease of implementation in real power plant, and effective in predicting tube leaks.
Kalman filter algorithm [104]	Complete Subsystems of the boiler.	Practical application with high accuracy.

3.2.2. Data-Driven-Based Methods

Recently, data-driven-based methods [86] are increasingly being used to detect and diagnose faults in TPPs, including boiler tube leakage. This approach incorporates the expertise and experience of operators in the industrial process, and can be used to support the analytical method. For example, techniques such as expert systems [105], wavelet analysis [106], pattern recognition, and ANNs (ANNs) have been used in the development of knowledge-based methods for fault detection. Data-driven FDD systems use machine learning algorithms to analyze data from sensors and other sources to identify patterns and anomalies that indicate a fault. These systems can be trained to recognize specific faults, such as boiler tube leakage, by learning from historical data, and can also be updated over time to improve accuracy. One example of a data-driven-based FDD system for boiler tube leakage is the use of predictive maintenance. This involves using AI-based algorithms to analyze data from sensors, such as temperature and pressure sensors, to predict when a fault is likely to occur [86]. This allows maintenance crews to proactively address the fault before it causes a significant problem, reducing downtime and costs. The process control data can provide sufficient information for effective tube leakage detection [107]. Rostek et al. [108] proposed a method for detecting and predicting tube leaks in fluidized bed boilers using an ANN. However, the use of ANNs requires a large amount of data for accurate predictions during the training phase, and obtaining comprehensive data sets, particularly from commercial units, can be difficult due to proprietary restrictions. These limitations may negatively impact the prediction capabilities of the ANN model. In their study, the team trained their neural networks on a five-year data set, and found promising results in early leak detection, leak prediction, and coarse fault isolation through the use of an ANN model. Figure 10 shows the design of the developed multilayer perceptron ANN.

Sohaib et al. [20] used wavelet packet analysis and deep neural networks to detect leaks in boiler tubes. The proposed method extracted salient features from acoustic signals, resulting in a high classification accuracy of 99.2%. Afgan et al. [105] applied an expert system to detect boiler tube leaks, using radiation heat flux measurements and a three-dimensional mathematical model of the furnace. The results of the case studies showed that the system was effective in detecting small leaks. Khalid et al. [15] proposed a machine learning-based waterwall tube leak detection algorithm. The approach consisted of two steps. Firstly, the most effective sensors were selected through correlation analysis. Secondly, various machine learning algorithms were applied to determine the accuracy of the proposed algorithm. The results showed that optimal sensor selection improved the accuracy of the machine learning classification. Ramezani et al. [109] developed a bidirectional long short-term memory recurrent neural network to detect tube leaks in power plant boilers. The system identifies abnormal acoustic signals that deviate from the reference or normal data it was trained on. The network was trained using data from a sample boiler, and was tested on the same boiler to determine its ability to detect leak presence. The results of the test indicate that this novel approach can accurately detect anomalies in signal levels, which indicate tube defects, with an acceptable level of accuracy. Table 5 compares various data-driven fault detection algorithms for detecting boiler tube leaks.

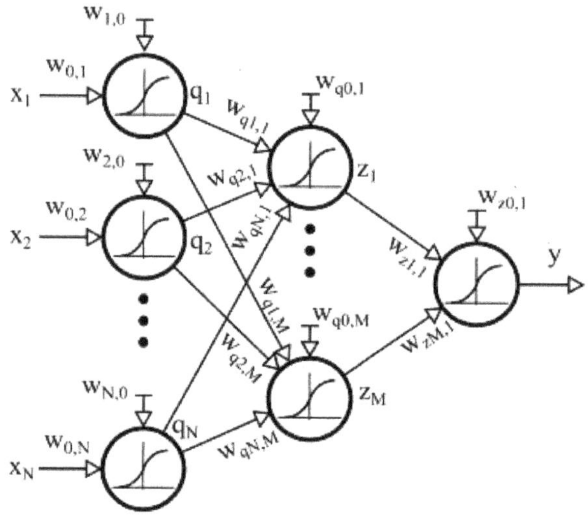

Figure 10. Representation of a developed Multilayer Perceptron Structure [108].

Table 5. Comparison of Different Data-Driven Algorithms for Boiler Tube Leak Detection.

Approach	Fault	Outcomes
ANN [42]	Various faults, including 12 faults of fluidized bed boiler.	Real world industrial applicability.
Expert system [105]	Waterwall tube leakage.	High accuracy using radiation heat flux measurements and three-dimensional model of furnace.
LSTM-based Model [109]	Various subsystems of the boiler.	High performance of the proposed model utilizing acoustic emission signals.
Machine learning-based optimal sensor selection algorithm [15]	Waterwall tube leakage detection.	Developed algorithm showed higher performance and ease of implementation in real power plant.
Deep neural network [20]	For all boiler tubes components.	High classification accuracy and applicable for practical implementation.
Multiplayer back propagation neural network [110]	Boiler burner system.	Used data mining technology to develop intelligent alarm.

3.2.3. Statistical Analysis Method

For many years, statistical methods have proven to be an effective tool in fault diagnosis applications. These methods include limit checking, frequency analysis, and data characteristic analysis, among others. Currently, one of the most popular signal processing-based algorithms for process monitoring is PCA [111]. PCA is widely used in process monitoring, as it reduces the dimension of the process variables. Yu et al. [112] proposed a novel method for detecting and identifying plugged tubes in the final superheater (FSH) tube banks. The method uses PCA for plugging detection and identification, and was applied to temperature data collected from an FSH tube bank in an 870 MW power plant. The results showed that the method was successful in detecting and identifying tube plugging and prevented severe failures by avoiding overheating. Figure 11 shows K-type thermocouples installed by banding on the FSH outlet header section to measure tube temperatures. These thermocouples are commonly used for temperature measurement due to their simplicity, cost-effectiveness, fast response time, and reasonable accuracy. They are also reliable in extreme environments such as boilers, ovens, and aircraft engines. K-type thermocouples are widely used in various industrial fields due to their accuracy and affordability. The temperature range they can measure depends on their diameters.

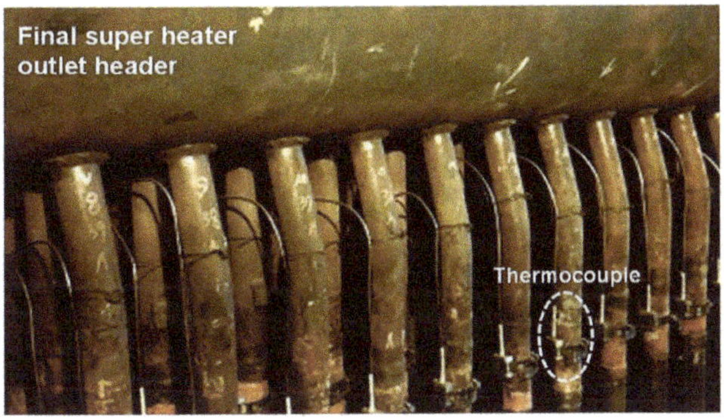

Figure 11. K-type thermocouples affixed to each tube in the outlet header section using banding [112].

Swiercz et al. [107] employed the Multiway PCA (MPCA) method for the early detection of leakages in the pipeline system of a steam boiler in a thermal-electrical power plant. The process variables were long segmented, so they were divided into smaller batches to represent the behavior of the power plant. MPCA was used to train the model for the healthy state of the boiler, and was periodically updated. The model was able to detect leakage when leak data were inputted. Several case studies confirmed the effectiveness of the model in the early prediction of boiler tube leakages. Xi Sun et al. [113] improved the PCA method for leak detection by effectively extracting fault information, and reducing the impact of noise and disturbances. The improved method was successfully used to detect a leak in a Syncrude Canada utility plant. Table 6 compares different statistical analysis-based algorithms for boiler tube leak detection.

Table 6. Comparison of Different Statistical analysis-based Algorithms for Boiler Tube Leak Detection.

Approach	Fault	Outcomes
PCA [112]	Final superheater tube leakage.	Successful in detecting and identifying tube plugging and prevented severe failures by avoiding overheating.
Improved PCA [113]	Boiler water/Steam leak.	The proposed method was tested on real data from a utility plant in Fort McMurray, Canada, for boiler water and steam leak detection.
Multiway PCA [107]	Riser and downcomer tube leakage.	High performance of the proposed Multiway PCA.
Clustering-based method [114]	Boiler tube leakage.	The proposed approach leverages unsupervised learning, and does not require labeled training samples.

3.2.4. Comparative Analysis of Intelligent Techniques for TPPs

This section provides a comparison of state-of-the-art intelligent techniques used in thermal power plants. Table 7 presents an overview of the different intelligent techniques employed, their corresponding applications, the performance metrics evaluated, and key findings and conclusions. The table provides a clear understanding of the effectiveness of various intelligent techniques in different applications. These techniques have been used for applications such as fault detection and diagnosis, predictive maintenance, and optimization. The evaluation of these techniques was based on metrics such as accuracy, efficiency, and cost savings. The key findings of this comparison highlight the effectiveness of intelligent techniques in improving the overall performance of thermal power plants.

Table 7. Comparison of Intelligent Techniques for Thermal Power Plant Applications.

Intelligent Technique	Key Findings and Conclusions	Performance Metrics	TPP Application
Deep neural network (DNN) [20]	Proposed classification mechanism using wavelet packet transform analysis of the acoustic emission signal	99.2% (classification accuracy)	Boiler tube leakage detection
Whole Process model [115]	Developed monitoring platform with the functions of online estimation of key state variables	1.1 % (mean relative deviation)	Boiler tube leak detection
SVM [116]	Prediction of the unburned carbon content of fly ash in the boiler and the exhaust steam enthalpy in turbine	0.068 % (mean relative error)	Online monitoring of 300 MW TPP
Deep learning flexible boundary regression [117]	Proposed impulse detection methodology that employs deep learning methodology	99.8% (classification accuracy)	Boiler tube leak detection
Hybrid intelligent system [118]	A Hybrid fault detection approach based on Decision fusion technique	99.99% (classification accuracy)	Steam generator unit transient condition
Residual network [90]	Proposed a fault diagnosis method based on Knowledge Graph and Bayesian Network	99.1% detection accuracy	Steam turbine rotor fault diagnosis
Graph neural network [119]	Fault representation through Graph neural network	86% inference accuracy	Steam turbine system
Vibration signal analysis [120]	Wavelet transform and statistical pattern recognition employed in the proposed approach	100% fault detection accuracy	Rolling element bearing in rotating machinery
Probability neural networks (PNNs) [121]	Proposed approach based on PNNs to fuse three information entropy	100% classification accuracy on training data and 80% accuracy on unseen data	Steam turbine rotor

4. Challenges, Limitations, and Future Research Directions

This section outlines the challenges and potential areas of future research for FDD techniques in the context of TPPs.

4.1. Current Challenges and Limitations of FDD Techniques in TPPs

FDD is an essential part of the maintenance and operation of TPPs, particularly for boilers and turbines. Despite its importance, FDD faces a number of challenges and limitations as mentioned below, which must be addressed to ensure its effectiveness.

- One of the main challenges of FDD in TPPs is the complexity of the systems involved. Boilers and turbines are highly complex systems that involve a large number of components and processes, which can make it difficult to identify faults and diagnose problems. Additionally, the variability in the performance of these systems can make it difficult to establish normal operating conditions, which is essential for effective FDD.

- Another challenge of FDD in TPPs is the limited availability of data. In many cases, the data used for FDD are based on sensor readings, and these readings are often limited by the frequency and accuracy of the sensors. This can make it difficult to accurately diagnose problems and identify faults, especially when the data are incomplete or noisy.
- A third challenge of FDD in TPPs is the complexity of the algorithms used for analysis. Many of the FDD algorithms used in TPPs are based on artificial intelligence and machine learning techniques, which can be complex and difficult to implement. Additionally, these algorithms require significant computational resources, which can limit their ability to be applied in real-time.
- The limitations of FDD in TPPs also include issues related to maintenance and repair. In some cases, FDD algorithms may identify faults that are difficult to repair, or the cost of repair may be high. Additionally, the time required to repair faults may be longer than the time required to detect the faults, which can reduce the effectiveness of FDD.
- Another limitation of FDD in TPPs is the potential for false alarms. FDD algorithms can sometimes generate false alarms, which can result in unnecessary maintenance and repair activities. This can lead to increased costs, decreased efficiency, and reduced reliability of the power plant.
- Finally, FDD algorithms may not always be effective in detecting faults in all components of a TPP. For example, some faults may not be detectable by current FDD algorithms, or the algorithms may not be effective in detecting faults in certain types of equipment or processes.

In summary, while FDD is an essential part of the maintenance and operation of TPPs, it faces a number of challenges and limitations that must be addressed to ensure its effectiveness. These challenges and limitations include the complexity of the systems involved, the limited availability of data, the complexity of the algorithms used for analysis, and issues related to maintenance and repair. Additionally, FDD may not always be effective in detecting faults in all components of a TPP, and the potential for false alarms must also be considered. To address these challenges and limitations, it is necessary to continue to improve the FDD algorithms and methods used in TPPs, and to develop new approaches that can better detect and diagnose faults in these complex systems.

4.2. Future Research Directions for FDD Techniques in TPPs

FDD techniques play a crucial role in the maintenance and operation of TPPs, particularly for boilers and turbines. To continue to improve the effectiveness of FDD in this context, ongoing research and development are needed. The following are some of the potential areas of future research for FDD techniques in TPPs:

- Big Data and Advanced Analytics: With the increasing availability of data from sensors, SCADA systems, and other sources, advanced analytics techniques are needed to process these data and improve the accuracy of FDD algorithms. This could involve the use of machine learning and artificial intelligence algorithms, as well as the development of new approaches to data analysis that can better handle the complexity and variability of the data generated by TPPs.
- Real-Time Monitoring: To ensure the timely detection of faults and the effective diagnosis of problems, real-time monitoring techniques are required that can process data from sensors and other sources in near real-time. This will require the development of new algorithms and techniques that can process large amounts of data quickly and accurately, and the deployment of these algorithms in real-world TPPs.

- Integration of Multiple Sensors: To improve the accuracy of FDD algorithms, there is a need for the integration of multiple sensors and sources of data. This could involve the use of sensor fusion techniques, which can combine data from multiple sources to provide a more comprehensive view of the state of a system, as well as the development of new sensors and measurement techniques that can provide additional information about the operation of boilers and turbines.
- Predictive Maintenance: To improve the efficiency and reliability of TPPs, predictive maintenance techniques are required that can anticipate faults and problems before they occur. This could involve the use of machine learning and artificial intelligence algorithms to analyze data from sensors and other sources, as well as the development of new approaches to data analysis that can identify patterns and trends in the data.
- Energy Efficiency: To improve the energy efficiency of TPPs, FDD techniques are needed that can identify inefficiencies and opportunities for improvement. This could involve the use of advanced analytics techniques to analyze data from sensors and other sources, as well as the development of new algorithms and approaches that can better identify inefficiencies and improve the energy efficiency of boilers and turbines.
- Context-Aware FDD: To improve the accuracy of FDD algorithms, there is a need for context-aware techniques that can take into account the specific context of a TPP. This could involve the use of machine learning and artificial intelligence algorithms to analyze data from sensors and other sources, as well as the development of new algorithms that can better understand the context of a system and identify faults and problems more effectively.
- Cybersecurity: To ensure the security of TPPs, FDD techniques are needed that can detect and respond to cyber threats. These could involve the use of machine learning and artificial intelligence algorithms to detect and respond to cyberattacks, as well as the development of new techniques that can better protect TPPs from cyber threats.
- Cost-Effective Solutions: To ensure the widespread adoption of FDD techniques in TPPs, cost-effective solutions are necessary that can be implemented in real-world scenarios. These will require the development of new algorithms and techniques that can be implemented with limited computational resources, and the deployment of these algorithms in real-world TPPs.

In summary, the future of FDD techniques in TPPs is promising, and ongoing research and development are needed to continue to improve their accuracy and efficiency.

5. Conclusions

Advances in FDD for TPPs have greatly improved the efficiency, reliability, and safety of these systems. The use of model-based, data-driven, and statistical-based algorithms has enabled the development of sophisticated systems for the detection and diagnosis of faults in real-time.

- Model-based algorithms have become increasingly important in the operation of TPPs. These algorithms, which are based on mathematical models and simulations, allow power plants to analyze large amounts of data, and identify patterns and anomalies that may indicate faults. The use of model-based algorithms in conjunction with other digital technologies, such as artificial intelligence and machine learning, has enabled the development of sophisticated systems for continuous monitoring of the health of power plants and the detection of potential faults in real-time.
- Data-driven algorithms, such as statistical process control and condition monitoring, are also playing an important role in FDD. These algorithms allow power plants to collect and analyze vast amounts of data, providing insights into the performance and health of the system.
- Statistical methods, such as principal component analysis (PCA) and multivariate statistical analysis, are used to identify patterns and correlations in the data that can be used to detect faults. These methods can provide a quantitative measure of the relationship between different variables, and can be combined with other

techniques, such as pattern recognition or machine learning algorithms, to enhance their performance.

Overall, the use of these advanced algorithms is contributing to the development of predictive maintenance systems, which allow power plants to proactively address faults, and minimize downtime and costs. As these algorithms continue to evolve and become more sophisticated, they will play an increasingly important role in ensuring the long-term viability of thermal power generation. In conclusion, advances in FDD algorithms are a critical component of the future of thermal power generation. By improving the efficiency, reliability, and safety of these systems, these technologies are contributing to the sustainable development of the energy sector. As these algorithms continue to develop and evolve, they will enable the creation of even more advanced systems that will help ensure the long-term viability of thermal power generation.

Author Contributions: Conceptualization, S.K. and H.S.K.; content preparation, S.K., J.S. and I.R.; writing—original draft preparation S.K., J.S. and I.R.; writing—review and editing, S.K., J.S., I.R. and H.S.K.; supervision, H.S.K. All authors have read and agreed to the published version of the manuscript.

Funding: This work was funded by project for Smart Manufacturing Innovation R&D funded Korea Ministry of SMEs and Startups in 2022. (Project No. RS-2022-00140460) and BK-21 four.

Data Availability Statement: Not applicable.

Conflicts of Interest: The authors declare no conflict of interest.

Abbreviations

ANN	Artificial neural network
EMA	Exponential moving average filter
FDD	Fault detection and diagnosis
MPCA	Multiway PCA
PCA	Principal component analysis
SVM	Support vector machine
TPP	Thermal Power Plant

References

1. Holechek, J.L.; Geli, H.M.E.; Sawalhah, M.N.; Valdez, R. A Global Assessment: Can Renewable Energy Replace Fossil Fuels by 2050? *Sustainability* **2022**, *14*, 4792. [CrossRef]
2. Gao, Z.; Cecati, C.; Ding, S.X. A Survey of Fault Diagnosis and Fault-Tolerant Techniques—Part I: Fault Diagnosis with Model-Based and Signal-Based Approaches. *IEEE Trans. Ind. Electron.* **2015**, *62*, 3757–3767. [CrossRef]
3. Eguchi, S.; Takayabu, H.; Lin, C. Sources of Inefficient Power Generation by Coal-Fired Thermal Power Plants in China: A Metafrontier DEA Decomposition Approach. *Renew. Sustain. Energy Rev.* **2021**, *138*, 110562. [CrossRef]
4. Mayadevi, N.; Vinodchandra, S.; Ushakumari, S. A Review on Expert System Applications in Power Plants. *Int. J. Electr. Comput. Eng.* **2014**, *4*, 116.
5. Chen, H.; Pan, P.; Chen, X.; Wang, Y.; Zhao, Q. Fouling of the Flue Gas Cooler in a Large-Scale Coal-Fired Power Plant. *Appl. Therm. Eng.* **2017**, *117*, 698–707. [CrossRef]
6. Shen, C.; Cirone, C.; Jacobi, A.M.; Wang, X. Fouling of Enhanced Tubes for Condensers Used in Cooling Tower Systems: A Literature Review. *Appl. Therm. Eng.* **2015**, *79*, 74–87. [CrossRef]
7. Rahmani, K.; Jadidian, R.; Haghtalab, S. Evaluation of Inhibitors and Biocides on the Corrosion, Scaling and Biofouling Control of Carbon Steel and Copper–Nickel Alloys in a Power Plant Cooling Water System. *Desalination* **2016**, *393*, 174–185. [CrossRef]
8. Wang, Y.; Yin, X.; Qiao, J.; Tan, L.; Xu, W.; Li, W. Generator Stator Windings Ground Fault Diagnosis for Generator–Grid Directly Connected System of Floating Nuclear Power Plant. *Energy Rep.* **2021**, *7*, 460–469. [CrossRef]
9. Ciupek, B.; Gołoś, K.; Jankowski, R.; Nadolny, Z. Effect of Hard Coal Combustion in Water Steam Environment on Chemical Composition of Exhaust Gases. *Energies* **2021**, *14*, 6530. [CrossRef]
10. Shahzad Baig, K.; Yousaf, M. Coal Fired Power Plants: Emission Problems and Controlling Techniques. *J. Earth Sci. Clim. Chang.* **2017**, *8*, 2.
11. Chen, J.; Patton, R.J. *Robust. Model-Based Fault Diagnosis for Dynamic Systems*; Springer Science & Business Media: Berlin, Germany, 2012; Volume 3, ISBN 1-4615-5149-8.
12. Ding, S.X. *Model-Based Fault Diagnosis Techniques: Design Schemes, Algorithms, and Tools*; Springer Science & Business Media: Berlin, Germany, 2008; ISBN 3-540-76304-X.

13. Xu, G.; Liu, M.; Wang, J.; Ma, Y.; Wang, J.; Li, F.; Shen, W. Data-Driven Fault Diagnostics and Prognostics for Predictive Maintenance: A Brief Overview. In Proceedings of the 2019 IEEE 15th International Conference on Automation Science and Engineering (CASE), Vancouver, BC, Canada, 22–26 August 2019; pp. 103–108.
14. Gangsar, P.; Tiwari, R. Signal Based Condition Monitoring Techniques for Fault Detection and Diagnosis of Induction Motors: A State-of-the-Art Review. *Mech. Syst. Signal. Process.* **2020**, *144*, 106908. [CrossRef]
15. Khalid, S.; Lim, W.; Kim, H.S.; Oh, Y.T.; Youn, B.D.; Kim, H.-S.; Bae, Y.-C. Intelligent Steam Power Plant Boiler Waterwall Tube Leakage Detection via Machine Learning-Based Optimal Sensor Selection. *Sensors* **2020**, *20*, 6356. [CrossRef]
16. Ali, J.B.; Fnaiech, N.; Saidi, L.; Chebel-Morello, B.; Fnaiech, F. Application of Empirical Mode Decomposition and Artificial Neural Network for Automatic Bearing Fault Diagnosis Based on Vibration Signals. *Appl. Acoust.* **2015**, *89*, 16–27.
17. Zhou, P.; Zhang, R.; Xie, J.; Liu, J.; Wang, H.; Chai, T. Data-Driven Monitoring and Diagnosing of Abnormal Furnace Conditions in Blast Furnace Ironmaking: An Integrated PCA-ICA Method. *IEEE Trans. Ind. Electron.* **2020**, *68*, 622–631. [CrossRef]
18. Chemweno, P.K.; Pintelon, L. Towards E-Maintenance: An Exploration Approach for Aircraft Maintenance Data. In *Applications and Challenges of Maintenance and Safety Engineering in Industry 4.0*; IGI Global: Hershey, PA, USA, 2020; pp. 189–212.
19. Razmi-Farooji, A.; Kropsu-Vehkaperä, H.; Härkönen, J.; Haapasalo, H. Advantages and Potential Challenges of Data Management in E-Maintenance. *J. Qual. Maint. Eng.* **2019**, *25*, 378–396. [CrossRef]
20. Sohaib, M.; Kim, J.-M. Data Driven Leakage Detection and Classification of a Boiler Tube. *Appl. Sci.* **2019**, *9*, 2450. [CrossRef]
21. Sohaib, M.; Islam, M.; Kim, J.; Jeon, D.-C.; Kim, J.-M. Leakage Detection of a Spherical Water Storage Tank in a Chemical Industry Using Acoustic Emissions. *Appl. Sci.* **2019**, *9*, 196. [CrossRef]
22. Khalid, S.; Hwang, H.; Kim, H.S. Real-World Data-Driven Machine-Learning-Based Optimal Sensor Selection Approach for Equipment Fault Detection in a Thermal Power Plant. *Mathematics* **2021**, *9*, 2814. [CrossRef]
23. Nurbanasari, M. Abdurrachim Investigation of Leakage on Water Wall Tube in a 660 MW Supercritical Boiler. *J. Fail. Anal. Preven.* **2014**, *14*, 657–661. [CrossRef]
24. Kim, Y.-H.; Kim, J.; Kim, J.-M. Leakage Detection of a Boiler Tube Using a Genetic Algorithm-like Method and Support Vector Machines. In Proceedings of the 10th International Conference on Soft Computing and Pattern Recognition (SoCPaR 2018), Porto, Portugal, 13–15 December 2018. [CrossRef]
25. Kokkinos, A. Coal R&D Beyond 2020. In *DOE-NETL-EPRI Technical Exchange Meeting*; EPRI: Pittsburgh, PA, USA, 2019.
26. Lang, F.D.; Rodgers, D.A.; Mayer, L.E. *Detection of Tube Leaks and Their Location Using Input/Loss Methods*; AMSE: New York, NY, USA, 2004; Volume 41626, pp. 143–150.
27. Qiu, J.; Wu, Q.; Ding, G.; Xu, Y.; Feng, S. A Survey of Machine Learning for Big Data Processing. *EURASIP J. Adv. Signal. Process.* **2016**, *2016*, 1–16.
28. Zhou, L.; Pan, S.; Wang, J.; Vasilakos, A.V. Machine Learning on Big Data: Opportunities and Challenges. *Neurocomputing* **2017**, *237*, 350–361. [CrossRef]
29. Chen, F.; Fu, Z.; Zhen, L. Thermal Power Generation Fault Diagnosis and Prediction Model Based on Deep Learning and Multimedia Systems. *Multimed. Tools Appl.* **2019**, *78*, 4673–4692. [CrossRef]
30. Hundi, P.; Shahsavari, R. Comparative Studies among Machine Learning Models for Performance Estimation and Health Monitoring of Thermal Power Plants. *Appl. Energy* **2020**, *265*, 114775. [CrossRef]
31. Cui, Y.; Xia, L.; Huang, Y.; Ma, X. Research on Fault Diagnosis and Early Warning of Power Plant Boiler Reheater Temperature Deviation Based on Machine Learning Algorithm. In Proceedings of the 2020 IEEE 6th International Conference on Control Science and Systems Engineering (ICCSSE), Beijing, China, 17–19 July 2020; pp. 212–216.
32. Dhini, A.; Surjandari, I.; Kusumoputro, B.; Kusiak, A. Extreme Learning Machine–Radial Basis Function (ELM-RBF) Networks for Diagnosing Faults in a Steam Turbine. *J. Ind. Prod. Eng.* **2022**, *39*, 572–580. [CrossRef]
33. Ghiasi, M.; Niknam, T.; Dehghani, M.; Baghaee, H.R.; Wang, Z.; Ghanbarian, M.M.; Blaabjerg, F.; Dragicevic, T. Multipurpose FCS Model Predictive Control of VSC-Based Microgrids for Islanded and Grid-Connected Operation Modes. *IEEE Syst. J.* **2022**, 1–12. [CrossRef]
34. Ghiasi, M.; Wang, Z.; Mehrandezh, M.; Jalilian, S.; Ghadimi, N. Evolution of Smart Grids towards the Internet of Energy: Concept and Essential Components for Deep Decarbonisation. *IET Smart Grid* **2023**, *6*, 86–102. [CrossRef]
35. Ghiasi, M. Detailed Study, Multi-Objective Optimization, and Design of an AC-DC Smart Microgrid with Hybrid Renewable Energy Resources. *Energy* **2019**, *169*, 496–507. [CrossRef]
36. Alobaid, F.; Mertens, N.; Starkloff, R.; Lanz, T.; Heinze, C.; Epple, B. Progress in Dynamic Simulation of Thermal Power Plants. *Prog. Energy Combust. Sci.* **2017**, *59*, 79–162. [CrossRef]
37. Dmitrienko, M.A.; Strizhak, P.A. Coal-Water Slurries Containing Petrochemicals to Solve Problems of Air Pollution by Coal Thermal Power Stations and Boiler Plants: An Introductory Review. *Sci. Total Environ.* **2018**, *613*, 1117–1129. [CrossRef]
38. Chaibakhsh, A.; Ghaffari, A. Steam Turbine Model. *Simul. Model. Pract. Theory* **2008**, *16*, 1145–1162. [CrossRef]
39. Drbal, L.; Westra, K.; Boston, P. *Power Plant Engineering*; Springer Science & Business Media: Berlin, Germany, 2012; ISBN 1-4613-0427-X.
40. Attia, S.I. The Influence of Condenser Cooling Water Temperature on the Thermal Efficiency of a Nuclear Power Plant. *Ann. Nucl. Energy* **2015**, *80*, 371–378. [CrossRef]
41. Lakzian, E.; Yazdani, S.; Lee, B.J. Passive Control Optimization of Condensation Flow in Steam Turbine Blades. *Int. J. Mech. Sci.* **2022**, *237*, 107804. [CrossRef]

42. Dhini, A.; Kusumoputro, B.; Surjandari, I. Neural Network Based System for Detecting and Diagnosing Faults in Steam Turbine of Thermal Power Plant. In Proceedings of the 2017 IEEE 8th International Conference on Awareness Science and Technology (iCAST), Taichung, Taiwan, 8–10 November 2017; pp. 149–154.
43. Cai, W.; Lu, S.; Wu, Z.; Ying, G.; Wu, W. Strategy and Technique of High Efficiency Balancing in Field for Turbo-Generator Units with Large Capacity. In Proceedings of the Journal of Physics: Conference Series; IOP Publishing: Bristol, UK, 2021; Volume 2101, p. 012011.
44. Hou, P.; Ma, H.; Liu, B.; Chen, X.; Zhu, C.; Tan, F. Mechanical Fault Diagnosis of Reactor Core Winding Looseness Based on Multi-Feature Fusion and Improved KELM. In Proceedings of the 2021 IEEE Sustainable Power and Energy Conference (iSPEC), Nanjing, China, 23–25 December 2021; pp. 3927–3932.
45. Reyes-Martínez, J.; Astorga-Zaragoza, C.-M.; Madrigal-Espinosa, G.; Chadli, M.; Vargas-Méndez, R.-A.; Osorio-Gordillo, G.-L.; Reyes-Reyes, J. Actuator Fault Compensation Based on a Takagi-Sugeno PI Observer: Application to a Thermoelectric Steam Generator. *Int. J. Fuzzy Syst.* **2022**, *24*, 855–866. [CrossRef]
46. Weigel, B.V.; Odenbach, S.; Uffrecht, W.; Polklas, T. Thermal Characterization of a Steam Turbine Casing Including Measuring of Adiabatic Wall Temperatures Using Proprietary Sensors. In Proceedings of the Turbo Expo: Power for Land, Sea, and Air; American Society of Mechanical Engineers: New York, NY, USA, 2021; Volume 85017, p. V008T22A011.
47. Nayeri, M.R.; Araabi, B.; Moshiri, B. Fault Detection and Isolation of Gas Turbine: Hierarchical Classification and Confidence Rate Computation. *J. Frankl. Inst.* **2022**, *17*, 10120–10144. [CrossRef]
48. Zhao, W.; Li, Y.; Xue, M.; Wang, P.; Jiang, J. Vibration Analysis for Failure Detection in Low Pressure Steam Turbine Blades in Nuclear Power Plant. *Eng. Fail. Anal.* **2018**, *84*, 11–24. [CrossRef]
49. Talai, S.M.; Desai, D.A.; Heyns, P.S. Infrared Thermography Applied to the Prediction of Structural Vibration Behaviour. *Alex. Eng. J.* **2019**, *58*, 603–610. [CrossRef]
50. Uekita, M.; Takaya, Y. Tool Condition Monitoring for Form Milling of Large Parts by Combining Spindle Motor Current and Acoustic Emission Signals. *Int. J. Adv. Manuf. Technol.* **2017**, *89*, 65–75. [CrossRef]
51. Pondini, M.; Colla, V.; Signorini, A. Models of Control Valve and Actuation System for Dynamics Analysis of Steam Turbines. *Appl. Energy* **2017**, *207*, 208–217. [CrossRef]
52. Szymański, K.; Hernas, A.; Moskal, G.; Myalska, H. Thermally Sprayed Coatings Resistant to Erosion and Corrosion for Power Plant Boilers—A Review. *Surf. Coat. Technol.* **2015**, *268*, 153–164. [CrossRef]
53. Singh, P.M.; Mahmood, J. Stress Assisted Corrosion of Waterwall Tubes in Recovery Boiler Tubes: Failure Analysis. *J. Fail. Anal. Preven.* **2007**, *7*, 361–370. [CrossRef]
54. Lee, N.-H.; Kim, S.; Choe, B.-H.; Yoon, K.-B.; Kwon, D. Failure Analysis of a Boiler Tube in USC Coal Power Plant. *Eng. Fail. Anal.* **2009**, *16*, 2031–2035. [CrossRef]
55. Indrawan, N.; Shadle, L.J.; Breault, R.W.; Panday, R.; Chitnis, U.K. Data Analytics for Leak Detection in a Subcritical Boiler. *Energy* **2021**, *220*, 119667. [CrossRef]
56. Che, C.; Qian, G.; Yang, X.; Liu, X. Fatigue Damage of Waterwall Tubes in a 1000 MW USC Boiler. In *Proceedings of the 7th International Conference on Fracture Fatigue and Wear*; Lecture Notes in Mechanical Engineering; Abdel Wahab, M., Ed.; Springer: Singapore, 2019; pp. 314–324. ISBN 9789811304101.
57. Singh, W.S.; Rao, B.P.; Mukhopadhyay, C.K.; Jayakumar, T. Detection of Localized Damage in Water Wall Tubes of Thermal Power Plants Using GMR Sensor Array Based Magnetic Flux Leakage Technique. *J. Nondestruct. Eval.* **2015**, *34*, 19. [CrossRef]
58. Yang, G.; Gou, Y.; Liu, X.; Zhang, X.; Zhang, T. Failure Analysis of the Corroded Water Wall Tube in a 50MW Thermal Power Plant. *High Temp. Mater. Process.* **2018**, *37*, 995–999. [CrossRef]
59. Xue, S.; Guo, R.; Hu, F.; Ding, K.; Liu, L.; Zheng, L.; Yang, T. Analysis of the Causes of Leakages and Preventive Strategies of Boiler Water-Wall Tubes in a Thermal Power Plant. *Eng. Fail. Anal.* **2020**, *110*, 104381. [CrossRef]
60. Purbolaksono, J.; Ahmad, J.; Beng, L.; Rashid, A.; Khinani, A.; Ali, A. Failure Analysis on a Primary Superheater Tube of a Power Plant. *Eng. Fail. Anal.* **2010**, *17*, 158–167. [CrossRef]
61. Ranjbar, K. Failure Analysis of Boiler Cold and Hot Reheater Tubes. *Eng. Fail. Anal.* **2007**, *14*, 620–625. [CrossRef]
62. Ahmad, J.; Purbolaksono, J.; Beng, L.C.; Rashid, A.Z.; Khinani, A.; Ali, A.A. Failure Investigation on Rear Water Wall Tube of Boiler. *Eng. Fail. Anal.* **2009**, *16*, 2325–2332. [CrossRef]
63. Mandeliya, M.; Vishwakarma, M. A Review on Boiler Tube Assessment in Power Plant Using Ultrasonic Testing. *Int. Res. J. Eng. Technol.* **2018**, *5*, 708–714.
64. Thekkuden, D.T.; Mourad, A.-H.I.; Bouzid, A.-H. Failures and Leak Inspection Techniques of Tube-to-Tubesheet Joints: A Review. *Eng. Fail. Anal.* **2021**, *130*, 105798. [CrossRef]
65. Erenburg, B.; Zilberberg, A.; Iskevitch, E. Cracking of AISI T22 Reheater Pendant Assembly Tubing of Steam Boiler. *J. Fail. Anal. Prev.* **2019**, *19*, 320–327. [CrossRef]
66. Guan, H.; Xiao, T.; Luo, W.; Gu, J.; He, R.; Xu, P. Automatic Fault Diagnosis Algorithm for Hot Water Pipes Based on Infrared Thermal Images. *Build. Environ.* **2022**, *218*, 109111. [CrossRef]
67. Zhang, S.; Shen, G.; An, L. Online Monitoring of Furnace Exit Gas Temperature in Power Plants. *Appl. Therm. Eng.* **2019**, *147*, 917–926. [CrossRef]
68. Zhang, C.; Li, D.; Mu, Y.; Song, D. An Interval-Valued Hesitant Fuzzy Multigranulation Rough Set over Two Universes Model for Steam Turbine Fault Diagnosis. *Appl. Math. Model.* **2017**, *42*, 693–704. [CrossRef]

69. Sun, X.; Chen, T.; Marquez, H.J. Boiler Leak Detection Using a System Identification Technique. *Ind. Eng. Chem. Res.* **2002**, *41*, 5447–5454. [CrossRef]
70. Que, Z.; Xu, Z. A Data-Driven Health Prognostics Approach for Steam Turbines Based on Xgboost and Dtw. *IEEE Access* **2019**, *7*, 93131–93138. [CrossRef]
71. Ko, J.U.; Na, K.; Oh, J.-S.; Kim, J.; Youn, B.D. A New Auto-Encoder-Based Dynamic Threshold to Reduce False Alarm Rate for Anomaly Detection of Steam Turbines. *Expert Syst. Appl.* **2022**, *189*, 116094. [CrossRef]
72. Diatte, K.; O'Halloran, B.; Van Bossuyt, D.L. The Integration of Reliability, Availability, and Maintainability into Model-Based Systems Engineering. *Systems* **2022**, *10*, 101. [CrossRef]
73. Cano, S.; Rodríguez, J.; Rodríguez, J.; García, J.; Sierra, F.; Casolco, S.; Herrera, M. Detection of Damage in Steam Turbine Blades Caused by Low Cycle and Strain Cycling Fatigue. *Eng. Fail. Anal.* **2019**, *97*, 579–588. [CrossRef]
74. Salahshoor, K.; Kordestani, M.; Khoshro, M.S. Fault Detection and Diagnosis of an Industrial Steam Turbine Using Fusion of SVM (Support Vector Machine) and ANFIS (Adaptive Neuro-Fuzzy Inference System) Classifiers. *Energy* **2010**, *35*, 5472–5482. [CrossRef]
75. Salahshoor, K.; Khoshro, M.S.; Kordestani, M. Fault Detection and Diagnosis of an Industrial Steam Turbine Using a Distributed Configuration of Adaptive Neuro-Fuzzy Inference Systems. *Simul. Model. Pract. Theory* **2011**, *19*, 1280–1293. [CrossRef]
76. Li, G.; Zhao, Q. Minimum Entropy Deconvolution Optimized Sinusoidal Synthesis and Its Application to Vibration Based Fault Detection. *J. Sound Vib.* **2017**, *390*, 218–231. [CrossRef]
77. Hassan Shah, M.Z.; Ahmed, Z.; Hu, L. Feature Extraction and Fault Detection Scheme via Improved Locality Preserving Projection and SVDD. *Trans. Inst. Meas. Control* **2022**, *45*, 01423312221099855. [CrossRef]
78. Huang, B.; Hu, L.-S. A Geometrically Inspired Quantification Approach for Valve Stiction Using Riemannian Logarithmic Map. *Measurement* **2022**, *199*, 111562. [CrossRef]
79. Salahshoor, K.; Kordestani, M. Design of an Active Fault Tolerant Control System for a Simulated Industrial Steam Turbine. *Appl. Math. Model.* **2014**, *38*, 1753–1774. [CrossRef]
80. Zhang, Y.-J.; Yuan, Y.; Hu, L.-S. Fault Detection Based on Graph Model for Dead Zone of Steam Turbine Control Valve. *Int. J. Control Autom. Syst.* **2022**, *20*, 2759–2767. [CrossRef]
81. Shah, M.Z.H.; Hu, L.; Ahmed, Z. Modified LPP Based on Riemannian Metric for Feature Extraction and Fault Detection. *Measurement* **2022**, *193*, 110923. [CrossRef]
82. Yan, J.; Lv, M.; Wang, P.; Wang, M. Kalman Filter Based Neural Network Methodology for Predictive Maintenance: A Case Study on Steam Turbine Blade Performance Prognostics. In Proceedings of the ASME International Mechanical Engineering Congress and Exposition, Chicago, IL, USA, 5–10 November 2006; Volume 47748, pp. 271–276.
83. Baraldi, P.; Di Maio, F.; Rigamonti, M.; Zio, E.; Seraoui, R. Clustering for Unsupervised Fault Diagnosis in Nuclear Turbine Shut-down Transients. *Mech. Syst. Signal Process.* **2015**, *58*, 160–178. [CrossRef]
84. Jiang, J.; Ma, X.; Ouyang, D.; Williams, R.O. Emerging Artificial Intelligence (AI) Technologies Used in the Development of Solid Dosage Forms. *Pharmaceutics* **2022**, *14*, 2257. [CrossRef]
85. Chen, Z.; Wang, Y.; Wu, J.; Deng, C.; Jiang, W. Wide Residual Relation Network-Based Intelligent Fault Diagnosis of Rotating Machines with Small Samples. *Sensors* **2022**, *22*, 4161. [CrossRef] [PubMed]
86. Chen, K.-Y.; Chen, L.-S.; Chen, M.-C.; Lee, C.-L. Using SVM Based Method for Equipment Fault Detection in a Thermal Power Plant. *Comput. Ind.* **2011**, *62*, 42–50. [CrossRef]
87. Ashraf, W.M.; Rafique, Y.; Uddin, G.M.; Riaz, F.; Asim, M.; Farooq, M.; Hussain, A.; Salman, C.A. Artificial Intelligence Based Operational Strategy Development and Implementation for Vibration Reduction of a Supercritical Steam Turbine Shaft Bearing. *Alex. Eng. J.* **2022**, *61*, 1864–1880. [CrossRef]
88. Que, Z.J.; Xiong, Y.; Xu, Z.G. A Semi-Supervised Approach for Steam Turbine Health Prognostics Based on GAN and PF. In Proceedings of the 2019 IEEE International Conference on Industrial Engineering and Engineering Management (IEEM), Macao, China, 15–18 December 2019; pp. 1476–1480.
89. Fang, M.; Xu, Z. Vibration Fault Diagnosis for Steam Turbine-Generators Based on History Cases and Artificial Neural Network. In Proceedings of the 2018 2nd IEEE Advanced Information Management, Communicates, Electronic and Automation Control Conference (IMCEC), Xi'an, China, 25–27 May 2018; pp. 747–753.
90. Wang, C.; Zhang, D.; Xie, Y. Research on Fault Diagnosis of Steam Turbine Rotor Unbalance and Parallel Misalignment Based on Numerical Simulation and Convolutional Neural Network. In *Proceedings of the Turbo Expo: Power for Land, Sea, and Air*; American Society of Mechanical Engineers: New York, NY, USA, 2021; Volume 85017, p. V008T22A019.
91. Helin, M. Fault Detection in Steam Turbines Using Data-Driven Methods. Master's Thesis, Aalto University, Espoo, Finland, 2020.
92. Satyanarayana, K.; Sarcar, M.M.M.; Purushothaman, S. Implementation of Locally Weighted Projection Regression Network for Condition Monitoring of a Steam Turbine. *Artif. Intell. Syst. Mach. Learn.* **2012**, *4*, 574–577.
93. Komatsu, K.; Miyazawa, H.; Yiran, C.; Sato, M.; Furusawa, T.; Yamamoto, S.; Kobayashi, H. Detection of Machinery Failure Signs From Big Time-Series Data Obtained by Flow Simulation of Intermediate-Pressure Steam Turbines. *J. Eng. Gas Turbines Power* **2022**, *144*, 011007. [CrossRef]
94. Wu, Y.; Li, W.; Sheng, D.; Chen, J.; Yu, Z. Fault Diagnosis Method of Peak-Load-Regulation Steam Turbine Based on Improved PCA-HKNN Artificial Neural Network. *Proc. Inst. Mech. Eng. Part O J. Risk Reliab.* **2021**, *235*, 1026–1040. [CrossRef]

95. Zhao, G.; Jiang, D.; Diao, J.; Qian, L. Application of Wavelet Time-Frequency Analysis on Fault Diagnosis for Steam Turbine. In Proceedings of the 5th International Conference of Acoustical and Vibratory Surveillance Methods and Diagnostic Techniques, Senlis, France, 11–13 October 2004.
96. Ajami, A.; Daneshvar, M. Data Driven Approach for Fault Detection and Diagnosis of Turbine in Thermal Power Plant Using Independent Component Analysis (ICA). *Int. J. Electr. Power Energy Syst.* **2012**, *43*, 728–735. [CrossRef]
97. Mubaraali, L.; Kuppuswamy, N.; Muthukumar, R. Intelligent Fault Diagnosis in Microprocessor Systems for Vibration Analysis in Roller Bearings in Whirlpool Turbine Generators Real Time Processor Applications. *Microprocess. Microsyst.* **2020**, *76*, 103079. [CrossRef]
98. Lin, W.-M.; Wu, C.-H.; Lin, C.-H.; Su, C.-H. Grey Clustering Analysis Based Classifier for Steam Turbine-Generator Fault Diagnosis. In Proceedings of the 2007 International Conference on Intelligent Systems Applications to Power Systems, Kaohsiung, Taiwan, 5–8 November 2007; pp. 1–6.
99. Zhang, X.; Chen, S.; Zhu, Y.; Yan, W. Fault Detection and Diagnosis for Steam Turbine Based on Kernel GDA. In Proceedings of the Proceedings of 2011 International Conference on Modelling, Identification and Control, Shanghai, China, 26–29 June 2011; pp. 58–62.
100. Bae, S.J.; Mun, B.M.; Chang, W.; Vidakovic, B. Condition Monitoring of a Steam Turbine Generator Using Wavelet Spectrum Based Control Chart. *Reliab. Eng. Syst. Saf.* **2019**, *184*, 13–20. [CrossRef]
101. Panday, R.; Indrawan, N.; Shadle, L.J.; Vesel, R.W. Leak Detection in a Subcritical Boiler. *Appl. Therm. Eng.* **2021**, *185*, 116371. [CrossRef]
102. Sun, X.; Chen, T.; Marquez, H.J. Efficient Model-Based Leak Detection in Boiler Steam-Water Systems. *Comput. Chem. Eng.* **2002**, *26*, 1643–1647. [CrossRef]
103. Li, F.; Upadhyaya, B.R.; Coffey, L.A. Model-Based Monitoring and Fault Diagnosis of Fossil Power Plant Process Units Using Group Method of Data Handling. *ISA Trans.* **2009**, *48*, 213–219. [CrossRef]
104. David, N.P.; Swaminathan, B. Modeling, Identification and Detection of Faults in Industrial Boiler(July2015). In Proceedings of the 2015 IEEE Technological Innovation in ICT for Agriculture and Rural Development (TIAR), Chennai, India, 10–12 July 2015; pp. 197–201.
105. Afgan, N.; Coelho, P.J.; Carvalho, M.G. Boiler Tube Leakage Detection Expert System. *Appl. Therm. Eng.* **1998**, *18*, 317–326. [CrossRef]
106. Wang, Z.; Zhang, Q.; Xiong, J.; Xiao, M.; Sun, G.; He, J. Fault Diagnosis of a Rolling Bearing Using Wavelet Packet Denoising and Random Forests. *IEEE Sens. J.* **2017**, *17*, 5581–5588. [CrossRef]
107. Swiercz, M.; Mroczkowska, H. Multiway PCA for Early Leak Detection in a Pipeline System of a Steam Boiler—Selected Case Studies. *Sensors* **2020**, *20*, 1561. [CrossRef]
108. Rostek, K.; Morytko, Ł.; Jankowska, A. Early Detection and Prediction of Leaks in Fluidized-Bed Boilers Using Artificial Neural Networks. *Energy* **2015**, *89*, 914–923. [CrossRef]
109. Ramezani, M.G.; Hasanian, M.; Golchinfar, B.; Saboonchi, H. Automatic Boiler Tube Leak Detection with Deep Bidirectional LSTM Neural Networks of Acoustic Emission Signals. *Sens. Smart Struct. Technol. Civ. Mech. Aerosp. Syst.* **2020**, *11379*, 113791I. [CrossRef]
110. Rakhshani, E.; Sariri, I.; Rouzbehi, K. Application of Data Mining on Fault Detection and Prediction in Boiler of Power Plant Using Artificial Neural Network. In Proceedings of the 2009 International Conference on Power Engineering, Energy and Electrical Drives, Lisbon, Portugal, 18–20 March 2009; pp. 473–478.
111. Jing, C.; Hou, J. SVM and PCA Based Fault Classification Approaches for Complicated Industrial Process. *Neurocomputing* **2015**, *167*, 636–642. [CrossRef]
112. Yu, J.; Yoo, J.; Jang, J.; Park, J.H.; Kim, S. A Novel Plugged Tube Detection and Identification Approach for Final Super Heater in Thermal Power Plant Using Principal Component Analysis. *Energy* **2017**, *126*, 404–418. [CrossRef]
113. Sun, X.; Marquez, H.J.; Chen, T.; Riaz, M. An Improved PCA Method with Application to Boiler Leak Detection. *ISA Trans.* **2005**, *44*, 379–397. [CrossRef] [PubMed]
114. Yu, J.; Jang, J.; Yoo, J.; Park, J.H.; Kim, S. A Clustering-Based Fault Detection Method for Steam Boiler Tube in Thermal Power Plant. *J. Electr. Eng. Technol.* **2016**, *11*, 848–859. [CrossRef]
115. Tian, Z.; Xu, L.; Yuan, J.; Zhang, X.; Wang, J. Online Performance Monitoring Platform Based on the Whole Process Models of Subcritical Coal-Fired Power Plants. *Appl. Therm. Eng.* **2017**, *124*, 1368–1381. [CrossRef]
116. Cai, J.; Ma, X.; Li, Q. On-Line Monitoring the Performance of Coal-Fired Power Unit: A Method Based on Support Vector Machine. *Appl. Therm. Eng.* **2009**, *29*, 2308–2319. [CrossRef]
117. Duong, B.P.; Kim, J.; Kim, C.-H.; Kim, J.-M. Deep Learning Object-Impulse Detection for Enhancing Leakage Detection of a Boiler Tube Using Acoustic Emission Signal. *Appl. Sci.* **2019**, *9*, 4368. [CrossRef]
118. Moradi, M.; Chaibakhsh, A.; Ramezani, A. An Intelligent Hybrid Technique for Fault Detection and Condition Monitoring of a Thermal Power Plant. *Appl. Math. Model.* **2018**, *60*, 34–47. [CrossRef]
119. Zhang, Y.-J.; Hu, L.-S. Fault Propagation Inference Based on a Graph Neural Network for Steam Turbine Systems. *Energies* **2021**, *14*, 309. [CrossRef]

120. Brkovic, A.; Gajic, D.; Gligorijevic, J.; Savic-Gajic, I.; Georgieva, O.; Di Gennaro, S. Early Fault Detection and Diagnosis in Bearings for More Efficient Operation of Rotating Machinery. *Energy* **2017**, *136*, 63–71. [CrossRef]
121. Zhang, Y.; Huang, S.; Gao, W.; Shen, T. Vibration Fault Diagnosis of Steam Turbine Shafting Based on Probability Neural Networks. In Proceedings of the 2008 Congress on Image and Signal Processing, Sanya, China, 27–30 May 2008; Volume 5, pp. 582–585.

MDPI AG
Grosspeteranlage 5
4052 Basel
Switzerland
Tel.: +41 61 683 77 34

Mathematics Editorial Office
E-mail: mathematics@mdpi.com
www.mdpi.com/journal/mathematics

www.ingramcontent.com/pod-product-compliance
Lightning Source LLC
Chambersburg PA
CBHW041017270926
51850CB00024B/1277